W9-BKR-638

Freedoms Given, Freedoms Won

Freedoms Given, Freedoms Won

AFRO-BRAZILIANS IN POST-ABOLITION SÃO PAULO AND SALVADOR

KIM D. BUTLER

Rutgers University Press

New Brunswick, New Jersey, and London

Second paperback printing, 2000

Library of Congress Cataloging-in-Publication Data

Butler, Kim D., 1960—
  Freedoms given, freedoms won : Afro-Brazilians in post-abolition São Paulo and Salvador / Kim D. Butler.
  Includes bibliographical references and index.
  ISBN 0–8135–2503–9 (cloth : alk. paper). — ISBN 0–8135–2504–7 (pbk. : alk. paper)
  1. Blacks—Brazil—São Paulo—Politics and government. 2. São Paulo (Brazil)—Politics and government. 3. Blacks—Brazil—Salvador—Politics and government.
4. Salvador (Brazil)—Politics and government. 5. Slaves—Emancipation—Brazil. 6. Social movements—Brazil—History. 7. Blacks—Civil rights—Brazil. 8. Brazil—Race relations.
I. Title.
F2651.S2B85   1998
305.896081—dc21   97–43478
                                                                       CIP
British Cataloging-in-Publication information available

Interior graphics by Dean Hogarth

Copyright © 1998 by Kim D. Butler
All rights reserved
No part of this book may be reproduced or utilized in any form or by any means, electronic or mechanical, or by any information storage and retrieval system, without written permission from the publisher. Please contact Rutgers University Press, Livingston Campus, Bldg. 4161, P.O. Box 5062, New Brunswick, New Jersey 08903. The only exception to this prohibition is "fair use" as defined by U.S. copyright law.

Manufactured in the United States of America.

Dedicated with love to my mother,
Claudia Richards Butler

CONTENTS

ILLUSTRATIONS

Illustrations

Figures

TABLES

Acknowledgments

This book is the result of a decade of research that began as a master's thesis at Howard University. I was able to develop this project further as a doctoral candidate at Johns Hopkins University, where I had the good fortune of working with Dr. A.J.R. Russell-Wood. I am deeply indebted to him for his meticulous review of this work and for his wise and caring counsel. My thanks go also to the other professors who helped guide this work: Dr. Asunción Lavrin, my thesis advisor at Howard University, and Drs. Ronald Walters, Sidney Mintz, and Franklin Knight of Johns Hopkins University. Dr. Anani Dzidzienyo of Brown University and Dr. Robert M. Levine commented extensively on the manuscript, and their support is deeply appreciated. Dr. Michael Mitchell was kind enough to talk with me often throughout the early stages of my research. He facilitated my initial meetings with São Paulo activists and was a much-needed sounding board and guide who helped me get my bearings.

Individuals at a number of institutions have been very supportive. I worked for several years at the Smithsonian Institution while in graduate school. Words cannot express the encouragement I received from many kind and talented people at the National Museum of American History, especially Dr. Spencer Crew, Lonnie Bunch, Niani Kilkenny, and Dr. Bernice Johnson Reagon. The Africana Studies Department at Rutgers University helped me through the difficulties of balancing teaching and dissertation writing. I am grateful to Drs. Gayle Tate, Gerald Davis, and all my Rutgers colleagues for their support during this time, and to Gustavo Carerra and John Dizgun, who helped locate the illustrations. My thanks go also to Leslie Mitchner, of Rutgers University Press, and to Elizabeth Gretz, who painstakingly edited the text. The idiosyncrasies that remain are my own.

Several institutions provided financial support at different stages of this project. Howard University funded my first research trip to Brazil, and I am especially indebted to Dr. Genna Rae MacNeil for helping secure my initial grant. Johns Hopkins University awarded me the George Owens Fellowship, which supported three years of graduate study. The Fulbright Foundation provided a Dissertation Research Fellowship that enabled me to conduct my most extensive fieldwork between 1991 and 1992. The Department of History at Johns Hopkins University generously funded all other expenses during my graduate studies.

The emotional support of friends and family helped me through my various stages of career exploration and anchored me throughout seven years of graduate study. I thank my godmothers Daphne Osayade Dumas and Dora Sutton. I am grateful also to my friends Toko, Cary, Millicent, Judy, Claudia, Sandy, Rhett, Joe, Donna, Caroline, Virginia Thomas, and all the people who are my roots on Midwood Street in Brooklyn. Very special thanks also to my dear friend Mwangaza Michael-Bandele.

I was fortunate to meet a number of Brazilians who have struggled to make full freedom for people of African descent a reality. They include my interviewees and the people affiliated with Ilê do Axé Opô Afonjá, Casa Branca, Gantois, Sociedade Protectora dos Desvalidos, Venerável Ordem Terceira do Rosário às Portas do Carmo, Centro de Cultura Negra de Maranhão, Grupo de União e Conciencia Negra, and Ilê Aiye.

My friends Edson, Nelson, Ilmaci, Alda, Ben, Mãe Stella, Mãe Detinha, Mãe Cantulina, and especially Lino made Brazil my second home. Bob and Amelia Verhine, the Justino family of Santos, Hedimar Silva, Heliana Hemeterio, and the Leite and Cunha families also provided kind help at critical junctures. The staffs at the Arquivo Público do Estado da Bahia and the Arquivo Municipal de Salvador graciously allowed me access to many uncatalogued materials.

It is with deep love and respect that I recall those who have departed. José Correia Leite was a tireless defender of Afro-Brazilians who sacrificed much of his personal life and comforts in the struggle for his people. He remains an inspiration to me. My late uncles Henry and John Richards, and all my ancestors, helped make it possible for me to reach this milestone.

Finally, my greatest thanks and gratitude go to my family. They have been by my side every step of the way, most especially my parents, Claudia and Milledge Butler, my sister, Katrina, and my aunt Ruth Richards. Their spiritual support and love are the rock upon which I stand.

What illusions! The slaves having been restored to liberty, we believed our Brazil was about to initiate an era of peace, happiness, and unceasing progress—the "golden age" which the philanthropists always imagined would be around the corner but which, nevertheless, is still far, very far, centuries away.
     —André Rebouças, Afro-Brazilian abolitionist (1895)

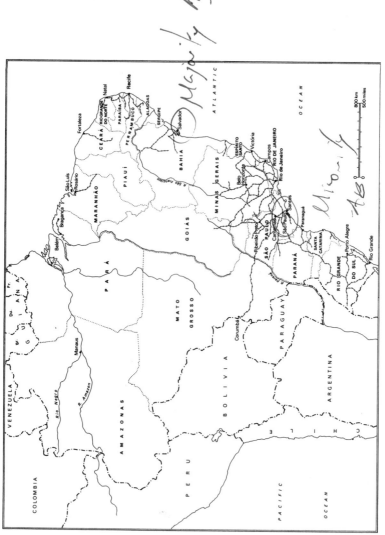

ILL. 1. Brazil during the First Republic, 1889–1930. From *Brazil: Empire and Republic: 1822–1930*, ed. Leslie Bethell (Cambridge: Cambridge University Press, 1989), p. 216.

Brazil and the Afro-Atlantic Diaspora

RECONTEXTUALIZING ABOLITION

The struggle of the Black people of Brazil is an aspect of a much larger struggle:
the struggle of the Black people of the world.
—Lélia Gonzalez, Afro-Brazilian activist (1985)[1]

$\mathcal{T}$he year was 1910 and in the hillsides of northeastern Brazil that once harbored fugitive slaves, Eugenia Anna dos Santos inaugurated a sacred community so that African ancestors and deities could give direction and strength to their children in the diaspora. Assisted by a *babalawo,* a diviner trained in Nigeria, she dedicated the land to Xangô, the patron deity of the kings of the Oyo Empire. In rituals learned from elders on both sides of the Atlantic, the first of many generations of spiritual children entered this special land to become African. Physical Africa may have been forever lost to them, yet they had bridged time and space to shape, in the twentieth century, lives informed by African cultures and sensibilities in the heart of the Americas.

The decades immediately following abolition in each of the slave societies of the Americas and the Caribbean opened a unique opportunity for African descendants to redefine themselves and their roles in the nations in which they lived. For dos Santos and her followers, this meant reconnecting themselves to an African heritage and spirituality. For others it meant narrowing the distance between themselves and a powerful white elite through cultural assimilation. Regardless of the way slavery ended in any specific nation, the post-abolition years in the Afro-Atlantic diaspora were characterized by a struggle for self-determination that set the tone for ethnic politics throughout the twentieth century.

The term Afro-Atlantic refers to the massive diaspora of Africans brought to the Americas and the Caribbean during the transatlantic slave trade, as well as their descendants. By even conservative estimates, at least nine and a half million Africans made the Middle Passage, a psychological journey as much as a physical one. Africans affected virtually every aspect of the developing American colonies—economically, socially, culturally, genetically. This was especially true in Brazil, the destination of approximately 38 percent of enslaved Africans overall and 60 percent during the last century of the trade. Despite demographic concentrations of Africans in such places as Brazil, Barbados, Haiti, and Jamaica and in coastal cities generally, certain aspects of slavery in the Americas were common to all. Among these was the practice of granting liberty to individuals while keeping the system intact. Not until the Haitian Revolution (1791–1804) did an entire slave population obtain its freedom. Slavery was subsequently ended by decree or warfare, with Brazil becoming the last nation to proclaim abolition in 1888.

To those who bore the brands of servitude, abolition was a simple concept—freedom. It was the word spoken when Africans dreamed of escape, when an individual received manumission, and even when a slave found release in death. With the wholesale abolition of slavery, the descendants of Africans looked to a new freedom as citizens. But abolition was more complex than the mere freeing of the enslaved, an act often attributed to the humanitarian natures of heads of state such as Princess Isabel of Brazil or Abraham Lincoln of the United States. Abolition was a complicated and protracted process, one that wrenched whole economies and societies from their very foundations. They did not go easily, especially in those nations in which large and influential interest groups had reaped fortunes from slavery. Emancipation transformed a marginalized, oppressed segment of the population into citizens, roughly at the very time the new nations of the Americas were defining the parameters of citizenship. In many American and Caribbean nations, abolition was carefully engineered to limit freedoms and to coerce former slaves into subservient roles in post-emancipation society. The fundamental problem was that people of African descent viewed abolition as freedom from the oppression they had suffered since colonial times. In contrast, the privileged classes of the Americas perceived abolition as a structural shift that could be prevented from jeopardizing race-based social relations of power. The freedoms given were far more paltry than the freedoms people of African descent hoped to win.

American elites soon learned that, although they enjoyed the prerogatives conferred upon them by slave society, such as the privileges of light skin and high social status, they could not simply impose their will on the new class of freedpersons. In the high-stakes game of reshaping society, both sides struggled to position themselves to their best advantage. The terms of the new freedom had to be negotiated in an ongoing dialectic of initiative and response.

Recognition of this dynamic opens new possibilities for historical analysis of the post-abolition era. The choices and initiatives of African descendants have frequently been obscured in studies of the transitional period after the demise of slavery. Too often they appear as victims of the historical forces and powerful protagonists able to set the social, economic, and cultural tenor of national life. Yet careful study of the experiences of African descendants in the Americas and Caribbean shows that they were actively involved in shaping their own identities and social roles despite efforts to perpetuate the limitations on them engendered under slave society.

This book revisits abolition and its aftermath in two Brazilian cities in an attempt to better understand the processes by which peoples of the Afro-Atlantic diaspora attempted to redefine their roles and prerogatives and, in so doing, the society at large. It focuses on the intersection of the freedpersons' choices and initiatives with specific socioeconomic and cultural conditions extant at the time of abolition. As Afro-Brazilians discovered the limitations on the freedoms granted by abolition, they realized that the "full free" they had envisioned could only be won through struggle. That struggle was rooted in the right of self-determination in the face of the dictates of a ruling class. Thus the many ways in which people of African descent asserted their humanity and right to full and equal participation in all aspects of society, both individually and collectively, were all part of the post-abolition struggle of self-determination.

Brazilian Abolition in Afro-Atlantic Perspective

With an estimated 120 million people of African descent, Brazil is home to the largest population of the African diaspora. They arrived in Portuguese slave ships to produce the sugar that made Brazil one of the richest American colonies in the sixteenth and seventeenth centuries. While continuing in the diversifying agricultural economy, Africans also mined gold and precious minerals during the brief gold rush of 1695–1750, worked as artisans, porters, and domestic workers in the cities, and formed the backbone of the first generation of export coffee plantations in the nineteenth century. Officially, this was the role of Africans—laborers bought and sold to produce wealth. In reality, however, these were human beings who composed the majority of the colonial population and left a lasting legacy in Brazilian society and culture.

The Afro-Brazilian experience may be understood in many contexts. It was part of the first global trade network which, centered in Portugal, stretched from the Americas to Africa to Asia. Afro-Brazilian history may be understood as a component of either the Brazilian experience, or of Latin America in general. Afro-Brazilians are also part of the African diaspora, and this book looks at them in the context of the Afro-Atlantic segment of that diaspora. Brazilian history is marked by factors that shaped the Afro-Atlantic world—slavery, resistance, slave culture, acculturation issues, the formation of new identities, racism, and problems of integration and egalitarianism. In that regard, Afro-Brazilian history shares references with Afro-Americans and Afro-Caribbeans throughout the hemisphere. These historical commonalities are echoed in the struggles of African descendants in the Atlantic world today. In understanding the persistent inability of people of African descent to achieve full parity in modern society, purely national explanations do not suffice. The descendants of slaves throughout the Americas and the Caribbean continue to suffer inequality well into the second century after abolition.[3] Lélia Gonzalez, an Afro-Brazilian activist, wrote that "the struggle of the Black people of Brazil is an aspect of a much larger struggle: the struggle of the Black people of the world."[4] A framework grounded in the African diaspora experience, by shifting perspective, makes possible an alternative analysis of the connection between those two struggles. A more nuanced understanding of the Afro-Brazilian adaptations to the new conditions of post-emancipation society may well shed light on those of other Afro-Atlantic peoples.

African diaspora history is often confused with popular notions of "black" history as the inclusion of the experiences of African descendants where they have previously been overlooked. Although this is a necessary dimension of much diasporan research, another significant component of diasporan studies is the application of alternative comparative frameworks. Diasporization scatters a group from its homeland to diverse locations around the world. To study its members as a diaspora rather than as immigrants to a particular nation requires a framework that transcends national boundaries.

This book seeks to form a diasporan framework that will illuminate the role of African descendants in setting the parameters for freedom after the final abolition of slavery. Freedom came with no handbook; it was left up to those who lived in post-emancipation societies to determine exactly how freedpersons would fit in. This work explores the collective strategies of two Afro-Brazilian urban communities as case studies from which models may be derived for testing in other Afro-Atlantic societies. In so doing, it will touch only tangentially upon some issues that may be of great importance in the interpretation of Brazilian or Latin American history. In contrast, extra attention will be paid to those topics essential to Afro-Atlantic diaspora history.

Abolition marked the end of the forced presence of people of African descent in the Americas, a people who had come unwillingly to a hostile and oppressive environment. It gave them the theoretical option of either "returning" to Africa or remaining in the countries in which most had been born. The choice to stay or the impossibility of an African return meant the acceptance of citizenship in their countries of residence. The terms of that citizenship, however, had yet to be negotiated. Ethnic politics during the first decades after abolition redefined the relationships of African descendants to Atlantic nations. At least four common themes link the Afro-Brazilian case to the rest of the Afro-Atlantic diaspora.

First, the shared experience of slavery established a relationship wherein one segment of the population decided the position and function of another. Across a vast hemisphere, the Portuguese, Spanish, British, French, and Dutch financed the wholesale transfer of Africans to the Americas as a subservient labor force for the express purpose of generating wealth for others. Only through constant pressure and resistance did Africans and their descendants carve roles for themselves beyond the boundaries of brute labor. Neither Africans nor indigenous peoples were originally viewed as participating members of civil society, notwithstanding their essential roles as laborers, caregivers, and contributors to the development of creole cultures. The colonial understanding of "Brazilians," for example, referred to the white descendants of the Portuguese; the brown and black descendants of Africans and indigenous peoples—albeit a numerical majority—were seen as interlopers who had to find their own way into Brazilian society.[5] Their strategies varied depending on conditions existing in diverse colonial settings and with the aspirations of each individual. The notion that the labor and lives of African descendants were subject to the dictates of governments and slave masters not only lingered after abolition, but was frequently included in emancipation legislation. The penultimate law of abolition in Brazil, passed in 1885, granted masters "the use of the services of the *freed* slave for five years" and confined former slaves to their municipality of residence for five years on pain of arrest.[6]

Second, Brazil's abolition was a state-directed initiative, as was the case throughout the Atlantic nations with the exception of Haiti, the Dominican Republic, and the United States. The desire to forestall revolt on the part of the enslaved converged with international economic pressures to move governments to assume this responsibility. Only in the violent Haitian Revolution did slaves take full control of their own liberation. State-controlled abolition had the benefit of permitting elites to shape the initial terms of abolition to their advantage, notwithstanding the fact that the ultimate outcome would be affected by the initiatives of freedpersons as well as by world market conditions. Abolition is considered in this regard not as a single legislative act but, rather, as a series of related laws and policies affecting labor and ethnic relations.

③

Third, Brazilian abolition was not philanthropic; it was part of a general program of economic modernization that entailed coercing freedmen into specific sectors of employment. Throughout the Americas, slaveowners expressed great concern over their ability to maintain pre-abolition levels of production. Because of this, measures to ensure the profit levels of slaveowners, including compensation for lost investments, became integral to debates over abolitionist legislation. Theirs was a pragmatic concern given the fact that in Haiti, sugar production decreased by 98 percent after the revolution and did not regain its colonial level until the 1960s. The greatest threat to American economies was the desertion of freedpersons from the productive roles they had exercised as slaves. The most common mechanism to prevent such flight was the implementation of transition labor policies oriented toward maintaining freedmen in their pre-abolition roles.[7] Numerous demographic, economic, and political factors affected the ability of former slaveowners to protect their interests, and local modifications to labor and economic legislation are best understood as a protracted process extending over decades and continuing to be refined well after abolition. What these colonies shared was the fact that abolition did not become a revolutionary act changing the basic relations of power and property (with the obvious exception of Haiti). The mere declaration of abolition did not automatically remove the barriers containing former slaves in their previous class position. Indeed, the orientation of social, political, and economic objectives toward the preservation of elite prerogatives served to handicap freedpersons in their pursuit of higher socioeconomic echelons, pressuring them instead into disadvantageous positions in free society.

④

The fourth issue that Afro-Brazilians shared with their Atlantic counterparts was the construction of an ethnicity that could be used to their advantage. Despite the fact that their differential treatment was linked to their common African heritage, the concept of a unified "black" ethnic group developed late and gradually in most of the Afro-Atlantic diaspora.[8] Diasporan communities were, in fact, extremely heterogeneous. The transatlantic trade drew Africans from hundreds of ethnic groups. They intermingled in the Americas, where slave owners emphasized further subdivisions based on such factors as color, degree of assimilation, trade, class, and civil status (free versus slave). A keen sense of internal differentiation served the regime; Africans and their descendants, including free blacks, slaves, and mixed-bloods, made up the majority population of many slave societies. Acting together, they could well have toppled the ruling class. What happened to those cleavages after abolition? To what degree was racial identity as a basis for group solidarity further hampered by the dual stigmas of the supposed barbarity of Africa and the shameful heritage of slavery? Were other forms of ethnicity developed, and how did these affect the strategic position of blacks? One way to approach these questions is through the study of collective actions of African descendants in the post-abolition era.

The emancipation decree of 1888 did not free many slaves. Brazil's slave population, which had been as high as 50 percent of the national total in 1822, had dwindled to 5 percent by the time of abolition.[9] The rapid pace of attrition was due to the restructuring of the labor force, technological advances in automation, and the cumulative effect of abolitionist legislation. A ban on the trafficking of slaves across the Atlantic, passed in 1817, was actively enforced after 1850. The Rio Branco Law of 1871 freed the children born to slave mothers, and a law in 1885 granted freedom to sexagenarians. The enslaved could also purchase their freedom or run away—both options exercised liberally throughout the nineteenth century. The post-abolition period in Brazil, therefore, did not begin with an abrupt mass liberation. It began with two terse sentences that legislated a freedom left undefined.

> From the date of this Law slavery is declared abolished in Brazil.
> All contrary provisions are revoked.[10]

With these words, the Golden Law abolishing slavery was approved by the General Assembly and sanctioned by the Princess Regent Isabel on May 13, 1888. A new republic was declared in November 1889. In 1890 Finance Minister Rui Barbosa burned the government's slave registers, signaling the start of a new era in Brazilian history. Progress was the order of the day, and Brazil proudly announced to the world that all its citizens were welcome to share in that progress in the spirit of racial democracy. Yet four centuries of slavery could not be brushed away with the ashes of Rui Barbosa's bonfire. A date on the calendar was only the final moment of a process that had spanned seventy years. Beneath what appeared to be a smooth and orderly transition to modernity, no one in 1888 knew what the true meaning of Brazilian abolition would ultimately be.

Emancipation was more than the sum of individual transitions to free society. It forced Brazilians to grapple with the larger issue of the social position of African descendants in national life. On this matter, opinions contrasted sharply. The elite perspective is possible to reconstruct because its members left a vast written record. The many voices of Afro-Brazilians are rarely found in documents. Instead, it is necessary to turn to their actions. What became the points of contention, the unacceptable restrictions on freedom and citizenship that Afro-Brazilians found important to fight? With whom did they associate? To what degree did identification and loyalty to nation contrast with loyalty to an ethnic group, and how was that ethnic group defined? These are some of the questions explored here in the context of São Paulo and Salvador.

In different ways, São Paulo and Salvador are perhaps the most important cities in twentieth-century Afro-Brazilian history. São Paulo is traditionally regarded as the vanguard of political activism. It is the single richest source of the written political ideology of Afro-Brazilians during the post-abolition period, recorded in dozens of Afro-Brazilian newspapers beginning around 1915.[11] Brazil's first race-based political activist organization, the Centro Cívico Palmares, was founded there in 1926. In 1931 former members of that group founded the Frente Negra Brasileira, the nation's first and only Afro-Brazilian political party. It was also in São Paulo that the Movimento Negro Unificado was founded in 1978. Salvador is popularly known as the African capital of Brazil.[12] It is home to world-renowned centers of the Afro-Brazilian religion of candomblé, derived primarily from the culture of the Yoruba peoples of Nigeria. The elaborate rituals of Bahian candomblé have long been heralded as a clear example of African retentions in the diaspora. But Africa informs many other aspects of Bahian life. On street corners, for example, Afro-Bahian women sell the food of the African gods known as orixás—*acarajé*, *abara*, pastries, and coconut sweets; popular festivals feature gifts of flowers and prayers to Iemanjá, the goddess of the oceans; African drumming animates the weekly rehearsals of Carnival clubs; and the Angolan-inspired *capoeira*, a martial art, flourishes both informally and in academies throughout the city of Salvador. The trajectory of each of these cities stems not only from historical antecedents in the nineteenth century but also from the dynamics of the post-abolition era that link past and present.

The collective responses to abolition in São Paulo and Salvador are clues to the profound changes taking place as Afro-Brazilians determined for themselves the roles they wished to play in national society and took steps to realize their objectives. Yet they raise more questions than they answer. The striking regional differences may have been due to different local political cultures or to other factors, such as whether the Afro-Brazilian population was a minority, as in São Paulo, or a majority, as in Salvador. What types of patterns emerge when post-emancipation conditions are compared not between Brazilian cities, but with other diasporan communities where conditions are more similar? In addition, this study focuses exclusively on cities. Is there an urban model of abolition that differs from that of the seignorial structure of agricultural economies?

This book begins with only the most basic assumptions. The first is that the objectives of economic and social elites differed from those of freedpersons. Second, African descendants, in their efforts to reshape their lives, became dynamic historical actors and not mere victims of white objectives in post-emancipation society. Beyond that, the only way to begin to understand abolition for the people of the African diaspora in its many nuances is to go back into the past to examine their actions and discern possible patterns.

Chapter 1 examines the contextual factors affecting elite initiatives and Afro-Brazilian responses. Social, political, and economic conditions, at both the local and the national levels, clearly affected the nature of Brazilian abolition. It will be argued, however, that an entirely different set of internal factors related to the nature of the Afro-Brazilian community itself had an equally powerful effect on the range of its members' choices as they adapted to the changing conditions of post-abolition life. These internal factors are discussed in detail in Chapter 2. The case studies of São Paulo and Salvador in Chapters 3–6 each begin with an overview of their Afro-Brazilian communities. These overviews attempt to go beyond the limited statistical record to outline more clearly the contours of ethnic, philosophical, and economic diversity that characterized a truly heterogeneous population. Finally, after examining specific Afro-Brazilian initiatives, I suggest a framework for categorizing and analyzing post-abolition responses within the context of the Afro-Atlantic diaspora.

Sources of Afro-Brazilian History

In many instances, source material is scarce for this period of Afro-Brazilian history. There exists a serious lacuna in Afro-Brazilian historiography attributable, in part, to the fact that the raw data of social history—census, health, demographic, educational, and other records—have proved exceedingly difficult to collect for Afro-Brazilians during the First Republic (1889–1930). This information is needed to assess demographic, economic, and social changes among people of African descent. Prior to abolition, statisticians routinely noted slave status, color, and African nationality, thereby enabling historians to reconstruct significant aspects of the African and Afro-Brazilian experience. After 1888 race began disappearing as a statistical category in many essential records. Sacramental records of births, baptisms, marriages, and deaths dropped racial identifications in the early 1890s.[13] Racial classifications were absent from forms used by police to record arrests and prison movement.[14] The national censuses of 1900 and 1920 did not include race and only reintroduced the category in 1940. Whereas some of this information is gradually being uncovered, it is often difficult to establish uniform bases of comparison. In addition, financial constraints on Brazilian archives have meant that the administrative records of the First Republic are not yet available in their entirety. Primary documents produced by Afro-Brazilians have also been hard to find, although the availability of an increasing number of oral histories conducted in recent years has proved a helpful complement for preliminary analyses.[15] Nonetheless, the net result is that it is virtually impossible to document Afro-Brazilian history in the post-abolition years with the depth and precision it merits.

The lack of essential data illustrates the problem faced then and now by Brazilians of African descent. They are ever present as color and context in Brazilian history, yet in many ways remain invisible at the same time. African descendants populate the margins of Brazilian society, but are at the heart of its national culture. In the luxurious residences of wealthy urbanites, Afro-Brazilians are kept out by electrified fences and high walls; inside, they serve as guardians and housekeepers, cooks and drivers, nannies and handymen. In the four volumes of the *Historia Geral da Civilização Brasileira* dedicated to the First Republic, there is no mention of the political activism of blacks in São Paulo that led to the creation of the Frente Negra Brasileira.

Nonetheless, Afro-Brazilians have been the subjects of a great deal of scholarly research, including significant works addressing their trajectory after abolition.[16] Raymundo Nina Rodrigues published the first major analysis of Afro-Brazilians and their role in national society in 1896.[17] His assessment, echoed by a host of late nineteenth- and early twentieth-century researchers, was that African social and cultural heritage had had a lingering and negative effect that limited Afro-Brazilians' assimilation into mainstream Brazilian culture. Some authors relied heavily on biological determinism to argue that blacks were inferior and incapable of succeeding in modern civilized society.

Gilberto Freyre shifted this interpretation in 1933 by contending that the ideas and relationships shaped during slavery, not African retentions, were the decisive factor determining post-abolition race relations.[18] Freyre championed the concept of Brazil as a racial democracy, a notion increasingly called into question as the twentieth century moved into its latter decades with no substantial change in patterns of racial inequities.

The work of Nina Rodrigues and Freyre paved the way for anthropological and ethnographic research, but the study of Afro-Brazilians as political actors remained relatively neglected. The existing literature focuses on Afro-Brazilian activists in São Paulo, the principal exponents of black political ideology during that era. Much of that ideology was captured in a flourishing black press. In the first two decades of the twentieth century, Afro-Brazilian social clubs in the city began publishing newspapers that included commentary on the position of blacks in society. Increased politicization in São Paulo led to the creation of racially based social advocacy groups, including the Centro Cívico Palmares, founded in 1926, and the Frente Negra Brasileira, founded in 1931. The appearance of activist organizations coincided with a trend toward a more doctrinaire press, as evidenced by such newspapers as *O Clarim da Alvorada, Progresso,* and *A Voz da Raça.* This period of Afro-

Brazilian activism ended with the establishment of the Estado Novo (New State) in 1937, when President Getúlio Vargas censured all forms of political expression.

The only contemporary study to touch upon this aspect of Afro-Brazilian history was a chapter in Arthur Ramos' *The Negro in Brazil*, published in 1939.[19] The first detailed analysis of Afro-Brazilian adjustment in the post-abolition years came in 1965 with the publication of *A Integração do Negro na Sociedade de Classes* by the Brazilian sociologist Florestan Fernandes.[20] Basing his work on the São Paulo experience, Fernandes set out to explain the relative inability of Afro-Brazilians to attain upward mobility in the modern economy. He concluded that the social problems plaguing blacks in the late twentieth century were the result of their inadequate adaptation to post-abolition conditions. "The psychological distortions induced by slavery," he wrote, "limited their ability to adjust to urban life under a capitalist system."[21] Whites and nonwhites, he maintained, had the same opportunities but, because of slavery, blacks began with a disadvantage at the time of abolition. Fernandes shared Freyre's fundamental premise that slavery was the single most important factor in assessing post-abolition developments. In his opinion, slave society made blacks unfamiliar with the free market and created a negative attitude toward work. This made freedmen unsuitable for the lucrative industrial jobs that European immigrant workers were better prepared to assume. Migrants from the rural interior and those without white benefactors had a harder time adjusting:

> Having little knowledge of the white, they feared to express themselves to him and submitted passively to his wishes. They did not risk looking for better jobs or transgressing the role expectations which condemned the Negro to a hard, thankless, and unrewarding life. Being both timid and naive, they preferred to suffer silently and to isolate themselves even from their more successful colleagues.[22]

Fernandes also maintained that blacks' aspirations were too high, causing them to "develop social ambitions that were disastrous to them."[23]

Fernandes devoted considerable attention to the efforts of black Paulistanos to organize politically.[24] He noted their chronic problems; "[p]redatory individualism and lack of consensus were the two specters that hovered continually over the rights movements."[25] Blacks, he maintained, never achieved the broad-based solidarity necessary to compete effectively in the political culture of the corporatist First Republic. To do so would have required institutionalized "patterns of organic solidarity that were typical of the class society."[26] In other words, black interest group activism was a doomed concept in the absence of a black community with strong group identity and social institutions.

There were many flaws in the Fernandes thesis, which has since been challenged by numerous scholars. Methodologically, Fernandes relied almost exclusively on the oral testimony of a handful of activists and therefore presented a limited view of the Afro-Paulistano community. He also engaged in sweeping generalizations about the character of "the Negro," such as the comment about being "timid and naive," based purely upon assumption and racialist folklore. Critics have challenged his "blaming the victim" approach and have identified other causes for Afro-Brazilian marginalization. Carlos Hasenbalg, a sociologist writing not long after Fernandes, rejected the reliance on slavery alone as an explanatory factor. He, along with Afro-Brazilians beginning to publish after the political détente of the mid-1970s, charged that the persistence of racial discrimination was equally responsible in accounting for the inferior social position of Afro-Brazilians in the late twentieth century.[27] Hasenbalg also noted the disproportionate concentration of Afro-Brazilians both geographically and occupationally in the less economically productive sectors of the economy. Other scholars, such as Nelson do Valle Silva, have documented the persistence of discrimination in hiring and its negative economic repercussions.[28]

Among the most recent revisions of the Fernandes thesis is George Reid Andrews' *Blacks and Whites in São Paulo, Brazil, 1888–1988*.[29] In this 1991 work, Andrews used employment records to document hiring patterns by race over time. He also revisited the black press and black organizations, which he analyzed in the context of local and national political changes. Andrews concluded that the principal factor in economic disparity between the races was the intervention of the Republican government in the post-abolition labor market. With regard to black activist groups, Andrews concentrated on their position within the Brazilian political spectrum. He recognized internal class differences and the situation of the activists at the upper end of the black social strata. He did not, however, dwell on the evolution of diverse political and social strategies within the black community, which is the focus of this study.

Despite legitimate objections to his analysis, Fernandes did address a major challenge to black political empowerment in Brazil. The political culture demanded a level of group solidarity that did not yet exist. In this regard, I differ with Fernandes' conclusion about the role of *negro* identity (he uses the term "negritude") as merely "an understanding of the past, present, and future that was consistent with the social perspective and longings for justice of the Negro people."[30] As will be seen, black leaders in São Paulo used ethnic identity strategically, transforming it from its traditionally divisive role into an instrument of group solidarity.

Roger Bastide, a colleague of Fernandes at the University of São Paulo, conducted the first substantive analysis of the black press.[31] Its principal audience was the membership of Afro-Brazilian social and recreational clubs. These journals chronicled the activities of black activist organizations and served as a forum for debates about ideology and political strategy, therein providing a window into a broad spectrum of the black Paulistano community. In 1977, drawing on the journals in conjunction with oral history, the political scientist Michael Mitchell outlined the evolution of a political agenda that later broke into divergent factions. With his work, the role of Afro-Brazilians themselves in molding their own futures became central to the analysis, unlike the work of Fernandes, who merely credited "certain specific sociohistorical incentives" with the fomentation of the social movement.[32]

Two Brazilian authors have made important contributions toward a social history of nonactivist black groups in São Paulo. Iêda Marques Britto published a study of the emergence of samba groups between 1900 and 1930, opening the possibility of studying the political implications of social collectives, although this was not her research objective.[33] José Carlos Gomes da Silva used the black community of Barra Funda as a counterpoint to what he termed the "social movements of the black elite." He provides valuable insights into the work, social problems, and culture of a previously understudied black community that was intimately related to the development of political agendas by Afro-Paulistas.[34]

Actual organizational archives were scattered and destroyed over the years. One of the few surviving records of the Frente Negra was the "Livrão" (the "Big Book"), which contained membership rolls, newspaper clippings, and organization documents. A former officer of the Frente, Francisco Lucrecio, kept it at his home for years until it was irreparably damaged by a leaky roof. A valuable collection of contemporary Afro-Brazilian newspapers, in the home of Henrique Cunha, an activist in several organizations, barely escaped a fire several years ago.[35] The scant documentary sources and their precarious state have led virtually all scholars to supplement their research by interviewing former participants in São Paulo's black organizations.

Oral history has played a particularly prominent role in the reconstruction of Afro-Paulista history. Fernandes' principal source was based upon interviews with José Correia Leite, co-founder of the newspaper *Clarim da Alvorada*.[36] Leite was the single source consulted by all researchers until his death in 1989.[37] Raul Joviano de Amaral was also interviewed for several studies, as were Francisco Lucrecio, Jayme de Aguiar, and Henrique Cunha. Each of these men played critical roles in their organizations, but only reflected the perspectives of a single generation of activists. Their political agendas were also similar, despite the fact that a rift developed between the

Clarim da Alvorada's collective and the Frente Negra. They all wanted to strengthen the black community through solidarity, and to use that unified base to advocate for equal opportunities. There were, however, many types of Afro-Brazilian collectives, as well as nonaffiliated individuals, embracing a broad spectrum of political thought. Recently more documentation and oral history have been preserved and collected from these sources. Gomes da Silva's thesis relies heavily on interviews with the workers and samba afficionados in São Paulo's Barra Funda neighborhood. I have conducted oral histories with former activists as well as members of the samba community and nonaffiliated individuals.[38]

Together, this body of literature and oral history helps mitigate the challenges to an informed analysis of black activism in São Paulo. This is not the case for Salvador, for which I was unable to find any research on black political involvement in post-abolition society. In terms of formal organizations, Salvador had no black political entity comparable to São Paulo's Frente Negra Brasileira.[39] Scholarship on Afro-Bahians has focused on explicitly cultural manifestations, addressing to a far lesser degree the political implications of those activities.[40] This contrast has given rise to a deceptive polarity in the representation of the south (São Paulo in particular) as the "political" center and the northeast (especially Salvador) as the "cultural" center for Afro-Brazilians.

If, however, we change the definition of what is political, the landscape of post-abolition activism becomes quite different. The efforts to deny Afro-Brazilian self-determination reflected entrenched relationships of power between whites and nonwhites. Any opposition, therefore, had political repercussions. In that regard, the activities of Afro-Bahians were extremely important in redefining the social identity of persons of African descent. There was a flourishing organizational life in Salvador, composed primarily of religious (both Catholic and Afro-Brazilian) institutions, which provided the infrastructure for post-abolition struggles against cultural repression and police brutality. Afro-Bahians reversed the national trend toward marginalization of Afro-Brazilian culture. They impressed their cultural stamp on mainstream Bahian society, albeit with the stigma of "low" culture or "primitive" folklore. They chose cultural confrontation over a bid for political power, which remained in the hands of a white minority. The scholarly literature has not yet addressed the reasons behind this choice, the subject of the Bahian section here.[41]

Among the most valuable sources for Bahian research is the archive of the Sociedade Protectora dos Desvalidos, a black mutual aid society founded in 1832 as a Catholic brotherhood. Its records provide insight into many diverse aspects of Afro-Bahian social life. I also consulted the organizational records of the Rosário brotherhood, contemporary newspapers, ecclesiastical archives, government documents, and the files of the Secretaria de Segurança Publica. This last group of records, which covered police activity, were partially destroyed prior to its transfer to the state archives. The archived collection to which I had access contains no reference to the ongoing covert police raids on candomblé houses that became more frequent in the 1920s and 1930s. Finally, secondary literature and informal conversations with older members of Bahia's black community provide important contextual background.

Scarcity of sources has proved a deterrent to many researchers, but cannot be used as an excuse to neglect a subject meriting serious study. Given the boom of Afro-Brazilian and African diaspora studies in the twentieth century, an understanding of Afro-Brazilian initiatives in the transformation from slavery to free citizenship is an indispensable prerequisite. A meticulous combing of personal and archival data, state agency records, iconography, and oral history may someday yield sufficient information to compile a social history of Afro-Brazilian life between 1888 and 1938. Such research is necessarily long-term and cumulative. What I have attempted here is a preliminary endeavor to move toward a better understanding of self-determination struggles in the Afro-Atlantic diaspora and of the ways in which African descendants have acted as protagonists in their own history. It is an effort to bring together sometimes disparate bits of information—pieces of an historical puzzle that may not constitute a full picture, but will enable us to perceive its general outlines.

CHAPTER 1

"Order and Progress"

ELITE OBJECTIVES AND THE
SHAPING OF ABOLITION

The black race in Brazil, as great as have been their undeniable services to our civilization, as justified as are our sympathies that they were enmeshed in the revolting abuse of slavery... will forever constitute one of the factors of our inferiority as a people.... We consider the predominance of the black race harmful to our nationality, their intolerable influence prejudicial in all cases to the progress and culture of our people.
—Raymundo Nina Rodrigues, *Os Africanos no Brasil*[1]

$\mathcal{T}$he post-abolition era, determined here as the first five decades following abolition, corresponds roughly with the political regime known as the First Republic (1889–1930). By then, Brazil had had various forms of government. Upon its foundation, the colony was divided into fifteen large land grants known as captaincies. Portugal instituted a formal colonial government in 1549, with its capital at Salvador, Bahia. In 1808 the royal family fled to Rio de Janeiro to escape Napoleon's invasion, and subsequently elevated Brazil to the status of kingdom in 1815. When the Court returned to Europe in 1822, Prince Pedro remained behind, declaring Brazil to be politically independent and transforming it into an empire. For the Brazilian-born upper classes, independence alone was incapable of quelling their desire for total control of national affairs, in which native Portuguese had historically played a major role. Only with the coup d'état of 1889 did Brazil definitively attain its autonomy from its European metropole.

"Order and Progress" was the motto of the elites who shaped the First Republic. The phrase captured their hopes that Brazil's vast potential, aptly managed, would propel it to the ranks of advanced societies. It was a time in which weaker nations throughout what would be called the "third world" were losing their autonomy to colonial powers and falling behind in economic development. Brazil, clearly wishing to avoid this fate, embarked upon a series of state-directed initiatives in social and economic engineering. This chapter explores the objectives of the Republican leaders, as encompassed by that motto, and the implications of these goals for Afro-Brazilians.

The challenge to the new Brazilian republic was to define itself as a nation. Part of that challenge was the development of a national identity and a sense of who was to be included in the new civil state. Would that include the African-born and their descendants, regardless of their length of residency in Brazil? Would it include the former slaves, heretofore regarded as property, or the sharecroppers, servants, and poor, many of them people of color, traditionally relegated to the margins of Brazilian society? Such a shift would require fundamental changes in Brazil's underlying principles. On the surface, Brazilian history is replete with radical changes in government, sweeping economic booms and depressions, and a host of social uprisings. Yet beneath it all lies a remarkable continuity of the principles of social organization that reaches back into the colonial era. Part of that organization was the confinement of people of color to the lower ranks of society and power. The persistence into the twentieth century of the ideologies, institutions, and social relationships shaped during slavery continued to constrain black mobility long after abolition.

It is important to analyze the intent of those who fostered elite initiatives in the post-abolition era, because these were the individuals who controlled the mechanisms of political and economic institutions. They framed abolition and its aftermath, placing persons of African descent in a reactive position. Freedpersons did assume initiative, but were forced to begin their response within a pre-arranged framework. It is therefore necessary to understand the conditions on freedom set by Brazilian society before turning to the Afro-Brazilian response.

Order

The word "order" has several meanings, all of which are intrinsic to understanding the Brazilian conceptualization of society. Order can refer to the organization of society in the sense of providing a rationale or guiding principle underlying social relationships. Order may also mean control, the forces by which stability is ensured. Finally, order can be used in the sense of hierarchy, the relationships of rank by which all segments of a society are interconnected. In each sense, order entails the factors of social cohesion. It is explored here because the dominant rationale of social order in Brazil prevented the equitable participation of blacks in national society. Attempts to break free of the constraints upon them constituted a challenge to order and, hence, stability. Accordingly, struggles to dismantle discrimination against people of African descent faced not only individual resistance but an entire national ethos in which race-based discrimination was ingrained. Brazil's relative lack of personalized expressions of racial animosity was often held up in favorable comparison with the United States to demonstrate that racism did not exist. Yet the inequities implicit in the national ethos proved to be as formidable as any explicit racial barrier.

The first concept of order is the understanding of how individual members of society relate to one another—the order of social relationships. In Brazil, the underlying principle of social relationships is patronage. It is the notion that social relationships are based upon an exchange of fealty and services for protection and economic support, and that disloyalty to one's patron merits punishment.[2] Historians have studied patronage as the basis for Brazil's political culture.[3] Here that concept is extended as a principle underlying all social relationships.

Evident in microcosm in the family, patronage dates back to colonial Brazil as a paternalistic structure in which the male head of the household acted as arbiter of the family's fate and fortunes. He was responsible for its actions and served as proxy for the other members in important decisions. He was also the owner of the wealth, including slaves and dependent workers. The patriarch stood as patron to a constituency of dependents of varying categories who, in return, gave him loyalty and support.

The interstitial bonds of marriage and cognatic kinship that linked Brazilian families to one another also embodied the principle of patronage. One of the most important institutions of this type was godparenthood. Parents from all social backgrounds, including slaves, sought individuals who could benefit their child in some way. Wealth was not the only consideration; the Brazilian saying that "a friend in the plaza is worth more than money in the bank" illustrates the importance of social connections. According to the historian Katia Mattoso, "In a society in which positions depended upon the help of third parties, the choice of a well-connected godfather and godmother was part of a strategy of social ascent or, at least, the preservation of a condition already attained."[4]

Within such a system, the support of a patron was essential for social mobility. A free person without connections could not realistically aspire to high-level positions in civil service or the military, for which recommendations were indispensable. Even average jobs were generally obtained through the references of family and friends. Those who were not under the aegis of a patron, generally the landless free population, often procured such relationships. The expression *protegido* (protected one), which refers to dependents of patrons, implicitly warns of the dangers of maneuvering alone through society.

At a broader level, the principle of patronage served as the basis for

Brazil's economic, political, and social structures. Latifundiary agriculture was the predominant mode of production for the colony, generating the bulk of its wealth and giving the patriarchs who owned the large sugar plantations and cattle ranches considerable political influence. It also organized the majority of the colonial population into spheres controlled by the landowners on whom they depended for their livelihood. The owner of a sugar mill *(senhor de engenho),* for example, supported an overseer, mill-master, and a cadre of slaves responsible for all the duties of the house, mill, fields, and livestock. Local farmers came to him to grind their cane at harvest time, and free laborers farmed plots as tenants, or hired out their specialized services.[5]

This early socioeconomic structure antedated the establishment of formal government in 1549.[6] Plantation culture carried its own political principle of autocratic rule. It was a particularly convenient colonial system because the dependency and coercion intrinsic to the system of patronage served as an effective mechanism of social organization and control. Control over an enslaved or otherwise dependent work force also ensured the smooth flow of profits, with which the metropolitan Portuguese government did not wish to interfere. As a result, political structures fit within the framework of plantation culture and patronage rather than serving as an organizing superstructure. The patrons who controlled the means of production also wielded considerable influence over local government, despite periodic power struggles between creole elites and Portuguese nationals. The interests of powerful landowners were well represented in the upper echelons of local politics and the military.

Patron status correlated directly with control over economic resources, but did not suffice to integrate the mobile population of landless freepersons into spheres of influence as clients or dependents. This required the command of force, for if wealth was the carrot of patronage, coercion was its stick. Herein lies a second concept of order as control. Coercion began with financial dependency, but extended to include punishment and violence. It was a major element in managing slave resistance to ensure the stability and economic viability of the colony in the agricultural northeast. Force took on different dimensions in the south and interior, where pastoral and migrant labor characterized the economy. Families banded together in clans and developed private armies to defend their territories. In both situations, there was little government intervention. Here again the government's role was to reinforce rather than to mitigate the power of patrons. Because the colonial and imperial armed forces were relatively small outside of the large coastal cities, they relied on the volunteer services of private armies.[7] Patrons enjoyed great latitude in exercising force and became the de facto administrators of political, judicial, and military matters affecting their constituents. The autocratic authority of patrons over virtually all areas of life left their constituents few alternatives for imposing checks and balances on that power. This type of concentration of power by either an individual or a clan is a pattern evidenced in the Brazilian backlands.[8] The presence of courts and governmental agencies in the large coastal cities diffused power, giving citizens more choices of patrons. Nonetheless, the patronage *mode* of accessing power remained the same.

The story of Josepha da Silva Santos provides an example of the way in which patronage functioned in Republican Brazil. In January 1895, she appeared at the office of the chief of police to ask his help in resolving her complicated domestic problems. Her husband, an alcoholic unable to support his family (and subsequently jailed for robbery and murder), had given their daughter to a Portuguese immigrant whom Josepha charged with "mistreating her as if she were his slave, every day keeping her barefoot, carrying water, doing all the kitchen work, and, to top that, not allowing her to receive my blessing."[9] When Josepha's son, a police officer, found out, he went to the immigrant's house, which resulted in what Josepha euphemistically referred to as a "disorder." Fearful of the Portuguese man's threats to have her son arrested, Josepha appealed to the chief of police in his role as patron to his employees. Without connections, there was nothing Josepha could have done to free her daughter from the Portuguese man, a situation compounded by the father's tacit right to dispose of his daughter as he pleased regardless of Josepha's wishes. Once her son became involved, however, she had recourse to a higher authority with an obligation to intervene on behalf of his *protegidos*. The records do not reveal what ultimately became of Josepha's daughter, but the case shows the avenues pursued within the patronage framework, different from other alternatives such as engaging a lawyer to defend one's constitutional protections.

A third dimension of the Brazilian concept of order is that of hierarchy. Although clear distinctions existed between upper and lower classes, the society may be more aptly described as a finely calibrated continuum in which each individual had his or her place. As described by Richard Graham, "This view meant that no one thought himself equal to anyone else; all met within a hierarchy and found themselves either above or below the others."[10] Graham notes that such a paradigm allowed virtually everyone to feel superior to someone else, and that the fact that people did move either up or down the continuum legitimized its existence.

Patronage as a social principle had important implications for Afro-Brazilian opportunities. In the context of Brazilian patronage, upward mobility was essentially an individual phenomenon. Group activism was rare; it took the form of isolated rebellions against government authority, such as the Inconfidencia Mineira in 1789, the mulatto-led Revolt of the Tailors in Bahia in 1798, the Pernambuco revolt of 1817, and the Islamic Revolt of the Malês in Bahia in 1835. In each of these cases, the objective was to reject or overthrow the existing government. This differs from activism on behalf of a social sector within the constitutional framework. Such activism did not become part of the political culture of Brazil until the corporatism of the 1930s.

Political culture is used here to refer to the aggregate of methods used to effect change and resolve disputes. It is the modus operandi of political and social change—the way things "get done." Brazilian political culture is based upon the patronage model, in which constituents appeal directly to an omnipotent patron, as illustrated by the case of Josepha. Because this method of political communication was so individualized, it discouraged the formation of interest groups. Afro-Brazilians were not collectively represented in the government and, therefore, were an aggregate of mostly powerless individuals.

Blacks as Brazilians: The Assimilation of the Ethos of Order by Afro-Brazilians

Like all Brazilians, people of African descent utilized the system of patronage and its principles, an integral part of the legacy of slavery. This was most evident structurally in patronage relationships between Afro-Brazilians and whites. Many freedpersons found advantages in continuing their relationships with former masters. Women commonly stayed on with white families to work as domestics. These women occupied positions of confidence, performing such intimate duties as food preparation and the nursing and rearing of children. Domestic work was the principal source of income for black women in the post-abolition years. Relationships of patronage between blacks and whites extended beyond the formal bonds of employment. Whites proved beneficial in other ways, helping to secure housing, job references, health care, or any number of services. White patronage became an important and highly desirable factor of social mobility among blacks in São Paulo. Many Afro-Paulistas had migrated from other states, and therefore did not have connections to white families to help them negotiate for employment and services.[11] Those from the city and the Paulista interior often maintained their ties to white families, but Florestan Fernandes noted that even these weakened over time. "Eventually the majority of [the Afro-Brazilian] population came to be unacquainted with and lacked access to the traditional white families. Thus the number of those who did not expect or seek to find a solution to their problems in 'my white man' steadily increased."[12] In Bahia, where the rate of black migration was much lower, relationships with white families could be sustained more easily. As late as 1955, the Bahian scholar Thales de Azevedo found that many politicians were assisted by Afro-Brazilian campaign workers "who today prolong the loyalty and dedication of their forebears to the families for whom they were slaves."[13]

Patronage was equally pervasive within the confines of Afro-Brazilian social circles. Its most common formal expression was the bond of godparenthood. When Fráncisco Lucrecio's parents died in the 1920s, for example, it was his godfather who took him to live in the interior and financed his dentistry studies.[14] Informal ties of patronage were also important. One such example was the practice of male family heads who supported friends and family newly arrived to the capital who needed help settling in. Henrique Cunha, Jr.'s grandfather brought his family to the city of São Paulo from the Paraíba Valley around the turn of the century. New arrivals from his hometown were welcomed into the household as part of an extended family. "It was a house that always had 'extras,' so to speak—the cousins that weren't necessarily relatives. . . . It was traditional with the black families in São Paulo in the old days, the people who came from the country."[15] In Bahia, some well-to-do blacks supported extensive networks of dependents in more archetypical patronage relationships. João Fernandes Galliza, an African freedman, supported three Yoruba slaves, their children, his own children, and a stepchild.[16]

Some Afro-Brazilians were important patrons within their communities. There was a longstanding tradition of black philanthropy in support of Afro-Brazilian brotherhoods. While the general membership contributed modest annual dues, board members donated considerably more. The financial records of two Bahian brotherhoods in the decade between 1890 and 1900 show a structure in which a regular member typically paid between 10 and 15 *milréis* in dues, while the highest-ranking male and female board members were expected to contribute 100 *milréis*. In practice, board members often failed to meet their obligations, but those who did were vital to the brotherhoods' financial security.[17] Board memberships were annual and, for some, represented a one-time large contribution. Others served on several boards over a period of years and constituted a class of philanthropists to Afro-Brazilian organizations. For example, Matheus Cruz served as a vice president at Salvador's Sociedade Protectora dos Desvalidos in 1894–95, as *vice-prior* of a chapter of the Rosário brotherhood in 1918, and as *mordomo* (senior board member) of the São Benedito devotion at the Rosário in 1925–26.[18] Such philanthropy positioned individual blacks as patrons within their community.

Afro-Brazilian institutions also acted as patrons, providing employment opportunities to members either as regular staff or as contracted laborers. The Sociedade Protectora dos Desvalidos, a beneficent organization in Salvador, occupied an old building in constant need of repairs. Made up primarily of artisans, the Sociedade contracted all its work with its own members. The Rosário às Portas do Carmo brotherhood employed one of its members as a resident janitor and watchman. Similarly, the Frente Negra Brasileira employed its members to staff its various services. Francisco Lucrecio worked at the Frente's dental clinic while serving on its executive board. A variation on this theme that may also be considered a form of patronage was that of the candomblé *terreiros* (religious communities).[19] The Iyalorixa or Babalorixa (senior priestess or priest) was the authority directly responsible for the spiritual well-being of all the devotees, which in turn affected their physical and material state. In return, they were expected to fully support the *terreiro,* in part by providing the financial resources necessary for its existence. Each example fits within the patronage model insofar as benefits were distributed in exchange for services and loyalty to a clearly delimited circle of clients.

Were Euro-Brazilian and Afro-Brazilian forms of patronage fundamentally different? The power and dependency institutionalized in patronage relationships in mainstream Brazilian society were not as readily apparent in Afro-Brazilian patronage. An important difference between white and black patrons is that the black patronage was limited in scope. Black patrons of brotherhoods did not hold sway over all aspects of the livelihood of constituents as did the white rural patriarchs. Nor did they have access to, or control over, the same means of coercive force wielded by the traditional patrons.[20] Thus it would appear that while patronage did exist within the Afro-Brazilian community, its social implications differed from those in the larger society.

Patronage as a mode of social interaction was a dimension of Brazilian culture fully embraced by Afro-Brazilians. Not only did it condition their relationships with whites and the larger society, but it informed the structure of relationships within the black milieu. Patronage had positive repercussions to the extent that it encouraged mutual support within the black community. Also, among Afro-Brazilians the dynamics of patronage did not encompass the abusive or violent aspect so frequently evident in the seigneurial model developed under slavery. As a national language of social discourse, patronage placed Afro-Brazilians in a role of dependency upon white patrons. The disproportionate representation of whites in positions of power helped institutionalize the relationship between whites and blacks as patrons and clients, respectively.

The sense of order as hierarchy also played a role in shaping the ideological orientation of Brazilians in relation to skin color. It was one of the factors used to position people socially, along with such others as wealth, education, and lineage. Because skin color was applied in this sense, Brazilians tended to conceptualize it as a spectrum and not merely a dichotomy between black and white. This way of thinking was to become a major factor affecting the conceptualization of a broadly defined black ethnicity encompassing all people of African descent.

"Order" in the motto of republican Brazil represented these dynamics of social organization and cohesion and, for its leaders, symbolized security and continuity. This order was to be the anchor against which change could take place. Above all, order signified control of what Torcuato di Tella referred to in Latin America as the "dangerous classes," the disenfranchised masses. In order for elites to enjoy the benefits of progress with no threat to their hegemony, they needed to maintain the principles of hierarchy and social control established in the colonial era. Indeed, elites themselves displayed a colonial way of thinking as they planned to manipulate people, technology, and the environment for their own benefit. Their visions for the future were captured in a single word of almost magical implications—progress.

Progress

The choice of the word "progress" in the Republican national motto reflects the roots of the Brazilian elite in the scientific ideology of the nineteenth century, steeped in the philosophical traditions of the Enlightenment, Darwinism, and Positivism. Darwinist science had also introduced the notions of biological and environmental determinism, both of which had serious negative implications for a tropical nation whose population was largely descended from what were believed to be lesser races. By the late nineteenth century, a new optimism had emerged based on the conviction that technology and careful planning could attenuate the effects of demography and environment. Brazilians, long attentive to developments in Europe and particularly influenced by France, were anxious to be ranked among the number of civilized modern societies. Leaders in the new Republic, after they seized control of the government, embarked on a revolutionary program of political and economic reform. Social and cultural reforms complemented the Republic's attempt to reinvent Brazil for the twentieth century.

For Republican Brazil, progress was a European affair. In science, politics, economics, and culture, Brazil's leaders embraced Europe as a yardstick against which they measured their accomplishments. Long before Gilberto Freyre coined the phrase, Brazilian elites were hard at work at the business of creating a "new world in the tropics." Indeed, Brazil was one of the rare places where such a concept was viable; an 1818 survey estimated that a scant 7 percent of the entire population was of indigenous descent. The remainder descended from Africans and Europeans, at a ratio of 2.5 to 1.[21] Notwithstanding the fact that European civilizations had developed out of their own unique historical factors, Brazilians took Europe's trajectory as a replicable model which they imposed upon a society that differed radically from Europe in geography, demographics, and economy. They were not alone in their efforts. By nineteenth-century standards, South America was a backward continent. It was peopled predominantly by Indians and Africans, both representatives of the most "primitive" stages of human development. Their intermingling with European creoles would serve merely to reverse or retard the evolutionary trend that had reached its highest expression in the Anglo-Saxons. Bad enough that the settlers were of Iberian stock, already considerably mingled with North African blood over seven centuries of Moorish rule.[22] Furthermore, their economies were based upon slave labor and export monoculture, they had produced no original science or technology, and their political systems were colonial dependencies. These were the deficits perceived by the leaders of the independence era and which, in Brazil, they set out to correct under the autonomy of the Empire and the First Republic.

By the time Afro-Brazilians began to move into free society in large numbers, the concept of progress as Europeanization was already institutionalized at all levels. The reinvention of Brazil as a European nation was to be a significant factor circumscribing Afro-Brazilian participation in post-abolition society as the nation's leaders sought to shape the future of politics, economics, society, and culture. The elite vision of Brazilian progress placed Afro-Brazilians at a disadvantage on each of these fronts and simultaneously set the context for their efforts toward self-determination. Such an approach necessarily situates Afro-Brazilians in a reactive position just after abolition, even though there eventually developed a process of negotiation through which they were able to take charge of their own destinies.

Political and Economic Progress

The First Republic signaled Brazil's transition from an agriculturally based monarchy to a modern industrial nation. Its leadership consisted mostly of landed elites from the coffee-growing states of São Paulo and Minas Gerais and, to a lesser degree, the livestock ranchers of Rio Grande do Sul in the far south. The salient feature of the new governmental structure, as expressed in the 1891 constitution, was the decentralization of authority.[23] Its federative bent gave states and their governors the balance of power; militias and even political parties operated only on the state level. The power of individual states was directly related to their economic importance. Such a structure permitted the richest states, São Paulo and Minas Gerais, to dominate national politics. The sugar and tobacco states of the northeast, so important in the colonial and imperial eras, saw their influence greatly diminished in the Republic. Coffee profits from São Paulo and Minas Gerais provided a cash flow allowing for monetary stability, economic expansion, and favorable international trade. In 1889, the first year of the new regime, coffee alone accounted for 67 percent of total exports.[24] São Paulo assumed early political leadership, providing the first three civilian presidents between 1898 and 1906. The presidency subsequently alternated between São Paulo and Minas Gerais, a practice that continued until 1930. The political influence attendant to the economic power of commercial exporters led to the development of a governmental system nicknamed *Café com Leite* ("coffee with milk") because of its dominance by southern politicians from the coffee and cattle states of Minas Gerais, São Paulo, Rio Grande do Sul, and Rio de Janeiro.

The First Republic represented the consolidation of political power by coffee oligarchs, financiers of the boom product of the nineteenth century. The rise of coffee became the linchpin of Republican efforts to modernize the Brazilian economy and, by extension, the society at large. Originally cultivated in the Paraíba Valley, coffee found its greatest success in the fertile soil of the São Paulo interior, replacing sugar as the province's leading export in 1850. The completion of railroads in São Paulo created a vital link between the agricultural zone, the port at Santos, and the capital city.[25] Coffee could now be exported in mass quantities at greatly reduced expense. As a result, investors scrambled to capitalize and develop new plantations. Slaves provided most of the early labor despite British pressure on the Brazilian imperial government to end the trade. Brazil enacted several measures toward this end beginning in 1815, when the trade was abolished north of the equator. In 1830 the government passed legislation that declared all slaves entering Brazil to be free.[26] Nonetheless, lack of enforcement allowed slaves to continue to pour into the country. Most arrived in the southern ports for transport to the expanding coffee plantations of the Paraíba Valley and São Paulo. Between 1817 and 1834, Rio de Janeiro surpassed Bahia for the first time as the province with the largest number of slave imports, an estimated 73 percent of the national total. Bahia imported just under 11 percent and São Paulo became the third-largest importer with 35,100 slaves, or 6.8 percent of the national total. Philip Curtin estimates that 80 percent of the incoming African slaves were destined for the developing sugar and coffee estates of São Paulo.[27]

Between 1850 and 1852, the British government moved to actively enforce the ban by blockading Brazilian ports and seizing illegal slave ships. With the principal source of workers cut off, a labor crisis ensued, and southern planters searched for ways to maintain the labor force.[28] During the 1850s and early 1860s, failing cotton growers in the northeast often sold off slaves to the south for high prices. The rise in cotton prices during the U.S. Civil War, however, created a cotton expansion in the northeast and restricted this interregional trade.[29] In addition, by the 1870s it was becoming increasingly clear that abolition was inevitable.

The contribution coffee planters made to the national revenues gave them leverage with the imperial government, which they successfully used to help subsidize a transition labor program. São Paulo planters advocated state-funded immigration, notwithstanding the sizable free population of color and the potential for hiring the prospective freedpersons as wage laborers. Planters' organizations testified that they could not rely on former slaves to stay on as agricultural workers, and that Brazilian workers were inherently indolent.[30] The immigration program did not meet with early success. The government was reluctant to invest, forcing planters to raise most of the funds from private sources. The planters persisted nonetheless and, after coffee entered its expansion phase around 1850, immigrants began to arrive at the rate of 15,000 a year. São Paulo's private immigration societies alone sponsored 60,000 immigrants, known as *colonos*, in more than sixty agricultural colonies between 1847 and 1857.[31] These early immigrants discovered, much to their chagrin, that their living and working conditions were often barely distinguishable from slavery. Brazil was in competition for displaced European workers with the United States as well as with other South American countries such as Argentina and Chile.[32] The Brazilian government found it necessary to provide better incentives to prospective workers. It volunteered to cover most of the financing, including transportation costs, upon agreement that the *colono* would remain with the farmer until the entire debt was paid.[33] A form of profit sharing was offered, which supplemented the regular annual salary with variable wages scaled to crop value at harvest time. After 1870 the imperial government paid the transportation costs of immigrants destined for the coffee plantations; the planters covered expenses during the first year and provided a plot of land for subsistence farming.[34]

By the 1880s conditions for immigrant workers were considerably better than those for slaves. Many farmers constructed new housing for the *colonos*. Those who could not afford to rebuild instead converted old slave quarters into separate living units.[35] In 1886 immigration became the responsibility of the newly created Immigration Promotion Society. Over 90,000 Europeans arrived over the next three years.[36] Although the aim of state-subsidized immigration was to support São Paulo's coffee production, many of these immigrants ultimately settled in the capital as industrial and technical workers.

The immigration program was part of late nineteenth-century adjustments to the inevitable end of slavery, and reflects the issues affecting government policies. At the heart of the debate were the economic concerns of slaveowners, who wanted compensation for manumitted slaves and assurances that they could maintain adequate levels of production after abolition. Large-scale planters from southern Brazil fared much better than their counterparts elsewhere in the country on both counts, and were largely responsible for the failure of national indemnification. The immigration program, despite its inauspicious beginnings, provided influential planters with a fairly stable work force throughout the transition period. As for indemnification, while debates over a national plan dragged on, some provinces were able to execute local compensation programs. In São Paulo, ninety-six towns registered 158,093 freedmen liberated under the 1871 law, and slaveowners received a total compensation of 414:882$124.[37] Another form of indemnification was the traditional vehicle of self-purchase. Under the colonial legal structure, it was the slave's responsibility to remunerate the owner for his or her investment, thereby establishing the price of the *carta de alforria* (certificate of manumission). This same principle was intrinsic to the state's perception that indemnification applied to planters, not to the former slaves. Thus the debate that ensued after May 13, 1888, was led by planters seeking remuneration. Their efforts were undermined when Finance Minister Rui Barbosa burned the government's slave registers in December 1890.[38] São Paulo's planters also utilized the practice of *alforria* to their advantage, combining both freedpersons' contributions with state subsidies to net substantially more than the per capita allocations of the 1871 law.[39]

The broader implication of the indemnification debate for Afro-Brazilians was that the government would be of no assistance in their transition to free labor. There would be no financial compensation, nor would there be any formal government assistance. The purchase of letters of manumission depleted funds that could otherwise have been invested as seed capital. There were no state programs akin to the Freedmen's Bureau in the United States through which former slaves could receive the basic education, training, and placement assistance that would improve their chances of success in the free market. Afro-Brazilians were left to their own devices. As a result, there was no substantive shift in the position of blacks in the labor market attendant to the abolition of slavery.

Not all Afro-Brazilians followed the state-sanctioned avenues to freedom. A growing number of slaves, impatient with the delay of abolition, began organizing mass escapes to independent communities known as *quilombos*. The fugitive network joined forces with white abolitionists in the 1880s, when São Paulo became the scene of an "Underground Railroad."[40] In a movement spearheaded by Antônio Bento, a number of white sympathizers helped blacks escape from plantations in the state's interior and the Paraíba coffee valley. There is ample evidence of mass escapes during this period. Reports of groups of over one hundred slaves abandoning a single plantation were not uncommon, though probably exaggerated at times.[41] The "railroad" ran toward Santos, where former slaves often found jobs on the docks. Others settled in the *quilombo* of Jabaquara, in the hills of the Serra Maior between Santos and São Paulo.

Whether or not it was due to the marronage of the 1880s, coffee produc-

TABLE 1. *Quantity and Value of Coffee Exports, 1883–1893*

Year	(60K) bags	Value *(contos)*	Value/bag	% of total exports
1883	3,654,511	91,239	24$966	42.03
1884	3,897,113	105,495	27$070	46.62
1885	4,206,911	104,904	24$936	53.81
1886	3,580,965	99,436	27$768	37.73
1887	2,241,755	98,471	43$926	78.67
1888	3,444,311	103,205	29$964	43.50
1889	5,585,534	172,258	30$840	67.35
1890	5,108,862	189,896	37$170	58.17
1891	5,372,788	284,167	52$890	49.47
1892	7,109,277	441,443	62$094	56.27
1893	5,306,749	452,326	85$236	64.11

SOURCE: Brazil. Directoria Geral da Estatística. *Resumo de Varias Estatísticas Econômico-Financeiras* (Rio de Janeiro: Typografia da Estatística, 1924), 45.

tion dipped slightly just prior to abolition.[42] Because of fluctuations in international coffee prices, however, profits did not drop significantly and, by 1889, had fully entered the boom phase, as is apparent from Table 1. Coffee was Brazil's most important export product during the First Republic. Only three times in the four decades between 1883 and 1922 did it fall below 40 percent of total exports, and at no time did it fall below 30 percent.[43] At least in the coffee sector, the economy reached its apogee after the demise of slavery.

Important economic developments were also taking place in the state of Bahia, although it had a slower rate of industrialization and less of an impact on the national economy than São Paulo. The Bahian economy remained largely agricultural throughout the entire First Republic; by 1940, 85 percent of the state's working population was employed in agriculture, as compared with 11 percent in industry and 4 percent in commerce.[44] Unlike their counterparts in São Paulo, Bahian planters were unable to offset the loss of workers after abolition with foreign immigrants. They instead focused on improvements in agricultural technology, the most significant of which was the modernization of sugar production. Steam-powered sugar mills came into use in the 1870s and 1880s. These were soon replaced by *usinas,* centralized mills with far greater refining capability. *Usina* owners bought up unprofitable and undercapitalized plantations, displacing many agricultural workers and rising to prominence in yet another guise of patronage known as the *república das usinas.*[45]

Bahia's economy was nonetheless forging ahead in both commerce and industry (see Table 2). Small-scale food and beverage retailing made up nearly

TABLE 2. *New Commercial and Industrial Businesses,*
State of Bahia, through 1939

Years	Commercial	Industrial
Prior to 1900	112	22
1900–1909	165	29
1910–1919	505	83
1920–1929	1,289	215
1930–1939	7,953	824

SOURCE: Brazil, Instituto Brasileiro de Geografia e Estatística, *Rencens-*
eamento Geral do Brasil, 1⁰ de Setembro de 1940 (Rio de Janeiro: Serviço
Gráfico do Instituto Brasileiro de Geografia e Estatística, 1950), Censo
Commercial, Estado da Bahia, 328–329; Censo Industrial, Estado da
Bahia, 292–293.

two-thirds (63 percent) of commercial activity, which had grown to 13,082
businesses by the time of the census in September 1940. Of these, 87 percent
were exclusively retail operations.[46] The food industry was also the largest
sector of industrial enterprises. Makers of food products represented 33 percent of all new businesses prior to 1940, with another 8 percent in beverage
manufacturing. Bahia was not underdeveloped in industry overall but, rather,
in the most lucrative types of businesses. Textiles yielded a far greater profit
margin than all other industries besides utilities (electric, gas, water, and sew-
age). This sector, so central to São Paulo's economic development, was only 4
percent of the Bahian total, although 27 new businesses were founded between 1935 and 1939.[47] Without a strong economy, Bahia was unable to compete with the southern states for political prestige and influence in the national
government.

The inability or unwillingness of the First Republic's leaders to address
the concerns and facilitate the development of economically weaker states was
only one of its inherent systemic problems. The electoral system excluded 98
percent of the population. Political corruption, in the form of favors, bribes,
and fraud, went hand in hand with the institutionalization of the patronage
system. The Republic was also the heyday of *coronelismo,* the rule by fiat of
local leaders. *Coronel* is an honorific military title, but its practical usage during the Republic referred to political clients, who were expected to deliver
votes and military recruits and to guarantee social control. The Republic was,
in many ways, yet another incarnation of the same political principles that had
governed Brazil since the captaincy system of the sixteenth century.[48] It was a
government designed to accommodate a very restricted landed aristocracy, unwilling to adapt to changing times and new interests. The refusal of the old

elites to make concessions to the military or the emerging industrialist class set the stage for a host of problems that ultimately caused the Republic's downfall.

World War I was an important watershed. At the beginning of the war, hostilities interrupted foreign trade, causing inflation and unemployment. These problems fueled an urban workers' movement, dominated in the southern states by foreigners because of the massive immigration of the previous decades and their overrepresentation in the burgeoning industrial sector. Strikes shook São Paulo and Rio between 1917 and 1920, stirring popular discontent and an interest in the political ideology of anarcho-syndicalism. The anarchist position was favored by the immigrants, few of whom had adopted Brazilian citizenship and who had no opportunity to participate in electoral politics.[49] Elite opinion turned against the foreigners, and the government launched a virulent anti-immigrant campaign that resulted in the deportation of many labor activists.[50]

The military was also unhappy with Republican leaders. The armed forces had not been taken into account in the structure of political patronage and power and, since the institution of civilian government, many of their demands had gone unheeded. They argued for strengthening the military as a means of national security and progress. As early as 1901, officers were calling for a draft. An obligatory service bill, introduced in 1906, was not passed until 1908 and not enforced until 1916. Frank McCann notes that the military shifted toward political involvement, only to become disillusioned by institutionalized barriers against real change. "The [military] reformists had argued that aloofness from politics and loyalty to the federal government were marks of professionalism. . . . By the end of World War I they came to understand, vaguely at first, that the political system was set against army reform because such reform would endanger that system."[51] The military was further angered by President Epitácio Pessoa, who in 1922 appointed civilians to the posts of minister of the army and minister of the navy.[52] In protest, the military opposed his choice for successor, Artur da Silva Bernardes, the governor of Minas Gerais. In July, after Bernardes' victory, the officers revolted. This uprising was contained, but the young officers, especially the lieutenants *(tenentes)* continued with a series of revolts that in 1924 broke out in three weeks of fighting in São Paulo and Paraná. Bernardes again succeeded in controlling the unrest, although those loyal to the dissident captain Luís Carlos Prestes followed him along a 14,000-mile trek through the interior to recruit supporters that came to be known as the "Prestes Column."[53]

The poorer states and the military were not the only groups dissatisfied with the Republic. There was little opportunity for meaningful political involvement by the middle and lower classes, the illiterate, women, workers—

TABLE 3. *Coffee Prices, 1919–1931*

Marketing year	Cents per pound
1919–20	19.0
1920–21	10.4
1921–22	14.3
1922–23	14.8
1923–24	21.3
1924–25	24.5
1925–26	22.3
1926–27	18.7
1927–28	23.2
1928–29	22.1
1929–30	13.2
1930–31	8.7

SOURCE: Jordan M. Young, *The Brazilian Revolution of 1930 and the Aftermath* (New Brunswick, N.J.: Rutgers University Press, 1967), 70.

in general, people without economic power. Ruling elites excluded the Church from national politics and failed to adequately represent the rapidly growing industrial sector. Industry, which had accounted for 21 percent of gross national product in 1907 and 1919, reached 43 percent by 1939.[54] The government was primed for a fall, which occurred almost simultaneously with the end of the coffee boom.

In 1926 the presidency went to a Paulista, Washington Luís, who had to cope with the 1929 crash which toppled the coffee economy. Coffee had faced financial fluctuations in the past; prices had dropped between 1919 and 1921 in response to deflationary policies established by the United States after World War I. Paulista planters wanted the federal government to protect coffee profits through monetary policies, but were thwarted by President Bernardes and his supporters in Minas Gerais, who feared that such policies would benefit São Paulo disproportionately.[55] The Paulistas responded by establishing valorization mechanisms such as the Institute for the Permanent Defense of Coffee, which succeeded in boosting coffee prices temporarily.[56] Saddled by international debt, Washington Luís was able to do little to improve the situation, and the crash of 1929 only exacerbated the problem. This trajectory is apparent from Table 3.

Washington Luís made the critical mistake of sidestepping tradition by naming as his successor another Paulista, Governor Júlio Prestes. This angered the politicians from Minas Gerais, who formed an opposition party, the Liberal Alliance, for the 1930 presidential election. Their candidates were Getúlio Vargas of Rio Grande do Sul and João Pessôa of Paraíba. This move appealed to other states that had previously been excluded from the political inner circle at the federal level. Ironically, Vargas, a man who was to wield such great power in Brazil, was defeated in the election of 1930 and declined to contest the results. The September assassination of the Liberal Alliance's vice-presidential candidate (the result of a dispute with a local rival), however, prompted a military uprising that deposed Luís and placed Vargas in power.[57]

Early on, Vargas struck a responsive chord with Brazil's disenfranchised. He promised to open government to a broad spectrum of society through the principle of corporatism. The central tenet of corporatism is the conceptualization of the society as a body. Within the corporative body, each group is differentiated and ranked according to its function, as expressed in productive or economic terms. The central state acts as the brain, whose responsibility it is to regulate each of the component groups. In Brazil, elite groups became the principal actors, such as industrial plant owners, "who, rather than workers, were termed *classes productoras* [producing classes]."[58]

Vargas' interpretation of corporatism drew from the national tradition of patronage, but he modified it significantly by recasting it as clientelism. As opposed to group politics, in which interest groups seek to have their interests implemented as general policy, clientelistic politics rely on the direct distribution of concessions and benefits from the government to a specific constituency.[59]

Thus the Vargas coup changed Brazil's political culture, not by merely investing new sectors of the populace with political influence, but by offering new means to do so. Patronage was essentially a relationship between individuals. Clientelism enabled groups of people, who alone may have been powerless, to form interest groups and thereby wield collective influence. For a society so concerned with hierarchy and differentiation, the 1930s suddenly became a time for seeking commonality and group identity. This change opened an avenue by which Afro-Brazilians could shape a collective identity and seek political influence, which ultimately occurred with the advent of the Frente Negra Brasileira.

Society and Cultural Progress

The economic and political factors hampering Afro-Brazilians at abolition had social and cultural concomitants that proved equally disadvantageous. Stereotypes of African people and culture as "savage" were antithetical to elite notions of progress and development based on European models. Because establishing a modern civilization thus conceived represented a national goal, the mere fact of being Afro-Brazilian was, by extension, antipatriotic. This posed a serious challenge for post-abolition Brazil—would Afro-Brazilian ethnicity be reshaped to suit elite objectives or vice versa?

To understand elite initiatives on civic and cultural issues in the early twentieth century, it is necessary to recognize that the roots of these actions lie deep in the Positivist intellectual traditions of the eighteenth and nineteenth centuries. Throughout the eighteenth century, modern ideas, predominantly French, streamed across the Atlantic. Initially, this intellectual influence took the form of books shared among the private libraries of the elite and discussed in secret societies. Beginning early in the eighteenth century, organizations known as "academies" appeared in the principal provincial capitals, followed by Brazil's early Masonic lodges. The first lodge was inaugurated in Salvador in 1797, followed by one in Pernambuco in 1802 and three in Rio in 1803.[60] European influence also manifested itself in education. At the Olinda seminary, one of Brazil's oldest institutions of higher learning, its founder Azeredo Coutinho imbued the curriculum with the latest liberal ideas from Europe. His faculty, both clerical and secular, shared his modern views. The opening speech in 1800 by the professor of rhetoric quoted and made references to "Lacombe, Voltaire, Millot, Fleury, and a host of other Frenchmen."[61]

European intellectualism had two components of interest to Brazilians. The first was an integrated theory of natural sciences permitting greater control and utilization of the physical environment. Brazilians had become acutely aware of the wealth of their vast land and its potential for development. Second, European literature, supported by a scientific theory in which God played no role, challenged divine monarchic rule and began offering alternatives. Such a view positioned creole elites to situate themselves in leadership roles. As in other Latin American countries, European liberalism was to play a major role in the formulation of republican nationalism.

The scientific bent of the nineteenth century introduced an evolutionary notion of progress, namely, that humankind was progressing from African primitivism to European civility. Closely related was the concept of biological determinism, which held that the environment also played a major role in shaping distinct "types" of people. By those standards, a predominantly mestizo nation in the tropics could never hope for admission to the community of modern civilizations. Indeed, one of the most vocal advocates of this theory, the French ambassador to Brazil Count Arthur de Gobineau, publicly dismissed Brazil as a backward nation. In 1869 he described Brazilians as "a completely mulatto population, of polluted blood and spirit, and frighteningly ugly." Noting that "not a single Brazilian is of pure blood," he concluded that "all this has produced, from the lower to the upper classes, a most sad state of degeneration."[62] Such public ridicule engendered a crisis of national identity and a preoccupation with the prospect of social engineering in order to produce a population conducive to Brazilian progress as defined by elites.

Optimism and faith in their power to change society were critical components of the Brazilian elite's self-assessment. One of the hallmarks of

Brazilian national identity at the turn of the twentieth century was its conceptualization as a dynamic process and not a fixed reality. Most contemporary writers referred to Brazilians as a people still in the formative stage, which implied that actions could yet be taken to direct the nation's evolutionary development.

Brazil, as did other Latin American nations, went through an initial phase of nativist literature focusing on its indigenous heritage. The publication of *O Guaraní* in the mid-nineteenth century introduced this chapter in Brazilian literary history. The African element, however, was one that could not be ignored. In 1896 Raymundo Nina Rodrigues (1862–1906), a Bahian physician, published the first portions of his seminal study of Afro-Brazilian culture in the *Revista Brasileira*. He later compiled these chapters and published them in French as *L'Animisme Fétichiste des Nègres de Bahia* (The Fetishistic Animism of Blacks in Bahia). Although his work was essentially an ethnographic study of contemporary Afro-Bahian religious communities, Nina Rodrigues' own characterization reflected the concerns of his time. He introduced his writing as a contribution to "the elucidation of grave social questions relative to our destiny as a people in the process of formation," namely, "the problem of the black race in Portuguese America."[63] Nina Rodrigues not only described a people firmly rooted to "primitive" practices, but sought to demonstrate the pervasiveness of those practices in the context of one of Brazil's principal cities. It was a subtle warning that, unchecked, African-based culture could easily come to dominate.

A literary work published in 1902, buttressed by contemporary scientific theory, further condemned the African contribution to Brazilian civilization. In *Os Sertões,* a work about the Brazilian backlands and a millenarian revolt, Euclides da Cunha eloquently crystallized Brazilian theories of race and social evolution.[64] He painstakingly described how the racial mixture of Europeans, Africans, and indigenous peoples combined with the various climactic zones to form distinct Brazilian "types."[65] His depiction was unsettling to many Brazilians; a significant portion of the mixture came from what they deemed inferior races, inheritors of barbarism and savagery that would therefore contribute to the new Brazilian "race."[66]

By the turn of the twentieth century, elite perspectives on the role of blacks in Brazilian society had taken definitive shape. To a people who associated Africans with barbarity and paganism, their descendants were antithetical to modernization, a social ill and a national problem to be remedied. The African heritage was labeled inferior by both genetic and cultural standards. Nina Rodrigues' study appeared to prove that the attempt to acculturate Africans into Catholicism and European-based culture had not been entirely successful. At least in Bahia, external expressions of mainstream culture were, in fact, a veneer masking adherence to African culture. It was impossible to physically remove the population of African descent, tallied at 56 percent in 1890. The experience with immigration, however, suggested a possible solution; the breeding out of African genes through miscegenation would create a distinctly whiter Brazilian "race." The Aryan blood of mulattoes would endow them with the necessary qualities to become partners—junior partners—in national society. Even more hopeful were those who argued that "[i]n the fusion of the two races, the superior will triumph. The blacks of Brazil will disappear within seventy years."[67] João Batista Lacerda, director of the National Museum, was one of the first members of the scientific community to endorse "constructive miscegenation." In 1912 he calculated that by 2012 the black population would be reduced to zero, while mulattoes would make up merely 3 percent of the total population.[68] The principle that came to be known as "whitening" took shape during the First Republic, and became a social doctrine intimately related to Brazilian nationalism and patriotic ideals.

Miscegenation, or whitening, was not immediately accepted as a viable solution. Da Cunha was extremely skeptical:

> An intermingling of races highly diverse is, in the majority of cases, prejudicial. . . . [M]iscegenation, in addition to obliterating the pre-eminent qualities of the higher race, serves to stimulate the revival of the primitive attributes of the lower; so that the mestizo—a hyphen between the races, a brief individual existence into which are compressed age-old forces—is almost always an unbalanced type. . . . The mestizo . . . rather than an intermediary type, is a degenerate one, lacking the physical energy of his savage ancestors and without the intellectual elevation of his ancestors on the other side.[69]

The academic community in southern Brazil, however, was enthusiastic about the possibilities of whitening. The debate led to the emergence of eugenics as a scientific movement in the late 1910s. At least seventy-four major publications on eugenics were released between 1897 and 1933. Scientists subscribing to the tenets of eugenics first organized themelves into the São Paulo Eugenics Society in 1918, with the aim of producing "scientific studies, conferences, and propaganda on the physical and moral strengthening of the Brazilian people."[70] Upon the demise of this organization, its founder brought eugenics into the Liga de Hygiene Mental, founded in 1922. Brazilian eugenics embraced a broad conceptualization of whitening that went beyond the realm of genetics. The eugenicists advocated tempering racial "deficiencies" through such measures as education, sanitation, and social reform.[71]

Cultural whitening was a powerful approach because it had the potential to affect all of Brazil's citizens but, as noted by Nina Rodrigues, it was necessarily a long-term process with no guarantees. A much more promising "mechanical" approach was to whiten the population through immigration. A labor policy shaped by the contingencies of global economic conditions in the mid-nineteenth century suddenly took on new dimensions as a public policy of social engineering.

When the Republican government convened to write its first constitution, coffee planters were still interested in recruiting immigrant labor. Several planters, having observed the success of Asian labor in the United States and the Caribbean, suggested amending the legal prohibition against Asian and African immigration so that they could recruit Japanese workers. The government was ambivalent on the issue, but eventually passed legislation allowing immigration from China and Japan.[72] In the 1920s Japanese immigration was again defended against even greater challenges to restrict immigration to Europeans for eugenic purposes. "In no way," wrote Minas Gerais representative Fidelis Reis, "must we sacrifice for short-term interests the type of race we are creating with the introduction of unassimilable or prejudicially assimilable ethnic elements."[73] Representatives such as Oliveira Botelho argued that the Japanese were essential to agriculture, because whites tended not to stay on plantations and Brazilian workers were unproductive:

> The Turks and Syrians of white skin and good physical appearance, immigrants of their own accord, concern themselves only with business and do not venture outside the cities. Agriculture clamors for strong arms and will not ever forgive us if, on futile pretexts, we impede its development. . . . [I]f the thirty million Brazilians produced in the same proportion as the thirty thousand Japanese working here, Brazil would be the richest country in the world.[74]

Under pressure from such legislators as Fidelis Reis, Cincinato Braga, and Andrade Bezerra, the government ultimately agreed to limit the total number of Asians entering Brazil, while keeping the prohibition against black immigration intact.

The antiblack contingent went to great lengths to demonstrate that blacks represented a serious problem for Brazil:

> Our African blacks . . . fought with us in the most difficult battles of the formation of our nationality; they worked, suffered and, with their dedication, helped us to create the Brazil we have today. Yet it would have been preferable to not have had them. The case today is absolutely different. And they must constitute for us the motivation for serious apprehensions, an imminent danger weighing down our future.

Besides the ethnic, moral, political, social, and perhaps, economic reasons that lead us to repel *in limine* the entrance of the yellow and the black into this melting pot . . . is our hellenic concept of beauty which will never harmonize with the mixtures that would come of this sort of racial fusion.[75]

The debate over black immigration was sparked by an unexpected confluence of circumstances that resulted in black nationalists from the United States seeking to relocate to Brazil and, some hoped, to establish a black republic in South America. The post–World War I era was one of great political activity among United States blacks. Dissatisfied with the rising number of lynchings and race riots, Jim Crow segregation and lack of opportunities in the South, and the pervasiveness of racism at all levels, black Americans turned to a host of newly created political organizations. Some, like the National Urban League, directed their efforts toward helping blacks find employment and housing in northern cities. Others, such as Marcus Garvey's Universal Negro Improvement Association (UNIA) and Cyril Briggs' African Blood Brotherhood, represented many of those who had lost faith in the prospect of the United States ever accepting people of African descent as full and equal partners. Both organizations advocated black emigration, but whereas Garvey focused on Africa, Briggs raised the possibility of creating a "black republic" in South America in conjunction with the many people of African descent already living there. Briggs' vision was to unite the black struggles of Africa and America so that "with African liberty effected and Africa returned to the Africans[,] two rich continents would be dominated by the African races."[76]

Blacks from the United States were attracted to Brazil in part by its subsidized immigration program. In their efforts to recruit white immigrants, Brazilian representatives were actively promoting colonization packages in Europe and the United States. The other attraction for black Americans was their mistaken belief, based on widely published reports from blacks who had visited Brazil, that nonwhites were welcome there. Noting the many mulattoes in high positions who would have been considered "black" by United States standards (although not by prevalent Brazilian ideology), articles in such popular black newspapers as the *Chicago Defender, The Crisis,* and the *Negro World* seemed to confirm Brazil's public image as a racial democracy.[77] In 1920 a group of black Americans incorporated the Brazilian American Colonization Syndicate. Another group actively pursuing the possibility of emigration to Brazil was the Springfield, Massachussetts, chapter of the UNIA. This organization was infiltrated by the FBI which, through informants, reported that the economic objectives were part of a radical nationalist plan to establish a black republic along the lines indicated by Cyril Briggs. The Springfield UNIA branch had targeted northern Brazil, because of its greater number of blacks, as well as British Guiana on South America's northern coast. A letter published in the March 12, 1921, *Negro World* reveals the breadth of members' aspirations:

> What a source of strength our organization can have if only a part of that population can be brought into our camp; victory for our cause will be made easier and the commerical and financial aid can be obviously seen. . . . [I]f an effort is made to spread the doctrines of the Universal Negro Improvement Association and African Communities League and enroll them under the banner of the Red, Black and Green, we will find Negroes capable to fit in any position.[78]

For Republican leaders so eager to whiten Brazil, no prospect could have been more alarming. Many were willing to sacrifice the vision of economic progress. In the words of Fidelis Reis, "When we consider the possibility, distant or remote, of the emigration of black Americans to Brazil, we must accept the possibility of the disruption of peace on this continent if it is promoted or condoned by Washington. No advantage we might gain from a strengthening of relations with the United States would balance the disaster that such [immigration] would mean for us."[79] Their concerns about Washington were unfounded; the FBI apprised the Brazilian government of the colonization efforts, and the latter responded with confidential instructions to "discourage" black Americans seeking to emigrate. They refused to grant visas to individual blacks, and neither the Brazilian American Colonization Syndicate nor any other group of blacks from the United States was able to enter Brazil legally during the First Republic.[80]

The Brazilian government, despite its dedication to European immigration, had not had entirely positive relations with the *colonos*. In the nineteenth century agricultural workers, protesting slavelike conditions, forced planters to improve housing and contractual arrangements. By the twentieth century, immigrants made up a large percentage of the industrial labor force. Foreign factory workers took the lead in developing a proletarian political movement known as anarcho-syndicalism. Brazilians participated at all levels, but the government, in its efforts to quell the strike movements around 1917–1919, targeted foreigners as the subversive enemy working against national interests. Strongly anti-immigrant propaganda championed patriotism, and foreign agitators were deported. In São Paulo, one of the centers of the proletarian movement, black workers seized the opportunity to emphasize their Brazilian nationality as a strategy to advance in the labor market over the publicly derided foreigners. In 1920, however, the government reaffirmed its commitment to whites over blacks as a critical factor of the nation's development: "This is the exclusive work of the white man. The black and the Indian, throughout the long process of our social formation, do not give, as can be seen, to the superior guiding classes that realize the work of civilization and development, a single element of value. The two form a passive and unprogressive mass upon which works, not always with happy success, the formative action of the man of the white race."[81]

Part of the "formative action" was discipline; Brazilian elites were preoccupied with the maintenance of public "morals" and order. Public displays of Afro-Brazilian culture came under tight control with the demise of slavery. Police targeted Afro-Brazilian religious expressions, dance and music, and capoeira, considered uncivilized and hence inappropriate for public display. During the First Republic, nonwhites were disproportionately arrested for crimes of public order. The message was clear from the beginning; in the first full year of the regime, public order violations constituted 83 percent of all crimes recorded for males. Many of these arrests were the result of police surveillance of areas frequented by people of color.[82] Sam Adamo notes the emergence of cooptation as a complement to overt repression by the 1930s, when authorities began allowing such Afro-Brazilian cultural expressions as samba to appear publicly as long as participants curbed the objectionable elements of sexual suggestiveness and the accompanying public displays of drunkenness. In the religious arena, Adamo suggests that Afro-Brazilian candomblé and macumba traditions were strategically used by the government to obscure issues of race and promote the image of racial democracy by using these religions' fusion of Catholic and African elements as a social metaphor.[83]

The idealization of European norms included physical as well as cultural aesthetics. In the introduction to the 1920 census, Oliveira Vianna detailed the ethnic variations among the Africans who came to Brazil as they compared with Europeans.

> The blacks of the *yebu* tribe, for example, or the *cassange,* or *haussá,* though they have been reinforced and crossbred, have the repulsive ugliness of pure blacks. In contrast, those of the *mina* nation, or *fula, achanti,* or *felanin,* are types of great beauty, because of the proportionality of shapes, the softness of their features, their slender stature, their lighter color, and their hair, which is less kinky than that of the other nations. . . . In terms of physical beauty, none surpasses the *jolofos* and *sereres,* whose superior complexion has the purity, grace, and nobility of the European type.[84]

The social and cultural objectives of Brazilian elites in the post-abolition years directed them toward policies aimed at containing the African element in public life. An ideal of physical whitening combined with acculturation was intended to yield a new, European-based Brazilian culture.

Academic opinion on the historical and future role of blacks in Brazilian society developed along different lines during this period. The eugenicists, concentrated in the south and generally affiliated with governmental institutions, directed much of their scholarship toward pinpointing specific African contributions, particularly biological, to the developing Brazilian race. For some researchers, pre-Nazi Germany served as an inspiration:

> While modern Germany seeks to standardize its population, searching in the confines of the Black Forest for the pure Teutons . . . using this type of selection to constitute a homogeneous people with the qualities necessary for achieving the ideals of progress and supremacy of its current leaders, Brazil watches impassively the laboratory of its formidable human melting-pot, with its unorganized mix of so many different races and ethnicities, without making even a minimal effort to understand those elements that enter and the subsequent result.[85]

Of particular concern was the identification of clear delimiters of race. In Rio de Janeiro, the Department of Education's Research Institute was testing an index of radio-pelvic size developed in France as a determinant of African ancestry. In 1934 investigators concluded that "[t]he Lapique index . . . proves African ancestry, even in individuals apparently of the white race."[86] Meanwhile, researchers such as Abelardo Duarte were working on blood type as a "biochemical criterion" of race to supplement the "classic criteria of external morphology."[87] This raises the question of whether Brazilians would have developed a dichotomous color line as in the United States if they had had an acceptable criterion with which to draw clear distinctions between the races.

Demography may well have played a role in the orientation of regional scholarship. Whereas physical whitening captured the imagination of intellectuals in the predominantly white south, northeasterners generally accepted the permanent presence of Brazilians of African descent. Intellectuals in the northeast, focusing on culture, produced a prolific body of ethnographic scholarship that subsequently formed the basis of contemporary Afro-Brazilian studies. Much of the early work was in response to Nina Rodrigues. It included the writings of Manuel Querino (1851–1923), the first Afro-Brazilian to publish extensively on black history and culture and one of Nina Rodrigues' principal informants. Querino's works were collected and published in book form posthumously in 1938 as *Costumes Africanos no Brasil* (African Customs in Brazil). This volume included *The African Race and Their Customs in Bahia, The Black Immigrant as a Factor in Brazilian Civilization, Culinary Arts in Bahia,* and excerpts from *The Bahia of Yesteryear*. Querino provided an invaluable insider's perspective on Afro-Bahian culture, which had previously only been observed from outside.

These two avenues of scholarship—the natural sciences and cultural studies—were dramatically brought together and placed in the context of international anthropology in a 1934 conference organized by Gilberto Freyre. Freyre was the cousin and personal aide of Pernambuco's last governor under the First Republic, and had left Brazil after the coup of 1930. Already proficient in English as a result of a prior stay in the United States, he went to New York to study anthropology under Franz Boas at Columbia University.[88] There he met Melville Herskovits, a pioneer of African diaspora studies. Herskovits had first called attention to the lacuna in scholarship on Afro-Brazilian ethnography in 1930 in an article laying the foundation for the study of the "Negro in the New World."[89] He argued that the effect of biological race on cultural behavior had yet to be established. The Negro, he contended, offered the ideal test case, because "full-blooded" Africans existed in large numbers in climates similar to that of Africa as well as in subtropical and temperate zones. He went on to discuss the particular research opportunities offered by the various countries of the African diaspora in the Americas, but admitted that little information on Brazil was available: "Data on the physical anthropology of the Negroes of the western hemisphere are also sadly lacking. Up to five years ago, nothing had been done to study the Negroes of the United States. . . . Of the West Indians we know less, while of the Negroes of central America and northern South America we know practically nothing. And the culture and physical form of Brazilian negroes are *terra incognita*."[90] Freyre, well aware of Herskovits' work, must have seen an opportunity to make a timely contribution to anthropological research on New World Africans. In 1933 he published *The Masters and the Slaves*, a book of extraordinary impact.[91] Now considered stereotypical and outdated, in its day this work summarized widely held beliefs about the benign nature of Brazilian slavery. It also echoed popular concern with racial evolution and the progressive "whitening" of a new "Brazilian race" composed of African, European, and indigenous strains. Like many Brazilians, Freyre concluded that the African was rapidly disappearing from Brazilian life and culture.[92] Unlike the Brazilian attempt to eradicate Africanisms, however, Freyre introduced the contemporary concern of American anthropologists with preserving what they regarded as primitive cultures.

Immediately following the publication of his book, Freyre began organizing an Afro-Brazilian Congress in his home of Recife in the northeastern state of Pernambuco to bring together the academic establishment and the living culture in a format that had never before been attempted.[93] Freyre later published his reflections on the congress along with two volumes of the meeting's papers:

> The Recife Congress, with all its simplicity, gave new style [*feitio*] and new flavor to Afro-Brazilian studies, freeing it from the academic or scientific elitism of rigid "schools" on the one hand and, on the other, from the levity and lightness of those who follow the issue for the simple enjoyment of the picturesque, the literary value, the political value, or the aesthetic, devoid of any intellectual or scientific discipline, and without a social meaning beyond the facts. The participation of illiterates, cooks, and priests, alongside the doctors, somehow gave a new energy to the studies, the freshness and liveliness of direct contact with brute reality.[94]

The most popular topic of the papers was the effect of biological and physical characteristics on cultural behavior. This issue was a timely one in the 1930s for several reasons. First, the academic establishment was still studying the physical basis of cultural differences, a question of enormous importance for those who sought a biological justification for racial discrimination. Second, many Brazilians had embraced the concept that a new national race was emerging as a result of the intermingling of indigenous, African, and European blood. There was concern about any bio-cultural characteristics to be inherited, for these would, in turn, affect the national character. Third, the often-blurred racial lines in Brazil had given rise to a search for a definitive determinant of race. E. Roquette-Pinto, in his preface to the collection, noted that in his anthropological studies he had observed that "the common terms black, caboclo [Indian], mulatto, etc. are routinely assigned to every individual belonging to these groups, *without any definitive systematic anthropological characterization.*"[95]

Inspired by Freyre's efforts, a young mulatto scholar from Bahia named Edison Carneiro decided to organize a second Afro-Brazilian Congress in Salvador. Carneiro was not considered part of the academic elite, and certainly did not have Freyre's extensive network of connections. In fact, Freyre offered no assistance to Carneiro. He did not submit a paper and, prior to the congress, Freyre granted an interview to a Pernambuco newspaper in which he forecast its failure.[96] Nonetheless, the Afro-Brazilian Congress of Bahia took place over ten days in January 1937, proving its organizers as adept as Freyre in staging an eclectic conference of arts, culture, and scholarship.

The Bahian conference brought forth a wealth of ethnographic data on Afro-Brazilian cultural traditions in the northeast. Far less attention was given to eugenics, although some of the papers continued to reflect stereotypical attitudes. Ademar Vidal, for example, claimed that "the African is docile and submissive . . . the African rapidly adapted to [captivity]."[97] Most of the Bahian conference papers dealt with the documentation of Africanisms in Afro-Brazilian culture from an ethnographic perspective. They addressed the diverse aspects of this issue, including African origins, comparative ethnographies of African and New World cultures, and case studies of Afro-Brazilian traditions.

The second Afro-Brazilian Congress continued the direction set forth by Freyre in that it again represented predominantly white academic perspectives and concerns, although Afro-Brazilians were involved in the conference at all levels. Like the first congress, it offered a positive perspective on African contributions to Brazilian history and culture. Yet close examination reveals that this view was narrowed by stereotypes with which whites limited the *types* of socially acceptable contributions:

> The Negro gave us the tone and styles of life. It was he who, with his goodness, his incredible patience, his enormous capacity for moral fortitude, made us believe in the earth, and feel it deeply. He gave us also a great degree of unity based in our traditional cuisine which originated as a legacy of the slave quarter. This force converted the masses of Europeans and Africans and indigenous peoples into true Brazilians.[98]

In contrast, the contributions of blacks as intellectuals, politicians, poets, business people, and civic leaders were obscured by the tradition of ignoring the African backgrounds of individuals in these fields. Manuel Querino recognized this problem, and provided a lengthy list of prominent individuals in "O Colono Prêto como Factor da Civilização Brasileira."[99] José Correia Leite, an Afro-Brazilian activist who founded one of São Paulo's principal black newspapers in 1924, commented:

> [H]ere in Brasil mulattoes could easily "pass" when they were successful in life, as happened with Machado de Assis and other great mulattoes that Brazil has had and no one considered a mulatto, as a black. . . . Machado de Assis was a great Brazilian writer and he was black. In the American ethnic understanding he would have to add that he was black. Here, no. So only those mulattoes who weren't very successful stayed in the black circles. But those who were able, for whatever reason, to do well in life and become important, pass[ed] into the white circle. Whites accepted them . . . with great reservations. They would say these people were white, but they were mulatto, they were black.[100]

One contribution to the Bahian congress that departed from the white academic agenda focused on an issue of pressing concern to Afro-Brazilians. Presented by Dario de Bittencourt, this paper on Brazilian law and its relation to Afro-Brazilian religion addressed the contradiction between the constitutional rights of religious freedom and the widespread police oppression of Afro-Brazilian religions.[101] Bittencourt's article provided an important weapon for candomblé practitioners, giving them justification in Brazilian law with which they could defend their right to religious freedom. His research, and the momentum of the entire Bahian conference, led to the creation of the Union of Afro-Brazilian Sects in September 1937 to "advocate religious liberty for blacks."[102] Ironically, the scholarly congresses, which had begun with elements of overt racism, had now laid a foundation for a new stage of black activism.

Afro-Brazilians faced enormous pressures circumscribing their upward mobility in the post-abolition era. At the time of abolition, Afro-Brazilians were concentrated in the least productive sectors of the economy. The largest black *(prêto)* populations were, in descending order, in Minas Gerais, Bahia, Rio de Janeiro (excluding the capital district), and São Paulo—all primarily agricultural areas struggling to keep up with technological innovation and improve productivity. There were two pronounced patterns of Afro-Brazilian free labor in the agricultural sector. The areas of greatest growth attracted European contract laborers. In those areas of premium land, there was little space available for small-scale subsistence farming. Blacks were either forced out of the area or became dependents of the landowners. In the less productive areas where immigrants were not available, blacks continued in essentially the same roles they had performed as slaves.

In the post-abolition era, Brazil's most dynamic economic region was the industrialized south, with its related ports, transportation infrastructure, and major cities, including the national capital at Rio de Janeiro. It was in this sector that newly arrived Europeans, encouraged and financed by both governmental and private sources as substitutes for the newly freed slaves, established a foothold in the Brazilian economy.[103] In 1890, nonwhites made up only 32.7 percent of the population in the industrialized south (São Paulo, Paraná, Santa Catarina, and Rio Grande do Sul); in every other region, at least 60 percent of the population was *prêto, caboclo,* or *mestiço.*[104] Afro-Brazilians were decidedly underrepresented in the highest positions in the southern urban economy.[105] More generally, cities offered considerable opportunities for self-employment in trades and vending, but these low-level occupations offered limited prospects for a significant increase in socioeconomic status. Transitional labor policies privileging the concerns of former slaveowners provided little assistance to freedpersons. There was no outside aid in the form of government or charitable programming to assist their transition, and many families had depleted their savings to buy letters of freedom in the 1870s and 1880s.

The economic handicap borne by Afro-Brazilians and the distinct advantages enjoyed by immigrants and Brazilian whites were reinforced by prevalent cultural ideologies. Negative stereotypes about Africa and Africans, belief in inherent racial differences, and entrenched class prejudice contributed to the marginalization of Afro-Brazilians. Together, these economic and cultural obstacles made bridging the gap of inequality in the twentieth century a Herculean task.

The structures of elite hegemony should not be glossed over as a unilateral power relationship. Any close examination of oppressed peoples reveals myriad ways in which they develop mechanisms for ameliorating their situation. Afro-Brazilians in the post-abolition era continued traditions of resistance and contestation begun under slavery. From their origins as commoditized chattels, Afro-Brazilians helped establish roles for themselves in the social order both as slaves and as freedpersons. The threat and reality of revolts, alliances with whites as employees and political supporters, broadening prerogatives of urban slaves, and other negotiated relationships constantly reconfigured the boundaries of Afro-Brazilian social participation. A more nuanced understanding of the relationship between oppressor and oppressed reflects the fact that both used whatever means were at their disposal to protect their interests and advance their agendas. The next chapter takes a detailed look at how Afro-Brazilians transformed identity into a powerful tool of self-determination in the post-abolition era.

CHAPTER 2

Self-Determination

THE POLITICS OF IDENTITY

Something strange was happening in Bahia. On June 1, 1863, the Salvador police arrested a fifty-four-year-old carpenter named Vitório Aleixo José da Costa for having held "a meeting for that which is known as *candomblé*."[1] Throughout the city, police had been raiding these centers of African religious practices, confiscating ritual items and interrogating their leaders. Vitório was one of a growing number of *crioulos* (Brazilian-born blacks) discovered to be practicing candomblé rather than assimilating into the Catholic religious traditions of their native Brazil. Nearly a half-century later, with the overwhelming majority of blacks born and raised in Brazilian society, Nina Rodrigues described a Salvador in which candomblé *terreiros* were an important institution of everyday life.[3] In addition to performing sacred rituals pertaining to the relationship between the individual and Divine energy, *terreiro* leaders mediated disputes, healed the sick, and administered justice. Fifty years after Nina Rodrigues' observations, Edison Carneiro invited the international community into the world of candomblé, by then complete with dynasties, sprawling *terreiros,* and growing legions of followers that included high-ranking politicians.[4] Long after the abolition of slavery and the disappearance of African-born persons in Bahia's population, candomblés provided the infrastructure for the re-creation of African identity and the foundation of an African-based world that continues to flourish even at the dawn of the twenty-first century.

Far away to the south, quite a different process was taking place. Young Brazilians of color were suddenly rejecting old distinctions between blacks and mulattoes, embracing the pejorative label of *negro* that had come to be associated with a shameful heritage of slavery. Under the banner of negritude they formed numerous associations and eventually a race-based political party.

47

Black organizations overturned segregationist policies, and their successes shaped an enduring model for ethnic activism.[5]

In both Salvador and São Paulo, Africans and their descendants re-created social identity to their advantage. Ethnicity is vitally important in understanding collective activism because it is the organizing principle of group identity. Historically, divisions within the population mediated against solidarity. As Afro-Brazilians increasingly came to think of themselves as members of broader-based ethnic groups, they began acting along those lines. By the 1930s Afro-Brazilians had created new ethnic groups that did not exist even a century before. Regardless of whether the new ethnicities were as "blacks" or as "Africans," these redefined collective identities gave Afro-Brazilians new strength and political potential. Afro-Brazilians came to recognize ethnicity as a malleable concept that could be used as a strategy of social and political advancement just as it had been used traditionally as a tool of oppression. In the absence of other means of ascent, the development of empowering ethnic identities became a critical avenue to power for a people systematically denied that power by the societies in which they lived.

The fact that new collective identities varied around the country indicates an important distinction between form and function. The role ethnicity played is relatively clear; what is much more difficult to ascertain is exactly how specific ethnicities were constructed. In both São Paulo and Salvador, freedpersons shared African ancestry and Brazilian nationality, yet they devised quite different forms of ethnic identity. This difference suggests that other factors were at play in determining the contours of collective identities that could be used strategically by African descendants.

The Brazilian case therefore presents a rare opportunity to isolate factors other than ancestry and nationality in the construction of ethnic identity in the Afro-Atlantic diaspora. This chapter considers such factors as demographic differences among Afro-Brazilian communities, terms of marginalization by elites, and traditions of ethnic activism. It also examines the connection between specific identities and their role as strategies of social advancement.

The political implications of ethnicity were both simple and stark. To whom would the freedpersons pledge their allegiance—the nations that once enslaved them or, in Benedict Anderson's phrase, the "imagined community" represented by a distinct ethnonationalism? Would African descendants respond to exclusion by forcing their way into society, and would that integration take the form of assimilation or a pluralistic acceptance of the equal prerogatives of diverse groups? These were some of the questions that had yet to be determined in 1888. Fifty years later, patterns of ethnicity and ethnic strategy had already taken shape.

The Conceptualization of Race

It is always necessary to carefully outline the parameters of any discussion on race when speaking of Brazil, beginning with the social construction of race itself. Race, as we commonly conceive it, does not exist. As argued by Ashley Montagu in 1942, the choice of skin color to distinguish race is arbitrary.[6] It is grouped with other characteristics such as eye color and hair texture, but human genes do not mutate or travel in these conceptually convenient packages. The constant reconfigurations of the species' gene pool inevitably conflicts with the static concept of the racial "package." Socially conceived race must sometimes be contorted to accommodate this conflict. The contrasts between the United States and Brazil are striking in this regard. Intransigence characterized racial categorization in the United States. Former NAACP director Walter White, who was blond-haired and blue-eyed, was considered "black" because of his distant African ancestry. Brazil, in contrast, created a whole spectrum of racial terminology so fluid that a single individual might belong to several racial categories in a lifetime, even simultaneously. In one study, one hundred acquaintances were asked to identify the race of three full sisters and responses varied widely. The researcher, Marvin Harris, found that "[o]ne of the most striking consequences of the Brazilian system of racial identification is that parents and children and even brothers and sisters are frequently accepted as representatives of quite opposite racial types."[7] The social and genetic realities must be separated from each other and discussed in their local contexts.

The word "racism" is often substituted for "racialism." Popular usage of the former includes the concepts of belief in biological differences among races, racial hatred, discrimination, prejudice, and ethnocentrism. Only the first is literally accurate. Racism is the belief in the existences of "races" as biologically defined subdivisions of the human species. Racialism, which derives from this assumption, is the belief that those races may be compared hierarchically in such a way that one may be ranked superior to another. In discussions of racial ideology in Brazil, the assertion is frequently made that the nation is not "racist," often in reference to the absence of overt manifestations of racial hostilities. Although it is true that the horrors of racial terrorism, such as lynching, that occurred in the United States did not take place in Brazil, this alone does not negate the social impact of the ideologies of racism and racialism.[8] Such reasoning confuses racism with animosity, violence, and prejudice, none of which need be present to have a racist ideology. Racism in Brazil has produced a wide range of benign examples, such as the veneration of the erotic beauty of the *mulata*. Held as evidence of racial harmony, it actually derives from the paradigm that black and white races have distinct inherent qualities. The very term *mulata* validates the differentiation of the species by race. Both are powerful ideologies which, as noted by Richard Graham, not only shape society but also limit the range of intellectual response depending on the extent to which they are internalized and accepted by its members.[9] Regardless of whether social constructions of race are grounded in genetic reality, they nonetheless have a profound and very real impact on the lives of individuals. To analyze race in Brazil is, therefore, to work within a social paradigm that is no less powerful than if it had a basis in objective science.

Socially conceived race is a central issue in this study, which discusses the varieties of ways in which racial identity was perceived and the changes in racial ideology over the course of five decades. I have tried to represent accurately various perspectives on race, while retaining my own point of reference rooted in U.S. ideology.[10] I use "white" to include people of European descent. This term is applied with extra liberality in Salvador, where many fair-skinned elites perceive themselves as white and are acknowledged as such, despite the fact that they have a small degree of African ancestry.[11] I use "black" interchangeably with "Afro-Brazilian" for people of African descent. These terms include mulattoes as part of the reference group and represent the perspective of the author.[12] One of the major differences between U.S. and Brazilian racial terminology is the semantic separation of mulattoes from dark-skinned blacks. In the first national census, conducted in 1872, the government used *mestiço* (mixed) and *prêto* (black) to distinguish the two. The 1890 census, substituted *pardo* (brown) for *mestiço*. These were umbrella terms, used in official contexts, that embraced dozens of words and phrases describing a whole spectrum of colors. When necessary, I distinguish between mulattoes and dark-skinned blacks, although I have preferred to use Portuguese terms when representing Brazilian perspectives on race.

Demographic Change and Its Impact on Ethnicity in Salvador and São Paulo

The ethnicity of "blackness," a combination of somatic features and African cultural heritage, is neither fixed nor constant in the African diaspora. There is no intrinsic identification with blackness among people of African descent. In post-abolition Brazil, it was chosen only by a small group of people in the predominantly white south and expressed with the inclusive term *negro* instead of the traditional labels separating blacks and browns. As regional differences are explored, ethnicity appears as a fluid phenomenon both in response to, and as an outcome of, sociopolitical conditions. What has been referred to here as a "community" including all persons of African descent was, in fact, an extremely heterogeneous group. Although virtually all Afro-Brazilians shared some slave ancestry, important distinctions stratified the black population. Urbanity, free ancestry, genetic differences, education, income, profession, religious belief, degree of acculturation—all served to create subgroups within the black community. Addressing this issue in terms of what was assumed to be the "slave community" in U.S. historiography, Charles Joyner noted that "[h]istorians describe *the* slave community without having probed in depth any *particular* slave community. . . . The unity of the society and the integration of the culture have been assumed, when in fact that unity and that integration are merely hypotheses until they have been demonstrated in specific instances."[13]

Afro-Brazilians' concepts of race were far from homogeneous. In the minds of many Afro-Brazilians, there remained a sharp distinction between mulattoes and blacks.[14] Of the Afro-Brazilians who had achieved relative success in the abolition movement, politics, the arts, and other professions, many were mulattoes who did not acknowledge their African ancestry. Mobility was much easier for lighter-skinned Afro-Brazilians, and the ideology of "whitening" *(embranquecimento)* was firmly entrenched in most minds. The philosophy behind "whitening" was that a light-skinned person who assimilated Euro-Brazilian culture and entered spheres traditionally reserved for whites could be considered white and treated as such. The concept of blackness was so incompatible with social advancement that virtually any measure of success or social position sufficed for a person to be accorded whiteness in colloquial usages.[15] *Embranquecimento* also referred to the popular belief that the entire Brazilian population was gradually "whitening" through miscegenation.[16] Color was not the only means of "whitening." A special talent or good social connections could also help a person move away from "black" (that is, low) status. Machado de Assis was one of Brazil's greatest poets. When he died, one of his friends referred to him as a mulatto in a flattering eulogy. When Joaquim Nabuco, an abolitionist and member of Parliament, read the article, he asked the author to remove the racial reference on the grounds that "[t]he word is not literary, it is derogatory."[17] Gilberto Freyre once commented, "There are a number of colored men in high public office, though Brazilian courtesy would never describe them as 'negro.'"[18] The apparent facility with which mulattoes actually move into the "white" racial category has attracted a great deal of attention from researchers.[19]

It has been argued that the tripartite classification of whites, mulattoes, and blacks is the norm throughout the Afro-Atlantic diaspora, as opposed to the white-nonwhite dichotomy prevalent in the United States.[20] But while the three-tiered social reality is operative among Brazilians of all colors, there is an underlying supporting dichotomy distinguishing whites from nonwhites that cannot be denied. Freyre's comment juxtaposes behavioral conventions with an objective perception of certain politicians as "colored" in a classic Brazilian artifice. Underneath it all, the "whitened" black is still a black.

Color was not the sole criterion by which Afro-Brazilians defined themselves ethnically, nor was ethnicity the sole basis of social identity. In the nineteenth century, nationality was of great importance, particularly in areas with large African populations, as was slave versus free status. These bases of identity depended on demography. As the composition of the population changed—specifically, the decline of African-born persons in the general population—so did the mechanisms by which Afro-Brazilians defined themselves.

Changes in ethnic identity occurred differently in Salvador and São Paulo, concurrent with profound demographic transformations among the Afro-Brazilian population. Warfare in West Africa and new opportunities for international commerce caused an increased influx of Africans to Salvador in the late eighteenth and early nineteenth centuries. Over the course of the nineteenth century, ethnic identities changed as the Afro-Brazilian population shifted from a majority of African slaves to a majority of Brazilian-born free people. São Paulo's Afro-Brazilian community experienced a dramatic transformation as well. Shortly after abolition, Afro-Brazilian numbers swelled tenfold as new arrivals flocked to the capital from the Paulista interior and neighboring states. Gradually ethnicities shifted as newcomers adjusted to the conditions of urban life and developed new communities.

For Salvador, historic constructions of ethnicity in the nineteenth century are of great relevance in understanding the changes that occurred after abolition. Students of Brazilian history have described the many identities of Afro-Brazilian slaves.[21] They ultimately adapted their own formulations of ethnicity based upon these imposed identities. Slavers most often used the port of embarkation to denote an African's "nation" *(nação)*, such as "Mina" or "Angola." As the slave trade brought large numbers of captives from single areas, some came to be known by more specific geographic names, such as "Nagô" (Oyo Yoruba) or "Jêje" (Ewe). Within the black population, ethnicity based upon *nação* was limited to Africans. A secondary categorization for Africans determined their level of acculturation, with *bozal* referring to the unacculturated African and *ladino* referring to those relatively familiar with Portuguese language and customs. Still other classificatory measures distinguished the rest of the Afro-Brazilian population. The first was the differentiation by birthplace as either African or Brazilian. Color categories further stratified the Brazilian-born. *Creoulo* (alternatively spelled *crioulo*) described the darkest blacks. *Pardo* included the various intermediate shades of brown, each with its own name. In addition, the civil status of slave or free delineated an individual's position in society. This system of reference existed in these broadly sketched terms throughout the period of slavery.

The historian Mieko Nishida provides an overview of the changes in ethnic identity among Afro-Brazilians in the city of Salvador in the eight decades preceding abolition.[22] She divides this era into four stages. In the first (1808–1830), African-born persons constituted the majority of the city's population. They regarded Brazilians of all colors as outsiders, and formed their own brotherhoods from which Brazilians were excluded.[23] During this time, African ethnicity based upon *nação* was a primary form of self-identification. This trend is reflected in the actions of a chapter of the black brotherhood of Our Lady of the Rosary, founded in 1685 for the Catholic religious instruction of *prêtos,* a broad color category encompassing slave and free, African and Brazilian. The members themselves took note of both civil status and nationality; these are the only data recorded in the oldest surviving enrollment books. The brotherhood's shared *prêto* color category, however, was an imposed form of ethnicity that did not suffice to create a common bond among members. Conflicts between African-born Angolans and Brazilian-born *crioulos* had led to provisions to ensure representation for each group in seventeenth-century statutes, and these were restated in the revised statutes of 1820.[24] Each group elected its own Juiz and Juiza, the male and female leaders. The other offices of the board, including the scribe, treasurer, and procurador geral, were to rotate between the two groups, with the stipulation that in the year that the scribe was Angolan, the treasurer would have to be *crioulo*, and vice versa.[25]

Nishida's second stage, 1831–1850, began with the increase of Brazilian-born blacks *(crioulos)* in the population, along with their own institutions. The prohibition of the African slave trade suddenly curtailed the ability of African *nações* to revitalize themselves with new arrivals. An interethnic "African" identity gradually came to supersede individual *nação* identity, particularly after the 1835 slave revolt when reprisals and public sentiment targeted "Africans" generically. Rather than a *nação* community extending throughout the urban and suburban areas, there emerged a locally based "African" community. In the third stage (1851–1870), pan-African identity solidified, with a greater reliance on personal networks over formal institutions for mutual assistance. Finally, between 1871 and 1888, Brazilian-born mulattoes came to outnumber blacks for the first time in Salvador's history. Ethnicity denoting color *(prêto* and *pardo)* now replaced the old labels denoting nationality, such as *crioulo*.

The factor of Brazilian versus African birth was an important delimiter of ethnicity in the nineteenth century. It had profound impact because of its emphasis on assimilation into the dominant culture. Brazilian-born *crioulos* and acculturated *ladinos* had been valued for their knowledge of Portuguese Brazilian language and customs. Status increased with their degree of acculturation and tended to correlate with color gradations. Thus the fair-skinned individual with a command of Brazilian culture ranked far above the darker individual who still retained many African cultural forms. To set oneself apart from Africans and darker Afro-Brazilians was an affirmation of that higher status as determined by prevalent norms. There were important financial incentives; rank frequently translated into concrete benefits. People of lighter skin were far more likely to attain their freedom; close association with whites usually brought better employment opportunities. Afro-Brazilians, positioned as they were on the lowest rungs of the social ladder, sought to improve their standing using the traditional determinants of social stature: color, wealth, and culture. Of these, culture was the easiest to change. Rather than embrace African cultural heritage and collectives of people of African descent, many Afro-Brazilians took their first step toward social mobility by disassociating themselves from what was deprecatingly called *a creoulada*—the black masses. For most Afro-Brazilians, being African and/or black was synonymous with servitude, poverty, and barbarity. Within the context of Brazilian society, distancing oneself from other blacks seemed a rational choice of the option with the greatest potential for benefits.

A diachronic overview of Salvador's Afro-Brazilian community in the nineteenth century reveals two patterns of ethnicity. The *africanos—jêjes, angolas, minas,* and others—tended toward ethnic solidarity around the concept of *nação*. As their numbers decreased, *nação* came broadly to mean Africa, although specific nationalities were recognized as secondary identifications. The smaller size of the group promoted greater solidarity. The Brazilians of African descent—*prêtos* and *pardos*—more readily adopted the national hierarchies of color and culture. Katia Mattoso noted that "[t]he bonds among new arrivals from Africa made a better cement than the creoles' desire for assimilation."[26] These patterns cannot be drawn too rigidly, however, because of the presence of an intermediate group, the Brazilian-born *crioulo* children of Africans. This group was to play a major role in reshaping ethnicity in the post-abolition years.

The story of Eugenia Anna dos Santos illustrates these changing notions of ethnicity toward the end of the nineteenth century. She was born in Salvador on July 13, 1869, to Sergio dos Santos and Lucinda Maria da Conceição, also known as Aniyó and Azambriyó. Her parents used two names because they belonged to two nations; they were Brazilians but they were also Gruncis, one of the African *nações* of Bahia. As a young woman, Aninha (as she was called) came to know Maria Julia Figueiredo, the daughter of the senior priestess of a candomblé house founded by Africans from the Yoruba nation of Ketu. When Maria Julia initiated Aninha as a devotee, she assumed the name Oba Biyi and became a child of Ketu. In her later life, Aninha became the most ardent defender of Yoruba traditions in Bahia, founding her own candomblé in 1910 and insisting upon adherence to customs and the adoption of the Yoruba language.[27]

Afro-Brazilians like Aninha were redefining ethnicity in Bahia at a time when Africans born on the continent were becoming increasingly rare. Whereas Aninha might have been called *crioula* because of her birthplace, her contemporaries referred to her as "Grunci" because of her parents. Particularly in the candomblés, where lineage determined succession, African ethnicity was extended into descending generations rather than applied exclusively to indigenous Africans. Aninha's story also illustrates a new conceptualization of *nação* as an *assumed* ethnicity, thus allowing a Brazilian to "become" African or an African to adopt a new nation—within the context of candomblé.

The role of candomblé is especially important, for it appears to match a process noted elsewhere in the African diaspora in which an African-based religion served as the basis for pan-African identity and solidarity. When enslaved Africans first arrived in Jamaica, those from numerically stronger national groups isolated themselves as a means of coping with a hostile environment. One such group was the Akan, which organized exclusively Akan slave revolts throughout the eighteenth century. Toward the end of that century, a decrease in Akan arrivals, an increase in the Jamaican-born population, and the emergence of Myalism as a pan-African religious culture led to a shift from national isolation to pan-African cooperation. In 1789 Akan, Kongo, and Mandinka people together took part in a slave revolt.[28] When a new influx of Africans arrived as replacement laborers in the early nineteenth century and became situated within a predominantly Jamaican-born black population, their national ethnicities became subordinate to an overarching African identity.[29] Here again, their gradual assimilation into Afro-Christianity eventually smoothed over ethnic differences, incorporating the new arrivals into a broader ethnic construct.

Candomblé played a similar role in Salvador. It was nominally *nação*-specific, with its sect designations such as Angola, *caboclo,* Jêje, and Ketu, but by the late nineteenth century these distinctions were unrelated to the specific ancestry of devotees, as seen in the case of Aninha. With the exception of the Islamic community (Malê), the Bahian candomblés seemed to share an ability to address the spiritual and social needs of the broad Afro-Bahian community, perhaps because they had not been able to retain nation-specific cosmological constructs once Africans born in those societies stopped arriving via the slave trade. Distinctions among the various sects had to do with factors not always related to national traditions, such as the predominance of men in the Angola and *caboclo* sects (see Chapter 6).

The flexibility of the *nação* concept, associated with its application in the context of candomblé, coincided with a general decrease in its usage elsewhere. *Prêto* became more widely used to include blacks of various African heritages, and the distinction between Brazilian and African birth ceased to be of relevance. By the time the Rosário brotherhood revised its statutes in 1872, rivalries between Angolans and *crioulos* no longer threatened to tear the organization apart. A single governing board sufficed for all members. The Rosário had ceased to be a brotherhood of Angolans and *crioulos*, becoming instead a brotherhood of *prêtos*.[30] The Sociedade Protectora dos Desvalidos, created in 1832 by and for free Brazilian-born *crioulos*, a term emphasizing nationality and civil status, by the post-abolition years had adopted the term *prêto*, with its emphasis on color, to establish membership restrictions. Precisely at a time when white Brazilians were publicly discounting the importance of color, it was becoming more significant as a basis of ethnic identity among Afro-Brazilians.

Color was to be of primary importance in determining ethnicity among Afro-Brazilians in São Paulo. It is difficult to compare São Paulo and Bahia in terms of ethnic identity before and after abolition. This is partly because little research exists on the pre-abolition Afro-Brazilian population of São Paulo, but also because much of its post-abolition population arrived only after 1888. The urban black population, estimated at 26,380 in 1910, rose to 108,682 by 1940.[31] Because of this, I examine developments in ethnicity in the city of São Paulo principally as a phenomenon of the post-abolition period and not as an evolution of preexisting patterns.

Over 50,000 Afro-Brazilians arrived in the state's capital city between 1910 and 1934, most of them from the agricultural regions of the Paulista interior and the neighboring states of Rio de Janeiro and Minas Gerais.[32] They formed between 8 and 12 percent of a population consisting mainly of European immigrants. This latter group was similar to the Bahian Africans in that its members represented many distinct communities that, once in Brazil, took slightly more generic formulations as Italian, German, Portuguese, Spanish, and so forth. In a pattern common to immigrant communities, hometown networks helped new arrivals settle in, with friends and family from home assisting in the procurement of jobs and housing. Blacks, following the same patterns as the European immigrants, established networks based upon region of origin. Also like the Europeans, the Brazilians began to reshape ethnicity in the context of a culturally pluralistic society.

Most blacks shared a common pattern of immigration. Descended from slaves, they came from areas that had shifted to free labor, a process that frequently left blacks in jobs with little potential for growth. They arrived in poverty, and settled in with fellows in similar circumstances. This pattern led to the formation of clusters of black residential concentrations that set them aside from their white Brazilian counterparts. Different in color, socioeconomic status, and residential distribution around the city, separate "white" and "black" ethnicities were easy to create. This was further compounded by the attitudes of Europeans who specifically excluded blacks from their social circles. People of African descent who wanted to join clubs, attend parties, play on soccer teams, or engage in other social activities typically had to do so through black organizations. Divisions of ethnicity were less important for São Paulo's black community than for Salvador's; there is no evidence that African ethnic communities had taken root in São Paulo as they had done in Salvador. The small number of blacks relative to the total population also facilitated group solidarity. If any distinctions of origin held importance, they were those based upon the cities and towns from which they had emigrated.

Around the turn of the century, a small group of activists in São Paulo began to articulate a racial ideology that rejected the traditional distinction between blacks and mulattoes, assuming instead a *negro* ethnic identity that incorporated all of the many color categories of people of African descent. Not only did they criticize this common differentiation, they occasionally referred to well-known mulattos as *negros,* holding them as role models for the race as a whole.[33] The redefinition of blackness to include mulattoes became an important tenet of Afro-Brazilian political philosophy throughout the twentieth century.

This constituted a drastic departure from traditional Brazilian racial ideology. During slavery, the word *negro* had pejorative connotations. Afro-Brazilians preferred other appellations, such as *prêto*. The historian Mary Karasch notes that *negro* "was almost synonymous with *escravo* (slave)."[34] Many early twentieth-century Afro-Brazilian newspapers used the term *homens de côr* ("colored" or, literally, "men of color") on their mastheads.[35] Others avoided any racial reference at all. Progressive journals such as *Clarim da Alvorada* and *Progresso* preferred to use *prêto* in their early stages.[36] *Clarim* became one of the first to use the word *negro* on its masthead when it declared itself the "Legitimate Organ of Black Youth" *(mocidade negra)* in 1928. It was the Frente Negra Brasileira, however, that launched the almost militant use of the word *negro* after 1931. Never before had anyone used the term so aggressively. Its official journal, *A Voz da Raça* (The Voice of the Race), boldly challenged the prevailing notion of a racial democracy with the words, "Color prejudice, in Brazil, is something only we blacks [*negros*] can feel," a banner that ran across the masthead for three years. One masthead admonished its readers, "BLACKS, don't be ashamed of being black!" *(NEGRO não te envergonhes de ser negro!).*[37] Such radical usage sought to imbue the term with positive connotations and unite all Afro-Brazilians under a single racial banner. The politically strategic use of *negro* identity was a prerequisite for creating a power base among a potentially large constituency, and closely resembles the changing terminology of self-determination among people of African descent in the United States. When, in the 1960s, African-Americans in the United States began to assume the word "black," their usage paralleled the Brazilian experience in terms of bringing positive connotations to a traditionally negative and derogatory appellation. In an attempt to clarify the social significance of these terms for readers from the United States, I will translate *homens de côr* as "colored" or "people of color," *prêto* as "Negro," and *negro* as "black."

Important demographic changes in both Salvador and São Paulo redefined the ways in which Afro-Brazilians formulated their ethnicity. The decline of African-born persons in Bahia led to the de-emphasis of nationality as a primary ethnic identity. The influx of blacks to São Paulo created a new community whose identity derived from the dynamics of immigration. In each case, new forms of ethnic identity gradually took shape in the post-abolition era.

To summarize, as Brazilian-born blacks became the majority of the population of African descent, Brazilian cultural concepts came to predominate in the Afro-Brazilian community. Color differences between *prêtos* and *pardos* increased in importance as a delimiter of subgroups within the overall black population. Where they were a small population in an ethnically diverse city, *prêto* and *pardo* Afro-Brazilians often found themselves grouped together as "black." It was harder to do so in Bahia, where *prêtos* and *pardos* were each large groups with their own institutions.

Another important difference between Salvador and São Paulo was the continuing viability of the concept of African nations. As *nação* was redefined in the post-abolition era, it emphasized cultural practices and beliefs. Although Africans ceased to be a large demographic group, African culture in some form was always viable in Salvador, either in the person of the African-born or as preserved culture by adherents of African traditions regardless of natal ethnicity. Afro-Brazilians in São Paulo also developed unique cultural forms, including the samba styles that grew out of the parties given by black social clubs. The process of creating diasporan culture was the same in both cities, but whereas Bahians could assert an "African" ethnicity, the Paulistas viewed themselves as Brazilians who differed only in that they were "black." A cultural ethnicity prevailed in the former instance, and a racial ethnicity in the latter. The cultural ethnicity was made possible by a large and diverse black population, but tended to exclude Afro-Brazilians who chose not to adhere to African cultural traditions. In contrast, the racial ethnicity was all-inclusive, but only arose where the black population was small in number. Neither situation was conducive to the formation of a powerful Afro-Brazilian interest group able to advocate on its members' behalf in post-abolition society, which would have required a broad-ranging collective identity and a common sociopolitical agenda.[38]

Identity, Social Strategy, and Self-Determination

Abolition resurrected the most fundamental political issue of all for people of the Afro-Atlantic diaspora in a new light. Brought against their will, their lives and those of their children marked forever by the specter of slavery, African-Americans were nonetheless an integral part of the new societies in which they lived. This problematic relationship and the duality of identity it engendered constitutes the crux of the political issue facing all people of the Afro-Atlantic diaspora: integration or separatism. There is a broad spectrum between integration and separatism, including back-to-Africa movements, maroon and other separatist societies, acculturation, "passing," and a host of intermediate options such as participation in separate social worlds while being dedicated to political participation in the mainstream. It must be stressed that these general categories are not mutually exclusive, and most ideologies combine elements of the two. Each is a political strategy of self-determination. Locating oneself ideologically on the integration-separatism spectrum has been part of the individual reality of African descendants since the arrival of the first African. With abolition, it became a matter of collective choice, the tenor of which would affect all persons of African descent and the societies in which they lived.

There was much variety in the Atlantic world in the ways African descendants identified themselves and their objectives after abolition. This is one of the reasons Brazil provides such an excellent case for study. In the city of São Paulo, Afro-Brazilians created the nation's first and only race-based political party in 1931, the Frente Negra Brasileira (Brazilian Black Front). It was an unprecedented form of activism by Afro-Brazilians and, though it lasted only six years, achieved important successes that had an enduring impact on race relations and race politics. Yet the Frente was unable to win broad support throughout Brazil, in part because, for many Afro-Brazilians, a race-based identity of "blackness" conflicted with their social realities and practical self-identities in their everyday lives. As already noted, the demographic contours of individual Afro-Brazilian communities had played an important role in shaping ethnic identity. To analyze expressions of self-determination—the identities people wanted to protect and promote in post-emancipation society—it is necessary to take a closer look at the factors affecting the formulation of identity.

Self-determination is a protagonistic form of identity that challenges

(challenge)

relationships of power between groups of people/ It is the rejection of determination by an "other." This became the struggle of Afro-Brazilians in São Paulo after abolition as they encountered multiple forms of discrimination against "black" people. *Blacks* were not welcomed in certain public spaces, *blacks* were not hired for certain jobs, *blacks* could not attend certain parties or live wherever they might like. Although Afro-Paulistas did not originally think of themselves primarily as "black," blackness eventually became a shared experience and identity as a result of its role as a basis for exclusion and subordination. Ultimately, resistance against racial discrimination paved the way for a new collective identity and race-based organizations such as the Frente Negra.[39]

Of the many external pressures affecting the identity of Afro-Brazilians, the most significant was the exclusion they experienced. Regardless of whether or not they chose to exercise it, many Afro-Brazilians believed they had earned the right of full and equitable inclusion in all spheres of national life. Indeed, as nearly one thousand supporters gathered in September 1931 to ratify the statutes of the Frente Negra Brasileira, the very first of these was the call to foster the "political and social union of the Black People of this Nation for the affirmation of the historic rights of same by virtue of their moral and material activity in the past, and to demand their social and political rights in the Brazilian community."[40]

Closer examination of the nature of the marginalization of African descendants reveals an important distinction between the *basis* (why) and the *mode* (how) of that exclusion. The basis of exclusion is its rationale. In the case of São Paulo, "whites" discriminated against "blacks." In contrast, "Brazilians" in Salvador discriminated against "Africans." This differs from the mode of exclusion, which centers on the regulation of social gateways.

Every polity creates socially sanctioned forms of access. In Brazil, light skin color, command of Euro-Brazilian culture, wealth, and connections were keys to upward mobility. Within the Afro-Brazilian community, some individuals held more of these keys than did others and therefore experienced discrimination differently. The social experience of the individual is unique in this regard. Thus a stereotypical denigration of people of African descent followed by the disclaimer "but I like *you*, you're different," legitimizes and perpetuates both the basis and the mode of marginalization.

Lacking the civil status of slavery as a justification for social, political, and economic exclusion, societies devised new mechanisms based on their specific demographic and historical contexts. This, in turn, affected both the basis and the mode of exclusion of Afro-Brazilians after abolition. The shift in forms of exclusion provided an impetus for the creation of new and politicized collective identities on the part of Afro-Brazilians. Although discriminatory ideologies were intended as a form of maintaining hegemony, they simultaneously had the potential to become a new basis for group solidarity and mobilization to address that discrimination. For Afro-Atlantic peoples, it was particularly important because their historic heterogeneity had tended to mitigate against mass action.

But another process was also taking place that became a factor facilitating the rise of newer broad-based ethnicities. African diaspora communities were becoming more culturally homogeneous as the African-born population diminished after the end of the slave trade. Beginning with the Middle Passage, the bridging of ethnic differences and the creation of creole diasporan cultures had been a fundamental part of Afro-Atlantic cultures that was often vital for survival.[41] These distinct cultures became a critical mechanism of psychological health and survival in the highly discriminatory societies in which most Afro-Atlantic peoples lived. Under pressure to adopt an oppressive worldview, Africans and their descendants consistently strove to shape their own from the cultural wreckage that survived the Middle Passage. Throughout the Americas, African philosophy, spirituality, aesthetics, and arts informed diasporan culture, especially in such places as northeastern Brazil, the islands of Jamaica and Haiti, or the southern United States, where there were demographic concentrations of blacks.[42] Thus the desolation and anomie resulting from the loss of one's cultural traditions described by Eldridge Cleaver in *Soul on Ice* coexisted with the world described in the works of Zora Neale Hurston. These were the private worlds of black folk, the plantation villages and urban ghettos, the worlds of samba and capoeira, the Maypole celebrations of Afro-Nicaraguans in Bluefields and Corn Island, the sacred ceremonies of African ancestors from candomblé to the Holy Rollers. Kwame Anthony Appiah characterizes it as "a black world on which the white American world impinged in ways that were culturally marginal even though formally politically overwhelming."[43] These "moments of cultural autonomy," in Appiah's words, helped the peoples of the Afro-Atlantic diaspora to "achieve, against far greater ideological odds than ever faced the majority of Africa's colonized peoples, an equally resilient sense of their own worth."[44]

The degree to which this was possible in the Afro-Atlantic world varied greatly; it must be recognized that European America impinged on the lives of its population of African descent in ways that ranged from the virtual extinction of the African heritage to a minimal involvement that affected only the most superficial levels of personal life. However, it was not necessary to have clearly identifiable African cultural components to have autonomist diasporan societies. In her study of nineteenth-century Jamaica, Monica Schuler points to the Myal religious tradition as a key factor bridging ethnic differences and forging Afro-Jamaican cultural identity. Religion often served this function;

Christianity brought slaves of diverse origins together in congregations and sodalities. African based-religions such as candomblé, santeria, and vodoun did the same by bringing together elements from both Central African and West African cosmologies.[45]

Whether African descendants directly retained cultural practices or reinterpreted European constructs to their sensibilities, the creation of distinct African diaspora cultures informed identities that differed from Euro-American creole society. This led to the creation of parallel and alternative communities coexisting within national cultures. A parallel community replicates the institutions of mainstream society but, by limiting participation to members of the oppressed group, factors out discrimination against individuals not possessing the characteristics determining elite status. For example, black mutual aid societies, brotherhoods, financial institutions, newspapers, and social clubs were parallel in structure and function to those found in mainstream society. An alternative community, in contrast, creates its own institutions and social networks in which its values differ from those in the mainstream.

Although completely autonomous societies have been attempted in the African diaspora,[46] they are virtually impossible to sustain. A semiautonomous model, in which participants live in both mainstream and alternative societies, is more common. In such a model, the values of the mainstream society are often inverted in the alternative, so that qualities which are deemed lower status by mainstream standards may become attributes of high status in the alternative. To use a Brazilian example, the age, ethnicity, and gender of older African women were social liabilities in mainstream culture, but, in the world of candomblé, were respected attributes.

Both alternative and parallel communities invalidate the bases of discrimination inherent in the dominant society. The extent to which African descendants were able to create these social collectives was to affect the viability of separatism, which depended upon the existence of a societal infrastructure, as a strategic option. This infrastructure requires not only a sufficient number of people but also institutions within the community. Where that infrastructure is small, it can at the very least serve to form parallel institutions, regarded here as a variant of separatism.

All acts of self-determination in the Afro-Atlantic diaspora can be situated along a political spectrum ranging from integration to separatism. Integration via assimilation was a choice sanctioned by Brazilian society. It came to be known as "whitening," and encompassed both somatic and cultural dimensions. Such an approach did not threaten the principles upon which rested white hegemony. Assimilation reinforced the notion of a white ideal and validated the marginalization of individuals who refused to assimilate. Voluntary separatism, in contrast, was a rejection of involvement with an oppressive society that included the psychology of oppression. As such, it was a liberatory ideology.[47]

The politics of identity revolve around barriers. For members of the dominant group, it is the ability to keep out those who pose a threat to their power. Leo Spitzer observes that this type of barrier regulates access in such a way that reinforces the hierarchical structure, but does not prevent the absorption of the dominant culture by the subordinate group.[48] For the oppressed, it is the extent to which they are able to prevent the encroachment of an oppressive society and its attendant ideology.

The availability of integration as an option, therefore, depended on the dominant society; it was this group that possessed the power of regulating access. With African traditions portrayed as manifestations of a more primitive stage of human development, Afro-Brazilians, to move upward, were expected to relinquish their African cultural identity, a problem commonly faced by immigrants and ethnic minorities seeking to succeed in a different, dominant culture. They must choose which cultural components they will adopt, and which of their own they will or will not relinquish. They are faced with a choice of integration versus separatism. I use the term integration ("to become part of") rather than assimilation ("to become similar to") because its objective is equality of opportunity and full participation in the social, economic, and political life of the nation. Assimilation may be seen as a means to achieve this end but, as will be seen, is not the only way. At the other extreme, separatism emphasizes maintenance of a distinct set of cultural values and practices (ethnonationalism). The availability of separatism, however, depended on the oppressed sector of society, insofar as its members were able to create either alternative or parallel communities.

The above conditions are structural factors established by both the dominant and the oppressed sectors of society that determined the viability of integrationist and separatist strategies. Given these conditions, individuals made personal choices about the strategies they wished to pursue in order to situate themselves in Brazilian society. Three tendencies were present, which I have categorized as integrationist, alternative integrationist, and separatist. Each of these relates to command of the tools of social mobility and the desired relationship with the dominant culture.

The integrationist seeks to become part of society using the mechanisms of access sanctioned by the dominant sector. In Brazil, this meant utilization of color, culture, wealth, and gender privilege. The alternative integrationist seeks to become part of society using alternative mechanisms. The Frente Negra Brasileira exemplified this strategy by using a "black" *(negro)* ethnic identity to form a mass-based pressure group advocating equal access to Brazilian society. The separatist does not focus on participation in the dominant society. Rather, the separatist retreats to enclaves of alternative or parallel societies as a survival mechanism within the context of dominant society.

One strategy is rarely embraced by an entire community, although it is common for a single strategy to become prominent at different historical moments. Sometimes either separatism or integrationism tends to prevail in a community because of its historical antecedents. The tradition of marronage, for example, is an important indicator of a diasporan community's ability to create alternative or parallel worlds and, hence, its proclivity for separatist strategies.

Given the heterogeneity of the Afro-Brazilian population, it should be no surprise that its history is replete with manifestations of self-determination that derive from both integrationism and separatism. Each has its own particular qualities. Integration was generally motivated by the very real promise of material gain, and reflected the personal choice of individuals to seek positions and affiliations within the structure of Brazilian society, such as military and civil service posts. Antônio Pereira Rebouças, son of a Portuguese immigrant and a mulata freedwoman, exemplified this strategy by taking advantage of Brazil's "mulatto escape hatch." His rise to prominence was partially attributable to his own initiative, but would not have been possible had he not also embraced the standards of the dominant world he sought to enter. "The social and economic rewards that Rebouças earned by passing through the 'escape hatch,' and by his involvement in the process of *embranquecimento,* also reinforced his motivation to continue striving to achieve within the dominant realm, and influenced him to identify less with the world he was leaving behind," observed Spitzer in his biographical sketch.[49] Integrationism was easily pursued as an individual strategy, thus fitting within the personalized nature of Brazilian patronage. Integration also had a pronounced gender bias, especially in colonial Brazil when the availability of marriageable white women was low. The veneration of the *mulata* woman as an erotic enchantress was a stereotype that these women were able to exploit in the selection of marriage partners. Spitzer offers the verses of Capistrano de Abreu as illustration:

Uma mulata bonita
Não carece de rezar:
Basta o mimo que tem
Para a sua alma salvar

A pretty mulatto girl
Need not practice her devotions;
All she needs are her graces
For her soul's salvation.[50]

② I term the second modality alternative integrationist because, although it shares general goals with the first, it endorses alternative mechanisms of social mobility. The extremely vocal black activist groups from São Paulo in the 1920s and 1930s fit this category. For them, *negritude,* the formulation of group identity based on race, became a new strategy, an alternative means of social ascent based on the interest-group model. I use the term *negritude* as opposed to "Africanity" because it was color specific, not culturally specific, as the Paulistas stressed their commonality as Brazilians. In order to consolidate their interest group, they had to valorize blackness and provide some benefit to membership that would counterbalance the perceived benefits of traditional integration. It was not necessary that they present a whole range of radical alternatives. The people embracing this modality may be characterized as aspirants. They were people who did not, or could not, use color privilege or wealth as mechanisms to increase their power or social stature, but nonetheless sought to share equally in the prerogatives and benefits of citizenship. They therefore created their own strategies to obtain fuller participation within the system. This group essentially believed in the promise of a racial democracy (as opposed to a caste society) in which individuals could improve their condition based on merit. Their organizations advocated not fundamental social change but, rather, broader access. A significant characteristic of alternative integrationism is that it incorporates an agenda of social change and is, therefore, the sector generating most social activism.

③ Whereas the first two modalities were oriented toward integration, the final was separatist. It was composed of outsiders, people who did not seek or anticipate significantly increased participation within the system. They developed alternative and parallel social structures to meet their needs.[51] "Outsider" endeavors such as candomblé communities and samba groups generated the institutional infrastructure necessary for the formulation of ethnonationalism.

Separatism had quite different qualities, most notably its collective nature. The premise of separatism is the establishment of a distinct society, with its own institutions, that serves as an alternative to the dominant culture. Such a society can only be established collectively, and its prerequisite is a group ideology to function as an organizing principle for that collective. This principle can be broadly classified as nationalism.[52] Ethnonationalism is the organizing principle for the political ideology of separatism. There is a fine distinction here, but one that is important, between the ethnonationalism of the separatists and that of the integrationists and alternative integrationists. The former is both cause and result of distinct institutions grounded in a shared culture, as expressed by alternative societies. The latter form of nationalism was born in response to exclusion. Thus if the exclusion no longer exists, the ideological rationale for the group's existence also dissipates.

The element of personal choice to pursue any of these patterns of self-determination—integrationist, alternative integrationist, or separatist—is important to recognize, for social-somatic factors alone did not automatically dictate an individual's political perspectives. Although mulattoes, by dint of their skin color, had privileges that would facilitate their use of traditional modes of social ascent, some nonetheless chose to cast their lot with darker blacks in demanding racial equity though collective activism. Others participated in separatist institutions. The options chosen by each individual were influenced by ethnic identity, but also by their own preferences with regard to integration versus separatism.

These modalities refer to individual choices, but may also be extended to include collective strategies. Many, and conflicting, political tendencies always exist in diverse communities. At certain historical moments, distinct ideologies become salient and come to characterize the mainstream thinking of the African-descended population. In the United States, the integrationist leanings of the civil rights movements in the 1950s and early 1960s gave way to a significant separatist strain, especially after 1968. In one of the Brazilian cases, one political agenda attained little popularity in 1928 but three years later constituted the ideological core of the first mass Afro-Brazilian organization. We must understand what makes a particular leader or movement "right" for a specific time and place. Both the sociopolitical framework of the society at large and internal factors among people of African descent determine the predominance of a political ideology at any given time.

These are some of the principles underlying the politics of self-determination that came into play for African descendants after abolition. We turn now to the actual experiences of Afro-Brazilians, to the extent possible given the limitations of the sources, to explore how they used these factors to shape their new lives in the post-abolition years. Freedoms had been given, but they had not been defined. Afro-Brazilians set out to give meaning to that freedom, and to struggle for its realization.

CHAPTER 3

São Paulo

THE NEW CITY—THE NEW *NEGRO*

We lived on a farm near Mococa. Then we moved to Mococa itself, which is a city.
We were always striving for better things. And from the city of Mococa we moved here
[to São Paulo]. In truth, all these moves we made were the yearnings of the ex-slave.
Because, when you think about it, those of us born in 1921 were born just about three
decades after slavery ended. So that longing was still in the heart of the black man.
So much so that, by the time I arrived in São Paulo [in 1935] the ideals of the black
movement had already been ingrained in me.
—Aristides Barbosa, former member of the Frente Negra Brasileira[1]

$\mathcal{T}$he story of Afro-Brazilians in post-abolition São Paulo is essentially a tale of immigrants and dreams. By the tens of thousands, they flocked to the burgeoning urban hub from the agricultural areas of the Paulista interior, Rio de Janeiro, and Minas Gerais.[2] By 1940 the Afro-Brazilian population had swelled over tenfold, from an 1890 total of 10,842 to 109,076.[3] Their story is not one of long-established communities faced with the challenge of changing deeply rooted institutions and relationships in an old slave society. Theirs is the story of the Barbosas echoed many times over, black families who saw no opportunities in the towns where their parents and grandparents had worked as slaves and who opted to start a new life in a city full of promise. What they eventually discovered was that São Paulo's promise had its limits; its welcome seemingly extended more to Europe than to Brazil, more to white than to black. It was a city that regarded its black population as a social problem to be tightly controlled and, if possible, shunted away from public view. For a while, Afro-Brazilians struggled quietly to succeed against the odds of marginalization but, by the 1920s, their young people, most of them raised in São Paulo, decided to demand more of their adopted city. A vocal breed of black youth opened a new chapter in Brazilian history by bringing the taboo subject of race politics into the open arena of public discourse. The unprecedented advocacy of São Paulo's race organizations also hinted at the existence of a "New Negro" community in the heart of South America.

The phrase "New *Negro*" is deliberately evocative of the Harlem Renaissance. Significant parallels exist between the changing consciousness in post–World War I New York City and in São Paulo. In both cases, people of African descent deserted the agricultural regions for the promise of a better life in a modern city. Like the blacks of Harlem, Afro-Brazilians in São Paulo shaped their own renaissance, a new type of Afro-Brazilian to be known as the *negro*—proud, united, and a full participant in all aspects of Brazilian society.

The New City: São Paulo, 1890 to 1940

The experiences of Afro-Brazilians in São Paulo after abolition must be set within the context of the city's overall development during that time.[4] The newness of São Paulo was its wholesale transformation into a modern industrial city at a lightning pace that peaked during the First Republic. Yet São Paulo was one of Brazil's oldest cities, a provincial capital that began as a Jesuit settlement in 1554.[5] Although persons of African descent had been essential to the development of the economy of the captaincy and later province of São Paulo, prior to abolition they had not been prominent in the history of the city of São Paulo. This apparent anomaly is in part attributable to the Portuguese and Brazilian penchant to use a single name—in this case São Paulo (but also applicable to Bahia)—to apply to both city and state. Ambiguities at times make it difficult to identify Afro-Brazilians in the city's history specifically. But their absence is also traceable back to the colonial era. Whereas São Paulo was established at the outset of Portuguese settlement in Brazil, only in the early eighteenth century was it accorded royal recognition. Prior to 1710, the regions that were to become the autonomous captaincies of São Paulo and Minas Gerais were part of the larger captaincy of Rio de Janeiro. In response to demands for a more active administration and regulation of gold mining, in 1710 the crown created the independent captaincy of São Paulo and Minas Gerais. Its capital was São Paulo which, two years later (1712), was accorded city status. In 1721 the two independent captaincies of Minas Gerais and São Paulo were created. The motivation for such crown initiative lay solely in developing an administrative response to discoveries of placer gold in the interior, the influx of miners and others imbued with gold rush fever, and the specter of lawlessness and disorder. But the major centers of such feverish mining activity that witnessed black labor of hitherto unparalleled intensity were far removed from the city of São Paulo.

The advent of commercial coffee agriculture profoundly revolutionized Paulista economy and society. The Paraíba Valley between Rio and São Paulo was the first area devoted principally to coffee, but it was soon discovered that the gentle hills and rocky soils of the Paulista interior were ideal for the profitable crop. Unburdened by a traditional socioeconomic monoculture, and with the opening of railroad links to the port at Santos, coffee became São Paulo's leading export by mid-century.[6] African slaves provided the labor; although São Paulo never became Brazil's largest slaveholding province, by 1874 its slave population surpassed those of both Bahia and Pernambuco.[7]

The free population of color in the city of São Paulo grew substantially just prior to abolition. In 1872 *pardos* and *prêtos* made up 37 percent of the population of 31,385. A third of the capital's Afro-Brazilian population (3,828) were enslaved. Rates of enslavement, however, varied greatly by color. Only 14 percent of *pardos* were slaves compared with 58 percent of *prêtos*. By 1886 only 593 (1.2 percent) slaves lived in the capital, with the vast majority of all slaves (95 percent) in the province's agricultural zones.[8]

Afro-Brazilians found their employment options after abolition limited by regional economic patterns. Florestan Fernandes notes that in the areas of slowest growth, where labor was scarce, manumitted slaves continued to work on plantations with few changes. Where labor was abundant, freedmen who left the plantations were quickly and easily replaced by immigrants.[9] In the agricultural colonies between 1908 and 1912, despite an increase in the work force from 4,380 to 12,193, the percentage of Brazilian workers shrank from 43.9 percent in 1908 to 28.7 percent in 1912.[10] In the early decades of the twentieth century, Japanese immigrants also began arriving to work on the coffee plantations.[11] There is some evidence that blacks attempted to establish private businesses.[12] Cut off from agricultural employment opportunities, however, many black Paulistas looked to the growing urban hub in the capital.

São Paulo in 1890 was still a predominantly rural state, with only 4.7 percent of its population residing in the capital. Of just under 400,000 Afro-Brazilians in the state, 10,872, or 2.7 percent of the total, lived in the city. Throughout the post-abolition decades, Afro-Brazilians increasingly abandoned the countryside for urban opportunities. By 1940 the percentage of Afro-Paulistas living in the capital had risen to 12.6 percent.[13] Despite the size and significance of black migration to the city of São Paulo, it was dwarfed by that of immigrants from abroad. Since the mid-nineteenth century, foreigners had become a critical segment of the Paulista economy, not only as agricultural *colonos* but also as a developing urban proletariat. In 1894 foreigners in the city of São Paulo outnumbered Brazilians in domestic work, manufacturing, crafts, transportation, and commerce. In manufacturing, 79 percent of workers were immigrants.[14] Foreigners operated as important entrepreneurs in

TABLE 4. *Population of City of São Paulo, 1872–1940*

Year	Population
1872	31,385
1890	64,934
1900	239,820
1910	346,410
1920	479,033
1934	1,060,120
1936	1,167,862
1940	1,326,261

SOURCE: Brazil, Ministerio da Agricultura, Industria e Comercio, Dire-
toria Geral de Estatística, Anuario Estatístico do Brasil, Anno I (1908–
1912), vol. 1, pp. 260–261, 268–269; Florestan Fernandes, *The Negro in
Brazilian Society* (New York: Atheneum, 1971), 61; Robert M. Levine,
The Vargas Regime: The Critical Years, 1934–1938 (New York: Columbia University Press, 1970), 191.

the growth technologies of industry, transportation, and utilities. The English
were principal investors in the railroad system; the Companhia Ingleza held a
lucrative monopoly on the rail line to Santos. European and American interests capitalized the trolley system run by the São Paulo Tramway, Light and
Power Company; the Brazilian Traction, Light and Power Company, a conglomerate of power, telephone, and gas companies, was incorporated in
Canada.[15] By 1940 foreigners, most notably Italians, Syrians, and Portuguese,
controlled 44 percent of the capital earned in industrial enterprises.[16]

São Paulo was emerging as a major industrial city with extraordinary
population growth (see Table 4). The economy enjoyed a boom around 1915,
when production increased to meet wartime demand. The principal industries
in the capital were textiles, food processing, clothing, chemicals, and pharma-
ceuticals. In 1907 São Paulo accounted for 16 percent of the nation's total industrial production; by 1915 this figure had nearly doubled to 31 percent.[17]

Immigrants had begun establishing nuclear communities in the capital
in the mid-nineteenth century. Central to this process were the consolidation
of national identity and the formation of collective organizations. São Paulo's
first mutual aid society was the Portuguese Society of Beneficence, founded
in 1859. The Germans followed with their own Society of Beneficence in
1863, and a recreational and educational society known as Germania in 1868,
a strategy characteristic of immigrant adaptations during the nineteenth and
twentieth centuries.[18]

Alongside the European immigrant communities was a growing population of African descent, with new Afro-Brazilian arrivals increasing steadily

throughout the 1920s and 1930s. Florestan Fernandes estimates that between 1910 and 1934, the Afro-Brazilian population grew from 26,380 to 90,110, with the majority coming from the state's interior.[19] By 1940, although the proportion of blacks had decreased to 8 percent owing to the higher rate of white immigration, there were more blacks in the city (108,682) than anywhere else in the state.[20]

Why did they come? Part of the reason was undoubtedly lack of opportunity in the agricultural areas of the Paulista interior and neighboring states because of the availability of foreign workers. Negative stereotypes about Brazilian workers, particularly those of African descent, compounded their weakened bargaining power. One of the most ardent proponents of anti-Brazilian sentiment in developing national labor policy, Fidelis Reis of Minas Gerais, described Brazilian workers as "of a deplorable color, emaciated, weak . . . with a vague and melancholy look—such is the moral and ethnic portrait of the Brazilian, descended from these [interracial] unions, aggravated by the harshness of the environment, alcohol, malnutrition and a general lack of the most rudimentary hygiene"—an overall picture he characterized as "painful and distressing."[21]

Henrique Cunha, whose family moved to São Paulo from the interior town of Pindamonhangaba around 1904, tells of some of the conflicts that erupted when Afro-Brazilians refused to continue tolerating racism.

> My father and my uncle were from the interior. They came to São Paulo because there [in the interior] they had had problems: my father, with the priest, and my uncle, with the police. Once they went to a circus and there was a clown who made jokes; when the bear came onstage, there was a whole degrading comedy. All the scenes made fun of blacks. And the clown sang:
>
> > The white drinks champagne
> > The mulatto Port wine
> > The caboclo drinks *pinga*
> > And the black the piss of pigs
>
> Well, they tried to burn down the circus. . . .
>   . . . And in the church, that business that the black was poor and had to resign himself to poverty, shouldn't fight, and should be good to his master, was all in the priest's sermon. My father protested, so he couldn't remain in the city because the priest had the backing of the town.[22]

Perhaps the most common reason for migration echoed by the São Paulo families I interviewed was one of hope. Aristides Barbosa's was a typical

ILL. 2. Afro-Brazilians in São Paulo, c. 1880–1900. Courtesy of Photographs and Prints Division, Schomburg Center for Research in Black Culture, The New York Public Library, Astor, Lenox and Tilden Foundations.

story. His family eventually made its way from a rural plantation to the capital, "always looking for better things." Barbosa's maternal grandfather, who had been a slave, urged his children to struggle to realize their aspirations. "They always taught us to do, to seek, to progress," recalled Barbosa.[23]

Afro-Brazilians flocked to the capital with much the same motivations as the European immigrants. They were risk takers who typically relocated entire nuclear families in search of jobs for which there were no guarantees. São Paulo offered the promise of employment in the expanding industrial sector, a compelling opportunity for blacks to escape the agricultural occupations so closely linked with slavery. The people who tested their luck in São Paulo envisioned a new productive role for themselves as black Brazilians, an independent professional role that would afford them higher socioeconomic status and a more meaningful participation in Brazilian society. Fernandes suggests that those who came to São Paulo tended to possess prior skills and aptitudes that would facilitate employment in the urban economy.[24]

For all the hope they might have brought, Afro-Paulistas lacked the seed capital necessary to establish a foothold in private business. In this regard, the mechanisms of abolition sometimes imposed economic handicaps on the freedpersons who purchased letters of manumission in the 1870s and 1880s. Provincial funds had been created to remunerate slaveowners, yet they supplemented their payments from the state with contributions from the enslaved. When Antônio, a thirty-six-year-old married man, sought his freedom from Arthur Barros, he paid 200$000 *milréis*. With the government's contribution, Barros netted 1:146$750 after legal fees of 26$750. In separate cases, Theodoro, aged forty-five, paid 264$000 for his freedom, and Sophia, aged forty-two, paid 300$000.[25] Each was married, which increased the impact of the emancipation fee. Laws enacted in 1871 and 1885 freed children and the elderly, respectively, but not those of working age.[26] Ties to enslaved family members would necessarily have been an additional burden for individuals seeking to purchase their own freedom letters, resulting in delaying freedom for the entire family or physical separation. Those able to buy themselves out of slavery would then have had scant resources with which to begin their new lives.

Recollections garnered from interviews, coupled with extant published information, permit some patterns to be traced of black migration.[27] First, migration occurred in phases, beginning with the families who left the coffee regions of the interior in the 1880s and 1890s. This first wave settled in the downtown section of Bela Vista known as Bexiga, the oldest black enclave in São Paulo. Originally a farm, it was bought in 1878 by Antônio José Leite Braga, who subdivided the land into plots advertised as *baratissimo* (very cheap) the following year. It came to be populated predominantly by Italian immigrants who subsequently rented their basements to black families. Public services such as water and electricity were inadequate for the densely populated neighborhood. It was distant from the factories, most of which were situated in the newer sections of the capital. Small workshops, mostly mechanical, dotted the neighborhood, whose population included many artisans. By the 1920s immigrant women had established cottage industries as laundresses and seamstresses, and they used part of their income to employ black women as domestics. Bexiga's central location was convenient for those black men working as clerks, office boys, and janitors in government offices.[28]

As the pace of migration increased around the turn of the century and space became scarce in the old neighborhoods, newer arrivals settled in outlying areas such as Barra Funda and Campos Eliseos. Earlier urban expansion had caused demographic shifts that transformed both these communities. The inauguration of the São Paulo Railway in 1867 set off a burst of residential construction directed by Italian builders.[29] Their architectural style included the storage basements *(porões)* that would become the future homes of black immigrants. By 1910–1915, the Italian immigrants who had prospered in skilled trades began moving to those newer sections of the city that enjoyed improved services. Upscale residents of Campos Eliseos moved to fashionable areas such as Higienopolis, neighborhoods "sanitized" from the epidemics of smallpox and yellow fever that plagued Brazilian cities during the first decades of the twentieth century.[30] Those who departed were rapidly replaced by Afro-Brazilians, along with white workers, the majority of whom were leaving the interior. The original homeowners converted *porões* into apartments, and subdivided the large houses of Campos Eliseos into tenements *(cortiços)*.[31]

The development of the black enclave in Barra Funda illustrates the forces that gave shape to the new community. It was located relatively near the upper-class neighborhoods of Santa Cecilia and Higienopolis, making transportation easy for domestic workers. A trolley line installed in 1900 provided rapid access to downtown. Barra Funda's most important attraction, however, was that it was a principal terminal and storage area for the agricultural products from the interior destined for the city's markets. When trains arrived, the heavy sacks of coffee, fruit, salt, and other produce needed to be quickly unloaded and stored. Barra Funda was also a stockyard for the São Paulo and Sorocabana railroads, where the cars were lined up in the proper order before returning to the interior.

All this required heavy labor. Many black men found work as jobbers, hired on the spot as needed. They were paid by the load or job, and a portion of their fee was customarily in produce. Most often they received bananas, which they then resold in front of the station in an area that became known as the Largo da Banana. A common practice was to increase the share of fruit by tossing one underneath the freight car for every four that were unloaded. The boys from the neighborhood would pick them up and add them to the official share for later sale in the market.[32]

⟩ In the phase of rapid growth after World War I, blacks poured into São Paulo from the Paraíba Valley and began to arrive from the northeast as well. These people settled in the expanding eastern section of the city, creating black enclaves such as that in Penha. A critical factor in facilitating Afro-Brazilian migration to São Paulo from an ever-widening radius was the railway system, which employed many black men. As employees, they traveled frequently around the countryside, creating an important network of communication among blacks in the greater São Paulo area and into the surrounding states, particularly Minas Gerais and Rio de Janeiro. Albertino Alves da Silva was an employee of the Central do Brasil railroad who was originally from Rio de Janeiro. After his first two wives died, he asked for a transfer and moved to Minas Gerais. His new job on the engine crew took him on runs through the city of Santos Dumont, where he met and married his third wife. When the family grew to nine children, Albertino decided to try his luck in São Paulo. In 1932 they settled in Vila Matilde, a predominantly Spanish and Italian neighborhood on the eastern side of the city.[33]

The second characteristic of Afro-Brazilian migration was that families did not always travel together. It was common for one or two family members to settle in the city before subsequently sending for other relatives. In the case of the Barbosa family, the oldest brother was the first to leave for São Paulo in 1933, followed by Aristides in 1934 and each sibling in turn until their parents finally arrived in 1940. They settled in Bela Vista.[34] Once families were settled, and with the communication provided by the railroads, it became relatively easy for people to leave the interior to stay with friends in the city until they could find places of their own. A close relationship with the interior became a hallmark of São Paulo's black neighborhoods and their clubs. It was generally more desirable to move the family together if at all possible, even though many rural families were quite large. The Lucrecios were a black family from Campinas with twelve children, headed by a father who worked as a carpenter and a mother who was a cook and laundress. When yellow fever and influenza broke out, they decided to take the children to São Paulo, moving to the neighborhood of Campos Eliseos in 1922. The grandparents also came along and worked to support the family, which eventually settled in Bela Vista.[35]

Third, São Paulo's Afro-Brazilian community settled in enclaves around the city. This was a matter of discrimination and segregation as well as one of convenience and practicality. Although there are no population statistics categorized by race for São Paulo neighborhoods during this period, a study of

TABLE 5. *Distribution of Live Afro-Brazilian Births by District,*
City of São Paulo, 1925 and 1929

District	1925		1929	
	(#)	(%)	(#)	(%)
Sé	8	0.8	7	0.6
Liberdade	91	9.2	79	7.0
Consolação	27	2.7	36	3.1
Bela Vista	406	41.4	583	51.6
Santa Efigenia	47	4.8	9	0.7
Bom Retiro	55	5.6	56	4.9
Santa Cecilia	81	8.2	94	8.3
Braz	29	2.9	52	4.6
Mooca	42	4.2	44	3.9
Belemzinho	66	6.7	40	3.5
Vila Mariana	49	5.0	26	2.3
Cambucy	40	4.0	28	2.4
Perdizes	38	3.8	74	6.5

SOURCE: Directoria do Serviço Sanitario do Estado de São Paulo, Secção de Estatística Demographo-Sanitaria, *Boletim Mensal de Estatística Demographo-Sanitaria de São Paulo,* anno VIII (January–December 1925), nos. 1–12; anno XII (January–December 1929), nos. 1–12.

NOTE: Afro-Brazilian includes *pardo* and *prêto* categories.

registered births between 1925 and 1929 (see Table 5) indicates strong residential patterns. The vast majority of Afro-Brazilian births were registered in Bela Vista, the district in which Bexiga was located. A 1934 school census also indicated Bela Vista as the neighborhood with the highest concentration of blacks.[36] Afro-Brazilians were disproportionately represented in the districts of Santa Cecilia and Liberdade as well.

Samuel Lowrie suggests that since blacks in service occupations required easy access to the whites for whom they worked, a pattern of black residential concentration emerged that combined proximity to whites and the availability of low-cost housing.[37] However, many, if not most, Afro-Brazilians living near whites (as opposed to those living with whites) probably did so not because they worked for them in service capacities but because numerous immigrant families had converted basements and backyards into rental properties. Another factor influencing residential concentration was proximity to friends and family. The Oliveira Galdinos came from the Paraíba Valley in the 1920s with a couple with whom they had grown up. Their daughter, one of five children, recalled how friends from their hometown of Engenheiros Passos sought and found help with her family.

We always lived in two bedrooms with a kitchen. We divided the space, separating the women on one side and the men on the other. . . People came with a characteristic respect, friendship, and desire to succeed. So they accepted the situation and stayed. They looked for work. For many, my father himself got them work with him until there was a room nearby. Then they'd stay in that room, but only if it was close so the women wouldn't be too far from each other, so that one could let the other know what was going on, what to do when you had a small baby: if it got sick, what [the illness] was like, what medicines to get at the pharmacy.[38]

Small enclaves of blacks, many of them linked by hometown affiliations, thus sprouted up around the city.

Conditions were not easy for the new arrivals, although they were mitigated by a spirit of mutual aid. Children, lovers, in-laws, distant relatives, and friends down on their luck or newly arrived to the city all found shelter under a single roof. So many people crowded into the *porões* and *cortiços* that the larger of these became miniature communities in which mutual assistance was indispensable. The journalist Francisco Branco, a longtime resident of Barra Funda, described the rapid process of settlement in the neighborhood, where "there was established an enormous black community [*colônia*], a vast *quilombo* installed in the basements. These, in turn, were linked and interlinked, converted into intricate subterranean labyrinths to which, impelled by economic pressure and seeking the support of racial fraternity [*fraternidade de côr*], flocked the blacks."[39] The Cunha family moved to São Paulo from the Paraíba Valley around the turn of the century. They opened their small house to those who needed help, "be they relatives, from the same city, compadre or comadre." When an epidemic hit São Paulo the house became a hospital, with the Cunhas laying pallets on the floor for ill friends and family.[40]

Educational opportunities were difficult in São Paulo. Economic circumstances forced many black children to work. Those who were able to study had to provide their own supplies and clothes. The 1934 school census revealed that of nearly 85,000 public school students, only 7 percent were black. Although this may appear proportional, the 1940 census revealed that only 3 percent of blacks and 2 percent of mulattoes had completed primary education, compared with 92 percent of whites.[41]

Lack of education exacerbated the difficulties encountered by Afro-Brazilians seeking work. São Paulo's principal industry, textiles, was characterized by its domination by foreign workers, many of whom were women and the Brazilian-born children of immigrants. Afro-Brazilians found it difficult to penetrate the growth industries, finding work (when they could) predominantly in domestic and other types of service positions or occasional work. George Reid Andrews notes the importance of the labor activism of the late 1910s that brought Afro-Brazilians into the work force as strikebreakers. They proved diligent and capable, thus paving the way for increased representation after the 1940s.[42]

The New Negro: *Afro-Brazilian Collectives and Changing Consciousness*

Afro-Brazilians in São Paulo created a variety of collectives after abolition that reflected new identities and needs as they adjusted to the changing pace of urban life. The most vocal of these were the social clubs, political advocacy groups, and newspaper cooperatives, but they were but one part of a broader spectrum of collective activities. The oldest form of Afro-Brazilian organization in São Paulo was the lay Catholic brotherhood, a social institution in existence since colonial times. Many sought to help enslaved members purchase their letters of freedom, although their typically meager resources were often insufficient. In the nineteenth and twentieth centuries, these religious associations in São Paulo assisted their members with such services as loans and burial expenses.[43] Some sodalities, such as the brotherhood at the Igreja da Bôa Morte, were restricted to mulattoes. Among the black brotherhoods were those of Santa Efigenia, São Bento, São Francisco, and São Benedito. The local branch of the Rosário brotherhood was founded in 1711.[44] Black churches were institutions central to the lives of the black slaves prior to the city's expansion. Some occupied prime downtown locations. The area around the Rosário church was appropriated by the city council in 1861 to widen the street and build a square. The building itself was appropriated in 1903 and the Largo do Rosário was renamed Praça Antônio Prado in honor of the mayor in 1905.[45] The city council gave the brotherhood a site on the Largo de Paissandú, where the new church presently stands. [46]

Although the brotherhoods continued into the post-abolition era, new forms of collectives and activities began reshaping the contours of Afro-Brazilian community life in the capital. An early cultural meeting point for Afro-Brazilians was the hometown picnic, an essential means for the large numbers of black migrants to São Paulo to reinforce their ties to family and friends. Trains linked the capital to virtually the entire interior, and since many blacks were employed by railroads in some capacity, excursions to hometowns were relatively easy to organize. The festivals of the towns' patron saints were invariably occasions for excursions, by no means limited to native sons and daughters. At the annual festival of Pirapora, held between August 3 and 7, delegations from all over the state sought to outdo one another every year. Blacks attending the festival stayed in an abandoned religious retreat. One of the two buildings had two floors, and families could stay in individual rooms with some degree of privacy. The other was in ruins, a giant open space where the majority of visitors lodged during the event.

As the sambas rolled on, each neighborhood or town had a favorite singer who would lead the improvisational lyrics in musical challenges in which one would sing a verse and another would respond, a style still popular in rural Brazil. In such a setting, the neighborhood became the basis for group identity, facilitating activities among the same circle of friends back in the city.[47] Neighborhood-based social groups organized around events such as excursions, picnics, dances, and Carnival were a new form of black collective in post-abolition São Paulo.

The veterans of the festivals in the interior re-created similar activities in the capital, making samba a cultural manifestation that developed along many lines. The samba world ranged from the highly structured Carnival associations to circles of friends who frequented nightclubs and house parties. Most of the important figures in Paulistano samba attended the Pirapora festivities during their youth. Among them were Dionisio Barbosa, a founder of the Barra Funda Carnival Group (later renamed Camisa Verde e Branco), Donata Ramos of Campos Eliseos, and Madrinha Eunice of Vai Vai, who subsequently co-founded Lavapés.[48]

Much of the samba world consisted of unstructured groups of acquaintances who socialized regularly at house parties and spontaneous gatherings. Because samba parties were so frequently based in domestic spaces, women became dominant figures. One of these was "Tia [Aunt] Olimpia," known for her house parties on the Rua Anhaguera in Barra Funda. In Lavapés, Eunice and Chico Pinga gave parties in the 1930s, and founded a samba school twenty years later.[49] This was a private world, Iêda Britto notes. "There is little information about these black spaces, but it is known that they were closed spaces within the black world itself and even more so to outsiders."[50] The private samba world was ongoing, unlike the occasional events such as empressario Zé Soldado's annual 13th of May party in the suburban neighborhood of Jabaquara.[51] In a tradition akin to that of the Bahian "aunts" in Rio de Janeiro, samba house parties gave rise to a distinct culture out of which developed the modern samba schools, the *escolas de samba*.[52]

Another social circle in which samba played a major role revolved around soccer. Neighborhood soccer clubs were more fluid in their membership, open as they were to players of all backgrounds. After games, players and their families typically gathered for informal parties. Alberto Alves da

Silva, whose family moved to the eastern end of São Paulo from Minas Gerais, became active in this community, earning himself the nickname "Nenê do Pandeiro."[53] He made his first *pandeiro* out of a tin of guava jelly and beer bottle caps, but his father, who worked on the railroads, found one forgotten by a passenger. His father was one of many railroad workers who belonged to local soccer clubs that played on Sundays.

> We had one in Vila Matilde. There were others in Bras, they had the "Fourth Stop" and "Fifth Stop," which today is called Caron. In Penha they had Guayaúna, Vila Matilde had Alturaví. . . . All these neighborhoods had ball clubs. So on Sundays, folks would have those *domingueiras* [Sunday get-togethers] in one of the neighborhoods. Folks would come from the others, bring pandeiros to make it fun, the good old days. Ay! Black folks came, black folks had fun.[54]

Soccer club circles were not exclusively black, as the other Afro-Brazilian collectives tended to be, and were probably the forum for the transformation of samba into the city's popular culture. Nenê's first performance was at a samba party alongside a white musician known as Russo do Pandeiro, and other whites were important influences in his adolescence. During his interview, Nenê sang sambas popular at the parties of the 1930s, many of which originated in, or were influenced by, Afro-Cuban and Puerto Rican music. The soccer club circles contributed to the development of multiethnic samba, whose various musical and dance styles eventually developed into modern Paulista samba. Vai Vai, the first Carnival group in Bexiga, originated from a soccer club of the same name.[55]

Organized samba became a fixture of black Paulistano culture with the emergence of *cordões carnavalescos,* precursors of modern *escolas de samba.* The first of these was the Barra Funda Carnival Group, whose debut was in 1914. The *cordões* enjoyed immense popularity and quickly sprang up wherever blacks were concentrated. An unstructured group from the Alameda Glette known as the Bloco dos Boêmios reorganized itself as the Campos Eliseos Carnival Group in 1917.[56]

Samba *cordões* provided the impetus for wider-ranging social clubs *(sociedades)* formalized through governing statutes and executive boards. It was their responsibility to sponsor activities throughout the year to raise money for Carnival expenses.[57] Some of these developed a political orientation, expressed in newsletters and auxiliary activities. The political and recreational dimensions coexisted for a time but eventually diverged along distinct paths in the 1920s with the creation of the explicitly political newspapers *Progresso* and *Clarim da Alvorada* and the Palmares advocacy organization.

By the 1920s samba consisted of the organized Carnival clubs and an unstructured world of parties and spontaneous gatherings. The clubs took on unique characteristics. Most important, they were family oriented, with entire families attending as a unit. If, for some reason, one member chose to leave a group, other relatives often left as well.[58] The importance of family was also evident in the leadership structure, passed along from one generation to the next within a single family. Dona Sinhá of Camisa Verde e Branco in Barra Funda was the daughter of the famous Felão de Pirapora. She subsequently brought her son Tobias into the leadership, who restructured the group into its modern incarnation as a samba school.[59]

There were less formal cultural manifestations taking shape in the poorer black communities, where bars *(botequins)* became a meeting point for music, billiards, dancing, and drinking. The *botequins* also served as a melting pot in which blacks from diverse regions of Brazil developed a distinct Afro-Paulistano musical and social culture, in the same way that the Praça Onze had given rise to samba in Rio. One such area was the Alameda Glette in Barra Funda, near the trolley terminal. It was the site of a crowded *cortiço*, several soccer fields, and numerous bars. Partying and alcohol became so associated with the area that *negro da Glette* became a common euphemism to refer with disdain to lowbrow Afro-Brazilian culture.[60] Black bars were targeted by the police, who made more arrests for drunkenness, disorderliness, and vagrancy than any other crimes. Between 1914 and 1916 Afro-Brazilians made up 28.5 percent of the prison population, despite the fact that they were only 10 percent of the general population. In 1923 *pardos* and *prêtos* were 33.5 percent of all detainees.[61]

A founder of one of Barra Funda's social clubs recalled the dynamic of the Glette *botequins:*

> [T]he Corote was a *botequim* on the Rua Cruzeiro, but we never entered from the street because if we entered from the street, the police were always around to get the blacks that had no jobs. We left from the Patio da Banana and entered from those bushes, and 1–2–3, we were there at the Corote to drink *pinga* [cachaça] in peace. . . . There were lots of black girls, we flirted with the black girls there. . . . In the *botequins* there was lots of silliness, drunken antics, but there was a good side. Folks [*Negro*] fought with each other, then when it was over they'd go drink *pinga* and make peace.[62]

Part of the stigma of the *botequins* derived from their location in the crowded tenements known as *cortiços*. The negative image of the *cortiços* and the "negros da Glette" was one the aspiring black working class strove to avoid. The *cortiços* represented squalor, whereas recently developed districts idealized clean living; city planners expressed this thought literally with the creation of the district named Higienopolis. In 1929 the black newspaper *Progresso* compared São Paulo's *cortiços* with the slums known as *favelas* in Rio de Janeiro: "barbarous, once even savage, nuclei of a life that contrasts in stark anachronism with the progress of the Paulista capital." The newspaper congratulated the city for having destroyed a particularly infamous *cortiço* known simply as Tressentos (Three Hundred) for the widening of the São João Avenue. It denounced the *cortiços* as an impediment to progress:

> It is possible that the *cortiços* have the picturesque quality of things that survive as relics of remote eras, but the attraction they might hold for the occasional antiquarian cannot compensate for the moral and material disadvantages caused by the persistence of these ugly fragments of antiquity in the Paulistana community. As regards sanitation, the *cortiços* are wellsprings of epidemic disease and it is certain that they played a role in the recent incursions of the [influenza] pandemic that so devastated São Paulo.[63]

The boisterousness of the *botequins*, though frequented by many whites, became a symbol of black marginality and evoked negative images of promiscuity, alcoholism, and crime incompatible with the image São Paulo cultivated of itself as a genteel and progressive city. It was a question of social values and lifestyles that took on class dimensions between an aspiring black middle class and a marginalized underclass. The differences were not great in terms of family income, but their social views led to radically different manifestations of Afro-Brazilian collectives in the social and cultural life of the city. Ironically, many of the clubs that became the backbone of the Afro-Paulista aspiring middle class were born in the *botequins*. Campos Eliseos, which later became a formal social club, began in the botequins on the Alameda Glette around 1915.[64] Formal black social clubs were also a response to the exclusion of Afro-Brazilians from white clubs. Those seeking a more "respectable" form of socializing discovered that Italian clubs and dances in mixed neighborhoods such as Bela Vista excluded blacks.[65] The only way for Afro-Brazilians to attend such functions was to sponsor their own. In the early years of the century, a number of clubs appeared in São Paulo's black neighborhoods. The first of these, Luvas Pretas (Black Gloves), was founded in 1904.[66] The main activity of the clubs *(gremios recreativos)* was to sponsor social functions, and they enjoyed enormous popularity. In order to circulate information to club members, the organizers published small newspapers.[67] Juxtaposed as they were to "white" groups and events, these early social clubs were instrumental in developing "black" ethnic identity among Afro-Paulistas. It is important to note that they were also juxtaposed to the lowbrow image of the social circles associated with the *cortiços* and the *botequins*.

After the appearance of the Luvas Pretas in 1904, black social clubs and newspapers gained widespread popularity. Well over twenty such clubs existed at any given time and some, such as Centro Recreativo Kosmos, Brinco de Princeza, 28 de Setembro, Elite Flor da Liberdade, and Centro Recreativo Smart, were maintained over several years. Kosmos, which survived into the late 1920s, had been founded as early as November 1908.[68] The clubs were fairly complex organizations; the directorate usually included a president, vice president, and two each of secretaries, treasurers, *procuradores* (official representatives, or proxies), *fiscais* (accountants), and a *mestre-sala* (host of the house, emcee at events). This type of organization is common in modern *escolas de samba*, and probably derives from the organizational structure of the Catholic brotherhoods.

The social clubs sponsored picnics, athletic events, dance contests, beauty pageants, and other entertainment. Some, like Kosmos, were able to develop educational components as well, but this was unusual. Occasionally large clubs would have a women's auxiliary, which maintained its own directorate. There were women's clubs, like G.R. (Gremio Recreativo) Flor da Mocidade ("Flower of Youth"), G.R. Princeza do Norte ("Northern Princess"), G.R. Rainha Paulista ("Paulista Queen"), G.R. 8 de Abril ("Eighth of April"), and the Grupo das Que Não Ligam Importancia ("The Group of Those Who Don't Care"), that were led by female directorates.[69] It appears that each club had a nucleus of highly loyal members, and marriages among members were not uncommon. Club affiliations identified people, and improper behavior reflected badly on their organizations. *A Liberdade,* a bi-weekly newspaper founded in 1919, carried neighborhood gossip using references to clubs as identifiers. "Madame Idalina of Kosmos," for example, was sent an anonymous message from someone unhappy with her choice of dance partners.[70] Mainstream newspapers regularly carried announcements from white groups. The black association newspapers such as *Menelick, Kosmos, Liberdade,* and *Bandeirante* emerged as parallel vehicles within the Afro-Paulistano community for circulating their own information, gossip, and social commentary.

The early Afro-Brazilian social press also served as a forum for the identification and discussion of racial issues. Using the black population of the United States as a model, a front-page editorial in *O Alfinete* called for Afro-Brazilians to recognize that they had the responsibility for improving their own situation.[71] The *Bandeirante* declared itself "A Combative Organ for the General Revitalization of the Class of Men of Color." It was one of several outlets complaining about police harassment and general racial discrimination. In one case, *Bandeirante* reported on a funeral procession that had been detained by the police. The coffin was being carried through the streets because the family could not afford a car. "They were jailed simply because the

ILL. 3. Early Afro-Brazilian newspapers in São Paulo. Clockwise, from top left:
O Menelick, Elite, A Liberdade, and *O Alfinete.*

issue involved only poor people of color." Four people who protested were also arrested. *Bandeirante* issued a terse warning. "These senseless jailings continue, and the innocent people will not forever be able to maintain the necessary calm in the face of the vexation to which they are subjected."[72] This was still a problem in the 1930s. The first issue of *A Voz da Raça* complained of an unprovoked attempt by the police to arrest some Frente Negra youths leaving a theater rehearsal.[73]

The black press often presented such issues as a point of departure for complex discussions about Afro-Brazilian political strategies. Accompanying *Bandeirante*'s story on the funeral was this editorial:

> Given the dispersion in which people of color are living, doing nothing to protect one another in the cosmopolitan environment, who have no solidarity, who do not join in a cause that would assure them relative tranquility in the face of any of life's eventualities, that would give them the means to confront anything that conspires to undermine their legitimate rights as free citizens, as Brazilian citizens, incidents such as that which Snr. Gastão [Silva] has reported are very natural.
>
> When the Bandeirantes club was founded, their extensive program was read at the inaugural festivities. It was this program that served as the platform for the appearance of this journal; among the many ideas contained therein and for whose fulfillment we asked for everyone's cooperation, whether or not they were members of Bandeirante, was the creation of a special fund to aid the sick and needy and those who were unjustly imprisoned.
>
> Very well. No one listened or even read our words of concern. Now Snr. Gastão comes to alert us to the bitter fact that four blacks were jailed without just cause, merely because they were returning from the cemetery where they had left the cold corpse of a brother who had died penniless!
>
> And we ask ourselves, why did that poor soul die destitute? Let those who did not heed us answer the question. And those well-intentioned blacks, have they been set free? Are they yet back in the bosom of their worried families?
>
> We do not know. Everything is unknown. Could it be that those poor souls, those unfortunate unprotected souls, have been sent away, working themselves to death in the gloomy Northeastern backlands?
>
> Ah! This bitter doubt that we now entertain would have had no reason to exist if our voice had been heeded. There would be a fund for a lawyer to aid those unfortunate prisoners.
>
> There would be a collective of all people of color in defense of

the rights of the sacrificed brothers. But our cry goes unheeded in an immense desert!

No one listened and no one will listen. If it had to do with collecting for dances every day, then there would be no lack of acclaim and support. But since it deals with a fund for defense and legal aid, no one steps forward. Why not embrace the Bandeirante's program?

What sadness! Always disunited! Always unprotected! Always persecuted and without a generous arm to defend us!

And, if we don't lift our heads and see it, in short order we will fall precipitously into the abyss of our criminality, and then, our final ruin!

All this is bitter, it is painful. But what can we do when it seems to us that it is the force of an adverse Destiny that impels us on this fatal march of disunity![74]

The editorial, written in 1919, touched upon three of the four themes that characterized black activism in post-abolition São Paulo. First was the need for unity. The young activists discovered that a program based on a concept as amorphous as unity was difficult to sell to a populace of Afro-Brazilians for many of whom politics and philosophy were too far removed from the everyday realities of work, family, relationships, parties, and basic survival. Nonetheless, such newspapers as *Clarim da Alvorada* consistently stressed this point. In the words of editor José Correia Leite, "We can do nothing unless we unite. This is the reason we live in endless retrocession, without the means to organize a financial base [*patrimônio*] to help ourselves."[75] Despite class, color, regional, and other differences, São Paulo's black activist leadership felt that unification was not only possible, but the indispensable prerequisite for the progress of all blacks. They were already articulating a color-based group identity, *homens de côr*, one that did not distinguish mulattoes from blacks. The second theme was that the social clubs and dances were a waste of valuable energy and resources that could be better spent in securing an economic base, social support mechanisms, and class advocacy. Third, the editorial depicted the predicament of visionary black leaders in convincing the rest of the community to go along with their programs. The message appears in the newsletter of a social club because, despite their criticisms, leaders needed the clubs as a vehicle for reaching the black constituency. A fourth theme, Afro-Brazilian patriotism, was to become more pronounced in the 1920s with the emergence of a new generation of urban activists.

This overview of black organizational life prior to 1940 highlights the fact that Afro-Brazilians in São Paulo pursued several strategies as they determined the roles they wished to occupy as free citizens. There existed a viable alternative cultural community built around music that served more than recreational purposes. It was a retreat from the unpleasant aspects of mainstream life into a black world in which music served a spiritually regenerative function. Samba stemmed directly from African slave cultural gatherings, the latter a ritual for the restoration of psychological and spiritual balance. Early descriptions of samba in Pirapora contained markedly African elements—the formation of musicians and dancers into a circle, the restriction of drumming to men, the call-and-response style of song, and the orientation of the dancer to the drums rather than to a partner.[76] As samba moved into the capital, it is likely that its essential role was very similar given the hostility of the environments in which Afro-Brazilians circulated. Black samba also reflected philosophical differences with the larger society. The unquestioned dynastic leadership of organized clubs reflected notions of governance moving in direct contrast to the increasingly democratic clamorings in mainstream Brazilian politics. In addition, women played significant roles as leaders and organizers whereas white Brazilian women had yet to overcome the weight of traditional stereotypes.

It is important that the history of the black samba community be placed alongside that of the activists as part of the larger history of Afro-Paulistas in the post-abolition period, because theirs was yet another adaptive strategy to the conditions of urban life. Until recently, many researchers have portrayed the organized political activism of the 1920s and 1930s as a "movement" expressing the aspirations of *the* black community.[77] That image is now subject to reassessment in light of the fact that the known number of participants was relatively small given the total number of blacks in the capital. Were the activists a black elite distinct from the majority of Afro-Paulistanos? To answer this, it will be important to conduct further research on the less visible strategies of those who retreated into universes of their own creation as yet another expression of self-determination in the post-abolition era.

Still another group of Afro-Paulistanos, whose story is not told here, pursued individual strategies, capitalizing on valued assets such as fair skin.[78] Although it is not possible to fully explore each of these adaptations, this chapter has sought to broaden the scope of analysis in the consideration of post-abolition responses in the city of São Paulo. For the collectives, new forms of organization only became possible after the consolidation of group identities around both race and geographic origins. The most vocal of these, as we shall see, were the political advocacy organizations of the 1920s and 1930s.

CHAPTER 4

The Politics of Race in São Paulo

[T]he day will come when it will be loudly proclaimed to the whole universe that [our children] are Brazilians as worthy as any other.
—*O Elite* (São Paulo), editorial, January 20, 1924

$\mathcal{T}$he question of why collective self-determination in São Paulo based itself on race and why it took the unprecedented form of political advocacy that emerged in the 1920s and 1930s is a complex one. Ethnicity centered on "blackness" during the first decades of black migration to São Paulo for several reasons, including the contextual factors considered in the preceding chapter. Whites, both Brazilian and immigrant, discriminated against Afro-Brazilians on the basis of color, as reflected in such areas as employment, housing, admission to social events, and government policies. This behavior strengthened the viability of race as a social construct. Equally integral to Afro-Brazilian collective identity was Brazilian nationality, an important basis of ethnicity in a city in which immigrant communities played a prominent role. National identity heightened awareness of race difference and discrimination by isolating color as the principal factor of difference. The structural composition of the Afro-Brazilian community in São Paulo further reinforced racial identity. The social groups and institutions that formed in response to a sense of commonality and isolation from other segments of Paulista society laid the foundation for a race-identified community. Residential concentration complemented the creation of a "black world" in the psychological sense. The degree of black community development cannot be exaggerated, of course. Afro-Brazilian institutions were still changing and growing in response to the pace of new arrivals. Another factor working against the creation of an alternative or parallel society was that São Paulo had no exclusively black neighborhoods. Even though physical spaces were clearly delineated between the residences and social ambits of whites and blacks, the fluidity of those barriers and the proximity of people of different ethnic backgrounds precluded the all-inclusive "black worlds" found in segregated environments.

This combination of factors helped steer some members of São Paulo's Afro-Brazilian community toward the goal of integration. The psychosocial black world created by Afro-Paulista collectives was not reinforced by sustaining institutions. Without a well-developed infrastructure of institutions in such fields as transportation, commerce, banking, medicine, law, and social services that would have given blacks a broader measure of autonomy from white institutions, there was no alternative or parallel economy in which blacks could establish themselves. In the United States, such an economy developed in the early twentieth century because forced segregation provided opportunities for black entrepreneurship in parallel institutions. In Brazil, the mainstream economy was the only viable and legitimate option for upward mobility. This was obviously the goal of a large number of Afro-Brazilians who had made the journey to the capital much as the European immigrants had done. In terms of individual goals, they were aspirants desiring to share in the benefits and promise of the modern economic revolution.

Unfortunately for the newcomers, social change did not go hand in hand with economic progress; the rules of access to money and power under the First Republic were the same as those under the Empire. Color, lineage, wealth, and connections continued to act as socioeconomic gatekeepers, and the late nineteenth-century fixation with European standards and eugenics reinforced the significance of color. In São Paulo specifically, blacks watched white immigrants use bonds of nationality as they helped compatriots enter the industrial labor force. Even though most factory jobs offered low wages and unsavory working conditions, they nonetheless represented a stable and respectable income. While there were some factors Afro-Brazilians felt they could control, such as adherence to certain cultural standards, there was nothing they could do about their color or nationality. Both as a response to insurmountable barriers of discrimination and as an expression of their desire to integrate into the most lucrative socioeconomic system available to them, the rise of alternative integrationism was a logical conclusion. This chapter examines the formulation of collective identity and social strategy as expressed by the newspapers and advocacy organizations that emerged in the 1920s and 1930s.

Shaping Ideology: The Black Press of São Paulo

The black press of the post-abolition era documents a developing consciousness in São Paulo as Afro-Brazilians came to grips with the multiple aspects of self-determination. These can be reduced to three fundamental questions: Who are we? Who do we want to be? How do we get there? The newspapers addressed these questions in an open ideological dialogue with opinions that became more nuanced and complex with the passage of time and with the growth of the black intellectual community. Despite inevitable philosophical differences, certain positions resonated and consensus was reached often enough that the black newspapers published between 1915 and 1937 constitute a body of literature that outlines a new identity and specific goals of a vocal segment of the Afro-Brazilian community. The serious divergences centered on the strategies for achieving those objectives.

Scholars of the black press have always recognized that it represented, in the words of Michael Mitchell, an "opinion elite."[1] Black newspapers were not commercial endeavors run by professional publishers and journalists. They were partnerships and collectives of young working men (joined, in rare instances, by young women) who were part of the Afro-Brazilian bourgeoisie.[2] These were people whose clubs distinguished them as the "Elite," the "Smart" set, and "Princesses."[3] They followed the society pages, took care to dress in the height of fashion, and demonstrated little sympathy for blacks living in squalor and poverty. Supporting the newspapers were dozens, perhaps scores, of clubs with a substantial membership organized into governing boards, committees, musical bands, theater groups, and much more. As such, the press is a vital window onto the thoughts of a large and significant segment of São Paulo's black population. Roger Bastide felt that the press represented an even broader cross-section of black Paulistanos because, for all its posturing, the black elite was not so far removed from its humble origins.[4] Mitchell's characterization is nonetheless accurate; the writers operated as an ideological vanguard within the Afro-Brazilian society world. As were the private samba circles, they too were a faction unique in some ways while yet sharing basic characterisics and concerns of the rest of the community.

Afro-Brazilian journals first appeared in the city of São Paulo around World War I, although Bastide reports that a black newspaper called *O Bandeirante* published its first edition in the nearby city of Campinas in 1910.[5] The capital's first known black paper was *O Menelick*, published in 1915 and named for the "great king of the black race, Menelick II, who died in 1913."[6] Many papers followed, generally affiliated with social clubs and frequently short-lived (see Table 6).

The black press prior to 1938 may be divided into three phases. During the first, 1915 to 1924, the journals contributed to consolidating popular notions of Afro-Paulista identity. They positioned blacks as patriotic and loyal Brazilian citizens by stressing their historical contributions to national development. Combating stereotypes of black inferiority, they emphasized their

TABLE 6. *Afro-Brazilian Newspapers of São Paulo, 1910–1935*

Title	City	First publication date
O Bandeirante	Campinas	1910
O Menelick	São Paulo	1915
Princeza do Oeste	São Paulo	1915
A Rua	São Paulo	1916
O Xauter	São Paulo	1916
O Alfinete	São Paulo	1918
A União	Campinas	1918
O Bandeirante	São Paulo	1918
A Liberdade	São Paulo	1919
A Protectora	Campinas	1919
A Sentinella	São Paulo	1920
O Kosmos	São Paulo	1922
O Getulino	Campinas	1923
O Clarim da Alvorada	São Paulo	1924
Elite	São Paulo	1924
Auriverde	São Paulo	1928
O Patrocinio	Piracicaba	1928
Progresso	São Paulo	1928
A Chibata	São Paulo	1932
Brazil Novo	São Paulo	1933
Evolução	São Paulo	1933
A Voz da Raça	São Paulo	1933
Cultura/O Clarim	São Paulo	1934/1935
Tribuna Negra	São Paulo	1935
O Estímulo	São Carlos	1935

SOURCES: Miriam Nicolau Ferrara, *A Imprensa Negra Paulista, 1915–1963* (São Paulo: FFLCH-USP, 1986), 278; Michael Mitchell, ed., *The Black Press of Brazil, 1916–1969* (Firestone Library; Princeton: Princeton University, n.d., microfilm); Roger Bastide, "A Imprensa Negra do Estado de São Paulo," Faculdade de Filosofia, Ciencias e Letras, *Boletim CSSI, Sociologia,* no. 2, *Estudos Afro-Brasileiros,* 2a serie (1951), 50–53.

equality by demonstrating mastery of mainstream culture and standards. Related to these concepts was an emphasis on blacks as Brazilians vis-à-vis European immigrants and meriting parity, if not preference, in opportunities and prerogatives. In the second phase, 1924–1930, organizers implemented the early ideologies in shaping political activist efforts. Out of the experience with civil rights activism grew an ideologically oriented press. Blacks experimented with modes of advocacy that, in turn, refined political ideology. This led to the third phase, 1931–1937, which coincided with the flourishing of the Frente Negra Brasileira. Its popularity over other modes of activism in São Paulo at the time lent credence to the organization's claim of representing the predominant political sentiments of the era. During this time it was the journal of the Frente Negra, *A Voz da Raça*, that emerged as black São Paulo's preeminent publication.

Sponsored as most were by social clubs, one of the primary functions of the early Afro-Paulista newspapers was to publicize the activities of those clubs and their members. This included regular announcements of governing board elections, upcoming meetings and events, and reminders about annual Catholic feast days, such as the Pirapora festival, that had become part of the popular Afro-Paulista social calendar.[7] Oratory was an integral element of club parties, particularly anniversary commemorations, and papers listed the honored speakers culled from the elites of black society. An afternoon waltz given by the "genteel ladies" of the Princeza d'Oeste club featured speeches by delegations from the capital and from Jundiaí.[8] When the São Geraldo soccer club opened its 1920 anniversary party with a series of toasts and the presentation of a silver trophy, *A Liberdade* was there to record all the proceedings.[9] Lapses in decorum elicited outspoken criticism. When a jealous fight erupted at a "beautifully chic" dance given by Brinco de Princeza, *A Liberdade* censured the directorate for having only suspended, rather than expelled, the guilty parties.[10] Journals commended those clubs that maintained order and "good taste." *O Elite* praised the decorations, dress, and orderly proceedings of the 6 de Maio recreational club, and the reporter from *A Liberdade,* having visited an auction given by the Paulistano club, remarked, "I have not seen such order and respect in quite some time as I saw that Sunday."[11] When the Princeza do Norte club took steps toward more respectable behavior, *O Elite* expressed the hope that it would continue, "because our people need the press to defend their interests rather than to criticize them."[12] The press helped solidify certain standards of behavior to which it strictly held the black social elite as an example for the rest of the Afro-Paulista community.

Complementing the club news were society columns featuring announcements peppered with a good deal of gossip. Much of it was playful teasing, such as *A Liberdade*'s comments about Maria da Conceição's being seen in the cemetery with her boyfriend, or Maria Guedes' disappearance from social circles without having finished the installment payments on her new shoes.[13] As was the case with the coverage of organized events, these also served the purpose of instruction in proper behavior. Some papers referred to this feature as *crítica* (literally, criticism), in which editors instructed, chided, and corrected Afro-Paulistas to bring them to an idealized standard of proper behavior. *A Rua* devoted considerable space to its *secção crítica,* organized by neighborhood. Assessing the doings in Belemzinho in 1916, its editors saw fit to chasten:

—Olguinha and her friend on 21 April Street for climbing a lightpost
late at night in front of her house. Goodness! What a bad habit!

—A certain lanky fellow who, in the same neighborhood, was all over
a young lady in her doorway late at night. Goodness! Does the gentleman think himself a locust?

—A certain *gaúcho* [native of Rio Grande do Sul] who waits for the
lights to go out in the cinema to kiss his girl. Is that how she likes
it? *A Rua* was in the next row and we saw everything.[14]

The papers did not limit themselves to questions of morality. *A Liberdade* de-
plored the use of tennis shoes by black youth, popularized during the 1919
Carnival. The author begged his audience not to be offended; "[m]y only in-
tention is to try and show my compatriots that, in matters of fashion, many are
misguided." He was concerned that "those who dress themselves without
knowing whether their attire is appropriate for the avenue or for the beach"
ran the risk of ridicule. He also pointed out that the choice of footwear did not
stem from financial constraints, "because our young men and women of color
in São Paulo never worry about sacrifices in order to dress in the height of
fashion, and we have seen many young men and women of color . . . in attire
that does honor to our Capital and our people."[15]

This criticism served multiple functions. As a type of society column, it
elevated certain individuals to the status of public figures meriting appraisal in
the press. It also served as a primer on etiquette. These were, however, corol-
laries to a far more fundamental goal recognized by a contributor to *Elite* in
1924. "We shall increase our efforts one hundred-fold, we will educate our
children, we will sacrifice everything to raise them to the status of the perfect
citizen, and the day will come when it will be loudly proclaimed to the whole
universe that they are Brazilians as worthy as any other."[16]

To that end, the press emphasized all points of similarity and equality with
whites. One vehicle for demonstrating Afro-Brazilian mastery of European-
based culture was through original literary pieces, mainly poetry and short
prose pieces known as *crónicas*. Literature was a mainstay of the black press,
especially in its early days. The desire to display cultural "refinement" revealed itself in other ways as well. When the editors of *O Xauter* became furi-
ous with *A Rua* and *O Menelick,* apparently over an insult in their "criticism"
columns, they chose to retaliate by deriding the lack of education of their ad-
versaries. "These men who make such a great to-do about their knowledge apparently make no use of it. In their effort to preach morality to one of our
associates, they begin their discussion in the second person plural and end in
the second person singular!" *O Xauter*, citing Shakespeare, Victor Hugo, and

John Stuart Mill, and quoting in Latin, chided them for "error[s] that a school-child would not commit."[17] Not only were the *Xauter* writers attempting to prove themselves superior, but they were also seeking to demonstrate a mastery of the cultural standards applied to Brazil's elite.

Thus did the journals address one of the central elements in the issue of self-determination, "who do we want to be"—their conceptualization of an ideal Afro-Brazilian identity to which they aspired. Related to this was an assessment of present identity and those problematic aspects requiring modification. The papers readily accepted that Afro-Brazilians needed to assume responsibility for improving their standard of living through behavior modification. When *O Alfinete* rhetorically asked who was to blame for the fact that Brazilian abolition had "ended official slavery and begun private servility," their answer was "us, and only us, we who live in the most shameful ignorance, the most profound moral abyss [*absecamento*], we who do not comprehend the distressing situation in which we live."[18] Simultaneously, they recognized that race prejudice constituted an obstacle to black progress that had to be dismantled in order to achieve their dream of equity.

O Bandeirante, which first appeared in 1918, was a pioneer in identifying racism in Brazilian society and in analyzing its implications for the Afro-Paulista community. Its subtitle, "a monthly organ in defense of the class of men of color," expressed its advocacy of racial solidarity as a basis for class interest. The choice of the word "defense" is also significant. Until then, the press had looked primarily to faults within the black community when identifying obstacles to their progress. *O Bandeirante*'s subtitle implied an adversarial relationship between Afro-Brazilians and an external force that the journal identified as race prejudice. Even more significant, *O Bandeirante* took the position that racial discrimination was no longer acceptable. In response to disparaging remarks published in the mainstream press about the election in Sergipe of a black congressman, Joaquim Cambará asked, "In regard to his color, ought that to impede him from being elected? Does he not enjoy full civil and political rights? Is he not protected under our Constitution? What, then, caused such surprise to this reporter? It was the eternal disrespect of our laws and the unacceptable race prejudice that exists in our country."[19] Cambará's positioning of racial prejudice as antipatriotic and disrespectful of Brazilian law was to become an integral tenet of Afro-Brazilian political ideology. It was a shrewd strategy that elevated the struggle against racism from a special interest issue to an act of national patriotism on behalf of the nation as a whole. Within months two new journals, *O Alfinete* and *A Liberdade*, joined *O Bandeirante* as self-declared defenders of blacks. They too sought out examples of prejudice and active discrimination. *A Liberdade* exposed a dance hall owner who had previously kept a sign posted prohibiting blacks from entering and had recently reopened under the aegis of a private club to circumvent the laws of equal access to public functions.[20] The newer journals continued the tradition of correcting shortcomings within the community, and this did not exclude color discrimination. A 1919 editorial in *A Liberdade* criticized "certain dark people at some clubs, who think they are light," for using the word *negro* as a form of disrespect, rather than *moreno,* which the author felt was more acceptable.[21] The topic of color discrimination by lighter Afro-Brazilians appeared very rarely in the black press, which strove to promote racial unity.

As the number of newspapers and writers expanded, so too did analyses of the state of the Afro-Brazilian community and strategies of uplift. Even those journals that concentrated on society news had one or more contributors whose analytical pieces soon became standard fare for the cover pages. During this time, there appeared themes that were to become part of the dominant Afro-Brazilian political ideology by the late 1920s. One of these was the need to emulate foreigners. "It is necessary that all people of color follow the fine example of the immigrant community," wrote José Benedicto Martins in *O Alfinete* in 1918, "sending your children to learn a profession so that they may earn a living in the future." He described how immigrants had left plantation agriculture to make their own way in the capital, and criticized blacks for not wanting to learn a trade: "Blacks must aspire to be something in the future; therefore it is necessary that all have the strength of will to teach our children what our parents did not have the opportunity to learn."[22] Another was the creation of an Afro-Brazilian voting bloc. A small notice in 1919 advised residents of Vila Mariana that Gastão Rodrigues da Silva, editor-in-chief of *O Bandeirante* and president of the Centro Recreativo Smart, was registering black voters with the intent of increasing their political importance and visibility.[23]

A parable in the second issue of *O Menelick* entitled "An Episode from the Revolt of Saint Domingue" offered an interesting path to black redemption. In this story, a marauding band of escaped slaves roams the countryside seeking revenge. They come across a white family who owned no slaves, with a daughter described as "pretty, blonde, blonder than a child of Albion." When the chief of the former slaves raises a knife to murder the girl, one of his men stops him "because of love. He loved that girl with all his soul." At that moment, she suddenly repents having shouted in her anger and fear that "blacks were not human." The black chief sentences the man to hang for insubordination, "and he died peacefully, he died like a hero, he died for love of a white girl. . . . And now, beside his cadaver it could be said: that blacks are just as human as whites."[24] The story was a striking use of the biblical concept of redemption through love of one's enemy. In the Brazilian context, it instructed blacks not to focus their attention on reparations for their enslavement. Indeed, the concept of retribution against whites never gained popular currency in the Afro-Paulista press.

While the journals upheld morality and industriousness as avenues to personal improvement, the strategy of community uplift most commonly echoed in the black press was that of racial unity. Frustrated by their inability to develop cooperative initiatives among organizations, activists turned to the journals to voice their concerns to the public. In 1924, *O Elite* lamented the inability of black organizations to reconcile dissidence effectively, causing "disunity in the heart of a race that still needs the cooperation of all without distinction of faith or creed." The writer Abilio Rodrigues sadly characterized his "one desire to someday witness the perfect unification of all people of color of São Paulo" as a "complete illusion."[25]

These voices articulated elements of an Afro-Paulista political and ideological platform that were to become dominant among activists in the 1920s and 1930s. It took shape in response to race prejudice, the identification of which determined the strategic choice of ideology. Journals such as *O Bandeirante, O Alfinete,* and *A Liberdade* focused on race prejudice as an obstacle to Afro-Brazilian progress and as a subversion of the stated objectives of the Constitution. This, in turn, directed Afro-Paulista self-determination along the following lines.

1. *Who are we?* Journals positioned blacks as patriotic and loyal Brazilian citizens by stressing their historical contributions to national development. As such, the black press' condemnation of prejudice and discrimination became a patriotic act on behalf of the nation as a whole as opposed to special interest activism.

2. *Who do we want to be?* As articulated in *Elite*'s editorial, Afro-Brazilians sought to be considered on a par with all other Brazilians. They chose assimilation as a path to full integration, striving to meet mainstream sociocultural standards. They therefore minimized any cultural differences that might have distinguished them from their white counterparts.

3. *How do we get there?* The Afro-Paulista activists worked simultaneously on two strategies. They first concentrated on initiatives that blacks themselves could undertake. These included promoting Afro-Brazilian interest group unity and adherence to mainstream sociocultural standards. Second, they sought to remove prejudice and discrimination as external obstacles to Afro-Brazilian upward mobility.

Journals such as *O Bandeirante* and *A Liberdade* were pioneers in advancing the development of a political ideology. Yet it was not until the mid-1920s that the writers involved with the black press integrated theory with issue activism. The most influential journals of the late 1920s were *O Clarim da Alvorada, Progresso,* and, in the 1930s, *A Voz da Raça.*[26] This era witnessed the emergence of an activist cadre of young Afro-Brazilian men determined to dismantle discriminatory practices. Among the most influential were José Correia Leite, co-founder of *O Clarim da Alvorada* and the driving force behind numerous efforts to create coalitions of Afro-Brazilian organizations, and Arlindo Veiga dos Santos, involved with some of the earliest efforts toward political activism and the leader of the Frente Negra Brasileira. Although both men had long careers of activism, they each left their mark on distinct periods of the self-determination struggle in São Paulo. In the last years of the First Republic, Leite's efforts to organize a confederated black organization created a political platform that became the foundation for the Frente Negra Brasileira immediately thereafter.

José Correia Leite was born in downtown São Paulo on August 23, 1900. Child of a white father who did not acknowledge his paternity, Leite and his younger sister lived with their mother Ricarda, a domestic worker and daughter of a slave. Leite described his childhood as difficult. His mother died while he was still young, and José had to support himself by working odd jobs. He was taken in as a domestic worker by an Italian family. On various occasions Leite talked his way into school by persuading directors to let him attend classes in return for helping with chores, or found his way into charitable programs. But he was unable to sustain his education long enough to learn to read properly until around age twenty, when, at the black social clubs, he renewed a childhood acquaintanceship with Jayme de Aguiar. Aguiar, who had been to school and had literary aspirations, helped Leite learn to read and do mathematics.

One day Aguiar approached Leite with the idea of starting a monthly literary journal. They decided to call it *O Clarim* (The Clarion). *Clarim* first appeared on January 6, 1924. The "office" was Leite's living room, where he and Aguiar set the type to be sent to the printers. The two also made up the entire staff of the paper, which they financed themselves. Leite worked as a guard at city hall, and often used much of his paycheck to cover *Clarim's* costs. Aguiar thought of using pseudonyms (such as "Jim de Araguary") in imitation of a popular literary fad, and they used other names to make it seem as if they had more writers. Shortly thereafter, a man came to Leite's home claiming previous ownership of the journal's name. Leite and Aguiar pondered a replacement. According to Leite, "We thought of 'The Clarion of Victory' or 'The Clarion of Dawn.' But I said, 'What victory? We haven't even begun.'"[27] Aguiar agreed, and the paper became *O Clarim da Alvorada* (The Clarion of Dawn), subtitled "A Journal of Literature, News, and Humor." The subtitles until 1928 (the end of the paper's first phase) reflected subtle changes in orientation, first "A Journal of Literature, News, and Science" and, later, "A Journal of Literature, News, and Politics."

Although Leite credits Aguiar as his mentor, their differences in vision and style were apparent from the start. Aguiar wrote poetry and *crónicas*. Leite's work was of a critical nature, examining the problems facing the Afro-Brazilian community and proposing solutions.[28] An article by Leite in the fourth issue called for the unification of existing organizations:

> If we analyze the valor of our forebears in history, we shall see the sub-lime courage of a race which, though enslaved, did not let itself be domi-nated in the struggle for its rights. . . . How many tears did the liberty of those poor martyrs cost, those who were among the first workers for the progress and order of our country. . . .
>
> The good name of our people depends on our actions. It is our responsibility to bring the value of our race to the development of society. . . . For this it is necessary [that we form] a general convoca-tion of Negro men and work to establish a beneficent fund, elect a di-rectorate, send manifestos to all states of Brazil, and finally, found a society, "Confederation of Negro Men [Confederação dos Homens Prêtos]," in accordance with the ideas of various patricians.
>
> Dear readers, this seems difficult, but it is not. In São Paulo there are a great number of dance societies. If all their presidents would come together we would already have a sufficient number for the first meet-ing, and if each president promoted the noble principles of the confed-eration in his association, we would have a good number of members as well.[29]

Leite continued to appeal for unity in *Clarim* editorials, and this became the journal's central theme. In an editorial commemorating *Clarim*'s first anni-versary, Leite and Aguiar asked of their readers, "We want from all of you a great promise, and a great gift. . . . You have this gift of great value in your hands. They call it UNITY."[30] It would be five years before Leite could begin to see his dream approach reality.

Leite also picked up themes introduced in earlier journals. In the excerpt above, he underscored the role of Afro-Brazilians in the nation's history. His use of the phrase "progress and order" took on those elites who felt blacks were detrimental to Brazil's development. Also like the first generation of journals, *Clarim* focused on self-criticism rather than blaming white society. "It is our fault that we live despised not only by foreigners, but also by our white compatriots."[31] This perspective was evident among other Afro-Brazilian social critics as well.[32]

Clarim placed great emphasis on Afro-Brazilian history. Most important was the commemoration of abolition, and each year the May issue was dated May 13 in honor of the decree's anniversary. The May editions were devoted

O CLARIM D'ALVORADA

ORGAM LITERARIO, NOTICIOSO E HUMORISTICO

Direcção: JIM DE ARAGUARY & LEITE

| ANNO IV | SÃO PAULO, 15 DE JANEIRO DE 1927 | NUM. 28 |

JAYME DE AGUIAR

Apezar dos pezares...

É felizmente, hoje, com enthusiasmo, ante os applausos daquelles que nos têm ouvido, admiradores de bom senso, que aqui esentamos o presente numeri, commemorativo do nosso anniversario.

Em se tratando de uma data significativa, cumpre-nos, pois, antes de qualquer outra asseveridade, deixar bem acclarados os nossos effusivos agradecimentos a todos os nossos presados leitores e assignantes e bem assim á aquelles que se deixam ainda dominar pelo despeito ou mau intendido inqualificavel; os seus ideaes, embora circundados de imagens bem representativas, pelo pincel de um artista de pulso, jamais hão de salientar ao lado das grandiosas e soberbas paizagens que se nos deparam nestes ultimos tempos de um encantamento admiravel, de uma evolução assombradora, feitas e baseadas num criterio, com arte; nellas ha o encantamento, a attracção, tudo bem norteado na combinação das cores! Não podemos representar os nossos sentimentos de satisfação e de enthusiasmo sem os imprescindiveis pezares; aos falsos idealizadores de fancaria que se julgam compridores dos seus deveres sociaes e dos impostos pelo Creador. Entramos no 3.º anno de vida; ja não nos esquecçamos das promessas passadas, das ideas por nós combatidas, nem tampouco do evoluir da nossa gente nestes ultimos tempos.

Cumpre-nos, pois, embora contrafeitos, em primeiro lugar identificar os nossos sentimentos de agradecimentos a todos os nossos presados collaboradores, admiradores sensatos, pelas ajudas constantes e dignas de reconhecimentos profundos; são estas as nossas sinceras demonstrações de gratidão que lhes endereçamos, aos despeitados por excellencia, tambem os nossos agradecimentos, pelas grandiosidades dos seus feitos de desprestigiadores da boa ordem, do bom senso e das constantes irregularidades. Ha dois annos passados surgimos com este pequeno jornal, idealizando á nossa gente, demonstrando-lhe o caminho a trilhar, para que se realizassem quanto breve o nosso tão falado problema racial, que de ha muito já deveria ter sido posto em pratica.

Permitta-nos, o Redemptor, que outros tantos annos de existencia se nos apresentem conquistando o apoio de todos aquelles que reconhecem as nossas labutas, a nossa boa vontade para elevar sempre ao triumpho merecedor, se conseguirmos o apogeu da nossa identidade moral e social.

Então, todos nós, em coro entoaremos em altas vozes, o solemne Te-Deum, ante o altar magestoso do grande templo do Dever da nossa digna Ascensão, harmoniosamente, com amor proprio dos nossos sentimentos de alegria, enthusiasmo, crentes no polvir valoroso que será por certo, o psalmo rithmado dos idealizadores sensatos de hoje, e da mocidade estudiosa e luctadora de amanhã!...

J. DE AGUIAR.

Anno Velho e Novo!

A noite esta magnifica. Diante de mim não muito longe vejo uma linda creança morena, que com um suave sorriso a brincar-lhe nos labios, pede gentilmente ao velho tremulo e cançado que se setire.

Adeus, ó velho de barbas brancas e rosto enrugado. Os homens esperam anciosamente o teu ultimo suspiro. Vae-te.

Foste bom ou mau? Querido ou amaldiçoado? Deixas bôas ou más recordações?

Tu roubaste ao avô ao neto, o neto ao avô; o pae ao filho, o filho ao pae; o irmão ao irmão; o amigo ao amigo. Tu despedaçaste cadeias de amor delaceraste corações enamorados... Velho fatal, parte!

Mas em compensação, espalhaste tambem pelo mundo muitas alegrias. Encheste berços vasios, uniste corações apaixonados, deste-nos novos amigos e encheste-nos de alegria o coração e a alma. Vae, pobre velho parte e leva contigo dôres e alegria, risos e prantos, tristezas e esperanças.

E tu ó linda creança vem! Ouves? Um grande barrulho annuncia a tua chegada; os homens saudam-te com gritos de alegria dizendo: — «Bom' Anno!»

Vêm, ó linda creança a tua vida é breve. Hoje és festejada e abançoado; mas daqui a doze mezes o que acontecerá?

Vêm, ó creança! Eu te saudo e te peço; auxilia os pobres e os desamparados, dá pão a quem tem fome, consolo a quem soffre. Protege os velhos e as creanças, os pobres e os ricos.

Sê bon para udos...

E vós, ó leitores do Clarim d'Alvorada ó amigos gentis, ó irmãs no sentir, juntae a vossa voz á minha e digamos: «Sê propria, ó Anno Novo, a quem fundou esse querido jornal que espalha por todos os lados bellas paginas cheias de conselhos e instrucções; fazei que Elle resee por todo o nosso querido Brasil que encerre em si o triumpho da raça preta o amor santo da Patria e de Deus.

EVANGELINA XAVIER DE CARVALHO.

BOAS FESTAS

O nosso jornal O Clarim d'Alvorada, pelo motivo de commemorar hoje o seu anniversario occorrido á 6 do corrente, embora já sejam decorridos quinze dias das tradicionaes festas do Santo Natal, Anno Bom e Reis, vem cumprimentar todos os seus admiradores, e ás associações dançantes desta capital que têm emprestado auxilios quanto a sua distribuição, augurando-lhes innumeros progressos, felicidades no decorrer do NOVO ANNO; ás sociedades abaixo mencionadas:

- Auri - Verde
- Brinco de Princezas
- Campos Elyseos
- Elite da Liberdade
- 15 de Novembro
- 28 de Setembro
- 6 de Maio
- 13 de Maio
- Barão do Rio Branco
- Eden Juvenil
- Paulistano
- Kosmos
- Cravos Vermelhos
- Princeza do Norte
- União Militar
- União de Mocidade.
- Barra Funda.

Ás associações: Centro Civico dos Palmares, e C. B. José do Patrocinio, que tanto têm labutado com verdadeiro amor e carinho para elevar ao triumpho merecedor e a educação imprescindivel, de todos aquelles que, de bom grado, concorrem para a evolução civica moral e social da nossa gente, nestes tempos de um evoluir de progresso assombrador!

São estes os ardentes votos, sinceros, deste pequeno mensageiro dos brasileiros de cor, no dia de hoje.

JOSÉ CORRÊIA LEITE

Muito agradecido...

Completou mais um anniversario, o nosso pequeno porta voz, apartario, é mais um anno de luctas assiduas que passa, tão cheio de chimeras para nos outros, que alimejamos um futuro de grandeza para raça que descendemos. O Clarim, apresenta-se hoje, tal qual o cavalheiro andante que, por um momento estanca firme para saccudir o pó, unico trophéu que traz da grande jornada. Mas está contente com a sua conquista, que se resume no pó da longa estrada. É nesse trajecto que se aprende a ter fé e a esperança de vencer. Vencer ao lado dos innumeros patricios que nos acompanha com a mesma crença, com a mesma vontade de luctar em pról da gente preta brasileira. Agradecemos com franqueza, sem selecção, não sómente os que nos acompanha quer emprestando seus apoios intellectuaes ou financeiros; mas tambem não podemos esquecer dos outros que luctam do outro lado, para o mesmo fim, e para o mesmo ideal.

O anniversario da nossa folha, não representa para nós uma data festiva, porque, ainda não attingimos o ponto capital da nossa vontade terrea de fazer do Clarim, o orgam tumultuario o istemonto defensor da classe dos homens pretos, de nossa terra. Mas isto por ora será somente um sonho, emquanto o despeito campear como até aqui tem campeado no seio da nossa gente. É por este facto que ainda não possuimos nada, e tambem não somos unidos. A nossa folha é simplesmente um signal de esforço de um pugilo de moços, dispostos a luctar ao lado dos que luctam. O Clarim é dirigido por rapazes, logo é para a nossa mocidade, que elle vive; a essa juventude esperançosa que floresce tão risonha lançamos hoje a nossa saudação, para que não se esqueçam do nosso antepassado glorioso. Os agradecimentos que aqui deixamos fazemos um timbre na nossa classe, sem porque quem beneficio o Clarim, com sinceridade e não com promessas petulantes raras vezes compridas... Como já nós fizeram. Esses são julguem que estão beneficiando os humildes dirigentes desta folha, não façam pelo amor de Deus, em troca de recompensas de nossa parte, ou para receberem homenagem. Mas sim esperem a recompensa do futuro.

As sociedades dançantes desta capital e do interior os nossos agradecimentos, pelo acolhimento cavalheiresco do Clarim, em suas sédes, como pelo interesse e o reconhecimento do seu valor.

Aos nossos collaboradores, não encontramos palavras, para enaltecer os seus altos predicados de homens esforçados, e dignos companheiros de lucta. Em fim a todos em geral os nossos agradecimentos sinceros, unica recompensa que podemos apresentar aos nossos amigos.

Dentro de alguns dias completará tambem o primeiro anniversario do nosso appello para fundação nesta capital, da Confederação dos homens de cor. Não podemos deixar passar desapercebido este facto de summa importancia para nos e para os nossos leitores sensatos. Temos ainda mais esperanças de ver realisado esse nosso intento, não por nós

ILL. 5. Staff of *Clarim d'Alvorada* at their typesetting machine in the home of José Correia Leite. Standing, fourth from left, is Henrique Cunha.

to stories about the abolitionists, the way abolition was celebrated in Afro-Brazilian homes, and related literary works. The heroes most frequently eulogized were the Afro-Brazilian abolitionists Luiz Gama and José do Patrocinio. The editors also gave great attention to Princess Isabel, Rui Barbosa, José Antônio Bento, José Bonifacio, and Joaquim Nabuco, each of whom played important roles in the abolition process. For the first two years of the journal's existence, Afro-Brazilian history appeared only on May 13, but in 1926 *Clarim* began commemorating the September 28 anniversary of the Law of the Free Womb (the Rio Branco Law), and Afro-Brazilian history quickly became a regular feature. As yet there was no mention of either African events or information about the African diaspora. *Clarim* did not greatly expand its scope until 1928, when it began its second phase, a major reorientation toward political ideology and advocacy. This was the fruit of two years of involvement by Afro-Paulista youth in a pioneering organization, the Centro Cívico Palmares. From that point on, the black press was to become an integral instrument in the campaign for political mobilization.

Integrating Ideology and Strategy: Early Activism and the Politicization of Race

The growing politicization of black journals in the 1920s was not an isolated event, for several reasons. George Reid Andrews explains the genesis of black activism as the result of the marginalization of blacks in politics. Barred as they were from meaningful participation as military officers or members of political parties, blacks created their own political institutions, the first of which was the Centro Cívico Palmares. To this must be added the fact that the political culture of São Paulo had changed by opening new avenues of oppositional politics. São Paulo, along with Rio de Janeiro and Santos, had become a major center of public manifestations of dissidence. In the late 1910s it was one of the principal sites of labor activism. In 1922, a military revolt by junior officers transformed the streets of downtown São Paulo into a battlefield. The national government, heavily influenced by the entrenched agricultural barons of São Paulo, faced an ever-rising tide of discontent that had its partisans among Afro-Brazilians. Because the abolition decree had been an act of the Empire, and because the ruling elites of the Republican government had been the principal enslavers of Africans in the previous century, black allegiance to the Republican Party was often ambivalent.

There was another factor that undoubtedly had great impact on the journals. In 1923 Robert Abbott, the publisher of the *Chicago Defender,* visited Rio and São Paulo. In his lectures comparing the racial situations of the United States and Brazil, Abbott, an African American, concluded that there was no race prejudice in Brazil. His Afro-Brazilian audience objected strongly, pointing out the prevalence of employment and social discrimination.[33] Abbott's visit, and the newspapers he sent to friends in São Paulo, opened the way for the debate and contextualization of Afro-Brazilian issues from an international perspective.

External factors alone do not fully explain shifts in political sentiment. The experiences of Palmares members José Correia Leite and Henrique Cunha help shed light on activists' personal motivations. When asked why he, in contrast to Aguiar, had shown such a concern for black protest, Leite replied: "My life was different from Jayme's. Jayme was a well-educated boy, protected by his family. Jayme's family still had ties with white families. . . . But I had none of this. So I began to perceive, in the face of adversity, that blacks had to do everything necessary for unity and the work of uplift."[34] Henrique Cunha recounted an incident of discrimination as his motivation for joining Palmares and *Clarim:*

> One day I went to the plaza to look for a job. There was a plaza where everyone, whites and blacks, went to look for jobs. . . . I was there,

talking with someone next to me. Then a white guy came up, a friend of the one talking with me. . . . [They pointed out a man] and the guy said, "He came to find a houseboy." My friend . . . said to him, "Well, he [Cunha] is a good houseboy." But the other guy said, "No, the owner of the house says blacks can't go there." That upset me. I said to myself, "So, blacks don't have even an opportunity to work! So I began to seek out the movement. They used to have lots of meetings there in the plaza."[35]

Both these stories indicate the inability or unwillingness of aspirants to gain access to the material rewards of society using conventional methods. Leite's case is interesting because as a mulatto, he might have been expected to fare better than Aguiar, who was dark-skinned. Leite, however, lacked those vital connections that Aguiar enjoyed with white families, relationships of protection and patronage that enabled many blacks to finance their education and find employment. Once Aguiar assumed the financial responsibility of providing for his family, he dropped out of activism, although his sentiments did not significantly change.[36] Given the option of lucrative connections or social activism, many blacks chose the former, with its immediate benefits, over the latter, which demanded great commitment with no assurance of personal reward. Cunha's story depicts a black man seeking a job using the same methods as "everyone, whites and blacks." It was the failure of those methods that led him to seek alternatives.

Florestan Fernandes cites economics as the most significant incentive for social protest among black Paulistanos: "The majority of the black population came up against successive obstacles to their aspirations for social mobility. It was almost as impossible to secure, maintain, and improve a respectable source of income as it was impracticable, once secured, to make it yield the same material, psychological, and political fruits that such sources provided for whites."[37] Afro-Brazilians, unhappy with their socioeconomic status as a whole, responded both to social and to economic conditions. Social discontent provided the impetus for the development of black collectives. Over two decades, the social clubs helped create a group identity and solidarity. Economic frustrations led to protest against perceived injustices. Both forms of discrimination were based upon race. It was therefore logical that the protest group should come from the same race-based group formed as a response to social discrimination.

Common motivations and aspirations, and attitudes about how to pursue them, were perhaps the most important factor in converting an ethnic base into social advocacy. Many black Paulistanos shared the desire to partake of the city's financial prosperity. Overwhelmingly, they were migrants who aspired to succeed through the channels of education and hard work, as they had been taught. They sought integration; impeded by their race but not wanting to abandon their quest, a large number of black Paulistanos could easily agree that they needed an alternative method of achieving their goals.

Afro-Brazilian political organization in the 1920s was not new; indeed, there were political implications to virtually all Afro-Brazilian collectives throughout the nation's history. The conditions of post-abolition urban life in a city such as São Paulo, however, demanded new forms of response. The myriad factors contributing to the creation of race-based advocacy coalesced until, in 1926, conditions were ripe for the birth of the Centro Cívico Palmares.

The Centro Cívico Palmares, founded by Major Antônio Carlos of Minas Gerais, was the first Afro-Brazilian activist organization in São Paulo. The fact that Palmares was founded by a Mineiro is not incongruous, for São Paulo's black community was growing yearly with new arrivals from Minas, Rio, and the Paulista interior. On the night of October 29, 1926, Antônio Carlos convened a meeting of young men involved in black organizations and newspapers at the Apollo Theater for the purpose of creating a small library of black history and literature.[38] The organization's name is of significance; Palmares was an independent African republic founded in Brazil by fugitive slaves that lasted from approximately 1604 to 1696, and is the quintessential symbol of Afro-Brazilian resistance.[39]

The Centro Cívico Palmares formed a directorate of approximately 20 people, and membership reached somewhere between 100 and 150. Among those involved with Palmares were the future Frente Negra leaders Arlindo and Isaltino Veiga dos Santos and the renowned orators Alberto Orlando and Vicente Ferreira. Other members of Palmares included the publishers of black journals—Leite and Aguiar of *Clarim* and the poet Lino Guedes of *O Getulino* and, later, *Progresso.* Guedes, along with Benedito Florencio and Gervasio de Moraes, among others, left Campinas in 1926, ceased publication of *O Getulino,* and moved to São Paulo, where they joined the Centro Cívico Palmares.[40] It is significant that there is no evidence of involvement by any of the leaders of the recreational associations, with the possible exception of Frederico Baptista de Souza of Kosmos.[41]

The idea of the library soon mushroomed into a host of other projects when, as Leite recalls, "the distinctly cultural objective . . . was overcome by the force of the conditions in which we lived, the association coming to play a role in defense of blacks and their rights." Palmares offered secondary school courses that enabled many students to continue their education. By 1928 members had established a theater group and a medical clinic.[42] Membership income grew to 715$000 in July and by October had grown to 834$000.[43]

That same year Antônio Carlos returned to Minas Gerais and Joe Foyes-Gittens assumed the presidency.

Palmares carefully began cultivating ties to politicians who might be of help in the future, a proven tactic within the political culture of patronage and clientelism. In May of 1928, in collaboration with the Rosário brotherhood and the social clubs Campos Eliseos and Paulistano, the group commemorated the fortieth anniversary of abolition with a morning mass and a visit to the tombs of leading abolitionists. On that occasion Palmares held an unveiling ceremony of a portrait of Brazil's president, Washington Luís, painted by Palmares member Olavo Xavier, to mark Luís' selection as honorary president of the group. The president, the governor, and other local authorities were invited to an evening "civic session" featuring speeches by Vicente Ferreira and Gervasio de Moraes.[44] Later in May the group invited state delegate Orlando de Almeida Prado to speak (the delegate who, three months later, would support Palmares' struggle to integrate São Paulo's police force). Palmares also had Dr. Evaristo de Moraes present a special session on "The Psychological Factor of Race in Brazilian Civilization" when he was visiting São Paulo.[45] Thus Palmares positioned itself for its first foray into issue advocacy.

In August 1928 Palmares became involved in a protest concerning racial discrimination in the Civil Guard, the state police force. The group approached the desegregation of the Guard from two fronts. First, it educated the community about the problem through the usual outlets of speeches and editorials. It also experimented with theater as a strategy of political education. On Thursday nights during the winter, Palmares' theater group performed a play entitled "Negroes in the Civil Guard."[46] Second, as a representative advocacy organization, Palmares made direct appeals to government officials to hire blacks in the Guard. Group members lodged complaints with several state legislators and convinced the delegate Orlando Prado (who had been a guest of Palmares in May) to give a speech on the floor of the state legislature condemning discriminatory hiring practices.[47] The members also met with President Washington Luís, their honorary president, and Governor Júlio Prestes. Prestes rescinded the order barring blacks, although it was not until the early 1930s that pressure from the Frente Negra forced the state to actually hire black officers.[48] Orlando Prado came to Palmares demanding an unspecified quid pro quo for his efforts, but members protested on the grounds that he was merely doing his legislative duty. A dispute over whether Palmares owed a debt to Prado caused a serious schism, resulting in the departure of key members and an irreversible weakening of the group's base of support.[49]

Over the course of the year many Palmares members became involved with *Clarim* and a new journal, *Progresso*. When Jayme de Aguiar left to get married in early 1928, he suggested that *Clarim* cease publication, but Leite decided to continue with a stronger emphasis on social protest. In February *Clarim* reorganized as a collective. The journal, now in what it called its second phase, defined itself as a "Journal of Struggle." Along with Leite, Luiz de Souza became manager; Urcino dos Santos and João Soter da Silva joined as directors. Also joining *Clarim* from Palmares were Horacio da Cunha, Arlindo Veiga dos Santos, Gervasio de Moraes, and Lino Guedes. Jayme de Aguiar continued to contribute articles and poetry.[50] In June 1928 Lino Guedes and Argentino Wanderley started the newspaper *Progresso*.

Wanderley resigned from Palmares' management committee *(commissão de syndicancia)* in August, and by late 1928 *Progresso* had become openly critical of Palmares' leadership. When Joe Foyes-Gittens ran for reelection as Palmares president in December, *Progresso* expressed concern over the future direction of the organization. "If one looks at the initial plan, there is much that the Centro [Cívico Palmares] has placed on the list of forgotten things." The journal published the October budget, which showed a "disappearance" of 111$400 *milréis* in addition to a deficit of 44$900 *milréis,* which remained unaccounted for as late as the following January.[51]

Progresso was particularly concerned with Gittens' leadership style. The editors wrote, "Mr. Gittens is president, absolute president. On this point we do not agree with the untiring reformer of the Centro Cívico Palmares. . . . Palmares, because of the importance it has achieved in [the city of] São Paulo, must have a president who is representative and not absolute."[52] The influential orator Vicente Ferreira apparently agreed; *Progresso* quoted from an interview he gave to the *São Paulo Journal:*

> Unfortunately, the Centro Cívico Palmares is being directed by a true dictator, who has alienated old members and [caused it to lose its] prestige among the "Palmares" family.
>   It is true that the "Palmares" society has grown in volume with its apparent expansion, *but it has lost its essence, becoming a traitor to its goals of struggle on behalf of black Brazilians.*[53]

The depth of commitment to collective decision making reflected some consensus regarding the way black groups ought to be run, which did not necessarily derive from Afro-Brazilian organizational traditions. Groups such as the social clubs and brotherhoods, and even such informal collectives as the Carnival *cordões,* were structured in ways that facilitated autocracy. Conflict over "dictatorial" leadership was to become a major issue in the Frente Negra Brasileira.

Palmares continued for several years, but never regained its original popularity and influence. It nonetheless introduced a new method of struggle that many of its members subsequently took to new organizations. Palmares

ILL. 6. *Clarim d'Alvorada*, first edition of its "second phase."

combined social services, recreational activities, and protest in a way that no earlier groups had attempted. This model was especially evident in the Frente Negra Brasileira, whose first directorate included several former Palmares members. A retrospective article published in 1935 discussed and evaluated the experiences of Palmares. Its author wrote:

> 1926. The Centro Cívico Palmares is founded. A period of great agitation begins at this time around the problems of the Brazilian black. Speeches, conferences, articles, etc. . . .
>
> Black people came from everywhere and, through the media [i.e., black newspapers], came to feel themselves part of an intensive project of struggle for the ideals of the race—moral, material, and intellectual uplift.
>
> For more or less three years, Palmares dominated everyone's attention, and all those people imbued with a healthy sense of racial pride were part of the work of Palmares.

Yet, he concludes, Palmares was fraught with internal problems, a lack of cooperation, and "political maneuvering and petty interests." Personalizing

Palmares in his imagery, the author describes its metaphoric "death." "And after some months of serious illness, it went to the common grave—dances."[54]

The Palmares experience ushered in a new era of Afro-Brazilian journalism and activism reflected in the pages of *Clarim* and *Progresso*. At *Clarim,* the creation of a writers' collective under Leite's stewardship steered the paper toward more radical analyses of Afro-Brazilian politics and activist endeavors. *Progresso* also benefited from the contributions of new writers, but its salient feature was its effort to understand the politics of race from an international perspective.

The analysis of racism was important because the existence of racial discrimination was often denied in Brazil, a claim typically sustained by the fact that there were few outward manifestations of racial hostilities like those in the United States. As late as 1928 this view was defended by Horacio da Cunha in *Auriverde*. "There are many Negroes who maintain there is a little bit of prejudice in our country! It is not true, my countrymen of color." Da Cunha contended that charges of racism merely reflected the ignorance of people jealous because some blacks, several of whom he named, were ascending to new heights, ("and there are many more I am unable to cite because they do not consider themselves black").[55] The denial of racism placed the burden of black inability to achieve on the backs of Afro-Brazilians. Identifying and exposing racism allowed them to target a major external barrier to upward mobility. Both *Clarim* and *Progresso* hammered away at developing awareness of racism and its negative repercussions, thus preparing the way for eventual activism. This awareness was vital to the creation of a rationale for political action.[56]

Progresso targeted the terminology of race itself. The journal was in the vanguard in its regular use of the term *negro*. Although it had appeared occasionally in the newspapers, *prêto* was still used with greater frequency. In *Progresso*'s article on Juliano Moreira, president of the Brazilian Academy of Science and director general of psychiatric assistance in Rio de Janeiro, the editors identified him in the headline as "The Black Scientist *(O Cientista Negro)* Juliano Moreira."[57] *Progresso* imbued the traditionally negative term with positive connotations, using it for persons held in high esteem, such as "Tafari [Haile Selassie], the Black Emperor," and Josephine Baker, "the Black Salomé."[58] This practice was also followed by *Clarim*.

Another issue to which *Progresso* gave extensive coverage was the "medical caravan" of 1928. Brazil had planned a dramatic voyage of doctors to attend a European conference. A boat sailing northward was to pick up prominent doctors along the coastline and then cross the Atlantic. When they arrived in Bahia, they were shocked that the delegate, Dr. Enoch Carteado, was an Afro-Brazilian. The doctors from São Paulo protested, causing an embarrassing diplomatic entanglement. Carteado remained on board, and retaliated by contacting the Foreign Ministry. At that point, the government sided with Carteado, thus allowing it to publicize its image of "racial democracy."[59]

A new sensitivity to cultural manifestations of racism was also evident. A review by Horacio Cunha of the film "The Negro with the White Soul" is illustrative. "We don't understand this title," he wrote. "We do not agree with it. We will not, either." The film dealt with the "tragedy" of being black. The star performs a noble act for love of a white woman, but dies after she rejects him. Its theme was similar to *O Bandeirante*'s story of the Haitian Revolution, but *Progresso* analyzed it quite differently. "A fine gesture of a fine soul, a philanthropic soul, a big soul, but never, never a white soul."[60]

Progresso was concerned with redefining what it meant to be of African descent. The valorization of blackness was important to its editors, who recognized the implications of a lack of self-esteem that would lead to the exogamy so roundly encouraged by mainstream thought. "Because the black Brazilian, in contrast to his North American counterparts, makes a point of marrying white women," they warned, "in three quarters of a century he will belong to the past."[61] By showcasing the accomplishments of blacks around the world, they offered role models and countered the claims of black inferiority. When members of the Black Star Golf Club integrated and won a golf tournament in Chicago (to the horror of the local white press, which suggested sending the winnings to the Ku Klux Klan instead), *Progresso* announced, "The White Race Is Put in Check by the Black Race." The pages of *Progresso* opened a window onto the international arena: readers could learn about the activities of Africans in Paris, the Pan-African Congress, or Marcus Garvey's Universal Negro Improvement Association. They traced the history and activities of Emperor Haile Selassie and other prominent black political figures, without neglecting notables from the worlds of the arts and athletics. Josephine Baker was the subject of their first international item (in this collection), a small announcement in 1928 about the woman they nicknamed the "Ebony Venus" and the "Countess," when she traveled to Berlin.[62] Baker became a favorite with the editors, who published several articles about her.[63] The victory of an Afro-Panamanian in a world boxing championship held in New York was another early international news item.[64]

The expansion into international coverage was largely the result of two fortuitous contacts outside São Paulo. One of these was Robert Abbott, who, it appears, sent copies of the *Chicago Defender* to both *Clarim* and *Progresso*. The São Paulo newspapers rarely limited themselves to simple reprints in Portuguese. Instead, they used the articles as a springboard for commentary and analysis. Commenting on a *Defender* article about Herbert Hoover's visit to Brazil, *Progresso* noted that U.S. blacks had supported the Republican candi-

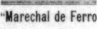

ILL. 7. *Progresso*, July 31, 1930. The lead story of this edition was "The Birth of the Race Question in South Africa."

date Alfred E. Smith. "Let us see if Hoover is able to achieve this coming together [of the races], because race hatred in the U.S. comes from very deep." In the same issue are articles about languages spoken in Africa, the visit of Juliano Moreira to receive an honor from Emperor Hirohito in Japan, and the crowning of Haile Selassie as Ras Tafari I of Ethiopia—along with an editorial about Josephine Baker.[65] The second contributor of great importance was Mario de Vasconcelos, a teacher of English in Bahia with a keen interest in the Garvey movement. Vasconcelos had seen *Clarim* and began sending translations to São Paulo through its representative in Bahia. In late 1930 *Clarim* introduced "O Mundo Negro," a regular column of translations from *The Negro World,* the publication of the Universal Negro Improvement Association.[66] As yet, there is no evidence that any UNIA branches were formed in São Paulo, but Garvey's ideas had a considerable impact on the *Clarim* collective. According to Leite, they especially liked Garvey's ideology of African unity, but disagreed about repatriation to Africa.[67]

Both *Clarim* and *Progresso* engaged in collective endeavors on behalf of the Afro-Paulistano community. *Progresso,* noting the erection of a statue in honor of the Syrian-Lebanese community, raised collections for a bust of the abolitionist Luiz Gama to be erected in the Largo de Arouche, a site near the neighborhoods of Campos Eliseos and Barra Funda. *Clarim's* principal project was the creation of an umbrella organization of all black organizations in the city. Since the inception of *O Clarim d'Alvorada,* José Correia Leite had been urging a federation of the diverse black associations in São Paulo. As early as 1924 Leite proposed the formation of a Confederation of Negro Men (Confederação dos Homens Prêtos). Such a confederation would begin with a meeting of the presidents of the recreational or "dance" clubs, who would then elect a directorate, send a manifesto to all other states, and promote the idea locally among their own members.[68] Although his idea was well received, Leite was not able to implement his plan at the time. Leite saw the inception of *Clarim's* new phase as a second opportunity, and in February 1929 he issued a call for a Congress of Black Youth (Congresso da Mocidade Negra), to be organized exactly along the lines of his earlier confederation idea.[69] "Blacks of São Paulo and Brazil," he wrote, "the Congress of Black Youth is the only true way to develop our struggle of resistance, to definitively form our united front, and to achieve the firm consolidation of our ideas. It is the fundamental base for the revival of our community."[70] He sent invitations to sixteen association presidents, arranged a provisional meeting place, and held the first planning session on March 8, 1929.[71] Leite presided at the meeting, and *Clarim* manager Luiz de Souza acted as secretary. The meeting opened with a standing ovation for Frederico Baptista de Souza, president of the well-established Kosmos social club. Next, a *Clarim* member, Gervasio de Moraes, gave a short speech focusing on the need for economic progress as a basis for progress in other realms. The debate centered on how the congress would be financed, finally resolving that each group would be responsible for raising funds from its members. Further, *Clarim* was charged with making contacts in the interior of the state and acting as congress promoter. Those attending nominated Jayme de Aguiar as congress president, and Frederico Baptista de Souza as secretary, but both declined in favor of Leite and Luiz de Souza, stating that this would be more expedient. The congress organizing committee included Frederico Baptista de Souza, Augusta Eusebio de Oliveira, Norberto Rocha, Lino de Oliveira, and Sebastião de Castro, each representing one of the ten associations attending the meeting. Before adjourning, a collection was taken that raised 26$000 in on-the-spot contributions. Within a month, G.R. União Militar had raised an additional 322$000.[72]

The manifesto of the planning commission, written by Arlindo Veiga dos Santos, appeared in *Clarim* in June. Veiga was explicit about the group's objectives: "The problem of the black Brazilian is that of the absolute, complete integration of the black man in all aspects of Brazilian life (politics, society, religion, economics, labor, the military, diplomacy, etc.); he must have complete training and complete acceptance everywhere and in everything, given comparable physical, technical, intellectual and moral conditions necessary for equality before the law."[73]

Soon after the manifesto was issued, the project began to stall. Money was still coming in, but more slowly. By June members had collected 437$000 and, after expenses, had a balance of 222$800.[74] In July *Clarim* reported that a delegation had been set up in the interior city of Botucatú.[75] By August, however, Luiz de Souza began to complain that only two of the associations (União Militar and Paulistano) had sent in money.[76] Particularly frustrating to the *Clarim* organizers must have been reports in *Progresso* about the success of similar efforts elsewhere, such as the Pan-African Congress in Europe.[77] Numerous appeals for support of the congress appeared in *Clarim* over the next few months by various authors.[78]

By the end of the year it was obvious that the plan had failed. *Clarim* attacked members of the community who refused to cooperate with the project in such editorials as "Open Letter to the Ghetto Aristocrats of Botucatú."[79] This unsigned editorial was characteristic of Leite, whose criticism of blacks was as sharp—if not more so—than that he gave to whites. This quality was to earn him the respect of many, but also the enmity of key figures.

The participants in the congress planning commission went their own way. Arlindo Veiga dos Santos became involved with the monarchist movement. An active member of the Monarchist Cultural, Social, and Political Center, he wrote a "Hymn of the Brazilian Monarchist Youth" with the theme "Race! Country! Labor! Religion!" In October 1929 he started a newspaper entitled *Patria Nova* as the monarchist center's official publication.[80] The monarchists were staunchly opposed to the Republican party and therefore did not support the candidacy of São Paulo's governor, Júlio Prestes, for president. In contrast, many influential former Palmares members, including *Clarim* members and the orator Vicente Ferreira, supported Prestes, who had been courted by the Centro Cívico Palmares and who, in return, had ordered the desegregation of the state police. [81] *Progresso* was vocal in its support of Prestes, and gave extensive coverage to his effort, assuring him in a front-page article that "we will never forget this act of his Excellency Dr. Júlio Prestes."[82] The public support of Prestes may have been payment in the currency of patronage, but there were mixed feelings on the subject. Indeed, in the same issue in which *Clarim* extolled Prestes' virtues, it published an editorial by Frederico Baptista de Souza of Kosmos in which he wrote that "blacks, up to the present date, have not known of a single Governor who in his political platform has included a single line in the interest of blacks."[83]

The Afro-Brazilian community of São Paulo was thus divided in its political sentiments at a crucial crossroads for the nation. Afro-Paulistas were one of many sectors of Brazilian society disappointed with liberal democracy under the Republic. The government had excluded the Church from national politics, concentrated political power in a small group of landed elites, and upheld social, racial, and sexual inequities. Some groups, including the Church, the military, and politicians from economically weaker states, had clearly defined objectives and strong organizational support. In contrast, the members of the Afro-Paulista community had yet to fully perceive of themselves as an interest group, although great progress had been made in this direction through the black press and efforts at activism. Their political affiliations varied; some may have felt indebted to Prestes, but the Republican government had done little for Afro-Brazilians. Black newspapers championed the Empire because it had been the regime to sign the abolition decree. Arlindo Veiga dos Santos, one of the most influential voices of the era, rejected the Republicans in favor of monarchism. Veiga dos Santos was also a staunch Catholic. In this regard he embodied an influence that, until his ascension, remained tacit, namely, that of the Church on Afro-Brazilian thought.

When the revolution of 1930 ousted the Republican government, disaffected groups rallied around the provisional president, Getúlio Vargas, in the hope that his government would offer them greater opportunities. The Vargas administration's early corporatist approach encouraged the formation of large interest groups to advocate directly with the president in support of their specific agendas. This was especially urgent as delegates were to be elected in 1933 to rewrite the Constitution.

The Catholic Church took an active role as a newly restored political force. It had been forced out of the public realm after 1889, and the 1891 Constitution had cut off its state subsidies. Within months of Vargas' assumption of the presidency, the Catholic Church organized two mass demonstrations of popular support under the leadership of Sebastião Cardinal Leme. These mobilizations indicated the strength of Catholic influence on the public, a point that Vargas grasped immediately.[84] Throughout the early years of his regime, he was to court the Catholic political bloc.

In 1931 the Brazilian Federation for the Advancement of Women organized its first national convention. When its members learned that the electoral reform commission was planning to require a married woman to obtain her husband's permission to vote, they sent a delegation directly to Vargas. He agreed to their demand of unconditional suffrage, signing a decree to that effect on February 24, 1932.[85]

São Paulo's blacks, as they had done so many times before, tried the methods that seemed to work for whites. On the night of September 16, 1931, Arlindo Veiga dos Santos called a mass meeting of the Afro-Brazilian community at the Working Classes Hall. His experience with the Centro Cívico Palmares and the Congress of Black Youth had taught him about organizing and acquainted him with most of the city's black activists. Veiga dos Santos opened the meeting with a few words about its general purpose. He then called Alberto Orlando, the renowned orator, to the front. In a stirring speech, Orlando traced the history of Africans in Brazil. He spoke of the African contribution to Brazilian literature and of popular opinions about race relations in the country. The *Diario de São Paulo,* reflecting Orlando's skill in conveying the message formulated over the past decade in the pages of the black press, reported that it was "the first seeds of a campaign of uplift of the people of color in Brazil. Because of the past and what they have represented in the life of the nation, they have the right to demand a situation more in accordance with their numbers and the sacrifices they have made for Brazil." Veiga returned to the stage and spoke of the strength of the Afro-Brazilian community, saying that its members should unite as "fearless soldiers bearing the cross [of the] struggle for their goals." Many other speakers followed, lending their support to the ideas expressed by Veiga dos Santos and Orlando. The meeting closed with a call to all supporters to bring their friends and family back in two weeks to vote on the statutes of a new organization, to be known as the Frente Negra Brasileira.[86]

On September 28, the statutes were read and approved by an audience of over one thousand Afro-Brazilians, in addition to a number of whites:

> Article 1—The "Frente Negra Brasileira" is herein founded in this city of São Paulo to foster the political and social unification of the Black People of this Nation, for the affirmation of the historic rights of same, by virtue of their moral and material activity in the past, and to demand their social and political rights in the Brazilian Community.
>
> Article 2—Membership in the "Frente Negra Brasileira" is open

to all productive Black People of this Nation, of both sexes, in accordance with the fundamental laws of Brazil.

Article 3—The "FRENTE NEGRA BRASILEIRA," as a social force, will work to promote the moral, intellectual, artistic, technical, professional, and physical advancement of the Black People. It will provide social, legal, economic, and labor assistance and defense of their rights in these fields.

§—For the execution of article 3, economic cooperatives, schools for technology, science, and the arts, and sporting fields will be created as strictly Brazilian institutions.

Article 4—To achieve more fully its social objectives, the "FRENTE NEGRA BRASILEIRA," as an organized political force, will, within the legal order instituted in Brazil, present candidates for the elective representative posts of the Brazilian Black People, effecting its politico-social action within a strictly Brazilian framework.

Article 5—All the legal means of organization necessary for the attainment of the objectives of the "FRENTE NEGRA BRASILEIRA" will be utilized by as many active organizational departments as are necessary, each of which will be mandated by special regulation.

Article 6—The "FRENTE NEGRA BRASILEIRA" is directed by a "GRAND COUNCIL," sovereign and responsible, consisting of 20 members, including a Chief and Secretary. Other necessary posts will be filled according to the criteria of the President. This Council is assisted in its activities by the Auxiliary Council, composed of the district heads of the Capital.

Article 7—The President of the "FRENTE NEGRA BRASILEIRA" is the maximum authority and supreme representative of the "FRENTE NEGRA BRASILEIRA," and his action is limited by its guiding principles.

Article 8—The "FRENTE NEGRA BRASILEIRA" is represented actively and passively, juridically and extra-juridically by the "GRAND COUNCIL," in the person of the President, and in his absence by one of the other directors.

Article 9—Regulations, orders, notices, and communications issued by the "GRAND COUNCIL" have the force of law, and cases not covered in these Statutes will be regulated by laws and practices in vigor in the Nation.

Article 10—The "FRENTE NEGRA BRASILEIRA" shall only be dissolved by the unanimous will of the "GRAND COUNCIL" and a majority of the Auxiliary Council and all members in the Special General Assembly, convened by the General President, in accordance with the "Grand Council." If, by chance, it should be dissolved, its assets shall be given to a charitable society of Black People worthy of the donation.

Articles 1, 2, 6, and 7 of these Statutes are unchangeable, unless by unanimous will of the Councillors.[87]

So began the Frente Negra Brasileira, an ambitious project of social protest, advocacy for civil rights, and mutual assistance.

Consolidation: The Era of the Frente Negra

According to Arlindo Veiga, once the group had been formed, "the order was to break taboos."[88] One of the Frente's earliest actions confronted discriminatory practices at the public skating rink in downtown São Paulo, which refused to admit blacks. The Frente protested to the police, reportedly threatening violence if the rinks were not closed down. On December 17, 1931, the police department circulated a memorandum assuring "colored men the common right of frequenting public skating establishments." The memorandum went on to state that only the police had the right to force someone to leave, and that "color prejudice, if it still exists, will not be accepted as sufficient reason for this, because it is against the Law and the principles of humanity."[89] Veiga and Francisco Lucrecio recalled breaking the "footing" taboo. "Footing" was an ambulatory form of "cruising"; young people strolled around the downtown gardens on weekends for social meetings. Afro-Brazilians were made to feel unwelcome, and generally did not frequent the public parks. Frente Negra followers broke this taboo by urging members to "foot" around the parks as well.[90] The Frente's involvement over the next year in integrating the Civil Guard was another significant social protest action.

As the Frente developed, it began to follow a tradition established in the nineteenth century by other ethnic groups in São Paulo and by the Afro-Brazilian brotherhoods active in São Paulo since colonial times. The Frente provided a wide range of social services to participating members, with the difference that it was an autonomous entity. The Frente ran several businesses, among them a hair salon for men and women, a dental clinic, and a medical office, which offered membership discounts. Members could participate in the band, the theater group, or a dance group. Education was an important component; the Frente had a licensed elementary school. Women were invited to join the Black Roses women's auxiliary, and all participated in the frequent dances, picnics, and athletic events. (See Figure 1.) Each member received a photo identification card that contained complete information, including fingerprints, and was fully respected by the police as legitimate identification.[91]

One of the most important Frente functions was the *domingueira,* the

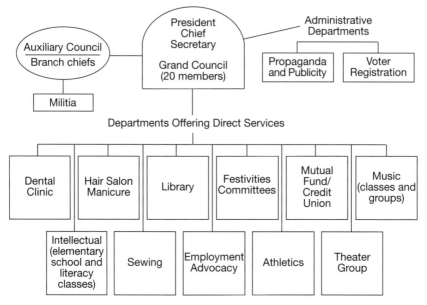

FIGURE 1. Structure of the Frente Negra Brasileira

Sunday meetings open to the public. Miriam Nicolau Ferrara describes these sessions as "doctrinaire meetings for educating and raising black consciousness. On these occasions classes were given in hygiene, child care, religion, and catechism; philatelic conferences were held; the poetry of Luiz Gama was discussed, as were national [historic] events. Also, blacks were encouraged to deposit their salaries in the Caixa Econômica [bank] to facilitate the acquisition of private homes."[92] Aristides Barbosa was one of the teenage members of the Frente Negra jazz and samba band. He points out that the *domingueiras* were social as well as educational: "The Frente Negra had a very big main hall which held more or less 200 people. Every Sunday we all met there. The directors came in and made their presentations. We used to call it "*fazendo cabeça,*" that is, raising the consciousness of blacks. . . . Then later, in the second part, we came in with the band, and people read poetry—it was very happy. Lots of music, lots of samba, lots of fun."[93] The *domingueiras* began around six in the evening and went on until almost midnight. Many people who weren't interested in the social programs found their way into the *domingueiras*. Barbosa remembers his brother, who never joined the Frente Negra but went to the Sunday sessions "because he liked to romance the girls. They had lots of girls. He later married a Frente Negra girl."[94]

The Frente created a social nexus in the community where people fell in love, found godparents for their children, and made useful social contacts. The directors actively recruited professionals and well-known people in the community such as Vicente Ferreira. José Correia Leite recalled, "The Frente Negra Brasileira had many teachers, doctors, lawyers, intellectuals—many important people, and that attracted many blacks. [Many] left the newspaper [*O Clarim da Alvorada*]—Jayme de Aguiar, Vicente Ferreira, they all went to the Frente Negra."[95]

Membership quickly grew into the thousands in the city and soon spread into the interior of São Paulo and to the neighboring states of Minas Gerais and Rio Grande do Sul. One of the Frente's strong points was its internal organization, which was called "regimentation." The group divided the city and its surrounding region into districts.[96] Each district was assigned a leader responsible for collecting dues. This process was tightly monitored. Occasionally doubts were raised about the trustworthiness of the recruiting/collecting teams. The Frente took prompt action against embezzlers, reporting them to the police and publishing their names in the official Frente Negra newspaper, *A Voz da Raça*.[97]

As membership grew, the Frente began to branch out in terms of new activities and national organization. Early on, the Frente sought a media outlet to help attract members. Initially, Arlindo Veiga dos Santos hoped to use the *Clarim da Alvorada* for such a purpose. Given Veiga and Leite's shared experience in the failed Congress of Black Youth, it was probably a reasonable expectation. During the revolution of 1930, however, Veiga had made public his political leanings in favor of the monarchists and Integralists, a view the *Clarim* group did not support. The struggle between *Clarim* and the Frente leadership became violent in early 1932, so the Frente went to *Progresso*, the monthly paper directed by Lino Guedes and Argentino Wanderley. A group from *Progresso* had formed to generate a mass committee to pressure the municipal government to erect a bust of Luiz Gama in downtown São Paulo. After 1930, when the bust was erected on the Largo de Arouche, the directors resigned.[98] Under *Progresso*'s new proprietorship, the Frente published official communications. In March 1933 it published the first issue of its own journal, *A Voz da Raça* (The Voice of the Race).

The *Voz* became a critical instrument for extending the Frente network. It was sold by Frente representatives across the country, from Rio Grande do Sul in the far south to Bahia in the northeast. Frente Negra chapters began to spring up in many cities, although the core of the network consisted of approximately twenty chapters in São Paulo, Minas Gerais, and Rio Grande do Sul.[99] It is very possible, however, that unofficial and unaffiliated "Frente Negras" were formed in other parts of the country where the *Voz da Raça* was distributed.

The growth of membership also brought a growth in income, with which the Frente Negra expanded its services. Each member contributed 1$000 *réis* upon joining. In 1933, the Frente purchased its own headquarters building, from which it expanded its operations. It assisted its members in disputes with employers on an individual case advocacy basis. Frente directors wrote letters on behalf of its members to the state Department of Labor. Case proceedings and correspondence were regularly published in *A Voz da Raça*. Florestan Fernandes describes Frente intervention on behalf of those of its members who were domestic workers.[100] The accredited elementary school and adult literacy courses also provided needed training in the community. The Frente Negra Brasileira had tapped into a real need at a propitious time.

Several characteristics of the organization contributed to its early success. It invoked the power of the spoken word, not unlike the preaching tradition of the black church in the United States, to direct and shape political ideology. It had proven successes with public activism in the desegregation of the parks, the skating rink, and the state police. Its well-coordinated organizational structure facilitated financial and membership growth. Recreational events provided a social nexus. While all these were important keys to the Frente's success, perhaps the most important was its ability to deliver vital services to members. For the constituents, these were more important than questions of political ideology, which remained more a concern of the directorate than of the general membership. The Frente recognized this strength and capitalized on it to draw members away from rival organizations. According to Moreira and Leite, "They accused the *Clarim* group of not taking action, of never having done anything for blacks except talk and criticize. [They said] 'our followers don't need intellectuals. We need more action and less talk.'"[101]

The ideology of the Frente was nevertheless of great significance, because its leaders sought to represent the interests of Afro-Brazilians across the entire nation. They intended to do so in the arena of party politics. The Frente became the first Afro-Brazilian organization to enter electoral politics with the candidacy of Arlindo Veiga dos Santos as a delegate to the Constituent Assembly. On April 29, 1933, Veiga dos Santos announced his candidacy as an independent. The Frente Negra had considered registering as a political party in order to run him as its candidate, but decided it would not have sufficient time to do so for the May elections.[102] Veiga's short and unsuccessful campaign helped solidify Frente support outside the capital. A "campaign caravan" visited Frente branches in Sorocaba, Itú, Rio Claro, Campinas, Limeira, Jundiaí, and Itatiba. The effort was also apparently helpful in earning respect for Afro-Brazilians, or at least for those in the Frente Negra, as an electoral force. The Rio Claro branch had the support of the local political boss, João

"O PRECONCEITO de CÔR, no BRASIL, SÓ NÓS, OS NEGROS, O PODEMOS SENTIR."— (Isaltino V. dos Santos)

A VOZ DA RAÇA

ÓRGÃO OFICIAL DA "FRENTE NEGRA BRASILEIRA"
SEMANARIO INDEPENDENTE

DEUS
PATRIA
RAÇA e
FAMILIA

A Frente Negra Brasileira

e um artigo do Snr. Austregesilo de Athayde

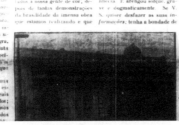

AGINDO DE MÁ FE

ILL. 8. *A Voz da Raça*, an official publication of the Frente Negra Brasileira. The masthead quotation is "Color Prejudice, in Brazil, Only We, the Blacks, Can Feel." The lower right corner of the masthead includes the Frente's slogan: "God, Country, Race, and Family."

Fina Sobrinho, who placed his name on ballots along with Veiga's. *A Voz da Raça* reported the attendance of Grand Council members at a gathering at the presidential palace, at which the guests showed great interest in the Frente's activities. One woman even ordered a subscription to the *Voz*.[103] Failing in its bid for a seat in the Constituent Assembly, the Frente postponed registration as a political party but oriented its activist strategies in the clientelistic pattern of appealing to the executive rather than the legislative branch to seek concessions for its constituents. In return for Getúlio Vargas' mild endorsements, the Frente threw its firm support behind him and gained great prestige in the black community for what was perceived as political leverage with the president of the Republic.[104]

As a candidate, Veiga dos Santos was forced to explain his political philosophy. He focused on a policy that attacked the democratic regime of the First Republic and what he perceived as a communist threat. Democracy, he felt, was a foreign aberration. "Any type of democracy, of egalitarianism, does not serve us," he wrote. "We do not want to be slaves to foreign errors."[105]

Veiga advocated the "nationalization of commerce, and government protection of agriculture and industry," which, he felt, would "lower the cost of living because we would export more national products."[106] He argued that this could be achieved through "educating the people organized in trade corporatives, whose techniques and functions, outlined in the colonial period, were restricted in the democratic era." This argument apparently combines basic corporatist ideology with socialist concepts of nationalization. Veiga argued ardently against socialism and communism, however. He warned of the "communist tyranny threatening our traditions, our homes, our waning economy and our land," which the "Muscovite bandits" would use as the "treasury to finance the judeo-cosmopolitan universal Bolshevik revolution."

Veiga supported Hitler, whom he defended as an advocate of patriotism and racial solidarity. He excused Hitler's persecution of Jews as the "natural exaggeration of one who has suffered so much Jewish cosmopolitanism." Veiga did, however, oppose Aryanism within the Brazilian context. He criticized the "mania of countless imbeciles who seek to make the Brazilian people an Aryan race, therein destroying the *mestiça* [mixed] race that the Brazilian is!"[107]

This philosophy was supplementary to the four basic points that made up his platform, all easily understood and endorsed by the majority of Afro-Paulistanos. First, he called for "Brazil for the Brazilians." Veiga transposed Marcus Garvey's advocacy of "Africa for the Africans" to reflect the patriotic orientation of Afro-Brazilians. Planks two and three continued the support of rights for blacks vis-à-vis immigrants: an "end to concessions to foreigners" and "suspension of immigration for twenty years."[108]

Veiga addressed the issue of race in his fourth plank. He called for the "moral, intellectual, physical and economic improvement of the black and mixed population so that they may subsequently ASSIMILATE NATIONALLY AND RACIALLY."[109] It is in this light that we can interpret his 1929 call in the manifesto for the Congress of Black Youth for the "absolute, complete integration of Blacks in all aspects of Brazilian life." Separatism, said Veiga, was the "dominion of international Jewish bankers."[110] Later he wrote that "if the spirit of the black Brazilian were one of separatism, I would be the first to oppose it."[111]

Social integration and the unification of blacks under a single front were twin goals of the Frente Negra. An often-repeated phrase was "separate now to unite later."[112] Such an ideology posited separatism not as an end in itself, but as a means to achieve integration through the use of interest group politics. Veiga's specification of "racial integration" endorsed the prevailing ideology of "whitening."

What brought Arlindo Veiga, an intelligent man who had shaped a powerful organization, to this line of political thought? In support of Afro-Brazilian civil rights and equity, he openly embraced anti-Semitism and ethnic persecution. A set of beliefs fraught with contradictions may be explained in part by the general context of Brazilian political ideology. During the 1930s, many different avenues of political thought flourished in Brazil. The large number of Italian and German immigrants led to the formation of groups supportive of Fascist and Nazi ideology. One such group, the Integralists, created a strong Fascist party. The Integralists were particularly influential in promoting anti-Semitism in the early 1930s.[113] Raul Joviano de Amaral, one of the Frente Negra leaders, underscored the impact of foreign ideas on the black community:

> When the Frente Negra was founded in mid-'31, São Paulo saw the enthusiasm with which the Italian community embraced the new Italian political ideas that arose with the advent of Fascism. Meetings in the [Italian] community were presided over by people in black shirts, who gave each other the Fascist salute. . . . The Germans, in turn, were enthused about Hitler's rise to power. The first stirrings of Integralism appeared at that point, similar in many respects to the monarchist [*patrianovista*] movement, directed by Dr. Arlindo Veiga dos Santos. . . . Because of this, the choice of Dr. Arlindo Veiga dos Santos for the presidency of the Frente Negra was accepted by some blacks with reservation, including the group formed around *O Clarim d'Alvorada*.[114]

The Catholic Church served as a bridge between Integralism and Frente Negra philosophy under Veiga. The Church had great influence in São Paulo where, even though the percentage of Catholics had declined after 1872, 92 percent of the state's population still described themselves as such in 1940.[115] African religions were banned, and cultural conditions did not permit even the illicit continuation of African traditions as had occurred in the northeast. The Afro-Brazilian community was exposed to Catholic political ideology, and Veiga was deeply attached to the Church. As a young boy attending the Church of São Bento, he had been singled out as a future leader and encouraged in his studies. Although it is not clear how he attained his title of "Doctor," often used merely as a sign of respect, Veiga did become a teacher in the church school.[116] Veiga borrowed the motto of the Integralists, "God, Homeland, Family" for the *Voz da Raça,* which used "God, Homeland, Race, and Family." In the Frente's regular meetings, Veiga upheld the Integralist doctrine of "total obedience to the Supreme Chief."[117] In 1933, setting this doctrine in the context of Afro-Brazilian history, he wrote: "In Palmares no one challenged its leader, Zambi [*sic*]. Likewise, the members of the Frente Negra

ILL. 9. Arlindo Veiga dos Santos

must not challenge the leader of the nation, because nothing comes to a people that is not through divine order. Nor should the members of the Frente Negra challenge their own leaders. . . . The Grand Council, in all it does, does it correctly, although at times it might not seem so from the point of view of an outside observer."[118]

If we understand Integralism as one of the most compelling popular ideologies of the day, and remember that Bexiga (the site of the Frente's headquarters) was the heart of both the Italian and the Afro-Brazilian activist communities in São Paulo, Veiga's ideologies are easier to place in context. Although many elements of Integralism are evident in his philosophy, he was known as a monarchist, and Veiga identified himself as an "organic syndicalist." This suggests that, in contemporary terms, there were concrete distinctions between Veiga and the Integralists. These differences were rooted in the ways Veiga and others tried to adapt prevailing ideologies to address Afro-Brazilian interests. It nonetheless remains the case that the Frente Negra's platform of liberation was problematic for many in the activist community. Whereas the black press was articulating and advancing a political ideology rooted in the Afro-Brazilian experience, Veiga was embracing oppressive Catholic and European theories.

The Frente came into conflict almost immediately with the group from *Clarim,* which opposed not only Veiga's right-wing sympathies but also his authoritarianism. When the first meeting of the Frente was held in September, Leite was not permitted to enter.[119] *Clarim* nonetheless gave its early support to the Frente. Leite no longer controlled the newspaper completely; he remained an editor, but the paper was under the direction of the Clarim association headed by the "elder statesman" Frederico Baptista de Souza. In November 1931 *Clarim* announced the formation of the League of the Friends of Struggle, headquartered (as was *Clarim*) in Leite's living room. The membership included the managerial staff of the newspaper: Secretary Luiz Gonzaga Braga, Editor Henrique Cunha, and News Editor José Correia Leite, along with Gervasio de Moraes and several others. Conspicuously absent was Frederico Baptista de Souza.[120]

Within a month, Leite had accepted Arlindo Veiga's invitation to sit on the Frente's Grand Council, which was still short of its full twenty members.[121] It is unclear how this came about; Veiga may have wanted to avoid creating a deeper rift, and Correia Leite may have sought an opportunity to redirect the Frente from within. This apparent attempt at either concession or cooptation was unsuccessful. The Frente wanted the *Clarim* group to "operate a black journal under the aegis of the Frente."[122] In protest, the League of the Friends of Struggle declared a strike at *Clarim* against "the Gandhi at the

Front." This may have been a reference to Frederico Baptista de Souza's acquiescence to the Frente's pressures. The result was the cancellation of the February 1932 issue.[123] Striking *Clarim* members replaced the February *Clarim* with a new journal, *A Chibata* ("The Whip"), replete with stinging satire and thinly veiled attacks aimed at the Frente leadership.

A Chibata's references were fairly obvious. In an article entitled "Patria Velha" ("Old Nation"—a play on "New Nation," as the monarchists were known), the editors ridiculed Veiga's ideology. They wrote, "[We] must abandon our race because blacks were born to live oppressed [*tapeado*], we must be illiterate, but we'd better know how to say our prayers—if not, we can't stay in the old nation."[124] Leite recalled that Veiga's political philosophy was an issue of extreme concern.[125] *Chibata* also challenged the morality and ethics of some Grand Council members. They made several attacks against "Xico" (Sebastião) da Costa, whom Correia Leite accused of unspecified "immoral acts."[126] Although the only editor listed was *homem negro* ("black man"), the Frente knew exactly who was behind *Chibata*. Francisco Lucrecio described the second issue as the "last straw."[127] One night in March the Frente Negra sent a group of men to ransack Leite's home and destroy the printing press, with Leite and his family present. Leite stood aside as they ripped out the plates for the third issue of *Chibata*. They threatened him as well, but stopped short of physical violence.[128] The incident caused considerable scandal and was covered in the São Paulo mainstream newspapers.[129] Although *Clarim* reappeared immediately to denounce the attack, it only published two more issues, the last appearing in May 1932. Many of its members had left during 1931 and 1932 to join the Frente by special invitation from Arlindo Veiga. Others, including Leite, joined a new and popular club, the Clube Negra de Cultura Social (Black Social Culture Club). There they started an Intellectual Department and eventually another newspaper, *Cultura*.

O Clarim was not the only Afro-Brazilian group to oppose the Frente. On May 13, 1932, two months before an anti-Vargas revolt in São Paulo, the black lawyer J. Guaraná Santana founded a socialist group known as the Radical Nationalist Party, commonly known as the Black Legion.[130] It opposed Getúlio Vargas, and therefore was able to organize in São Paulo's anti-Getúlio climate. In April 1933 Santana began publishing *Brasil Novo* (New Brazil), a weekly socialist paper. Its scope was international, and it covered European developments in detail. Interestingly, its only news on the black community took the form of attacks on the monarchist sentiments of Arlindo and his brother Isaltino Veiga dos Santos. Santana felt their position was absurd, considering that blacks had been slaves under the Empire.[131] The Frente rarely withstood attacks quietly, and was quick to denounce black "enemies" as "Judases of the race" or "false blacks."[132] Guaraná Santana's attacks came

ILL. 10. *Brasil Novo*, a socialist newspaper founded by J. Guaraná Santana, an Afro-Brazilian lawyer and activist with the Radical Nationalist party.

shortly after *A Voz da Raça* had begun publication, which gave the Frente a convenient outlet to respond. The journal issued a petition protesting Santana's allegations and reaffirming members' confidence in the Frente leadership. Santana's efforts lasted only a short time, however, and probably less than one year. He was eventually jailed under the Vargas regime for subversive activity.[133]

Despite controversy and ideological differences, the Frente maintained amicable relationships with many of São Paulo's Afro-Brazilian associations. The Frente remained the most powerful, but other groups continued to emerge and enjoy popularity. The Carnival groups expanded as they moved from marginality into mainstream popular culture.[134] Other organizations flourished; among the most popular was the Clube Negra de Cultura Social. The CNCS had begun as an entity devoted to sports, but gradually expanded its activities to include recreation and intellectual departments. Leite led a group of *Clarim* members to the CNCS after the attack by the Frente. In January 1934 the club's Intellectual Department began publishing a monthly journal, *Cultura*. Its first issue featured a photo of Leite's home after the ransacking with the words, "No comment! We are affirming from whence we came. And with this baptism of fire we will do everything possible . . . to continue in action toward our ideals."[135] Leite was not part of the directorate, but contributed articles. Even Mario Vasconcelos of Bahia continued sending news and articles concerning the African diaspora, such as a biographical note on Toussaint L'Ouverture.[136] In 1935 the paper changed its name to *O Clarim*.

Some groups attempted to replicate the Frente Negra's program. The May 1935 issue of *O Clarim* carried a notice about the formation of the Colored People's Collective Alliance, under the direction of Ernesto Ludgero J. Maria and Antônio Zeferino. Their program was to include "medical, pharmaceutical, dental, and legal assistance, funerals, schools, professional and business training, job placement, and aid to the needy, blind, and handicapped."[137] It is unclear whether the attempt was successful, but the group's structure does indicate that the Frente served as a model for successful activism in the Afro-Brazilian community. Years later, in 1945, José Correia Leite and other activists sought to institute a similarly comprehensive program under the Association of Brazilian Blacks (Associação dos Negros Brasileiros).[138]

Despite attempts at activism within the community, no group achieved the level of organization and influence enjoyed by the Frente Negra Brasileira. By the mid-1930s, black political activism was concentrated in the Frente Negra. Its massive support made the opposition of smaller groups relatively insignificant. The *Voz da Raça,* with its mass readership, apparently made smaller club newspapers extraneous. Even the popular Clube Negra de Cultura Social could not maintain either *Cultura* or *O Clarim* for more than one year each. Many clubs published their news and announcements in the social pages of *A Voz*. In this sense, the Frente operated as an unofficial "umbrella" organization. Frente Negra services and social events at other clubs complemented each other. Aristides Barbosa, a Frente Negra member, recalls that many members took advantage of the services of the Frente and spent their recreation time at dances sponsored by other clubs.[139] Such a high level of concentration thus made the closing of the Frente Negra devastating to the Afro-Brazilian community.

In late 1935 a military revolt in the northeast prompted Getúlio Vargas to declare a ninety-day state of emergency, which he renewed five times. By mid-1936 political observers began to sense that Vargas would not step down at the end of his four-year term. As potential presidential candidates began to maneuver for position in late 1936, Vargas quietly orchestrated a campaign that undermined each candidate. Then, on November 10, 1937, he had the congressional palace surrounded and distributed copies of a new constitution, the *Estado Novo* (New State). Under this constitution Vargas assumed near-dictatorial powers, which lasted until 1945.[140]

Vargas dissolved all political parties on December 2, 1937. The move took many of his staunch supporters by surprise, particularly the Integralists, who were effectively destroyed. Plinio Salgado, the leader of the Integralists, retreated to São Paulo, betrayed and defeated.[141] The case was much the same with the Frente Negra, which had registered as a political party and had consistently supported Getúlio Vargas. Aristides Barbosa recalls the day the Frente Negra Brasileira officially closed.

> At the time we had a theater group in the Frente Negra. . . . On the day the Frente Negra closed, we were putting on a play. Between the first and second acts, the curtains closed. Then Justiniano Costa, who was the president . . . opened the curtains and appeared, crying, with a telegram. He read the telegram. "By determination of the national government under Getúlio Vargas, et cetera, all political parties in Brazil are dissolved, and the Frente Negra is included in the dissolution of the political parties." The play ended right there. Everyone got up and started crying. And that's how the Frente Negra officially ended.[142]

In an attempt to salvage the organization, the Frente changed its name to the União Negra Brasileira (Brazilian Black Union), with Raul Joviano de Amaral as president. The renamed group lasted only until May 13, 1938, however, when the Afro-Brazilian community commemorated the fiftieth anniversary of abolition.[143]

The Frente Negra Brasileira was the culmination of a fifty-year process of self-determination as a modern Afro-Brazilian community came to life and took its place in the city of São Paulo. Out of many different identities and objectives, there came to the fore a popular ideology embodied by the Frente Negra. The orientation of identity was the first phase of this process. As Afro-Brazilians settled in the capital, discrimination and isolation enhanced their awareness of national and racial identity. Black social clubs and journals reinforced a sense of racial community; the dissemination of news from elsewhere in the African diaspora deepened this perception of an international ethnic community based on blackness.

Afro-Paulistanos created elements of alternative and parallel worlds in the psychosocial sense but were unable to fully sustain them with complementary institutions. The impetus for banding together in race-based associations therefore could not have translated into a separatist strategy for those who sought the material rewards of the modern economy. Without sufficient avenues for entrepreneurship within the black milieu, it was therefore necessary to wrest those benefits from the larger society.

The aspirants used racial identity as a base for ultimate integration—in Arlindo Veiga's words, to "separate now to unite later." Their strategy, however, could not be applied in a vacuum; it needed to be consistent with, and effective in, the larger political culture. When the Centro Cívico Palmares was founded, São Paulo was still functioning under the political culture of patronage, a remnant of the agricultural oligarchy in power during the Republic. When the organization appealed to politicians for assistance, its influence depended on the degree to which it could deliver the support of an interest group. Because voting rights were limited by literacy, the drive by black organizations to educate their members was directly related to amassing political power. By the late 1920s, black collectives had decided that the key to their success would be a unified interest group of voting citizens.

Did they achieve their objectives? They might have fallen short of the complete and colorblind integration envisioned by Arlindo Veiga dos Santos. Yet the black activists of the 1920s and 1930s achieved important victories. Their most significant immediate success was the prevention of legalized segregation through their protest activities. Beyond that, they left a lasting legacy in the history of Brazilian race relations. For the first time, Afro-Brazilians articulated ethnic unity as a national political strategy. Blacks around the country, but especially in the southern region, began not only to accept a corporate identity that included all people of African descent but also to use that identity as the basis for new modes of social and political dialogue. The Frente Negra's registration of a national Afro-Brazilian political party was one such effort. Many of the ideas that took root during this time were to flower during the black consciousness movement of the 1970s.

One of the most significant contributions of blacks in São Paulo was their effort to redefine the social meanings of race. Afro-Brazilians embraced an ethnic identity including both blacks and mulattoes, and sought to imbue the term *negro* with pride and positive associations. In addition to confronting racism, they contributed to the Afro-Brazilian cultural heritage through their associations, journals, and social networks.

In their own words, this was a sector of the Afro-Paulista community whose members demanded "complete and total integration" when they ran up against obstacles to their aspirations. They did not necessarily represent others who either had achieved integration via traditional modes of access or who were not seeking integration at all. These other responses are also major strategies of self-determination in the post-abolition African diaspora. The following chapters examine a separatist strategy as it evolved in what some consider the "heart" of black Brazil, the capital city of Salvador in Bahia.

CHAPTER 5

Salvador

AFRO-BAHIA IN AN ERA OF CHANGE

𝒯he Frente Negra Brasileira came to Bahia in the person of Marcos Rodrigues dos Santos, inspector general for the state chapter. One of his first official visits was to the hundredth anniversary celebration of the Sociedade Protectora dos Desvalidos on September 16, 1932. The Sociedade was one of the rare black institutions to possess its own headquarters, an aged but roomy townhouse on the Rua do Cruzeiro, the short street leading from the Terreiro de Jesus to the São Francisco church and monastery. The celebration took place in the main salon, filled to capacity with high-backed chairs. As with all important gatherings of the Protectora, the anniversary program began with the benediction of the group's patron saint, followed by the speeches of invited guests. To all appearances, there was little to distinguish this gathering of staid and respectable black folk from their counterparts at Frente Negra headquarters in São Paulo. It was to them that dos Santos turned for help in arranging a venue for his opening meeting in late November. Dos Santos hoped to organize a series of conferences "of a social and educational nature, for the congregation of our black and brown family, which up to now has only been the cart-horse of the Brazilian economy, exploited by savage politicking." Failing to elicit any response from the Sociedade's leadership, dos Santos nonetheless invited its members to the inauguration he had subsequently arranged at the hall of a nearby beneficent society. The only formal action taken by the Sociedade was to record dos Santos' letters into the minutes of the December meeting without further notation.[1]

Little is known about Marcos Rodrigues dos Santos. Born in the city of Santo Antonio de Jesus, he moved to Salvador at the age of fourteen. In a newspaper interview, dos Santos described himself as a "wandering Jew," having lived in numerous cities in Bahia, Minas Gerais, and São Paulo.[2] When he wrote to the Sociedade Protectora, he had only just returned to Salvador from a stay of several years in São Paulo. His roots, therefore, were not very deep in the Bahian capital, which may have hampered his ability to organize.

Despite his inability to win support from well-established Afro-Bahian organizations such as the Protectora, dos Santos found a niche with another constituency. He convened the first meeting of the Frente Negra of Bahia on November 15 at provisional headquarters and, by January 1933, had established a permanent office. The Bahian branch focused on literacy, long a personal concern of dos Santos, and the "moral elevation of the race," with a strong emphasis on family. Some of the Frente's activities seemed much like those of its counterparts in São Paulo, such as their visits to the tombs of abolitionists on the anniversary of abolition. In other respects, Bahia's Frente Negra took on very different dimensions.

When dos Santos organized a series of rallies of black workers in the commerical districts, he characterized the meetings' focus as literacy and suffrage in statements to the press. To the black working class, however, the Frente appeared to be a new avenue for voicing their concerns. Although dos Santos clearly expressed his desire to establish an organization similar in focus to the Frente Negra in São Paulo, it apparently proceeded along the lines of labor activism. The Frente's rallies were held in such areas as Sete Portas, the Largo do Tanque, and the docks, commercial areas where the city's predominantly black laborers and tradesmen were concentrated. Trade unions were an expression of class mobilization involving people of many ethnicities at the national level, and were therefore not a focus of this study. Yet the workers' movements of the early twentieth century may well have been a primary form of organized activism for some African descendants, especially men in urban areas. Afro-Brazilian men were well represented in trades that became unionized under Vargas' corporatist government between 1930 and 1937. In Bahia the unions opened a new avenue to political positions. Prior to 1930, the few blacks in public office were hand-picked by political bosses, although the story of Bahia's Frente Negra suggests that the autonomy of the unions was short-lived.[3]

In March 1933, the Frente Negra Bahiana announced Dionysio Silva as its candidate to the national constitutional congress. Two days before the election, however, the Frente withdrew its support in favor of an "eclectic ticket," in dos Santos' words, "of recognized candidates without regard to color preference." The organization itself was eventually absorbed by Ação Social Proletária (Proletarian Social Action) under the direction of Juracy Magalhães, one of approximately twenty labor unions under the control of the government.[4] The system of political clientelism in Bahia had adapted to the rise of unions by forcing them into the spheres of patronage.

The fate of the Frente Negra's political activity in Bahia was but one indication of the organization's inability to transplant itself from São Paulo. Another critical difference was the lack of support from Bahia's black middle
class. In São Paulo, race was a barrier to upward mobility at most levels of the
socioeconomic spectrum. In Bahia, where they were in the majority, people of
color were able to use other sanctioned mechanisms of ascent through most
levels of the middle class, with race becoming a serious obstacle only at the
uppermost strata. The same type of people that formed the backbone of the
Frente Negra's support in São Paulo were often able to successfully advance in
Bahian society. Middle-class Afro-Bahians did not embrace the Frente Negra
and were particularly offended by the marches that symbolically linked blackness with poverty.[5] These Afro-Bahians possessed means of social mobility
and were therefore unlikely to search for alternative methods of access. They
thus did not belong to the sector most associated with social activism, the alternative integrationists.[6]

Because race played such a different role in the public discourse of Bahia, the Frente Negra could not function as it had in São Paulo. Dos Santos
discovered that "worker" was a far more viable social identity than "black."
This raises important questions about the nature of Afro-Brazilian activism in
the post-abolition era. Further research into black labor unionism will shed
light on the relative importance of class-based and race-based interest group
formation. If blackness was not an operative category in ethnic activism, were
there other forms of ethnic identity expressed by African descendants in Bahia? Salvador had few race-based activist organizations, and civil rights did
not become a prominent issue in post-abolition politics.[7] This absence is incongruous if one accepts the premise in Chapter 2 that abolition signaled the
start of a new era in struggles for self-determination throughout the African
diaspora. The relative lack of ethnic activism in Salvador suggests that Afro-
Bahians took no new measures to broaden opportunities for African descendants in response to the new conditions of freedom. It also appears curious
that the idea of a black political party did not gain broad support in a city in
which blacks made up nearly two-thirds of the population.[8]

What appears to be an anomalous situation prevailing in Salvador may
be substantially reinterpreted if a new set of premises is accepted. First, the
demographic ethnicity studied by social scientists who predetermine the operative categories is not always the same as the social ethnicity experienced by
people in their everyday lives. In Salvador, the reality of ethnicity might have
been not a majority of "blacks" but, rather, many smaller minorities described
by more discrete determinants. A community divided into subgroups of ethnic
Nagôs, middle-class Brazilian mulattoes, Angolan candomblé practitioners,
and so on does not offer the same basis for political consensus that was a

necessary precondition for the creation of a mass interest group such as that found in São Paulo. In addition to ethnic differences, socioeconomic class was an important stratifier within the Afro-Bahian population. These schisms surfaced, for example, when the Frente Negra organized rallies of poor blacks. This chapter looks beyond the statistics of race in Salvador as recorded in censuses to explore a far more complex and nuanced Afro-Brazilian community.

Second, conditions in Salvador were not conducive to political mobilization along the same lines as in São Paulo. São Paulo was undergoing revolutionary changes in its demographic, economic, and political composition at a rate and an intensity unique in Brazilian history. The Republic catapulted its agrarian entrepreneurs into leadership roles in national politics and economics, which in turn facilitated the development of the capital into Latin America's premier industrial hub and magnet for immigrants. São Paulo became the epicenter for the power struggles of a new republic with a new economy and even a new population. When, in the 1920s, the decline of coffee's economic supremacy flung the door of political opportunity wide open, armed conflict broke out in the heart of the city, political organizations with paramilitary brigades proliferated, and a huge foreign contingent independent of the ties of patronage and clientelism represented their interests through new political structures.

Although Salvador also experienced changes under the Republic and into the Vargas era, its pace of change could not compare with that of São Paulo. There was no reorganization of the economy to introduce sectors capable of challenging the traditional power of the agricultural and commercial interests that had dominated political control of Bahia since colonial times. Salvador's transition into the twentieth century emphasized the continuity of a political culture in which popular interest groups played no significant autonomous role. The Republican years were the heyday of *coronelismo,* when the perquisites of political office were vigorously contested by men powerful in commerce, industry, and agriculture. The absorption of the Frente Negra of Bahia into the political sphere of Juracy Magalhães may well be an example of *coronelismo* in action. Mass constituencies were not viable as a power base in Salvador because its political culture was shaped by fiefdoms unable or unwilling to forge broader interest-based coalitions.[9] In contrast, the dismantling of extant local power bases and Getúlio Vargas' encouragement of corporatist politics created a greater potential for popular empowerment in São Paulo. Afro-Brazilians in São Paulo had options and incentives different from those of their counterparts in Salvador. Because of all these differences, it cannot be expected that expressions of the struggles for self-determination would follow the same politically oriented contours as had been the case in São Paulo.

This leads to the third and final premise, which is that the field of struggle in Salvador was not as quiet as it appeared. Manifestations of self-determination outside the strictly defined political world of formal parties and electoral processes could nonetheless have had important political repercussions. The most visible ethnic activism on the part of Afro-Bahian collectives between 1888 and 1938 was directed toward the protection of cultural freedoms. These included what became known as the "African" Carnival clubs and the many congregations of candomblé.[10] The simple act of manifesting African-based cultural forms was a political act of self-determination in that it counteracted the restrictive ideologies of the dominant culture. Viewed in that light, the underlying objectives of Afro-Brazilians did not differ so dramatically in the northeast and the south. Afro-Brazilians viewed abolition as an opportunity to redefine their position in Brazilian society and culture. In both areas, when the promise of freedom fell short, they staked out social spaces to be conquered through collective activism. By so doing, they forced Brazilian society to open its doors to a population of African descent no longer willing to accept the terms of its exclusion.

Afro-Brazilians in Post-Abolition Salvador: A Statistical Overview

In 1890 Bahia was Brazil's second most populous state, with slightly under two million residents. Nine percent (174,412) lived in the city of Salvador, which was more than twice the size of São Paulo (64,934). Most of Salvador's residents were people of color, classified in the 1890 census as *prêto* (black), *caboclo* (indigenous), and *mestiço* (mixed). The 1940 census replaced the 1890 designations of "race" with "color" labels, introducing the terms *pardo* (brown) to include mixed people of various combinations, *amarelo* (yellow) for Asians, and *côr não declarada* (undeclared color). The undeclared were combined with the *pardo* category in all but two of the 1940 census tables on the assumption that these were persons of at least partial African descent who would be offended by a designation as nonwhite.[11] I have therefore included those of undeclared race in aggregate figures for "Afro-Brazilians" in 1940. As is evident from Table 7, the racial composition of Salvador remained fairly constant over the five post-abolition decades. It was not greatly affected by immigration; in fact, the foreign population declined from 10,922 in 1890 to 5,439 in 1940. These statistics, however, fail to reveal the fundamental changes in the city's *ethnic* composition as the African-born majority of the early nineteenth century gave way to a new majority of Brazilian-born persons of color.

Whereas the post-abolition years saw a dramatic influx of Afro-Brazilians from the countryside to the city in São Paulo, census returns offer no evidence of a comparable phenomenon in Salvador. The proportion of Afro-Brazilians

TABLE 7. *Persons of African Descent in the City of Salvador, 1890 and 1940*

1890			1940		
Color	Number	% of city	Color	Number	% of city
Prêto	46,007	26.3	*Prêto*	76,472	26.3
Mestiço	61,243	35.1	*Pardo*	111,674	38.4
Afro-Brazilians[a]	107,250	61.4	Afro-Brazilians[a]	188,405	64.9

SOURCE: Brazil, Instituto Brasileiro de Geografia e Estatística, *Recenseamento Geral do Brasil, 1⁰ de Setembro de 1940* (Rio de Janeiro: Serviço Gráfico do Instituto Brasileiro de Geografia e Estatística, 1950).

[a]The category of Afro-Brazilians includes *prêtos* and *mestiços* for 1890 and *prêtos, pardos,* and *côr não declarada* for 1940.

in Salvador (using the aggregate categories just described), in relation to the rest of the state, decreased from 8.4 percent in 1890 to 6.7 percent in 1940, both proportions slightly lower than those for the total population. In contrast, São Paulo's Afro-Brazilian population made up only 2.7 percent of the state total in 1890 but rose to 12.6 percent in 1940 (see Table 8).

The large size of the eighteen districts in the 1890 census for Salvador precludes detailed inquiry as to whether race had an impact on the residential distribution of Afro-Brazilians. In 1890, Salvador's 107,250 *prêtos* and *mestiços* formed 61.4 percent of the city's population. Although each district tended to proportionally reflect the city's racial demography, the census noted several concentrations. *Prêtos* and *mestiços* exceeded by 10 percent or more their city average in seven districts: Paço (71 percent), Pirajá (77 percent), Itapoan (82 percent), Paripe (83 percent), S. Miguel de Cotegipe (87 percent), Piedade de Mattoim (86 percent), and Ilha da Maré (97 percent). Separating by color, the largest concentration of *prêtos* was in Piedade de Mattoim (26 percent of citywide population; 44 percent of district). The largest concentration of *mestiços* was in Ilha da Maré (35 percent of citywide population; 72 percent of district). Whites were distributed fairly evenly around the city, with only the district of Penha exceeding proportional representation by over 10 percent (32 percent of citywide population; 43 percent of district). Whites were underrepresented in Itapoan, where they made up only 4.9 percent of the district's population. *Caboclos,* only 6.5 percent of the city's population, were nearly a third (28.6 percent) of the population of the district of Passé.

Because domestic and service workers lived close to (or in) their place of work, as in São Paulo, statistics reflected racially heterogeneous districts. Some racial patterns were nonetheless discernible. *Prêtos,* as had Africans, tended to predominate along the coastline in districts connected either to the

TABLE 8. *Afro-Brazilian City Population as Percentage of State Total, Salvador and São Paulo, 1890 and 1940*

		1890		1940
Salvador				
	Prêtos	11.7	*Prêtos*	9.6
	Mestiços	6.9	*Pardos*	5.5
	All races	9.1	All races	7.4
São Paulo				
	Prêtos	2.4	*Prêtos*	12.1
	Mestiços	2.9	*Pardos*	13.3
	All races	4.7	All races	18.5

SOURCE: Brazil, Directoria Geral de Estastística, *Sexo, Raça, e Estado Civil, Nacionalidade, Filiaçao, Culto, e Analphabetismo da População Recenseada em 31 de Dezembro de 1890* (Rio de Janeiro: Oficina da Estatística, 1898); Brazil, Instituto Brasileiro de Geografia e Estatística, *Recenseamento Geral do Brazil, 1⁰ de Setembro de 1940* (Rio de Janeiro: Serviço Gráfico do Instituto Brasileiro de Geografia e Estatística, 1950).

port trade (such as Paripe and Pirajá) or to the fishing industry (such as Itapoan). Whites were disproportionately represented in the inland residential districts. Improvements in transportation allowed well-to-do whites to commute easily to and from recently modernized neighborhoods such as Vitória. Black and mulatto residents, historically a key segment of the downtown population as domestic workers, vendors, porters, and tradespeople, increased proportionally as whites relocated. The church of the black Brotherhood of the Rosário served as an anchor of this community which now took on a decidedly Afro-Brazilian character, and the square across from the medical school became known as a popular meeting point for the masters of capoeira and their protegés.[12] Two points should be underscored. First, although these racial breakdowns are suggestive, wealth was the single most important factor in spatial distribution. Second, there were no racially defined enclaves around the city; people of all races and occupations could be found in any district. This had important implications for the campaign to restrict Afro-Brazilian cultural manifestations on city streets. Public spaces belonged, at least in principle, to all.

Afro-Brazilian women in both *prêto* and *mestiço* categories slightly outnumbered men.[13] In 1890 there were 24,794 *prêtas* (women) and 21,213 *prêtos* (men); *mestiças* were 32,872 as compared with 28,371 *mestiços*. The 1890 census reveals significantly lower marriage rates for *prêtos* in Salvador than for all other groups. Only 9.2 percent of *prêtos* and 8.5 percent of *prêtas* in the total population had been married at least once.[14] This suggests either that there were fewer *prêtos* of marriageable age, or that prêtos had a lower propensity to marry. Although the census did not correlate age with race, 41 percent of Brazil's population was fourteen years old or under in 1890. If that proportion is used as a guide to calculate the adult population, the number of *prêto* men ever married was 38 percent that of white men, while *prêtas*' marriages were only 30 percent those of white women. The same percentages are obtained without separating the adult population. *Mestiços* were far more likely to marry; *prêto* male marriages were 66 percent of *mestiço* males, and *prêta* women's marriages were 61 percent of *mestiças*'. These figures appear to lend statistical support to the Brazilian saying, "White women for marriage, *mestiças* for sex, and black women for work." Salvador was not representative of the rest of Brazil in this regard. National totals indicate that 27 percent of *prêto* men and 27 percent of *mestiço* men had married at least once; for women the percentages were 27 percent for *prêtas* and 30 percent for *mestiças*. The failure of the 1940 census to cross-reference race and civil status precludes direct comparison. The marriage rate for the entire population, however, increased from 16.4 percent for men in 1890 to 21.5 percent in 1940, and for women from 17.0 percent to 24.8 percent. That this may have been the result of an increase in *prêto* marriages is purely speculative.[15]

The low incidence of formal marriages among *prêtos* meant that only occasionally were their children legally recognized. Unmarried African parents sometimes used their wills to recognize illegitimate offspring. The daughter of Manoel José Parra, an African freedman, used her father's surname although he had never married her mother, Antonia Pedreira de Cirqueira. Parra used his will specifically to recognize his daughter, as he had no material goods to bequeath.[16]

More detailed social data on Afro-Brazilian employment, health, and education are not available in the census and must be culled from disparate sources. Labor data indicating color are difficult to locate for this period, but anectodal references and random samples help construct working hypotheses. There is no evidence of signficant change in the labor market, such as the influx of a new class of workers either from the agricultural areas or from overseas, at the start of the Republican era. Afro-Brazilians continued in the same types of professions they had held during the nineteenth century as both slaves and free people of color. *Pardo* and *prêto* men worked mainly in skilled trades and manual labor. Women worked as domestics, sometimes specializing as seamstresses, laundresses, or cooks, in which case they had better opportunities for self-employment. Other women of color worked in commerce as itinerant vendors or in markets and small shops.

One sector of the labor market in which Africans specialized did not survive past the 1890s. African men had been a fixture of the nineteenth-century labor market as incidental laborers, particularly in the commercial dis-

ILL. 11. Afro-Brazilian workers in Bahia, late nineteenth century. Courtesy of Photographs and Prints Division, Schomburg Center for Research in Black Culture, The New York Public Library, Astor, Lenox and Tilden Foundations.

trict around the docks. They stationed themselves around the district in small ethnic *(nação)* groups known as *cantos*. Manuel Querino, the pioneer Afro-Bahian ethnographer, describes these *cantos* in the late nineteenth century as an option for emancipated Africans who did not want to work in agriculture. The *cantos* were stations where one could hire porters to transport merchandise, but the men filled the interim hours making such diverse items as rosaries, birdcages, brooms, and woven straw hats and mats. They also worked with African imports, creating bracelets of cowry shells and Moroccan leather. Clients could bring *panos-da-costa*, woven cloths from West Africa, for treatment at the *canto*. When new, the cloths were very stiff, so the men of the *canto* would beat them over a cylindrical wooden frame to soften them and bring out the shine. Querino notes that the men sculpted ritual art for their respective "sects," as well. Each *canto* was led by an elected "captain" whose responsibilities included contracting jobs for the members and collecting all salaries.[17]

African men also worked around the city as porters of traveling chairs, such as Roberto de Souza, who worked with a partner in Lapa.[18] These African freelancers began to disappear from Salvador's landscape in the 1890s, partly because of their decrease in the population but also because of the city's modernization. The expanding trolley car lines made transportation easier, obviating the need for the portered traveling chair. Bureaucracy may also have played a role, as the city struggled to regulate the many entrepreneurs and small business people plying their trades in the city streets. One of de Souza's passengers in 1890 was a woman who had been run over by a barrel in the street. Accidents such as this were frequent occurrences as people, carts, horses, and small vehicles transported all manner of merchandise along the narrow downtown streets. Not all were considerate of passersby; one Captain Joaquim dos Santos Correia was caught galloping his horse down the sidewalk. Salvador's local police sought to bring the bustling activity under control through a campaign to impose fines on all types of disorder. Fines were levied for taverns operating after legal hours (9:45 P.M. in one case) or on Sundays, for garbage or waste water tossed into the street, gambling, and even cursing. Salespeople's carts and draft animals could not be left unattended, trolley cars could not be overloaded, and one man received a fine merely for sitting on the shaft of a wagon.[19] This greater vigilance with regard to street commerce may also have imposed new burdens on black women working as itinerant vendors. The lives and livelihoods of all were affected by the increased regulation of trade, but especially those of African descent who played such a prominent role in the informal market. Roberto Moura, who studied the identical phenomenon in the city of Rio de Janeiro, noted that increased taxation and fines not only helped finance urbanization projects but also "attempted to end, or at least remove from the downtown area, those activities which gave some parts of the city the appearance of an African market."[20]

Afro-Brazilians participated actively in the trade associations that proliferated at the turn of the century. These organizations provided important social security and retirement benefits. Many represented trades exercised by people of color, such as the Barbers' Union Beneficent Society and the Artisans' Philanthropic Union Beneficent Society, occupations traditionally assigned to slaves in colonial times.[21] The trade associations do not appear to have been racially segregated to the extent of having parallel organizations for different racial groups exercising the same profession. It is more likely that the occupations themselves were divided along lines of color. Thus many trade associations took on the additional character of race-based collectives.

The records of the Sociedade Protectora dos Desvalidos offer a glimpse into the world of the trade associations. The Protectora was not itself a trade association, but a beneficent organization for *prêto* men open to all professions. Its members were mainly artisans in the building trades who also belonged to their professional associations. They maintained frequent correspondence with the city's trade organizations, advising one another of annual board elections, anniversary celebrations, and special events. One such organization was the Artisans' Pension Fund (Monte-Pio dos Artistas), located a few steps away from the Protectora. Although the fund was not formally established for men of color, they constituted the majority of the membership because of their concentration in those trades. Its leadership over the years was made up of men also active in black organizations such as the Protectora and the lay Catholic brotherhoods. In another artisans' group, the Artisans' Philanthropic Union, at least three Protectora members served on its board in 1898–99.[22]

Membership in multiple groups offered the assurance of an adequate pension for the member and his family in the event of retirement, disability, or death. Among working-class black men, it was common practice to join a second or third organization in addition to a trade association. Terencio Aranha Dantas was typical of this pattern; along with his membership in the Protectora, he served on the board of the Artisans' Philanthropic Union as first secretary in 1894–95 and president in 1897–98.[23] Some, such as Captain Bibiano Soares Cupim, were extremely active. A carpenter, he joined the Protectora in 1894 at age thirty. He became prior of the Third Order of the Rosário in 1907, vice president of the Centro Operário (Workingman's Center) in 1926, and a board member of the National Guard Officers' Association in 1927. Throughout the 1920s he also served on Protectora committees, including a long stint as General Council president.[24]

Two other samples from very different sources support the hypothesis that most Afro-Brazilian men in Salvador were employed as tradesmen and unskilled workers, whereas women worked mainly as domestics.[25] The first is a sample of arrest records from the city jail that noted both race and occupation (see Table 9). While too small to make any definitive statements, the sample draws from a group charged with criminal activity and suggests some directions for future inquiry into the relationship between occupation and social class. In this group, unskilled laborers are 18 percent of *pardo* occupations and 32 percent of *prêtos*. This may indicate a greater propensity of unskilled workers to be arrested for criminal offenses, and/or a higher concentration of *prêtos* over *pardos* in lower-status occupations. The women's sample is even smaller and does not indicate whether those who specialized in a domestic trade were self-employed or part of a household staff. Of the twenty-six women for whom criminal charges were recorded, twenty-one were accused of disorderly conduct and five charged with theft. These included two laundresses, two servants, and a cook. The second sample is of death certificates issued between 1919 and 1920 for the downtown district of Paço, located near both the commercial and the civic centers. Of fifty-five *pardo* and

TABLE 9. *Occupations of* Pardo *and* Prêto *Prisoners in Salvador, 1892*

Men	Pardo	Prêto
1. Skilled trades/artisans	16	12
2. Domestic/service	5	2
3. Business	1	1
4. Maritime	5	0
5. Agriculture	5	4
6. Unskilled manual labor	6	10
Total	38	29
Women	**Parda**	**Prêta**
1. Domestic	6	2
2. Domestic trades[a]	9	8
3. Other trades[b]	0	1
Total	15	11

SOURCE: APEB, Secretaria de Segurança Publica, Mappas de Presos, February, June, September 1892.

[a] Domestic trades includes specialized work (laundress, seamstress, and dressmaker).

[b] One woman was listed as *ganhadeira,* which probably referred to a street vendor, but also referred to fish retailers.

prêto men, thirty-one were skilled tradesmen. Of eighty-eight women in the same sample, seventy-eight worked as domestics.[26]

There is no evidence that, within the first fifty years after abolition, *pardos* and *prêtos* made significant inroads into professional positions in law, medicine, and politics, traditionally the preserve of whites. They were prominent, however, in efforts to forge proletarian solidarity. Members of the Protectora and the Third Order of the Rosário were active on the planning committee of the Centro Operário when, in 1893, it formed to "organize and unify" the "trades, crafts, and proletarian classes."[27] The Beneficent Society of the Proletarian Classes, founded in 1918, included two Protectora members on its governing board for 1925.[28] Rather than seeking to increase representation in those professions dominated by whites, Afro-Brazilians apparently chose to work toward the improvement of conditions within their traditional occupations.

Based as they are on statistical color categories of *prêtos* and *pardos,* official records do not fully reflect the contours of the post-abolition Afro-Brazilian community of Salvador. Formulations of ethnic identity in post-abolition Salvador evolved from antecedents deeply rooted in the historical conditions of the nineteenth century and earlier. Under slavery, distinctions between slave and free, *pardo* and *prêto,* African-born and Brazilian-born were significant stratifications of Salvador's population of color. The large African population was itself a conglomerate of many "nations" *(nações)* of different languages and ethnic backgrounds. Whites, in the minority and with a deep-seated fear of blacks uniting to overturn their hegemony, encouraged ethnic differentiation as a strategy of control. Hence Salvador's dark-hued majority was really an aggregate of many small social circles.

A radical demographic change had taken place in Salvador over the course of the nineteenth century. The number of Africans, once a large and vital segment of the city's population, had declined precipitously and irreversibly owing to the cessation of the slave trade at mid-century, natural decrease, and a back-to-Africa movement that had peaked between 1835 and the 1870s. Such a fundamental change undoubtedly had a profound impact on social ethnicity among persons of African descent.

In this context, social ethnicity refers to operative identities that differ from those reflected in statistics. The color categories used in the census represented one component of ethnicity. Given the size, diversity, and historical ethnic subdivisions of the Afro-Bahian community, it cannot be assumed that a "black" ethnicity was suddenly viable in the post-abolition years, especially since color had never been the sole basis of ethnic identity.

Collectives, based as they are on a sense of commonality, are one clue to the types of ethnic identity operative in the post-abolition Afro-Bahian community. Of the various forms of Afro-Bahian collectives explored here, only the Catholic brotherhoods and the Sociedade Protectora dos Desvalidos, a secular mutual aid society that originated as a brotherhood in 1832, explicitly restricted membership to *prêtos*. This prohibition was mandated during slavery, when sodalities were segregated by color, but sometimes was continued by these groups. Black soccer clubs, another response to segregation, declined in popularity with the loss of their best players once white clubs began admitting Afro-Brazilian players. Three types of collectives originated in the cultural heritage of the African community and their descendants. Candomblé, Carnival groups, and capoeira schools drew directly from African traditions, but, although their de facto membership was predominantly Afro-Brazilian, they were open to people of all backgrounds. Finally, a survey of wills reveals the continuity of informal networks of mutual assistance among Africans and their descendants. Other, less publicly visible forms of Afro-Brazilian collectives may yet be uncovered.

This range of collective behavior provides preliminary insights into Afro-Bahian ethnic identity. Only those groups formed in response to segregation were organized on the basis of color. In all other instances, Afro-Bahians sought associational bonds with those who shared specific traditions or family and community relationships. This pattern suggests a fundamental difference in perspectives of ethnicity. Whereas whites employed a color barrier separating themselves from *pardos* and *prêtos*, African cultural heritage served as the organizing principle for collective identity for at least a portion of the Afro-Brazilian community. It remains to be seen how the population of mixed descent viewed itself and what types of self-determination strategies it employed, for the institutions surveyed here had overwhelmingly *prêto* memberships.

The evidence of Afro-Brazilian collectives is thus concentrated among *prêtos,* who averaged about one-quarter of the city's population and just over 40 percent of the Afro-Brazilian population during the post-abolition period (see Table 7). None of these groups had mass memberships that would have included a majority of even the *prêto* population alone. It is therefore probable that collective organization was not the primary strategy employed by Afro-Bahians in their transition to post-abolition society.

Post-Abolition Adaptations: Three Perspectives

Because the issue of identity is so central to self-determination, a closer look at those examples of collective behavior in which identity and membership were clearly defined is useful. In this category are included informal networks of African-born persons and their descendants, and the exclusively *prêto* formal organizations. None was involved in advocacy on behalf of the larger social sector of *prêtos* to which they belonged; they sought, rather, to improve the lives of those within their membership circle. Each group faced particular challenges given societal changes that accompanied abolition. The *prêto* institutions had been created to fulfill specific needs under the conditions of slave society. After abolition, they needed to redefine their role in order to continue to meet the changing needs of their members. The African-born, having opted not to return to the continent, had to determine how to balance multiple options of identity and affiliations as members of African *nações, prêtos,* and the extended communities of Bahia and Brazil.

Salvador is a rare case in which, because of its close commercial ties with the African coast, return was a viable, though costly, option for freed-persons throughout the nineteenth century. The ethnographer Pierre Verger notes two patterns of behavior by emancipated slaves. "Some found themselves at home in Bahia and tended to integrate themselves into the life of the country, imitating and adapting themselves to its lifestyle; others remained tied to their African origins and sought to return to Africa."[29] This formulation posits a sharper dichotomy than actually existed. As we will see, not all those who remained in Brazil relinquished their ties to their African heritage.

Voluntary departure to Africa was one element of a major demographic change in Salvador that took place over the course of the nineteenth century. Africans, once a large and vital segment of the city's population, were in precipitous and irreversible decline. In addition to the back-to-Africa movement, natural decrease and the cessation of the slave trade at mid-century contributed to the diminishing proportion of Africans in the city's population.

In examining the return to Africa as a manifestation of self-determination, one must recognize it as a process begun prior to abolition, when manumissions were granted on an individual basis. The first major wave of departures took place in the wake of the 1835 Malê revolt, when a record 422 passports were issued to Africans "returning" to the Gulf of Benin. Although a substantial number of Africans hailed from that area, these voyages should not be confused with a direct return to place of origin. Many African-Brazilians ended up in areas of the continent new to them, where they undertook yet another cultural regenesis.[30] They settled as colonists in the "Brazilian" communities of Nigeria, Benin, and Togo. Another 319 followed in 1836. Between 1846 and 1868, 1,312 Africans obtained passports to travel to the coast. It might have been expected that, after the restriction of the slave trade after 1850, authorities would have been less willing to grant letters of freedom and passports. This was not the case; after a drop to less than 20 passports issued to Africans annually between 1851 and 1854, Africans left Brazil at an average rate of 67 per year from 1855 to 1868.[31] Not included in this number are the children of Africans, officially listed as "Brazilian."

Immediately after abolition there was a sharp rise in departures to Lagos. Only three ships sailed from Salvador to West Africa in 1888. The last two left just weeks after the abolition decree of May 13, taking only 54 passengers between them. In 1889, 227 passengers departed, an increase of 391 percent over the previous year. A total of twenty-one vessels left Salvador for Lagos between 1886 and 1892. Of the 637 passengers for whom nationality was recorded, a full two-thirds (421) were identified as African. These are assumed to be elderly people who would have arrived in Brazil sometime before 1850, when the illicit slave trade was halted. Another 193 were identified as Brazilian, and were probably the children and grandchildren of Africans. No matter how long they had lived in Brazil, African-born blacks were consistently referred to as *africano* and not *brasileiro*.[32] On the 1889 sailing of the Aurora, all passengers were listed as Brazilian. Three years later the logbook of the Bomfim, most of whose passengers had been recorded as African on previous sailings, recorded all 37 of its passengers as Brazilian. Either these passengers were Brazilian-born, or a change in policy had resulted in the labeling of Africans as Brazilian nationals. The figures for post-abolition departures are not exact because some passengers may have made the voyage more than once. Nonetheless, the annual average of 94 between 1882 and 1892 is higher than that of 67 at mid-nineteenth century.[33] Although significant, the

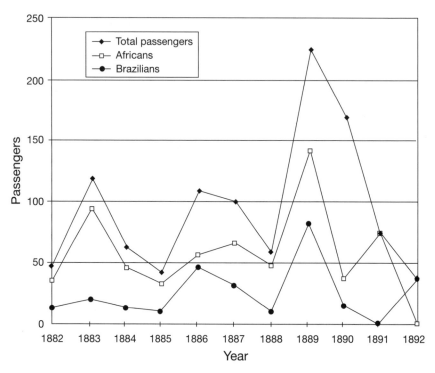

FIGURE 2. Passenger departures, Salvador to Lagos, 1882–1892. Data from Arquivo Público do Estado da Bahia, Commissariado da Policia, Registro de Sahida de Passageiros, bks. 54–56, 1882–1892.

returnees represented only a small percentage of the African-born population. The rest were left to shape their roles as citizens of the city of Salvador.

At the time of abolition, social networks of kinship and friendship were still a vital dimension of African life in the capital. Manuel Querino's account of the *cantos* hints at a parallel African world in which people could speak their native tongue, worship their own deities, and otherwise preserve such elements of culture as games, crafts, and cuisine. Evidence of extensive African networks also appears in the wills registered in the late nineteenth century. Although the testamentary records only refer to "African" nationality, it is likely that African-born persons engaged in these communal networks with others of the same *nação*. For West Africans, numerous in nineteenth-century Salvador, "African" ethnicity was a characterization most appropriately applied in the context of a Brazilian "other." Within an exclusively African context, more specific ethnicities prevailed, as with the *cantos*.[34]

African support networks were forged during slavery, illustrating how subject peoples are sometimes able to convert tools of oppression into avenues for empowerment. The Fernandes Galliza family, many members of whom became patrons of Afro-Brazilian institutions, is a particularly good example of this phenomenon. João Fernandes Galliza was born in Africa around 1815. He became the slave of Benedicto Fernandes Galliza, but had won his freedom by 1855, the year he drew up his will. Of his three children, one son was enslaved. His adult daughter lived independently and his youngest son lived with his mother. João himself had three slaves whom he identified as Nagô in his will. Two of them were women, and João was responsible for the women's three daughters. He willed two of the slaves to continue to care for his female companion Felicidade, and freed the third for her good services. To each of the three female *crias*[35] João bequeathed 200$000 *réis* and gold chains; his daughter received 100$000 *réis*. The money for the *crias* was to come from a debt owed by a freed African woman to whom he had lent 700$000.[36]

In the case of the Fernandes Gallizas, slaveholding among Africans seems to have incorporated dimensions of caretaking and patronage. It also appears as a mechanism for integrating the newly arrived African into a network of mutual assistance. João had become responsible for three slaves, their three children, a female companion and her daughter, though not directly for his own children. He had also granted a substantial loan to another African. Interestingly, his responsibility to his own children was nominal, illustrative of the ways in which blood relationships could be superseded by other bonds in the context of slave society. João's patron/owner, Benedicto Fernandes Galliza, along with his family, had also established close relationships of mutual help within the African-born community. Benedicto's wife, Henriqueta, acted as executrix of the will of an African-born woman, a position generally entrusted to an intimate associate of the testator. In the will in which Henriqueta was named, the woman left money to other African friends, family, and godchildren.[37] Benedicto's son, Manoel, left three of his six houses to the Rosário brotherhood.[38]

Outside of the context of slavery, African freedpersons maintained friendships with one another that filled the roles of the families they had lost. When Tito José Teixeira Ribeiro, a freed African, died without family in 1889, he left his possessions to be divided equally between two freed African women. A third freed African man served as executor.[39] Candida do Nascimento Paim was a childless widow. Her only possession was a house in Sant'Anna parish, which she left in equal parts to an African friend, her *crioula* goddaughter, and a woman who was probably her sister-in-law.[40]

The wills also reveal bonds of affection, such as godparenthood, that carried financial benefits such as personal loans extended to friends. The will of the African-born Pedro Pereira Marinho, written four months before his death in 1889, illustrates the types of networks of friends and cognatic kinship that helped the African community survive. He never married but by Delfina, who subsequently died, had two daughters named Eva and Paula. Pedro named two African friends as executors, one of whom was his *compadre* Achilles Serra.[41] Pedro was godfather to Achilles' son Manoel, who, like Pedro's own children, had lost his mother. Pedro had two other godchildren to whom he left 50 *milréis* each. Pedro also helped other friends financially. To his friend Agostinho dos Santos Correia he loaned over 700 *milréis* at 2 percent interest, a loan that had extended over four years. Pedro asked that his beneficiaries forgo the interest due on Agostinho's loan. He also had loaned 216 *milréis* to an African named Bernardo Coelho. Pedro had incurred some debt of his own as well. In return for 500 *milréis* borrowed from Esperança Francisca Marinho (relationship unspecified), he bequeathed her the house in which she had been living. Pedro himself lived with a woman named Ludovina Angelica, who had furnished the entire house.[42]

Pedro's loan from Esperança was not uncommon. African women often helped support African men. Cezar Victorino Botelho was an African who had a daughter by Felicidade, an African freedwoman. When he wanted to purchase a house on the Largo de Mouraria, he sought out an African woman named Constança Maria Antônia do Espírito Santo, from whom he borrowed the substantial sum of one *conto*.[43] Antonio Nunes Figueira, a freedman, had three children with Felicidade Adelaide. His house, however, was owned jointly with Maria Benedicta, also an African woman.

Izabel Innocencia de Araújo Sant'Anna was an African widow who had tried her hand at farming a small plot called "Pasto" on Salvador's outskirts. She had purchased it along with Abrahão de Barros Reis. She described herself as a poor woman who originally owned one slave, an African woman named Libania. Izabel came to own Libania's four children, and also cared for Libania's seven grandchildren who, born free, were classified as *ingenuos*. Having no children of her own, Izabel granted them all freedom in her will and left the entire farm to Libania and her family.[44]

The sample of wills, albeit small, suggests that Africans and their children maintained close ties of family and community that helped them adapt to Brazilian life. Those who owned slaves in the nineteenth century sometimes transformed that institution into one of beneficent patronage. They made loans, engaged in partnerships, and cared for godchildren and family members. These relationships were particularly important when legal problems arose. Antônia Maria da Conceição, an African woman, was jailed in 1893 on grounds of being mentally ill. Her sister, who could not read or write, dictated a letter to the chief of police requesting Antônia Maria's release since her only problem was the eccentricity typical of old age.[45] Without someone to advocate on her behalf, Antônia would likely have died in prison.

These support mechanisms were particularly important for people who began with as little as did the Africans. There was a long-standing tradition of gift giving from masters to slaves, notably trinkets and old jewelry, and sometimes slaves were remembered in wills. Yet Africans had no guarantee that their masters would be either wealthy or generous. Maria Roza da Conceição was a childless widow from Santo Amaro with two female slaves, Angelica and Henriqueta. She did not free her slaves in her will of 1871, transferring them instead to her niece, but did leave money and furniture to Angelica's three children.[46] Informal credit networks within the African community provided an alternative source of capital that helped individuals begin their new lives as free persons.

Thus for at least one portion of the Afro-Brazilian community of Salvador, the response to abolition was to remain in Brazil while retaining the supportive mechanisms of the African community.

The formal institutions of *prêtos* had already begun to change as the balance between African-born and Brazilian-born persons shifted over the course of the nineteenth century. As in the brotherhood of the Rosário (see Chapter 2), rivalries between Brazilian-born and African-born members subsided into irrelevance by the latter half of the century. Abolition brought a new challenge. In the early days of the colony, brotherhoods such as the Rosário were an essential part of African adaptation to Brazil. They served as cultural orientation centers, support networks, insurance funds, and provided a religious superstructure through which Afro-Brazilians could seek spiritual support from Catholic deities as well as the African deities with which they were syncretized.[47] After abolition, many of these roles came to be filled by new institutions. There were no longer new Africans needing cultural adaptation. Those who wished to worship African deities could do so in the supportive environment of the candomblé houses. Later, under Getúlio Vargas' administration of the 1930s, state-run social security provided health, disability, and retirement insurance. Brotherhoods found themselves duplicating services available elsewhere. In order to survive in the twentieth century, Afro-Brazilian brotherhoods needed to secure a niche in Bahian community life.

The history of the brotherhood of the Rosário às Portas do Carmo between 1888 and 1938 shows an organization in transition and in search of secure footing in a new society.[48] It was one of several branches of the Rosário brotherhood in Republican Salvador, including those at the Chapel of the Fifteen Mysteries, the Victória parish church, and the Rosário de João Ferrer downtown. Many other black brotherhoods were active in Salvador during this period, including those of Santa Barbara, located in the church of Corpo Santo, São Benedicto at the São Francisco church, São Vicente Ferrer at the Igreja da Sé, and Bôa Morte and Bom Jesus dos Martirios in the church of

Barroquinha.[49] The Rosário às Portas do Carmo began humbly in 1685 as a brotherhood of *prêtos,* but attained the singular distinction of elevation to the rank of Third Order in 1899.[50]

Dependent on the contributions of their members, many Afro-Brazilian brotherhoods struggled to survive. The Rosário brotherhood of Victória, recognized in 1767, was deeply in debt by the mid-nineteenth century. It owed an estimated 300$000. Its only property was a small house with an income of 120$000 annually, in addition to a small collection of religious ornaments valued at 100$000. Because of the group's poor financial management, a judge had named an administrator to oversee its affairs.[51] Annual membership dues and special collections for the feast days of patron saints were rarely enough to cover all the costs of a brotherhood, which included building maintenance and repair, clerical fees, taxes, utilities, and religious supplies. Financial security depended on a wise investment strategy that would cover operating expenses with interest income.

The Rosário às Portas do Carmo, despite its prestige, was not immune to the vagaries of precarious finances. It had once had active support from its members, despite the fact that many were slaves. It was they who had painstakingly built the Rosário's own church in the upper city, which permitted the brotherhood to move from its original home at the Conceição da Praia church. During slavery, the brotherhood had important secular functions, including mutual funds for the purchase of manumissions. After emancipation, the brotherhood's principal activity was the organization of the annual observances of the feast day of Our Lady of the Rosary, as well as other devotions throughout the year. It also continued to provide burial benefits and sacraments to members.

The zealous activities of the brotherhood's early days had given way to relative lethargy by the late 1870s. The brotherhood spent 413$000 on masses in 1876–77; the following year, only 385$000. By 1879 it had ceased regular masses altogether. The explanation the governing board gave to the archbishop in 1889 was that the roof was literally falling in. Upon taking office, the Rosário board of 1880 decided that the old church could not continue without sorely needed repairs. What ensued was a major renovation. The group rebuilt the roof, installed new iron railings, laid new floors of imported European marble and cedar, and repaired the cemetery.

During this time, it appears that no one had notified the archdiocese about the renovations. When the archbishop suspended the Rosário's charter in June 1889 because of their inactivity, the board members hastened to explain their situation. They acquiesced to the archbishop's demands that they immediately reopen their doors and elect a new board in accordance with the charter.[52] Ten years later, the archbishop elevated the brotherhood to Venerable

ILL. 12. View of the chapel at the Church of the Rosário.

Third Order, at the time the only black brotherhood for which I located such an honor.[53]

On the occasion of the Rosário's elevation, its leaders drafted a new set of statutes in 1900 that reflected their vision of broader service to the membership. They planned a pension fund in addition to providing the sacraments of communion and penance and arranging for the funerals of members and their families. This expansion was contingent upon an increase in the Rosário's endowment, representing the sum of all the group's assets in real estate and investments, to five *contos*. In the financial confusion and mismanagement of the Rosário's board in the early twentieth century, the pension program was never implemented. The brotherhood had also hoped to build an asylum for its poorest members, and promised to provide financial assistance until the asylum was ready for residents.[54] The board required applicants to submit their requests at the monthly meetings, but decisions were arbitrary. At the May 1917 meeting, Isabel Maria da Conceição asked for help for her mentally ill aunt who had no income of her own. The board immediately took up a collection. At the same meeting, Jovino Daniel da Silva repeated a request made in April for help because he was poor, ill, and nearly blind.[55] His case was deferred indefinitely. The asylum was never built.

Throughout the post-abolition period, the Rosário was intensely preoccupied with financial problems that would have threatened its existence were it not for a few fortuitous real estate acquisitions and interest income on government bonds. The Rosário owned several houses in the neighborhood around the church, as well as some land in the Quinta dos Lazaros cemetery. It acquired some properties through purchase, such as a house on the Rua dos Carvões purchased for 500 *milréis* in 1864.[56] Others were acquired through more creative measures in the nineteenth century. In one case, the group allowed Clara Maria do Monte Falco da Silva, a poor blind woman, to build a small house on a lot owned by the brotherhood. Upon her death, ownership of the house passed to the Rosário, with revenues from rent going to the cost of candles and masses.[57]

Although rent monies were an important source of income, the largest and most stable source in the early 1890s was the interest generated by government bonds.[58] In 1890–91 such interest accounted for 41 percent of the Rosário's income, followed by new member fees at 35 percent and annual dues at 23 percent.[59] Funeral costs were offset somewhat by the fact that members paid for their own burial plots.[60] The largest expenditure was the annual festival in honor of Our Lady of the Rosary, their patron saint.

On paper, the Rosário was well organized. In practice, it was often a disaster. The administrative unit of the brotherhood was the board *(mesa)*. After its elevation to Venerable Third Order, the board was comprised of the prior, sub-prior, secretary, treasurer, *procurador geral* (the previous prior), master of novitiates (to screen applicants), *vigario do culto* (responsible for the order's possessions), and approximately ten *definidores* (regular board members) with voting power but no specific responsibility. The statutes mandated monthly meetings, and elections were set to coincide with the annual festival of the patron saint in September. The regularity with which this schedule was met depended almost entirely upon the disposition of current members. Although the archbishop's office interceded several times to regularize the Rosário's administration when the board failed to hold elections, it operated with little oversight. This situation opened the door for widespread abuses. None of the candidates for the important office of treasurer had to demonstrate knowledge of bookkeeping. Every year, after approval by a review committee of three board members, outgoing officers were to submit all documents, receipts, and keys to their successors. Inevitably, transfers were delayed, receipts were misplaced, and errors went uncorrected. In one case, the board discovered in 1918 that the brotherhood owned a property for which rent had not been collected since 1868.[61]

José Martins, who joined in 1887 and served several times as treasurer, is a perfect illustration of the order's administrative weaknesses.[62] The board suspended him in 1905 because he refused to turn over the books to his successor. Moreover, they accused him of defaming the board to the archbishop's secretary.[63] Martins managed to get back on the board and was again serving as treasurer in 1916; how he accomplished this feat is impossible to know since there are no regular minutes for the period between 1907 and 1917. Because of the "enormous irregularities," the archbishop sent a commission in March 1917 to hold elections immediately. When the new officers were elected in April, Martins and Secretary Raymundo Erico de Miranda refused to turn over their documents. They did not appear at three successive meetings, forcing the board to ask the archbishop's office to intervene. A delegation of board members went to Martins' house and angrily demanded the books and key to the safe, which he finally turned over in May. By Martins' calculations, the Rosário's annual accounts were balanced; the order owned over 30 *contos,* a considerable sum, in federal bonds alone, in addition to other investments.[64] Only afterward did the discrepancies appear, such as a bill from a local newspaper for advertisements that Martins had declared paid.[65] Despite his apparent malfeasance, Martins eventually attained the posts of both prior and *procurador geral*. The board failed to hold annual elections until the archbishop again sent a commission in 1920. Martins insisted on becoming treasurer, but agreed to fill the post of prior that had been vacated since the death of the incumbent. At the same meeting, he was chided by the board for having printed flyers advertising a discounted membership fee

TABLE 10. *Net Income and Expenses,*
Rosário às Portas do Carmo, 1908–1926

Year	Net balance
1908–09	(24$670)
1909–10	(689$520)
1910–11	499$300
1911–12	690$300
1912–13	301$900
1913–14	(115$600)
1914–15	N.A.
1915–16	N.A.
1916–17	(863$600)
1917–18	(918$700)
1918–19	N.A.
1919–20	83$000
1920–21	(474$360)
1921–22	(3:697$690)
1922–23	(3:397$690)
1923–24	(6:078$340)
1924–25	818$760[a]
1926 (calendar year)[b]	(275$720)

SOURCE: Arquivo do Venerável Ordem Terceira do Rosário, boxes 13–1, 13–2. Numbers in parentheses are deficits.

[a] The outstanding debt from 1923–24 was not calculated in the fiscal report for 1924–25.

[b] The fiscal year customarily began in September; the shift in 1926 left unaccounted the period between September through December 1925.

N.A. indicates not available.

that had never been approved. Was Martins attempting to stack the membership with his supporters? His behavior certainly outraged some on the board, but he was allowed to continue. In August the board discovered that he had requested, and received, permission from the archbishop to wear a special medallion as part of the vestments worn at Rosário ceremonies. The next year he surreptitiously removed his portrait from the boardroom to have a special border placed on the frame. The secretary demanded its immediate removal. Martins was also accused of having called the archbishop's office, pretending to be someone else, to advise that no commission was necessary to oversee the next elections.[66]

The inability of the board members to deal with excesses was an open invitation to abuse, perhaps abetted by their confidence that the archdiocese was always willing to intercede in serious cases. The treasurer who replaced Martins in 1917, Affonso João Maria de Freitas, should have turned his books over to his successor elected in October 1920. At the September 1921 meeting, the board noted that not only had Freitas failed to submit his accounts, but he was in possession of several hundred *milréis* in cash belonging to the Rosário. Freitas finally submitted the books in May 1922, along with "explanations," but the secretary failed to give any details in the minutes.[67]

While the board engaged in heated diatribes over such issues as whose portraits were to be hung in the boardroom, cost overruns for building repairs were accumulating, and no one could accurately say how much money or property the group possessed. The financial records from this period are full of inaccuracies and accounting techniques vary, but it is clear that the Rosário survived from year to year on a very slim margin. The 1891 budget shows a deficit of 1:142$530, which is not atypical for the years studied. Under José Martins the accounting periods are irregular, and there are wide fluctuations in his reporting of the brotherhood's financial situation. He reported a positive balance of 80$900 for 1903–1904 and a deficit of 128$840 for 1903–1905.[68] Running totals are available for the period between 1908 and 1925. They illustrate the chaotic accounting that consistently forced the board to spend all its energies on resolving financial crises (see Table 10).

The net result of the continuing financial difficulties was the inability of the Rosário board to attend to expanding its membership base, let alone establish the programs it had planned in 1900. Some members recognized the dangers in neglecting the issue of recruitment, and proposed schemes to make membership more accessible. José Martins' plan to reduce induction fees could be interpreted in this light. One gauge of member support, the collections for the annual feast day of Our Lady of the Rosary, shows enormous fluctuation both in the number of contributors and in the amount pledged (see Table 11).

Through the festivals *(festas)*, it is possible to discern a more affluent sector of the Afro-Bahian community acting as patrons of *prêto* brotherhoods. The importance of the annual festival went beyond the spiritual veneration of the patron saint. It was the members' opportunity to parade the glory and prestige of their brotherhood, thus reflecting positively on their own status. Brotherhoods competed to outdo one another with the splendor of their festivals. J. da Silva Campos' description of the festival of the São Benedito brotherhood, housed in the São Francisco church, captures the exuberant ostentation that characterized the more popular festivals:

> The blacks [*a creoulada*] of the brotherhood took unheard-of steps so that the celebration would not be on a lesser level than that of Conceição da Praia of the Portuguese, Angustias of the local whites, or of Senhor da Cruz of the mulattoes [*pardos*].
>
> The blacks would go out on the street, on the day of the festival, with their "going to see God" clothes. The black women in those days

TABLE 11. *Annual Rosário Festival Contributions, 1901–1921*

Year	Number contributing	Total pledged (*milréis*)
1901	82	187
1902	60	109
1903	135	587
1904	95	408.1
1905	110	477
1906	N.A.	N.A.
1907	N.A.	N.A.
1908	N.A.	N.A.
1909	96	415.5
1910	95	395
1911	76	398
1912	71	463
1913	69	322.5
1914	43	263
1915	66	302
1916	39	229.5
1917	50	229.1
1918	32	215
1919	N.A.	N.A.
1920	45	226
1921	29	127

SOURCE: Archives of the Veneravel Ordem Terceira do Rosário, box 9–2, "Livro de Promessas de Irmãos, 1899–1921." This table should be regarded as a general indication of support, not a precise accounting. The actual amounts received (versus pledged) are not noted, except for 582$000 in 1903 and 366$000 in 1912. The totals for 1905, 1910, 1911, and 1921 have no signature of approval.

displayed wide skirts [*saias de beca*]—pressed by hand!—traditional shawls [*panos-da-costa*] . . . and silk headwraps, the most delicate blouses, beautifully embroidered, little velvet slippers of black grosgrain [a silk and wool blend], decorated with gold beads, and on ears, necks, arms almost up to the elbows, and fingers, an incredible profusion of costly jewelry. The finishing touch were the huge *balangandans* [a bracket of good-luck charms popularized by slave women] . . . hung from the waist. Old black women, apparently destitute, by day poorly dressed, beggarly, appeared now with so much gold they were the admiration of all. In fact, at all the big festivities in Bahia, the African, black and mulata women displayed themselves this way, wearing expensive materials, and ostentatiously displaying a copious quantity of gold. In no other region of Brazil was there ever greater personal wealth in gold belonging to poor people as here, except perhaps in Minas Gerais.[69]

A festival consisted of a parade through the streets by the members,

ILL. 13. Afro-Bahian woman, late nineteenth or early twentieth century. Courtesy of Photography and Prints Division, Schomburg Center for Research in Black Culture, The New York Public Library, Astor, Lenox and Tilden Foundations.

draped in the capes of the brotherhood. They often bore lit torches and carried statues representing the patron saint and other saints honored by the brotherhood on biers laden with fresh flowers. After the mass, there was usually a feast prepared under the auspices of the female members. Festivals were traditionally the occasion for the installation of the governing board for the coming year.

The brotherhoods did not plunder their endowments to meet the cost of the festivals, but depended instead on membership contributions. Most had separate male and female boards, with the highest officers contributing the most in annual dues. The extant financial records reveal the importance of female donors for such events, and the brotherhoods relied heavily on women's contributions. The dues at the São Benedicto brotherhood, for example, were 10$000 for regular members and 100$000 each for the Juiz and Juiza. When the collection for the patron saint's festival of 1891 yielded only 210$000, Dona Clementina, that year's Juiza, contributed an additional 328$000. Her contributions alone accounted for 23 percent of that year's income. The other sisters contributed a total of 128$000, as compared with the men's 70$000.[70] Women and men had distinct spheres of responsibility. In no case was I able to detect the direct involvement of women in the day-to-day management of the brotherhoods' affairs.[71] The offices of women were often nominally parallel, such as prioress and mistress of novitiates, but the men on the governing board handled all official business. It is probable that the women typically worked on the organization and food preparation for such activities as São Benedicto's fund-raising buffet, which raised 120$000 for the 1891 festival.

Because of the financial contributions expected of the leaders of the more popular brotherhoods, governing board rosters included some of the most well-to-do blacks in the city. There appears to have been a significant gap in financial status between members and leadership. If so, such a divide raises interesting questions about the formation of social groups within the Afro-Bahian community. The more prosperous individuals could have chosen to interact only among themselves, but the composition of the brotherhoods suggests they found other bases of communality. Was it ethnicity? Were descendants of specific *nação* groups continuing their associational networks through the brotherhoods? This is an important avenue of future research.

Brotherhood leaders, particularly those occupying the highest offices, played an important role as patrons to their institutions. Their financial contributions, as well as their participation on the governing boards, were essential to the organizations' survival. The Rosário leadership of the early twentieth century was a Who's Who of contemporary black Bahian society. It included Manoel de Bomfim Galliza and Manoel Friandes. Treasurer Manoel de Bomfim Galliza, whose profession I was unable to determine, was, if not wealthy, at least financially comfortable. He was the son of Benedicto Fernandes Galliza who, as already noted, was a well-connected patron within the African community. When Manoel died in 1908, his property was inventoried at a value of 33:180$000, including four houses and two *sobrados,* three of which he bequeathed to the Rosário.[72] Manoel Friandes, a master stonemason, was remembered by J. da Silva Campos as a dark black man, tall and thin, who wore a goatee. He was "almost illiterate. But intelligent and of forthright conduct. A talker, a swaggerer. One of the best-known people in Bahia." Friandes was also, at various times, an officer of the Sociedade Protectora dos Desvalidos, the Monte-Pio dos Artistas, and the São Benedito brotherhood. Regarding this last organization, Silva Campos asserts that Friandes long wanted to organize a grand festival. He realized his ambition when he became prior for 1887–88. For that year's festival, Friandes organized a huge celebration "never again seen or repeated till today."[73] It would be interesting to know if the size of the festival was related to the abolition of slavery that year.

The women who acted as patrons to brotherhoods were also drawn from the more affluent segments of black Bahian society, and probably commanded considerable prestige. Joanna Maria Ritta da Conceição, the daughter of an African woman, was a former Juiza of the Bôa Morte sisterhood.[74] When she died in 1919, she bequeathed 300$000 to pay for the bier of the statue of Mary carried in the procession. She was typical of active brotherhood members in that she belonged to multiple associations. Of the two houses she owned, Joanna left one to be divided among the brotherhoods to which she belonged—Senhor Bom Jesus dos Martírios da Barroquinha, Santa Barbara do Corpo Santo, São Benedicto, São Vicente Ferrer, and the Rosário às Portas do Carmo. She was particularly concerned with how the money would be spent, specifying that Bom Jesus dos Martírios would have to use its share to repair the altar, with the balance going to the purchase of a federal bond. She arranged for her clothes to be distributed among the poor and created a special fund for the donation of 1$000 to one hundred poor families and 500 *réis* to poor individuals.[75] Whether or not her will reflected her activities in life, Joanna was a philanthropist in the Afro-Brazilian community. Another woman who became one of the most memorable leaders of the Rosário was Eugenia Anna dos Santos (Aninha), prioress (1926-27), board member, and the founding Iyalorixa of one of Bahia's principal candomblés.[76] Aninha was a businesswoman who traded in African products. She began with a stall in the commercial district, later moving her business to her home next door to the Rosário church.

Aninha also exemplified the quiet disregard of some Africans and their descendants for restrictions on their religious freedom. Despite the official hostility of Catholic authorities to the candomblé and despite the requirement that members be Roman Catholic, the brotherhoods included various influential candomblé priests and priestesses in their ranks. In addition to dos Santos, Martiniano Eliseu do Bomfim, collaborator of Nina Rodrigues and a venerated *babalawo*,[77] was a Rosário board member from 1942 to 1944. Felizberto Sowzer, one of the priests who initiated Aninha, and Bibiano Soares Cupim, a priest and longtime leader of the Sociedade Protectora dos Desvalidos, are both buried in the Rosário. Another influential candomblé figure at the Rosário was Rodolfo Sowzer Bamboucher, whose remains are buried in the main chapel.[78] Regardless of the Church's position, these were respected figures in the Afro-Brazilian community, and the brotherhoods welcomed not only their financial contributions but also the prestige they lent to the organizations. In addition, although from the Catholic perspective it was only possible to belong to one religion, from the Afro-Brazilian perspective an eclectic worldview combining elements of several religious traditions was more than possible. It was an historical fact.

The second type of *prêto* institution making the transition into post-abolition society was the secular mutual aid society, the Sociedade Protectora dos Desvalidos. In 1832 a piano-carrier named Manoel Victor Serra founded the brotherhood of Nossa Senhora Protectora dos Desvalidos. The Protectora was required by imperial law to register as a religious institution, but its principal purpose was to function as a mutual beneficent society for *prêto* men. The group functioned first in the chapel of a small chapter of the Rosário at the Church of the Fifteen Mysteries, and moved later to the church of the Rosário às Portas do Carmo. A serious disagreement led to the group's forced departure from that church to their own quarters in a nearby house. They changed their name from "brotherhood" to Sociedade Protectora dos Desvalidos.

The Sociedade differed from the brotherhoods in its autonomy from the Catholic Church and in the peripheral importance of religious concerns.[79] The members concentrated on amassing an endowment that would provide for the care of those unable to work. Members contributed during their working lives until they earned the title of *remido,* conferred after payment of dues for eighteen years. Before 1888 the Sociedade did not have many assets, but it began to acquire both residential and commercial properties in subsequent decades. One of the reasons actual possession of properties was delayed was the frequent practice of usufruct. By his will of 1891, José Antônio Xavier de Jesus left a house to the Sociedade. He granted usufruct rights first to Carolina Francisca do Amor Divino, however, and upon her death, to his niece Maria José.[80] The Sociedade eventually came to own twelve buildings, most of which were located in the downtown area, used for both residential and commercial purposes.[81] The society purchased its headquarters, a large three-

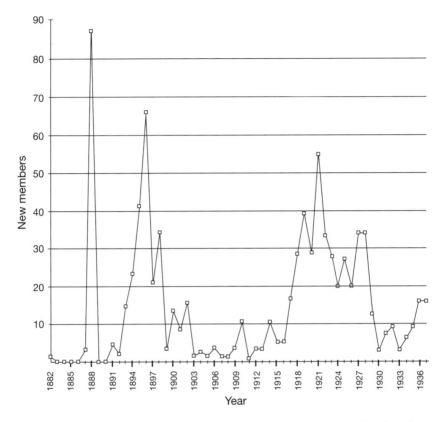

FIGURE 3. Sociedade Protectora dos Desvalidos, new members, 1882–1937. Data from Arquivo da Sociedade Protectora dos Desvalidos, Livro de Matriculas, 1882–1937.

story *sobrado,* for eight *contos* in 1883, subdividing the top floor into rooms for rent and the ground level into storefronts.

A total of 792 men joined the Sociedade Protectora dos Desvalidos between 1888 and 1938. Only *prêtos* were eligible, and applicants had to be nominated by a current member. The average age of new members was twenty-three, and 400 of the 656 men for whom occupations were recorded (61 percent) worked in construction-related trades.[82] Sociedade members, expecially those in elected offices, were often active in other organizations as well. Eloy Aleixo Franco, a stonemason who joined the Protectora in 1893, was a particularly active member. Between 1893 and 1897 he held the offices of treasurer, secretary, vice president, and president of the Artisans' Philanthropic Union, treasurer of the Artisans' Mutual Aid Society, and vice president of a trades school, and served on the planning commission of the Workingman's Center.[83] Florencio da Silva Friandes served simultaneously as a member of the Sociedade Protectora dos Desvalidos, president of the Sociedade Bolsa de Caridade, and first secretary of the Sociedade Beneficente 16 de Julho.[84] As tradesmen, members frequently belonged to one of the numerous trade associations in the city, particularly the Artisans' Philanthropic Union (União Philantropica dos Artistas), the Artisans' Mutual Aid Society (Monte-Pio dos Artistas) and the Workingman's Center (Centro Operário). Sociedade members frequently dominated the leadership of these organizations. At the Artisans' Philanthropic Union, Manoel Friandes and Eloy Aleixo Franco served as president and vice president, respectively, in 1893. The following year, a Sociedade member, Terencio Aranha Dantas, was first secretary. Two years later, Dantas nominated Faustino Gomes da Silva for membership in the Protectora, and the following year Dantas was president and Gomes da Silva first secretary of the Union. In 1898 the Protectora members Júlio Alves da Palma, Caetano Porphyrio da Silva Campos, and Ricardo Martins Ferreira served on the board, and in 1900 Faustino Gomes da Silva became president.[85] Many also belonged to the Rosário, in a strategy of combining benefits. Thus when Martinho Braga do Nascimento died in 1923, the Sociedade Protectora dos Desvalidos assisted with funeral costs and the Rosário buried him in one of their crypts.[86]

Unlike the Rosário, the Sociedade operated as a business, with the members themselves serving on active fiscal review committees and providing generally vigilant oversight. Members were required to pay their annual dues and to document requests for disability payments if necessary. In return the Protectora honored its responsibility to pay out disability income, funeral benefits, and pensions to widows and orphans.

The Sociedade made strategic use of the patronage process through a group known as "Socios Protectores." Because regular membership was restricted to *prêtos,* this was a special membership category open to persons not of African descent; it included politicians and other influential members of Bahian society. The Protectores were chosen for their ability to aid the organization, but had no voice in internal operations. Just how influential they could be was illustrated by the concessions secured by the Sociedade regarding payment of the municipal property tax *(décima).* In June 1883, the Sociedade paid 56$000 in taxes; this payment reached 59$384 for the following six-month period.[87] In the 1880s and 1890s, the city council frequently granted exemptions from this tax to charitable organizations.[88] The Protectora sent its initial request for exemption in 1885. In August 1889 the group awarded the diploma of Socio Protector to the provincial president and two imperial deputies, among them José Luis de Almeida Couto, "for the services [they] may provide."[89] With the aid of the two deputies, the Sociedade received the *décima* exemption in 1889. They also received an annual government subsidy of 1:000$000, approved by the provincial president. Political reorganization under the Republic required the Protectora to reapply in 1893. José Luis de Almeida Couto, the mayor at the time, personally intervened by sending a cover letter on behalf of the Protectora to the city council. Within 48 hours, the municipal fiscal committee approved the request.[90]

There are few references to political figures and events other than those directly related to the welfare of the organization. A search for Sociedade references to abolition in May 1888 yields only silence. In contrast, records noted the deaths of the king of Portugal in 1889 and of the former emperor Pedro II in 1891, the latter of whom was honored with a large portrait in the Sociedade's main meeting hall.[91]

A board of directors, elected by the members, ran the daily business of the Protectora. The General Assembly, consisting of all members, provided oversight and voted quarterly on important matters, generally pertaining to finances. There were factions within the assembly, and meetings sometimes became heated when fiscal irregularities surfaced. This was the case in 1893, when the members arrived for the General Assembly meeting at which the new board was to be installed, only to find the front door chained and locked. They proceeded to hold the meeting in the street. Eighty members arrived for the next meeting in April, but it had to be suspended after a shouting match could not be contained. A special meeting was called for later in the month. The former treasurer was accused of not having paid 224$000 in building taxes (this was the *imposto predial,* not the *décima*), and selling a filing cabinet for a sum far below its market value and without the consent of the assembly. The members quickly took sides: one faction defended the ex-treasurer's actions as "an oversight that could happen to anyone"; the other hurled insults. This meeting also dissolved in disorder. Twenty-three members drafted a petition requesting another special session in June; 101 members showed up. Manoel Cajueiro, president of the General Assembly, began to read Articles 32–43 of the statutes, pertaining to the maintenance of order, and was promptly interrupted by a senior member who insisted they get right to the business at hand. A vote was taken and the motion approved. Theodoro Gomes then rose and said he wanted the president to answer three questions. The minutes do not detail the questions, but as soon as they were asked the president had to call for order. Cajueiro told Gomes to wait for an answer. Gomes agreed. At that point Felipe da Costa e Souza muttered that Gomes should have waited in the first place, and immediately the assembly took sides in an argument that escalated to the point that one member, Felipe Benicio,

> protesting against the President, [attempted] to jump over the railing around the board's table, [but was] prevented by many members. From

that point on the session was tumultuous, all rising to their feet and the President calling for order and being ignored. There were great blows exchanged between members, even shouts demanding the ouster of the President, which resulted in one member leaving wounded, his nose bleeding. At that point the President called some members to order who were brandishing chairs, because he saw the damage they were about to do to the Sociedade. Realizing that his entreaties were being ignored, and seeing the lack of security, he declared he could not continue with the session. And not being able to deliberate anything whatsoever, he suspended the session.

When the General Assembly next met in October, the reading of the previous minutes almost precipitated another fight over the description of Felipe Benicio's attempt to jump over the railing. The ex-treasurer, whose action had provoked the initial outburst, wanted the entire account stricken from the record so that "this sad page would not remain in the annals of the Sociedade." His friend Terencio Aranha Dantas then chastened them all:

[F]or the respect due your race and this body, I make the same plea in light of the fact that these scenes lower our race and our Sociedade before our brothers and before the Public, demonstrating that black men do not know, or pretend not to know, how to conduct themselves in civilized society, to the point that the press [*Gazeta de Noticias*] published that our behavior was outside the bounds of civilized people.[92]

Terencio's comment reveals a sensitivity, also evident in the writings of the Frente Negra, to being included in the ranks of "civilized people." For people of the Afro-Atlantic diaspora, this type of commentary generally signals a desire to create distance between the negatively stereotyped blacks and those considered more "acceptable" because they conform to societal norms.

The fracas was not typical of the organization, nor did any other meetings become brawls, but it illustrates the extent to which the full membership was involved in the Sociedade. It was an active membership in that approximately 15–25 percent of all members sat on committees of either the Directorate or the General Assembly, the organization's governing units. Moreover, the Sociedade was an association of black men who had great personal and race pride. In the final analysis, it was that pride which proved great enough for them to set aside their serious personal differences for the good name of their race and their Sociedade. Although race is rarely mentioned in their discussions, the Protectora was adamant that only dark-skinned blacks (*prêtos*) be admitted.[93] They also conducted their business dealings with other blacks,

Ill. 14. Meeting hall, Sociedade Protectora dos Desvalidos.

whenever possible. When the hiring of an accountant was proposed in 1911, Terencio Dantas agreed, "so long as it is a person of our color who is already a member."[94]

The Protectora turned out to be a valuable resource for its members. Most were artisans engaged in building trades, and the Protectora owned old buildings in constant need of repair. The group contracted out virtually all maintenance and repair work to members. This was generally done through direct arrangements, as when Abílio José dos Santos was hired to do stonemasonry. Occasionally members subcontracted to one another. When the General Assembly needed a new table in 1921, the job was consigned to Franciso José da Costa, its president. He then got another member to do the actual carpentry for him.[95]

The Sociedade was valuable in other ways, particularly for its elderly members living alone. One of the offices of the Directorate was that of the *visitador,* who personally visited members to deliver their payments and check on the sick or delinquent. Jacintho Manoel dos Anjos, *visitador* in 1925, discovered that Americo Barros was "sick and in a state of complete abandonment." The directors immediately had him sign a document authorizing the Sociedade to sell his property. They bought the house for the organization, but this was not a ruse to take advantage of an incapacitated brother. The Sociedade agreed to manage the property throughout Barros' lifetime, giving him rents, his membership pension, and taking care of all repairs. After deducting taxes, *décimas,* and other costs, the balance would go to Barros. Barros also received 15$000 over the amount of his regular pension.[96] When another member, Luiz Antônio da Cruz, became sick, the directors hired a woman to care for him.[97]

Not all relationships were characterized by fraternal kindness. Manoel Raymundo Querino, the first Afro-Brazilian to publish books on Afro-Brazilian history and culture, was a member of the Sociedade. For reasons undisclosed in the archives, Querino had once left the organization, and requested readmission in 1892 while working in the Intendencia Municipal. The Directorate, in a secret ballot, denied his readmission by a vote of five to one. Querino, well aware of the prerequisites for membership, wrote back that he was perfectly qualified and that he would not accept their decision, "unless [the Sociedade] shows or declares on what moral or social principle you stood to reject this proposal." Another vote was taken. The result was the same, but the communication to Querino merely instructed him to await their response.[98] Querino again applied in 1894, and was approved.[99] In February 1896 Querino requested a disability allowance and enclosed a medical certification upholding his claim. The *visitador* duly went to his house, but Querino was not home. The directors debated over whether to authorize the payment, but decided to go ahead so that "no bad judgments be blamed on this directorate." A few days later Querino advised them that he would be sending a proxy to collect his money, as he had to leave the city for two months on medical grounds for a change of climate.

Always vigilant, the General Assembly convened a special meeting on March 9 to discuss Querino. Members noted that the Directorate had followed procedure by requiring a doctor's statement documenting his illness, but "it is well known that this gentleman has been seen lately in various places, parading in uniformed processions, staying up into the night at weddings, and taking strolls, et cetera, which proves quite the contrary." They voted 21 to 3 to discontinue Querino's payments, but Ricardo Ferreira warned that Querino, "being all involved in government, could avenge himself on the Sociedade by having the government stop its subsidy."[100]

By the time of the March meeting, not only had they failed to receive the subsidy, but Mattheus Cruz told the directors that rumors were circulating about the impropriety of demanding doctor's notes when they had a *visitador* perfectly able to see for himself whether a person was sick. When the subsidy still had not come by August, the treasurer made a proposal: "[G]iven that it is common practice for all the societies to confer titles on the heads of this Capital, [I suggest] that [we] bestow the title of Socio Benemerito on Conselheiro Luiz Vianna." By so honoring a city politician he hoped to gain a political ally to help reinstate the subsidy. The members agreed, but to no avail. Instead, they received a letter from a city official demanding a "minutely detailed report" of their most important activities of the past year.[101] The loss of the subsidy did not greatly hurt the organization. The Protectora's endowment had increased from just under 18 *contos* in 1888 to over 108 *contos* in 1910, attributable mainly to property acquisition, improved rent collection, and consistent investment in savings and bonds.[102] By 1923 those assets had grown to over 175 *contos*.[103]

Querino returned one final time, at age seventy-four, to request a retirement pension. He complained that his requests had been ignored and offered the curious criticism that "the Brazilian people, proclaiming Independence, gave proof they could not continue under the fierce tutelage of the Portuguese, but the Sociedade dos Desvalidos [*sic*] has not learned that lesson and has lived as though outside of social intercourse, without representation." The latter reference appears to be to the Sociedade's resistance to engaging in the politics of patronage in which Querino maneuvered, albeit without a black constituency of his own. At any rate, the Directorate decided that Querino "by his nature is no longer a member of this house," and rejected his request.[104]

The Querino case raises interesting questions about leadership and political strategies. Querino had risen to great prominence, as a politician, an elector (very few Brazilians of any race met the suffrage qualifications), and a scholar. He was a member of the prestigious Geographical and Historical Society of Bahia. He had joined both the Rosário brotherhood and the Sociedade Protectora dos Desvalidos, and was most likely a member of many other organizations. He was intimately acquainted with African Bahian life and customs, yet his experience with the Sociedade calls into question the nature of the relationships he maintained with various sectors of the community of African descent. He was well positioned to be a power broker between the community and the government, as illustrated by his apparent success in blocking the Sociedade's subsidy. There is no evidence that any black constituencies became involved with him in that capacity. Further research may shed light on whether blacks as a group resisted patronage politics, if they rejected Querino personally, or even if Querino sought such a role at all.

The case also raises the larger question of leadership patterns and political strategies within the Afro-Bahian community. It juxtaposes Querino, a black man who had attained an unparalleled degree of access to the political system, against the Protectora, which lacked political influence but maintained a solid constituency. Querino had nothing concrete to offer other than the vague promise of representation via an existing political system that held little potential for blacks. The failure of the Afro-Bahian community, and the Protectora in particular, to rally around Querino as a representative suggests a lack of faith in government even on the part of even those concerned about their inclusion in mainstream ("civilized") society. Their strategy was not to seek benefits from political authorities but, rather, to rely on their own entrepreneurship to ensure their financial security. This autonomous role served them well; when the Protectora's *décima* exemption was discontinued, members had an endowment that allowed them to stand by their principles in defiance of the manipulative Querino.

The Rosário and the Sociedade Protectora dos Desvalidos were both institutions that had originated in slavery and underwent changes after abolition. The Rosário, which continued to perform the same functions as it had in the colonial era, lost the bulk of its membership base. This loss is directly attributable to its failure to respond to the changing needs of the black constituency. In contrast, the Sociedade shifted toward a more secular orientation before abolition, making clear that its emphasis was on providing social security for its members as they became aged or infirm. This fulfilled a critical need, given the absence of such programs provided by the government. When the state instituted social security in the 1930s, however, the Sociedade found itself duplicating that function and thus redundant. Membership records suggest a gradual diminution in new enrollments. The pattern of membership had been cyclical; members typically entered as single men in their early twenties, and their sons followed some twenty-five years later (see Figure 3). Figures are available through 1937–38, but a more extensive longitudinal study is needed to fully assess this generational pattern. Despite a shrinking membership base, the Sociedade had already ensured its continued financial viability through its commercial real estate investments. Today, both the Rosário and the Sociedade Protectora dos Desvalidos are apprehensive about their ability to survive into the twenty-first century. Both have financial assets, but have lost their position as vital organs within the Afro-Bahian community.

This overview of the Afro-Bahian community and its post-abolition social institutions has sought to understand the role of collective activism as a form of self-determination among Afro-Bahians. It did not gain the popularity it enjoyed in São Paulo for several reasons. First, the population of color in Salvador was made up of many smaller communities bound by both formal and informal networks. Some of these evolved from the *nação* groups formulated during slavery. Africans assisted one another as friends and *compadres,* and fictive kinship ties bound one generation to the next. Retention of African social networks may well have impeded greater solidarity among *prêtos*. In addition, there is no evidence that *prêtos* and *pardos* pursued the type of inclusive *negro* identity used in São Paulo to forge solidarity within the entire population of African descent.

Second, the types of networks created by Afro-Brazilians in Salvador fit well within the model of patronage. The captain of a *canto* or the Iyalorixa of a candomblé community, for example, allocated benefits to recognized group members. To join the Sociedade Protectora, the sponsorship of a current member was mandatory; without it, entry was impossible. When that organization sought its tax exemption, it bestowed honorary titles on influential politicians. In each instance, Afro-Bahians operated within the political culture of patronage so central to the Brazilian ethos. The patronage model requires a clear distinction between group members and outsiders. As a guiding principle for Afro-Bahian collectives, patronage served to counteract a broader conceptualization of solidarity based on negritude.

Third, some of the oldest and best established Afro-Brazilian organizations, such as the brotherhoods and the Sociedade Protectora dos Desvalidos, were simply not engaged in the pursuit of political power. Their activities revolved around securing the future of their individual organizations. It is possible that they had little faith in a political system dominated by patronage and an entrenched group of elites, as was the case in post-abolition Bahia. Preoccupied as they were with the minutiae of day-to-day existence, these groups were not to be the source of collective activism.

The next chapter examines the central stage of action in post-abolition Bahia—the battle for cultural freedom. Afro-Bahians fought for their right to observe African religion and enjoy Afro-Bahian culture both in public and in private. The national bias against African culture had led to repression in this most African of Brazilian cities. Although no one paid much attention in 1932 to Marcos Rodrigues dos Santos and his Frente Negra agenda, constant illegal police raids on candomblés moved Afro-Brazilians to demand their full right to religious freedoms guaranteed all citizens under the constitution. It was a struggle with roots extending far back into Bahian history. Its first expression after abolition came in the public festivals, most notably, Carnival.

CHAPTER 6

The Politics of Culture
in Salvador

*[We] remind the police of the necessity, in the name of civilization and to the credit of
Bahia, to put a stop to these degrading parades of an entirely African character...*
—*Jornal de Noticias* (Salvador), January 22, 1902

Agua mole em pedra dura, tanto bate até que fura.
(*The steady drip of gentle water wears a hole in the hardest rock.*)
—Bahian saying

*I*n the ethnic spectrum of the city of
Salvador, the large mixed-race population obscured the existence of its two
extremes, the white and the African communities, each of which held very different objectives for the post-abolition era. These two groups clashed in a series of conflicts over cultural freedoms, underlying which were deeper
questions of power and hegemony. Throughout Salvador's existence as a slave
society, whites had determined the roles black people would play in the city's
political, social, economic, and cultural fabric. People of African descent, always in the majority, consistently tested and forced the limits of those boundaries. They had been most successful in the realm of culture. Africans had
reformulated the teachings of Catholicism into a syncretic cosmology with
African and indigenous influences.[1] The African women who fed Bahia introduced *acarajé, caruru, mungunzá,* and other continental dishes that became
staples of Bahian cuisine. Africans wore the cloths known as *panos-da-costa,*
protected themselves with charms and amulets, played games like *a-i-u,* and
spoke their own languages.[2] In these and many other ways, they refused to
adopt European-based culture as their own, formulating instead a blend based
upon African norms. Yet until the post-abolition years, this process proceeded
in an insular African world that coexisted with white Bahians and a pluralistic
society of people of color. Abolition brought a new sense of freedom for Africans and their descendants to fully express themselves and their culture. In so

doing on the public streets of Salvador during Carnival, they crossed a tacit boundary, unleashing a floodgate of anger at what was perceived as the Africanization of Bahian culture. White elites, supported by the legal system, government, and the armed forces, were determined to stamp out Africanisms, particularly the rapidly growing candomblé. Despite such opposition, Africans ultimately succeeded in making Salvador the city in the Americas most closely associated with African-based culture in the twentieth century.[3]

In speaking of Africans in this period, I am referring not only to the African-born but also to their descendants within the context of a redefined African ethnicity. When the self-described "African" clubs appeared in the Carnival of the 1890s, they stretched the meaning of the term in two significant ways. The designation "African" was now being applied to the Brazilian descendants of Africans, and as an umbrella term bringing together the various ethnic enclaves known as *nações*. "African" identity represented a choice based not on color (as in *prêto*) but, rather, culture. Not all *prêtos* were necessarily African; the choice of the latter identity in the late nineteenth and early twentieth centuries implied adherence to an African-derived set of values and cultural norms. Thus a Brazilian-born individual could adopt an African *nação*. Integral to the formulation of this African ethnicity was candomblé spirituality and culture.

A framework for interpreting this process is offered by Monica Schuler. In her history of post-abolition Jamaica, she notes the importance of the Afro-Jamaican religion known as Myalism. Afro-Jamaican religion had undergone a transformation strikingly similar to that taking place in Afro-Bahian religion, both coincident with the dismantling of slavery and the transition to free society. In Jamaica, as in Bahia, the decrease of African-born persons weakened the divisions among African ethnic groups *(nações)*. These ethnic groups had once been an important mechanism of support and adjustment for the uprooted Africans arriving as slaves. As their numbers declined, so too had the specificities of ethnic cultures in favor of a more pluralistic creole African culture.[4] Myalism, the cornerstone of this transition, drew on three basic elements of African religious traditions—explanation, prediction, and control. Although its external forms borrowed from several religions, notably Baptist, Myalism interpreted all phenomena as the result of forces that could be systematized, predicted, and manipulated. These fundamentals are shared by many African cosmologies, thus making them accessible to the broader Afro-Jamaican community. Myalism offered people a measure of control over their lives and, significantly, the forces working against them. It appealed to a wide range of Afro-Jamaicans regardless of ethnicity.[5] Myalism provided the institutional basis for a reformulation of identity and ethnicity.

Bahian candomblé was undergoing a similar transformation. New congregations of Brazilians spread rapidly as the numbers of African-born declined. Each congregation, or *terreiro,* established a ritual based on the traditions of one of the principal African ethnic groups *(nações),* which all followers then adopted as their own. This redefined African ethnicity made candomblé accessible to people of various ethnic backgrounds, including mulattoes.[6] It was a vital cross-cutting institution bridging ethnic and color lines and setting the foundation for an integrated Afro-Bahian society. The African Carnival groups also expressed this new pluralism with themes drawn from all over the continent, and with ample representation of the West and Central African cultures from which the majority of slaves had come. These groups also hinted at another possible reason for the shifting conceptualization of ethnicity. Although no specific data are available, Carnival groups are traditionally started by relatively young people in their twenties and thirties.[7] The founders of Bahia's African Carnival groups were not African-born, but the children and grandchildren of Africans. As the painful reality of being African and enslaved slipped into the past, this younger generation sought to preserve and venerate its own heritage.

The negative reaction of whites to the directions Afro-Bahian culture was taking was rooted in the experiences of the nineteenth century and strategies of social control dating back to the colonial era. Ever conscious of their minority status, Salvador's whites sought to foster intergroup rivalries among Africans by heightening *nação* consciousness. Among Brazilian-born persons of African descent, whites planted the seeds of disunity with the differential treatment accorded the various gradations of color categories. As in other American slave societies, the specter of the Haitian Revolution weighed heavily on the minds of slave masters surrounded by Africans. White fears were realized in the late eighteenth and early nineteenth centuries when several Afro-Brazilian revolts shook Salvador and the surrounding countryside.[8] The first, the Revolt of the Tailors in 1798, was led by mulattoes whose agenda included making Bahia an independent state in which slavery would be abolished.[9] Subsequent Muslim-led slave revolts had less clear political objectives, focusing instead on escaping slavery and obliterating anyone who stood in the way. The last of these, in 1835, resulted in a severe backlash against all Africans in the city. Government authorities ransacked the homes of Africans and suspended the rights of freedmen on the grounds that "[n]one of them has the rights of a Citizen, nor the privileges of Foreigners."[10] The Bahian historian João José Reis notes that in the wake of the uprising, "it is impressive how the presence of Africans and their cultures challenged the world-view, the daily habits, and even the psychological stability of many Bahians. The so-called African customs, which before had seemed so typically Bahian, suddenly emerge in the documents as alien and subversive and in need of prohibition and, if possible, extinction. Down with African Bahia! Indeed, in the heat of the anti-African backlash, not just the *abadás,* the Malê rosaries, and the Arabic writing constituted proof of rebelliousness. Musical instruments, necklaces, and African cloth were also considered harmful to law and order."[11]

Interestingly, whites felt increased hostility toward Africans, but not necessarily toward Afro-Brazilians. In the wake of that revolt, African cultural manifestations were cast as acts of potential sedition, suspected of providing Africans with secret forums for hatching new plots against the Brazilian state. In the polemic that ensued, Afro-Brazilians stood ambiguously, having to choose between casting their lot as "Brazilians" or as "Africans."[12] The polarity thus established was not one of race, as in São Paulo, but of culture. In Salvador, European and African cultural norms opposed each other with a large intermediate group of persons of mixed descent poised precariously between the two. The same dynamic characterized Bahian race relations in the post-abolition era and was the source of the conflicts that precipitated resistance.

The anti-African sentiment of the early nineteenth century continued, developing a new ideological underpinning as the historical context changed. By the time of abolition, whites feared not rebellion but, rather, the possibility that Afro-Bahian culture would become dominant. Bahia, once preeminent in the Brazilian power structure, was now reduced to backland status with the advance of coffee's economic success in the central-southern region, the establishment of the royal court in Rio, and the dynamics of artistic and cultural progress in the south. White Bahians became alarmed at the apparent proliferation of "barbaric" Africanisms, a trend diametrically opposed to what they viewed as the "progressive" regions of Brazil. They began a struggle to modernize, which meant the suppression of Africanisms in a city where most of the population was of African descent.

The history of Carnival during the First Republic illustrates the dynamics involved in the cultural war to bring Bahia into step with modernization. The Carnival groups, however, were merely symptomatic manifestations of what whites were most threatened by—the growing presence of the candomblé. Complaints about the *batuques* referred as much to the sacred drums and rhythms of the candomblé as they did to the Carnival celebrations.

The Social Geography of Ethnicity: The Fight for Public Space

The public streets and plazas of Salvador became the battleground of the culture wars of the post-abolition era. In the 1890s Salvador's white elites took steps to rid the city of what they perceived to be excessive displays of African culture, such as the *rodas de capoeira* in the plaza facing the prestigious medical school and the cathedral, the boisterous samba parties accompanying what they felt should be solemn Catholic festivals, and the seemingly ubiquitous *batuques*.[13] This is best illustrated in the history of Bahia's Carnival during that time.

Carnival is a unique window onto Brazilian life and thought. In those few pre-Lenten days of festivities is captured the essence of Brazilian culture, including its subtleties of class tensions, gender relations, and the important political issues of the day. As such, Carnival has grown and changed in pace with the nation itself. Even though Carnival was regarded as a time for merrymaking and the relaxation of social conventions, accounts from the mid-nineteenth century show that it respected prevailing social boundaries. The social changes accompanying Brazil's modernization in the late nineteenth century were reflected in Bahia's Carnival during the 1880s and 1890s. In the terminology of the era, Carnival, like the nation as a whole, became "civilized." The formula, not surprisingly, was "order and progress"—the imposition of order to ensure the progress of society toward modernity. The problem was that modernity was defined by a European standard, and the people animating Carnival were decidedly (and quite vocally) African.

Up until the 1880s Carnival had been characterized by the *entrudo*. Attributed to the early Portuguese settlers, the *entrudo* was a time for practical jokes. Pranksters ensconced in dark corners or at upper-story windows drenched unaware passers-by with buckets of water. Foreigners and blacks were favorite targets; in the case of blacks it was particularly popular to douse them with flour. Not all the missiles were harmless or inoffensive; some liked to use waste water, which inevitably provoked the quarrels and fights that caused the *entrudo* to be regarded as "barbaric" sport.

By the nineteenth century, the *entrudo* had developed a more refined, domestic side, consistent with the new urban lifestyles. The existing accounts come mostly from travelers who visited the principal cities of Rio de Janeiro and Salvador in the nineteenth century; it does not appear that the *entrudo* was equally popular in the rural areas.[14] Carnival was divided into the protective realm of the home and the "wild" realm of the streets.[15] Within the homes of the bourgeoisie, family members and guests of comparable social class shared in the merriment. The preparations began months in advance. The most popular *entrudo* game was mock warfare employing such munitions as water, flour, and perfume sealed in little wax limes and oranges that burst upon the slightest contact. The women of the household, including the lady and daughters of the house as well as the female slaves, confected the mock weaponry with wax procured by the men of the house.

Domestic *entrudo* games centered around coquetry in which women played the role of instigators. Their free-wheeling behavior led foreign observers to interpret Carnival as a general relaxation of social conventions. Fernando Denis commented that "[t]he Brazilian girls are naturally melancholic and live secluded, but when the *entrudo* comes they seem to change their character, and during three days they lose their graveness and natural shyness to forget themselves in their enjoyment."[16]

The *entrudo* was a time for women's open coquetry. Traveling in Rio, the Englishman John Luccock was doused by the *limõezinhos* (little wax limes) of the governor's daughters as he approached a church. He scrambled to safety, but they continued their "battle" with his friends.[17] The game was much the same in Bahia, where black women hawked their perfumed oranges with a song:

> Here they are, here they are
> The excellent little oranges
> Buy, Yayá, the little oranges
> To "entrude" your love
>
> It is Yayá, it is Yoyô
> Who want to "entrude" their love! . . .
>
> The one who "entrudes" his love
> It is a sign of intimacy
> Yayá entrudes Yoyô
> To become his close friend[18]

Of the game itself, Mello Morais Filho wrote: "The boys hit the bosoms of those beautiful girls who excited their senses, the girls sought the starched shirt-fronts of those boys who impressed them, or potential future fiancés. And the little oranges hitting the upper part of the wall broke and defoliated like little multicolored bouquets of moist perfumed flowers over the correct and beautiful bosoms of the *entrudo* players."[19]

Despite the apparent madness of the revelry, the boundaries of propriety were rarely breached. The flirtatious *entrudo* took place among people of similar social class. Women remained tied to the home and family; their participation in "street" Carnival was generally limited to tossing confetti or *limõezinhos* from doors and windows, protected by their advantageous position and the presence of men. The fact that women's participation was viewed as liberal underscores their circumscribed mobility throughout the rest of the year.

In these descriptions of Carnival, Afro-Brazilians play supporting roles to ensure the fullest enjoyment by white masters. Blacks were the butt of many practical jokes, particularly those in which their appearance was distorted with light-colored flour.[20] Blacks played *entrudo* games with one another, but were careful not to hit whites. The latter, however, readily doused blacks, therein reflecting the social inequalities in which whites enjoyed the advantage of a whole arsenal of social "weaponry" to which blacks had no access.[21] The question remains as to what form the Afro-Brazilian Carnival experience took. Jean Baptiste Debret recorded his observations of black participation during the *entrudo:*

> For Brazilians, then, Carnival is essentially the three "fat" days that begin at five o'clock in the morning on Sunday, amid the cheerful goings-on of the blacks already scattered in the streets to stock up on water and food for their masters, gathered in the marketplaces or around the public fountains and shops. We see them there, full of happiness and health, but possessors of little money, satisfying their innocent madness with the free water or cheap powder that costs them five *réis*. . . .
>
> . . . On these days of happiness, the most rowdy, although always respectful of whites, meet after supper on the beaches and in the plazas around the fountains to soak each other with water or dunk one another as a game. . . . As for the black women, one only sees old and poor ones in the streets, with their vending-trays atop their heads, full of perfume-filled limes, sold on behalf of their makers.

Indeed, for many blacks Carnival was a time of extra work in addition to their regular duties. They were responsible for providing each household with water, and undoubtedly faced excessive cleaning responsibilities in the laundry and around the house, not to mention cooking for the many guests. When they did have time to play, black women were not bold coquettes, as were their white counterparts. Instead, they were the objects of the black men's games: "With water and starch powder, the negro, on these days, exercises without reproof all the tyranny of his rude buffooneries on the negro women he meets; some oranges stolen from their masters become extra Carnival ammunition for the rest of the day. But the hapless steward negro woman, on the contrary, dressed voluntarily in her worst clothes, generally dark blue or black, comes back home with her bosom drenched and the rest of her dress marked with the hand prints of the negro who smeared her face and hair with white starch."[22]

It is difficult to ascertain whether the differential participation of black women indicates that they were poorly regarded and the butt of pranks by black men who, in turn, had been the victims of white men's jokes. It is also possible that different forms of Carnival play existed between black men and women, and that the games represented the flirtatious attentions of black men.

One interesting description of Afro-Brazilian Carnival observances bears striking similarity to the cakewalk popular among blacks in the southern United States. Debret noted "a certain Carnival in which some groups of masked and costumed blacks dressed as old Europeans imitated with great exaggeration their gestures as they greeted people in the balconies to the left and right; they were escorted by some musicians, also of color and equally costumed."[23] Imitation of whites was socially permissible because its impossibility made it a harmless farce. In contrast, a game of warfare in which blacks were permitted to attack whites, albeit symbolically, was dangerously suggestive and "too close to reality" to be allowed.[24]

On the streets, men engaged in a rougher form of play. These more aggressive *entrudos* garnered public disapproval of what was increasingly labeled "barbaric" behavior. The violent side of the *entrudo* led to repeated attempts to suppress it. Analyzing this process, Peter Fry and colleagues write: "This persecution appears related to certain historical processes occurring at that time, including the shift in the social meaning of public space, that is, the street itself. [The street] can no longer be merely an extension of each house in a modern version of the traditional grounds of the rural homestead. On the contrary, it must be prepared in aesthetic, hygienic and disciplinary terms, for the emergence of a republican and abolitionist urban elite in need of a setting compatible with the new political prerogatives it has taken for itself."[25] Underlying this line of thinking is the concept of ownership of public space, the conviction on the part of Salvador's elites that the streets were theirs to use as they saw fit. This was to be the source of subsequent conflicts with the African Carnival clubs.

In Bahia the *entrudo* persisted into the 1880s, and only began to disappear when it was supplanted by the organized processions and balls that came to characterize the modern Carnival. This new Carnival was spearheaded by the Euterpe Philharmonic Society. In 1883 it founded the Fantoches de Euterpe, the first of Bahia's three great "Carnival societies." The Cruz Vermelha was founded the next year, followed by Inocentes em Progresso in 1889. These clubs introduced the concept of a "civilized" Carnival, with entirely new types of festivities that permitted the orderly participation of both men and women under close supervision. Their changes literally "tamed" the *entrudo,* a goal consistent with the national ethos of "order and progress."

> Yes, now there is a reason for the proclamations of the city and the police, because now the people know that the *entrudo* is a crime against humanity and civilization. Yes, now the proclamations and edicts are accepted, aimed at producing effects on the delinquents [who infringe upon] the popular sovereignty, now that the carnival has been consecrated, its reign proclaimed. . . . Blessed, then, is the Carnival, that extinguished the *entrudo* and gave the public days of festivities and happiness.[26]

The clubs sponsored masquerade balls at the newly constructed Politeama Theater. Each chose annual themes from Greco-Roman mythology featured in the balls and in their parades through the downtown streets. There were also *carros de crítica,* floats and masqueraders satirizing politics and issues of the day.[27] Decorations, masks, costumes, and reams of confetti spurred a brisk trade, especially in the port district where many of these supplies arrived from Europe. City administrators arranged for transportation and security, but assigned responsibility for public decorations and lighting to citizens' committees from each neighborhood.[28] The entire cost of each club's presentation was borne by its members. By default, only the well-to-do could participate in the most lavish clubs.

This new style of Carnival took Bahia by storm. An estimated 80,000 visitors from the interior flocked to Salvador for the festivities in 1889.[29] Each year new clubs appeared, to the delight of crowds both in the streets and at the public balls. But just as the "Venetian"-style clubs reveled in the fantasy of a European Bahia, the children of Africans began to do the same with an idealized Africa. In the 1890s Bahia's Carnival witnessed the debut of the first of the great Afro-Brazilian Carnival clubs, the Embaixada Africana (African Embassy).[30] The first appearance of the Embaixada Africana was probably in 1895, "to resolve the question of *vatapá,* according to their widely distributed flyers."[31] An early spin-off and subsequent rival, the Pandegos da Africa (African Merrymakers), most likely appeared in 1896.[32] The first detailed account I located about these groups appeared in the *Jornal de Noticias* in 1896, the principal chronicle of Carnival celebrations. The popular Fantoches de Euterpe and Cruz Vermelha clubs had not participated that year, and only appeared intermittently throughout the 1890s. The Carnival editor at *Jornal de Noticias* feared that the absence of the major clubs would dampen the festivities, but the African clubs made them a huge success.

The members of the Embaixada Africana lived up to their club's name as African cultural ambassadors. Following the practice of the first clubs, which turned to Greek and Roman antiquity for their inspiration, these Afro-Brazilians reached back to their own cultural history and brought forth King Babá-Anin and Ajahy, escorted by the court of Oxalá, the Yoruba deity. For three days they paraded to applause and confetti through the streets of Salvador, accompanied by the music of the *agôgô,* the *atabaque* drums, and other "sonorous intruments from the temples of Africa." Their retine and the float that bore its standard were small, but they delighted the crowds. The *Jornal de Noticias* wrote that the Embaixada "gave *zing* to the Carnival of '96, and their presence in the future is not merely anticipated—it is indispensible."[33]

Also appearing in 1896 were the African Merrymakers, amid groups with such evocative names as the Sons of Venice, Sons of Pluto, Sons of Har-

mony, Lords of the Epoch, Poor Independents, Emigrants, Intimates, Para-
sites, Lost Souls, and the Invisible Ones. Suddenly, self-described "Africans"
had joined this public expression of the themes and issues of Brazil. Using the
social language of Carnival brought over by Europeans, they told of their own
antiquities and cultures. The moral of their story was that Africa and Africans
were inalienable components of Brazilian society and culture.

Public reaction was, at first, welcoming. Despite anti-African prejudices
and the equation of African culture with "savagery," the parades of clubs like
the Embaixada were nothing in comparison to what was remembered of the
old *entrudo*. Without the big clubs in the 1896 Carnival, some feared it would
return. Yet such fears proved groundless: "The barbaric and stupid *entrudo*
game has, to the honor of Bahia, even in these three days [of Carnival] disappeared from our customs, something which, sixteen years ago, seemed profoundly ingrained." Perhaps the Embaixada and the Pandegos seemed a quaint
novelty in 1896. Within a few years there were dozens of "African" clubs, including the African Knights, African Vagrants, African Hunters, African Warriors, Sons of Africa, Nephews of Africa, Grandsons of Africa, and the
Defenders of Africa.[34] In 1905 they were all banned from Carnival.

The return of Cruz Vermelha in 1897 did not dampen the enthusiasm for
the African clubs, joined that year by Chegada Africana (African Arrival). The
popular themes of antiquity and current events were back. Cruz Vermelha
chose time as its theme. Its procession began with the Knights of the Day, followed by a float entitled "Aurora" on which twelve girls represented the hours,
and the Knights of the Sun. The Sons of Venice represented the arts and sciences under the watchful eye of Father Time. There was a group that called
itself the "Fans of Antônio Conselheiro," the messianic leader of the backland
rebellion that was to become the subject of Euclides da Cunha's *Os Sertões*.
The African clubs prepared their processions with equal care, and were not
found lacking. The press noted that the standard of the Pandegos da Africa
was "one of the best we have seen, not only for its artistic taste, but also for its
luxury."[35] The Pandegos were always praised for their exuberance; a review in
1898 noted that they "identified with the name of their club and so great was
the merrymaking of the Merrymakers that the numerous cortege accompanying them merrymade as well!"[36]

The Embaixada, whose themes had come from West Africa in the past,
branched out to Ethiopia, choosing Menelik as their king. Along the street in
front of the Rosário they stopped to crown him with gold, repeating the ceremony
at the site of the colonial palace.[37] Both the Embaixada Africana and the Pandegos da Africa drew on a broad spectrum of African cultural and political
history in their Carnival themes. As reported in the Bahian press, the Embaixada Africana was unrivaled in its scope. Its 1898 processional announcement

makes clear the breadth of its knowledge of the African continent, its peoples, and their history. It is reproduced here as closely as possible to the original:

The Embaixada Africana

Opening the procession, thundering the winds with the strident notes of their instruments
TWO CLARIONS
to sound the herald
Beautiful costume from Tunis
As proof that civilization is not a Utopia on the black continent (as the ill-sayers have propagandized) there will follow a well organized
MUSICAL BAND
sent from one of the German possessions and costumed in
GROTESQUE GERMAN UNIFORM
Following in the procession an
ELEGANT CAVALRY
ceded by Soba N'DUMBA TEMPO—as a special favor to this embassy —and selected from the most dexterous and robust
[QUIOCO] HUNTERS
And now! Contain your admiration before the luxury and magnificence of the
Dazzling standard-float
Announcing the approaching float, so that all can maintain the respectful attitude due the high dignitaries that deign to visit this land
TWO PAGES
who will sound triumphant notes on their
EGYPTIAN TRUMPETS
Immediately following will be the exhibition of the unrivaled standard-float, on which all will appreciate the splendid and meaningful
African Allegory
The acclaimed and well-crafted standard of the popular *Embaixada* will be borne by
H[is] M[ajesty]
AGO LI-AGBO
King of Abomey
surrounded by his BA-CAMAS (wives), in formal dress
AFRICA IN PERSON
will be displayed in all the splendor of its beauty on the first level of the float, inspiring admiration on the front of same will be
The Cataranga Waterfall
Forming the honor guard will be the following important African dignitaries:

Muata Inhanvo (Cabeba of Lunda) **e Chanama** (heir apparent);
Two noblemen (Morocco);
Two tribal chiefs from ancient Ethiopia
Two dignitaries from Oran (Algeria)
Followed by AN ALLEGORY IN MINIATURE
THE
EMBASSADOR MUZUMBO-TEMBO and his secretaries
CHA-QUESSI AND CANGOMBE
dressed in an *elegant toilette* (purchased from an *ambaquista*[38] espe-
cially for presentation in this capital) will follow, cloaked in the gravity
that their positions demand. The untiring Africans living here, with the
aim of proving their patriotism, had imported from Paris, to transport
the embassadors

A car of mother-of-pearl
Possessed of the laudable desire to annihilate the detractors
of the great country of Chad, these same Africans prepared with
their own hands the interior of this car, that one may thereby evalu-
ate the advanced level attained by
AFRICAN ART
In the rearguard of the car will march the AMBASSADOR'S
TREASURER—bowed with the weight of his office
Forming the special guard of his excellency the Ambassador
THREE WARRIORS FROM MADAGASCAR
The distinguished African community of Bahia, promoters of
this tumultuous reception, will close the procession, forming
an original charanga [band]
Reformed with new instruments, not known here, brought from
the confines of Africa by the RENOWNED MAESTRO ABEDÉ, whose
baton he will allow to forget about Italian opera.[39]
The patriotic community will present
dressed à la great gala
A model made expressly for the reception of the Embassy[40]

The Embaixada Africana worked hard to present an image of Africa that
was comparable to that of the great European civilizations celebrated by the
traditional clubs. Members also demonstrated their concern about European
interventions in Africa, as in their allusion to the questionable results of the
German presence, whose "grotesque" soldiers were sent to "civilize" Africa.
Even more significant here are the repeated assertions of the organizers'
ethnicity—"the untiring Africans living here" and "the distinguished African
community of Bahia." By such public statements, the organizers were staking

claim to an identity and a heritage that contrasted sharply with the assimila-tionist tendencies of many Brazilian-born blacks.

The following year, the Embaixada opened its procession with Berber soldiers from Tunisia forming the escort of Prester John. Prester John was an interesting selection; tradition held that Prince Henry, known popularly as "The Navigator," had initiated Portugal's explorations to Africa to seek the aid of this African Christian king to crush the Moors. The main float centered on King Ptolemy of ancient Egypt. Responding to earlier criticism for its lack of female participants, the Embaixada surrounded Ptolemy with four ladies-in-waiting. It also entered the realm of contemporary political commentary with a *carro de crítica* about taxes and financial distress. It was a year in which Carnival was dampened metaphorically by economic difficulties and literally by torrential rains. Neither the Cruz Vermelha nor the Fantoches appeared that year, ceding the honors to the two African clubs. The *Jornal de Noticias* la-mented yet another year without the older clubs, but gave "thanks to those who came, principally two clubs who presented themselves stylishly, receiving applause and cheers from their numerous fans. These were the Embaixada Africana and the Pandegos da Africa, already appreciated by our public for the extent to which for three years they have contended for applause at these fes-tivities, whose energy truly owes much to them."[41]

Smaller African clubs, including the Chegada Africana and Filhos da Africa, had also organized Carnival processions. African clubs became so popular that the commissions responsible for each neighborhood's festivities and decorations solicited their appearance in the press. This was the case of the residents of the Largo da Mouraria, who published a request that the Embaixada change its parade route so that the club might pass along their street.[42] The African clubs also participated in the dances at the Politeama Theater. Their music had not yet become part of the popular Carnival reper-toire, although in subsequent decades Afro-Brazilian music was to become the driving force in Bahian Carnival. The musicians of the Politeama played popu-lar European styles, interpreted to suit Brazilian tastes. The *Jornal de Noticias* described a ball in 1899 and made reference to the maxixe, a turn-of-the-century Brazilian dance craze:

> The maxixe was colossal. They danced it to the sound of the waltz, the polka, the quadrille, even marches. Decidedly, [it should be recom-mended] to the maestro that he plan the following program: maxixe, more maxixe, always maxixe. And how they dance this national inven-tion—few correctly, many *à la diable*. At the dance we visited there was one couple who danced the maxixe so well they were toasted with ice-

cold beer. The lady was a little skinny, but she danced the maxixe like a Fluminense.

Around 11 o'clock the Pandegos da Africa entered the Politeama, covered in confetti, to the applause of their admirers. They left before midnight. The dance ended shortly afterwards, leaving a longing with all those who attended.[43]

Despite the success of African processional clubs, there were early signs of concern about the evolution of the Bahian Carnival. Vendors had taken to setting up food and drink stands along the main Carnival routes. The mayor of Salvador prohibited these "market shacks" in 1898.[44] This may have been an early manifestation of the desire to "civilize" Carnival. By 1902 the press had fully taken up the campaign, enjoining the assistance of the police. Concern had spread from the refreshment stands to a more insidious assault on the cultural overtones of Carnival.

> Once again, we remind the police of the necessity, in the name of *civilization* and to the credit of Bahia, to put a stop to these *degrading* parades of an entirely African character and people outside the bounds of taste and respect, who organize so that during Carnival they may traverse *our* streets with a joyless noise that brings no enjoyment whatsoever.
>
> The majority of these groups, bearing those instruments of *candomblés*, many in immoral costumes, often do not allow one to hear the music or the jokes of the clubs and independent masqueraders, such is the infernal racket they make.
>
> We have already made reference to this issue, and since we have not yet had the pleasure of reporting any official preventative measures by the police, we reiterate ourselves today in the hope that it will not be necessary to make such reference again.[45]

Apparently there was no official response, for three days later the *Jornal de Noticias* restated its protest:

> We recommend to those who animate the Carnival that you abandon the African batuque. We understand that the triumphal entrance of Menelik, so brilliantly staged by the Embaixada, was a cultural and superior event. What, however, we do not understand are these groups of *Africans* with their bodies smeared in black grease, making grimaces and causing all sorts of confusion, letting it be seen that in this land, good taste seems to be dying. There are so many good ideas that the Carnival partygoers could take advantage of.[46]

Somehow themes of the Embaixada were acceptable, but the cultural elite took offense at other expressions of Africanity. The juxtaposition of civilization versus barbarity, which had characterized the triumph of the modern Carnival over the *entrudo,* had now moved to a cultural level in which civilized Europe opposed barbaric Africa. Somewhere in between was the concept of civilized Africa introduced by the Embaixada Africana and the Pandegos da Africa. It is not clear whether any single event precipitated the anti-*batuque* effort, for it appears to have erupted suddenly in 1902 in the same newspaper that once had nothing but praise for the African clubs. As late as 1901, the *entrudo* was still the principal focus for criticism. Some revelers had engaged in *entrudo* games on the island of Itaparica, "violent and barbaric, against the law and against civilization," for which they were chided by the press in terms similar to those used against the *batuques*.[47]

Members of the cultural elite sought to delineate the boundaries of acceptable Brazilian culture and, in so doing, *who* the acceptable participants were. As had been the case with the *entrudo,* they sought to use the law as a weapon. By outlawing the *batuque,* they excluded an entire class of people whose culture was cast as an individual choice of a criminal nature.[48] The essence of the 1902 campaign was precisely the criminalization of the *batuques,* with regulatory licenses used as the mechanism for their exclusion. Drawing on the example of Rio de Janeiro, the *Jornal de Noticias* argued that the licenses issued there served to "maintain a degree of civilization even in festivals of this nature, not permitting any clubs to organize by themselves and parade in public without the appropriate review of their program."[49]

The vehemence of the attacks exposed the vulnerability sensed by the Bahian elite. Whereas the cosmopolitan whites of southern Brazil were speaking easily of a "whitening" of the population, in Bahia, given blacks' numerical preponderance, the same formula would inevitably yield a "blackening."

> Now if these groups of *africans* aroused a certain repugnance in Carnivals past, when enthusiasm burst forth at the sight of the victorious clubs and monopolized the attention of all, what will be the Carnival of 1902, if the police do nothing to prevent the appearance on our streets of these *terreiros* where fetichism reigns, with their cortege of *ogans* and their orchestras of *canzás* and pandeiros? . . . In particular, we beseech those who judge these offensive *sambas* to be entertaining to try to take their leave during these Carnival festivities.[50]

Whites spoke of the Africanisms in Bahian culture as a source of profound embarrassment. To them, these characteristics lowered their status vis-à-vis those societies they regarded as "civilized" and increased the growing disparity between themselves and the modernized south. A 1903 letter to the editor written by a high school professor just after the opening of Carnival captures the disdain and vulnerability felt by white Bahians.

> Dear Lellis,
>
> I appeal to your generous heart for shelter for these lines in the columns of the *Jornal*.
>
> This year's Carnival, despite the patriotic and civilizing request made by said newspaper, was yet again a public exhibition of *candomblé*, with rare exception.
>
> If someone from outside were to judge Bahia by its Carnival, they could not help but place it on a par with Africa, and note that, to our shame, lodging here is a commission of Austrian intellectuals, who naturally, with pens at the ready, are registering these facts, to divulge in the cultured European press their impressions of their visit.
>
> Really, it is sad and painful that Bahia, which once staged dazzling Carnivals greater than those of Rio de Janeiro, with extraordinary cavalries, fantastic historical processions, and exceedingly original allegories, should sink to the opposite extreme with this frightful barbarism.
>
> I see two means to correct this ill: the first is public indifference, and the second the interest which the police must take to demonstrate that this land has civilization. That part of the population which is civilized, which is the majority . . . should protest against this by not paying the slightest attention to this savage festival that Bahia displayed yesterday, and will yet display today and tomorrow.
>
> The genteel hands of our patricians ought not to toss a speck of confetti or streamers on this *African carnival,* nor should their lips betray a smile.
>
> In our humble household, this is being done, and the little money that was to be spent on these innocent sports, 5 *milreis,* I am sending you for your "Easter for the Poor," which is distributed by this newspaper.
>
> In that manner we register our protest against the *batuques* and provide comfort, albeit in a very small way, to some indigent brother of ours. Our needy brothers will benefit from this and, if everyone joins us in this protest, the *Jornal* will provide a good Easter for those it helps.[51]

The anonymous teacher was one of a growing number of conservative voices who feared the encroachment of African culture. This was to become a major issue in Bahian cultural politics during the twentieth century.

Some scholars have suggested that the members of the formal African clubs were "Negroes with white souls,"[52] and that their "conformist strategy" was also echoed in their social practices. In contrast, "the batuques seem to symbolize the black who is not very worried about the white values of the dominant class, or for whom these values make little sense. These groups (or what they represent) are what constitute a *public problem,* and it is they who, in the eyes of the press and their readers, are associated with barbarity, dirtiness, and the lack of appropriate behavior."[53]

Such an analysis places the *batuques* in the category of outsiders as outlined in Chapter 2. Using that framework, the clubs would be classified as alternative integrationists, because although they chose to participate in the Carnival of the dominant culture in the traditional fashion, they introduced their own themes. What differentiated the acceptable clubs and the detested *batuques* was the orientation of the former toward integration and, hence, the acceptance of the validity of mainstream culture.

Raymundo Nina Rodrigues, a contemporary, described an even subtler difference between the Embaixada and the Pandegos, but one that is quite important. The Africa invoked by the Embaixada, in his opinion, celebrated past glories and traditions, whereas the Pandegos demonstrated the very African traditions the police were attempting to destroy. "In fact, the fetichist blacks avenged themselves of the intermittent impertinences of the police, exhibiting their ritual [*festa*] in public."[54] Newspaper accounts are too scant to provide full corroboration of this interpretation, but they are not inconsistent with Nina Rodrigues' assessment. The Embaixada Africana seemed to have a broader scope than any of the other clubs. Its range of themes included distant history that was undoubtedly less threatening than was the public expression of the outlawed candomblé. The Embaixada used Carnival as a platform for promoting racial accommodation by staging processions quite similar to those of white clubs. If the Embaixada's 1901 motif was any indication, it was in fact moving beyond exclusively African themes. That year it focused on U.S. imperialism with costumes representing Haiti, the Philippines, Mexico, and American Indians. Uncle Sam sat atop a rock on the main float with "America for the Americans" emblazoned on his hat. The rock was inscribed "Cuba" and in his mouth was a fish representing the Brazilian territory of Acre, metaphors for U.S. expansionist policies in Latin America.[55] The Pandegos, in contrast, used Carnival as a political forum through which to challenge a society that denigrated and outlawed their religious traditions. Both groups were alternative integrationists using cultural expression as a form of political protest. Yet the Pandegos chose themes that directly asserted the Afro-Bahian community's rights of self-determination and religious freedom in post-abolition society.

It thus appears that there were three levels of Afro-Brazilian participation in the Carnival of the 1890s, with varying degrees of social acceptability.

Most acceptable was the Embaixada Africana, which organized its processions within the format established by white clubs and whose themes were not perceived as threatening. It portrayed a "cultured" Africa of kings and dignitaries. Nina Rodrigues referred to the club's members as "more intelligent or better adapted blacks" who celebrated the "refined peoples of Africa—Egyptians, Abyssinians, etc."[56] The Pandegos represented the next level. They also borrowed the format of their processions from the earlier white clubs, but transformed Carnival into a stage for social protest against candomblé repression. Finally, there were the smaller clubs and individual masqueraders, whose African instruments and black body paint so horrified the readers of the *Jornal de Noticias*. There are, however, grounds for caution in characterizing the Embaixada Africana as "Negroes with white souls." The label implies a rejection of identity that is unwarranted given the extraordinary efforts of the club organizers to study and promote such a broad scope of African cultural history. They made a pioneering effort to force the public to view Africa's classics and antiquities on a par with those of Europe. In this respect the Embaixada members appear to have had much in common with the members of the Frente Negra and São Paulo's black social clubs.

Part of the fear of the anti-*batuque* crusaders was that they were fighting a losing battle. The African clubs were growing in popularity among the general public, as their detractors readily admitted. Once a practice had become part of popular culture, it was difficult to eradicate. Nina Rodrigues noted that the *Jornal de Noticias* was merely echoing the complaints of a royal official in 1807 that Bahian blacks "gathered whenever and wherever; danced and played the strident and unmelodious *batuques* all over the city and at all hours; they dominated at get-togethers and parties, interrupting any other rhythms or songs."[57] Indeed, despite the prohibition of batuques after the Carnival of 1904, they were to be definitively institutionalized no later than the 1940s as an integral part of the annual festivities.[58]

Bahia's elites struggled to disassociate themselves from the African-based culture so characteristic of Salvador. The national sense of inferiority was heightened in Bahia, where whites were derogatorily referred to as "*branco da Bahia*," a term applied to very fair-skinned mulattoes who only classified as white in Bahia where few "true" whites were to be found. Popular culture, coming as it did from the lower classes, reflected African heritage and sensibilities. Carnival was only the most visible and important of the public festivals that abounded in Bahia; sacred, secular, familial, or invented, there were always occasions for celebration. A popular saying is that Salvador has 365 churches so that each day can be a feast day. These lesser festivals, like Carnival, came under increasingly virulent attacks for perceived Africanisms in the post-abolition years. One of these was the Bomfim festival, held in

January, in honor of the patron saint of the city of Salvador. This saint is equated with Oxalá, a deity of candomblé traditions stemming from the Nagô (Yoruba) cultures, and widely venerated in Salvador. The feast day of Senhor do Bomfim is traditionally held on the second Sunday of the new year. The facet of the festivities to which elites objected was the *lavagem,* a cleansing of the church, held on the preceding Thursday. Hundreds of faithful, dressed all in white (the color of Oxalá), converged upon the church high upon the hill overlooking the Itapagipe peninsula and the bay. Many came by boat. They bore gifts of flowers and gold; sometimes sailors would bring pieces of clothing torn by seawinds from which the Senhor do Bomfim had protected them. The women dressed in the traditional *Bahiana* full skirts, jewels, and turbans. During the *lavagem,* people sang, danced, and drank. The festivities continued long into the night. Just before the 1890 feast day, the archbishop Luiz Antônio dos Santos prohibited the *lavagem,* and the police showed up at the church to enforce the ban, confiscating brooms, vases and water jugs, guitars, and harmonicas.[59] In 1897, although they applauded the fact that the Bomfim feast was "happily free" of the *lavagem,* "a ceremony that implied great disrespect, if not immorality," the *Jornal de Noticias* noted that the popular festival was in decline.[60]

The Bomfim festival was not unique. Also attacked for its African element was that of Our Lady of Good Death, sponsored by a sisterhood of the same name that was frequented by Yoruba women from the African city of Ketu. Its members included the founders and priestesses of leading Bahian candomblés. Their festival has been noted for the predominance of its African symbolism incorporated into the Catholic rite as well as the secular samba danced after the procession, accompanied by popular songs, fireworks, capoeira, and steaming plates of feijoada eaten "slave" style, with the fingers. The festival was banned from 1930 to 1934. It returned in 1935 completely reorganized, the opulence of the African women in their gold jewelry and traditional Bahiana garb replaced by pale little girls dressed as angels. The sisterhood reorganized in the nearby town of Cachoeira, maintaining its traditions and becoming a symbol of cultural resistance within the Catholic Church to the present day.[61]

✗ Another African cultural expression facing constant repression was the martial art capoeira, derived from Angolan slaves. In Brazil, an entire culture had evolved from capoeira. Always discouraged, and outlawed in 1821, capoeira was often practiced to musical accompaniment, its graceful moves easily disguised as dance.[62] By the 1930s capoeira had its own complex folk music and distinctive instruments. A social culture had also evolved, with a process of apprenticeship, recognition of status as a master, symbolic clothing, and the division of the city into territories for different neighborhood groups of capoeiras. Until the 1930s capoeira was strongly identified with gang culture and violence. In actuality, capoeira songs champion not random aggression but the proud and valiant male who refuses to be bowed by the difficulties of life.

> Me trate com mais respeito
> Que é a sua obrigação
> Todo mundo é obrigado
> A possuí inducação
> Me trate com mais repeito
> Veja que eu lhe tratei bem . . .

> Treat me with more respect
> That is your obligation
> Everyone is obligated
> To be civil
> Treat me with more respect
> See how well I have treated you . . .[63]

This posture, in its orientation toward respect for black men normally subject to enforcement by violence, was a direct challenge to mainstream society. Altercations involving capoeiras, however, were almost invariably limited to the lower social classes in which they circulated.[64]

In 1932, the same year that new laws declared capoeiras "dangerous delinquents," an accomplished master, Mestre Bimba (Manuel dos Reis Machado), opened Brazil's first capoeira academy.[65] This unprecedented innovation signaled a change akin to the "civilization" of Carnival. In the controlled environment of the academy, capoeira was transformed. It now became accessible to a cross-section of students who ranged from the "simple man of the streets to politicians, former heads of state, doctors, artists and intellectuals."[66] Bimba's academy was followed in 1941 by Mestre (Vicente Ferreira) Pastinha's Centro Esportivo de Capoeira Angola and a host of others.[67] The academy became the principal form of capoeira instruction in the twentieth century. With the advent of the academy, capoeira became a source of income for its practitioners, and had the additional benefit of bringing them into relationships with the members of the bourgeoisie who began frequenting the schools. The price they paid was the commercialization and marketing of a popular cultural form to make it accessible to those selfsame outsiders that capoeira culture had evolved to protect itself from.[68]

The influence of African culture on Bahian life was pervasive and undeniable. Although no one seriously attempted to obliterate the traditions that characterized Bahia, there was constant pressure from both public and private

sectors to channel Africanisms into acceptable spheres. Local police un-
leashed a vigilante reign of terror on the candomblé houses, confiscating sacred objects and detaining priests. Private citizens often complained in the
press about those practices they felt gave Bahia an uncivilized image. Bahian
writers, in the press as well as in fiction, characterized Afro-Bahians and their
culture in terms evoking sensuality, mysticism, and a less than "civilized"
status.

> The dark multitudes boiled. *Batuques. Sambas. Capoeira* circles. One
> heard *pandeiros, cavaquinhos*, guitars, harmonicas, *berimbaus*, and the
> cadence of clapping hands. Pandemonium. Confused chatter. Licentious
> comments and gestures. The wheezy exclamations of drunks. The al-
> cohol unleashed the rude masses with their primitive instincts. An ac-
> rid odor of *cachaça,* of rankness, of sweat, of ripened fruit, made one
> giddy.[69]

Writers also cast Afro-Bahian culture as a vestige of slavery. Its continuance
indicated a failure to break with the past, and there were many public complaints about the resulting image of Bahia as a colonial backwater. An unsigned letter published in *A Tarde* bemoaned manifestations of slave culture in
contemporary urban life:

> "Down with Samba! . . . Old Customs Incompatible with Progress."
> The blacks, slaves, those that were more happy, those that did not
> live under the whip of oppression of unenlightened masters, would then
> go down to the Terreiro [de Jesus], and in that area between the Cathe-
> dral and the old hospital, now the Medical School, they would gather
> to dance samba and celebrate African rites.
> They would form a circle and the pagan festivities would go on
> to nine and ten o'clock, maintaining perfect order, and under the mo-
> notonous rhythms of the *canzá* and the *atabaques.*
> On Fridays the scene shifted, because the poor slaves were obliged
> to pray the *terço* and sing the "Senhor Deus Misericordia" in Pelourinho,
> in front of the church of the Rosário, that enormous plaza entirely filled
> with kneeling people, from down below to the very top.[70]

The author went on to complain that "in spite of progress . . . there is no lack
of people who like to maintain these primitive traditions." He referred specifically to the "Linha Circular" streetcar workers who, on off hours, played and
danced samba in front of the Lacerda Elevator, and the "ciranda africana" in
the Rio Branco (Municipal) Plaza where people sold sweets and ice cream.
The letter closed with a request that the Linha Circular attend to this.[71] Yet
there was little the authorities could do. The fact of the matter was that in Sal-

vador, an African-based culture was thriving and growing with a vitality that threatened the hegemony of European-based norms.

African Salvador

It may well be said that there were (at least) two Salvadors, one white and Brazilian, one black and African. Of all the social groups considered here, none so clearly exemplifies the concept of the alternative community as does the African-based culture of Salvador.[72] Occupying the same physical territory as did mainstream society, it was a multidimensional world unto itself. The *cantos* of the nineteenth century were the most visible manifestation of African Salvador, and serve as a convenient starting point for a tour of the city's alter ego. In addition to their role as employment sites for day laborers, the *cantos* were cultural meeting points for the various African "nations" *(nações)* represented in Salvador. During the heyday of the *cantos,* the capital could be mapped according to these ethnic nations. In the commercial district of the lower city, the Arcos de Santa Barbara belonged to the Guruncis. Near the Hotel das Nações were the Hausas. In the upper city the Minas stationed themselves on the Rua das Mercês, while the Nagôs occupied most of the other *cantos.* In Campo Grande they were joined by a few Jêjes. African women had their own *cantos,* also divided by ethnicity, at the docks, the Baixa dos Sapateiros, the Largo Dois de Julho, and other points around the city. The Geledes masked society of women met in a sacred area known today as the Dendezeiros do Bomfim.[73]

African spirits also had their special locations. Exu, the deity of the crossroads, watched over intersections, his presence marked by the occasional offering left inconspicuously on the street.[74] Rituals for Baba Igunnukó consecrated the area known today as Bonocô, and the Kongo *nkisi* deities roamed the hills of Cabula. To worship the Dahomean vodoun, one could visit the descendants of the Mahis and Dassa in a section of today's Federação.

There was yet another landscape, that of the candomblé houses, which represented a reorganization of the physical and spiritual spaces occupied by Africans into consecrated cultural enclaves known as *terreiros.* The term *candomblé* is used here to refer broadly to those religions derived principally from African theology and culture.[75] Despite the gradual diminution of African languages and cultural practices of the various "nations" after the end of the slave trade, numerous Africans in Salvador continued their spiritual traditions in congregations also known as candomblés. Most numerous were congregations of the descendants of the Yoruba and Fon, known in Salvador as the Nagô and Jêje, respectively, but the Kongo and Angola nations made up an important minority as well. Religious observances took place both in private residences and on specially consecrated plots of land known as *terreiros;* the number of the latter was still quite limited before the twentieth century.[76] The first detailed studies on Bahian candomblé, by Raymundo Nina Rodrigues and Manoel Querino, were based on their observations in the late nineteenth century.[77] The extensive literature that followed the work of these pioneers focused on the theology of candomblé, which was generally viewed synchronically, and on the relative purity of African retentions.[78] Such an approach makes it difficult to reconstruct the historical dynamics in the evolution of candomblé, which changed dramatically from its earliest expressions to its current form.

It is useful to divide the history of Bahian candomblé into four phases. In the first phase, religious expression was an integral component of community formation as African ethnic *nações* became established in Salvador.[79] Candomblé began to take its modern form in the second phase, coinciding with broader changes in the Afro-Bahian community around the mid-nineteenth century. The hallmarks of this phase were the consolidation of major features of African sacred and secular institutions into the Nagô liturgy, the proliferation of *terreiros,* and the rising influence of the Nagô houses. Repression of candomblé led to a third stage, in which the communities were forced to respond and assert their right to religious freedom. Finally, candomblé began to be absorbed into the general popular culture of Brazil. This last change began in the middle and latter decades of the twentieth century, and is therefore beyond the scope of this study.

The first phase dates from the foundation of the colony through the closure of the transatlantic slave trade in the mid-nineteenth century. Africans arriving in Brazil sought support in ethnic collectivity. Religion in the African tradition cannot be separated from other aspects of life; it organizes the individual's understanding of all phenomena, both natural and supernatural.[80] Ethnic communities therefore incorporated many elements of various African cosmologies as they developed distinct Afro-Brazilian cultures.[81] Candomblés began as ethnic clusters of people sharing the same nationality, language, and customs. Owing to both the spread of Islam in Africa and the forced conversion of slaves to Christianity, the religions practiced by those people could have included elements of Islam, Catholicism, and/or animism.

The importance of religion as a central pillar of the ethnic identity embodied in the concept of *nação* is highlighted in the experience of Africans from pluralistic societies. The history of the Malês, a generic term for Muslims in Salvador, exemplifies this process.[82] Islam was an adopted religion for many West Africans, and had only spread into the Oyo (Yoruba, or Nagô) Empire with the *jihad* of 1817. The Tapa, Fon, Hausa, and Nagô were among the nations in which Islam attracted large numbers of converts. In the case of the

Fon, their community in Salvador consisted of both animists (Jêje) and Muslims (Malês). The oral traditions of one of the older Jêje candomblés hint that Muslim Fon sought the help of their animist brethren during at least one Muslim slave revolt. The Zoogodo Bogum Malê Rundo is a candomblé located on the site of an old plantation in Salvador's Federação district. The exact date of its foundation is uncertain, but current members estimate its origin around 1620. They cite Bogum's early composition as "Fon [Jêje] peoples of old Dahomey, now the Republic of Benin, descendants of the cities of Mahis and Dassa." One oral tradition maintains that one Joaquim Gege Matos hid the chest containing contributions for the 1835 Malê revolt at Bogum. Others suggest a connection between Bogum and the various Muslim-led conspiracies between 1807 and 1835. The full name of the community even includes the term "Malê," referring to Muslims, although the religion is based on animistic traditional religions.[83] This example illustrates a sense of Fon solidarity, as collaborators in slave conspiracies, that supersedes religious differences. However, it also indicates that Jêje and Malê, not Fon, were the operative categories of ethnic identity, thus placing religion at the center of the concept of *nação*.

The beginning of candomblé's second phase may be conveniently marked by the establishment around 1830 of Ilê Iyá Nassô, although in its earliest years it was most likely typical of the first phase.[84] The newer candomblés were characterized by a transition from predominantly African to predominantly Brazilian membership, and they reflected the conscious choice of the Brazilian-born to maintain African culture as a source of moral and spiritual support.[85] The pivotal impetus for the change was the cessation of the transatlantic slave trade and, with it, new arrivals to revitalize African traditions practiced in Salvador. Once the slave trade ended, the religious communities became the principal repositories of African cultural traditions. They were able to flourish because candomblé provided an institutional basis for African-based culture and, thereby, continuity and formalization of its cultural components. In this I disagree with Melville Herskovits' observation that "the carriers [of culture] themselves are the crucial elements."[86] The individuals may be the *seminal* elements, but it is the institutions that form the basis of New World creole cultures.[87] Without them, there exists what took place in the first, "African" phase of candomblé, namely, the practices of a given congregation emerging as a compilation of the variations of traditions as remembered by individuals. "Brazilian" candomblés like Ilê Iyá Nassô were not the simple accumulation of cultural practices inherited from the days of slavery. The Ilê Iyá Nassô was founded and led by women with the mission of faithfully re-creating, in a modern Brazilian capital, the traditions of the Yoruba nation of Ketu. Their focus on institution building eventually established "standard" elements of candomblé by which others were measured, and which was imitated to varying degrees throughout Salvador.[88]

Nineteenth-century candomblé practiced by free persons of color held a social meaning quite different from that practiced by enslaved Africans. The latter discouraged pan-African solidarity and was therefore useful to the slave regime. Freedpersons engaging in candomblé, however, were seen as a threat to mainstream Bahian culture. The police began to target the free African community and subjected its members to arrest for participating in the sacred ceremonies known by mid-century as candomblé.

> . . . [A]rrested today . . . in the first district of the Santo Antonio parish . . . the Africans Benedicto Bastos, João Coieiro de Magalhães, Marcelina and Maria, *libertos* discovered in a meeting known commonly as *candomblé*.[89]

> . . . [A]rrested today . . . in the second district of Santo Antonio, Paulo Antônio Vieira, freed African, 58 years old, for questioning regarding a house he possesses which is used for meetings known commonly as *candomblé*.[90]

> . . . [A]rrested today and taken to the Algube jail, freed African Gonçalo Paraiso, sorcerer *(feiticeiro)* in whose house in the Rua do Paço parish in this city were discovered various ingredients and drinks he administered to ignorant persons who procured him as a healer and whom he abused, making those who were amenable to his demands suffer. In the absence of a solid base of evidence for the opening of a formal case against such a dangerous African, whom the public voice also accuses of sending some people to the grave with his remedies, I come to solicit of your Excellency the necessary authorization to have him deported to one of the ports on the Coast of Africa.[91]

These measures, however, could not stem the swelling tide of candomblé practitioners around the city, nor could they prevent the spread of the tradition to the descendants of Africans and into the broader population of color.

A distinguishing feature of this transitional phase of candomblé was the new conceptualization of the *terreiro* as re-created African homeland in microcosm. As late as the 1890s, Nina Rodrigues observed that the use of *terreiros* was largely restricted to special observances; "[t]hey have, on the outskirts of the cities, special temples [*terreiros*] for the great annual festivals, and small oratorios or chapels in private homes for regular ceremonies and prayers throughout the year."[92] Candomblé leaders of the post-abolition era transformed the *terreiro* into an alternative cultural enclave, evolving, by the mid-twentieth century, into a multifaceted world in which one could live with only limited contact with mainstream Brazilian culture.[93]

The Ilê Iyá Nassô, known subsequently in popular parlance as Engenho Velho, was the pioneer of this phase of candomblé history, although two off-shoot congregations, Gantois and Opô Afonjá, influenced to a far greater degree the changes occurring in candomblé as it moved into the twentieth century. Ilê Iyá Nassô was founded by African-born women from the nation of Ketu sometime early in the nineteenth century. The salient role of women was a departure from Yoruba tradition. Although women held important political and religious offices in the Oyo Empire, the key positions of state, such as the Alafin (King), administrative councils, and military commissions, were held by men. Enslaved women in Salvador, however, had resources at their disposal that gave them access to autonomy. One such institution was the Bôa Morte sisterhood, based in the Barroquinha parish church.

The names, and even the number, of Engenho Velho's founders have long been a matter of debate, but all may have been members of the Bôa Morte sisterhood. At that time Catholic sodalities were still divided along ethnic lines of *nação*. The Rosário às Portas do Carmo, founded at a time when Angolans were prominent in the slave population, came to be frequented predominantly by Jejes by the early nineteenth century. Jejes also had the brotherhoods of Bom Jesus das Necessidades e Redenção dos Homens Prêtos in the Corpo Santo church in the port district. Nagôs had two major organizations, the Bôa Morte sisterhood, whose membership was restricted to people from Ketu, and the brotherhood of Senhor dos Martírios.[94] According to Pierre Verger, a photographic ethnographer and initiate of Mãe Senhora (Maria Bibiana do Espírto Santo) of Opô Afonjá, the original name of the candomblé that came to be known as Engenho Velho was Iyá Omi Axé Airá Intilé, founded by Iyalussô Danadana and Iyanassô Akalá, with the help of a certain Baba Assiká.[95] This differs slightly from the version offered by Mãe Menininha of Gantois in the twentieth century, who maintained that the original founder was an Iyá Akalá, replaced after her permanent return to Africa by Iyanassô Oká.[96] Verger goes on to say that Iyalussô Danadana returned to Africa, where she later died. Iyanassô also traveled to Ketu, along with her daughter Marcelina da Silva (Obatossi) and her granddaughter Madalena. They returned to Salvador seven years later, with two children born to Madalena in Africa. Pregnant on the return voyage, Madalena gave birth in Bahia to a third child, Claudiana, the mother of Mãe Senhora of Opô Afonjá.[97]

The candomblé first functioned near the Barroquinha church, in a house on the street known today as Rua Visconde de Itaparica. After several relocations, Engenho Velho moved to its current site in the Federação district, where Marcelina assumed leadership following the death of Iyanassô. The degree to which Engenho Velho departed from established practices is unclear. The religious ritual itself, a matter restricted to the initiated priesthood, will not be discussed in detail here, but some features of the cultural transfer and reinterpretation are important to note.[98] Engenho Velho's highest administrative and religious office was that of the Iyalorixa, who was assisted by several titled officers in the candomblé hierarchy. These were lifelong positions restricted to women, and subject to confirmation through the Ifá divination system. For the precolonial Yoruba, the circumstances of birth determined many spiritual relationships and commitments. The new Brazilian model incorporated this principle through religious kinship. An initiate, regardless of his or her natal ethnicity, was "born" into the candomblé community. The subsequent relationships involved the initiate as a "child" of both a specific orixa (deity) and a spiritual family. The initiating priestess became the "mother" (*iyá* in Yoruba, *mãe* in Portuguese), the initiates became "daughters" or "sons," hence, siblings to one another. The initiation ritual entailed other spiritual relationships, such as those with assisting priests or with initiates of the same deity. Within the candomblé, age was based upon the date of initiation and superseded chronological age in the determination of seniority. With such a structure in place, Engenho Velho began as a nuclear family. As its children matured and began creating their own spiritual families, it became a larger clan of interrelated units.

According to Edison Carneiro, upon the death of Marcelina da Silva, the succession was contested by Maria Julia Figueiredo, her legal substitute, and Maria Julia da Conceição Nazareth. The details of the dispute have never been publicly clarified, but it resulted in the departure of Maria Julia da Conceição Nazareth. She left Engenho Velho with her followers and founded Ilê Iá Omin Iamassé, known popularly as the Terreiro de Gantois, the name of its French landlord. The registered statutes of Gantois give the date of Maria Julia's departure as 1849, but Marcelina da Silva, whose death supposedly sparked the controversy, lived until 1885.[99] If Gantois was indeed founded in 1849, the dispute may well have been between Marcelina and Maria Julia da Conceição Nazareth following the death of Iyanassô. The debate over the rules of succession illustrate the trend toward the establishment of fixed procedures within Bahian candomblés. At Gantois, Maria Julia da Conceição Nazareth restricted the title of Iyalorixa to female blood relatives. She trained her daughter Pulcheria to succeed her upon her death in 1900.[100]

Another departure from Engenho Velho in 1903 led to the creation of the last of the three pioneering candomblés of this era. Eugenia Anna dos Santos (Aninha), born in 1869 to African parents of the Gurunci nation, had been initiated into the Nagô tradition at Engenho Velho.[101] It is significant that although she never disavowed her natal ethnicity, Aninha assumed Nagô as a spiritual ethnicity. The parameters of ethnicity had been redefined such that one could become an African of a given nation by initiation into its cultural world.

Aninha's departure coincided with a disputed succession at Engenho Velho after the death of Ursulina (Sussu), the Iyalorixa who followed Maria Julia Figueiredo in 1890.[102] If blood kinship were indeed a prerequisite for the office of Iyalorixa, Aninha could never have assumed the title because of her Gurunci heritage. Carneiro suggests that Aninha supported the candidacy of Joaquim Vieira. When she first left Engenho Velho, she took her followers to his *terreiro* in Rio Vermelho.[103] It is doubtful, however, that a man would have been seriously considered for this traditionally female position. Maximiana Maria da Conceição (Tia Massi) became Iyalorixa at Engenho Velho, while Aninha began initiating godchildren with the assistance of other dissidents.[104] Aninha eventually inaugurated her *terreiro,* Ilê do Axé Opô Afonjá, in 1910 in São Gonçalo do Retiro. It was an outlying district not serviced by streetcars. Once the site of *quilombos,* it shared their strategic advantages, as did Gantois and the new Engenho Velho. Like the *quilombos,* the candomblés were routinely hunted and persecuted. They sought locations of difficult access; all three were located on hills from which they could espy intruders before they arrived.

Other candomblés surfaced and flourished in the late nineteenth century. The Ketu house of Alaketu and the Jêje house of Bogum trace their origins as far back as the seventeenth century. Houses from other traditions, including Kongo-Angola (Central African), and the *candomblé do caboclo* (syncretized with indigenous spirits), also became established and grew stronger into the turn of the century. There were still a few Muslim congregations when Nina Rodrigues conducted his research, although their influence was limited. None, however, engaged in as ambitious an effort to reinterpret African tradition in a Brazilian context as did the houses of Engenho Velho, Gantois, and Opô Afonjá.

Two salient features distinguish this era of Brazilianization and adaptation of candomblé. The first is the importance of women as entrepreneurs. This, in turn, is related to the second characteristic, namely, the reconceptualization of the candomblé as the institutional basis of an alternative culture. In this process, the changes in candomblé became rooted in the conscious choice of Afro-Brazilians to use African culture as a mode of support and survival in modern Brazilian society. This is significantly different from the perpetuation of African culture by African-born persons for whom this was the only worldview with which they were familiar. The Brazilian-born, and even Africans who had spent considerable time in Brazil, were sufficiently cognizant of Euro-Brazilian culture to choose between the two. There were measurable rewards attendant to assimilation—greater possibilities of upward mobility, social acceptance, employment, and even manumission. Yet not only did succeeding generations opt for maintaining a distinct African cultural reference, they also exhibited a growing tendency toward separatism in the alternative cultural mode throughout the post-abolition period.

The *terreiro* embodied this trend, but its new role was made possible only with the increasing financial security of the candomblé community. The *terreiros* were transformed from the groves and unclaimed spaces where the faithful gathered for special ceremonies to a new form as modern *quilombos,* where fugitives from mainstream society could find sanctuary in a society of their own creation. In order to do this, the candomblé had to move from a primary location of private homes to parcels of land devoted explicitly to this purpose. There were women in Bahia such as Aninha who were uniquely positioned to assume leadership roles in this regard. As noted in Chapter 5, a small number of Bahian women had disposable income sufficient to enable them to become critically important financial supporters of Catholic brotherhoods. Aninha was a businesswoman. She was a retailer of imported African products at the Mercado Modelo on the docks. Since the nineteenth century, Africans had been involved in commercial trade with Nigeria. She lived in the "upper city," not far from the Mercado, on the Ladeira da Praça.[105] Later she moved next door to the Church of the Rosário in Pelourinho, using her home as a retail outlet. By 1909, she had accumulated sufficient funds to purchase the land in São Gonçalo do Retiro for Opô Afonjá. Aninha's example illustrates the way in which some Africans and their descendants on both sides of the Atlantic were able to break into, and profit from, the lucrative retail trade in goods between Salvador and the Bight of Benin, although it does not explain what appears to be an income differential favoring a small group of Afro-Bahian women.

There exists the intriguing possibility that some female candomblé leaders were among the richest members of Salvador's African community. If this was indeed the case, it was the result of deft financial management. The women who founded Engenho Velho, Gantois, and Opô Afonjá began with little capital. Their constituency was overwhelmingly poor. Establishing a candomblé *terreiro* was no small feat; it required the construction and maintenance of residences and shrines, enormous quantities of food for the many ritual feasts, adornments, sacred objects, and countless other expenses including a reserve fund for problems with the police. Amassing money took time, and the wills of two nineteenth-century Iyalorixás at Engenho Velho indicate that, though they may have lived comfortably, they were far from wealthy. Marcelina da Silva's estate was valued at 1:698$000, and the combined value of Maria Julia Figueiredo's three houses totaled a mere 400$000.[106] The records of a bitter family dispute between Marcelina's husband and her daughter Madalena over the estate provide a glimpse into one of the financial strategies of these women. Marcelina and her husband Miguel Vieira combined their resources to buy at least three houses which, according to Miguel, were placed in his stepdaughter's name because Africans were prohibited from purchasing real estate.[107] By passing property along to daughters and nieces either during their lifetimes or through their wills, priestesses helped succeeding generations of women amass wealth. In addition, priestesses with well-connected congregations benefited directly from influential contacts.

In her travels in Bahia in 1938 and 1939, Ruth Landes commented upon what may have been another factor contributing to the financial security of the priestesses:

> Menininha did not marry . . . legally for the same reasons other mothers and priestesses did not marry. They would have lost too much. Under the law of this Latin Catholic country, a wife submits entirely to the authority of the husband. How incompatible this is with the beliefs and organizations of candomblé! How inconceivable to the dominant female authority! . . . Most of the women dream of a lover who can offer financial support at least to the extent of relieving her of continuous economic worry; but they do not think of legal marriage. Marriage means another world, something like being a white person. It brings prestige but not necessarily joy in living.[108]

Landes thus implies that women protected their estates by not entering into legal marriage.

However it was acquired, the priestesses of Engenho Velho, Gantois, and Opô Afonjá had money, and used it to procure property to be converted into *terreiros*. Reference to a French "landlord" at Gantois suggests that land was sometimes leased or rented rather than purchased outright. This was also the case at Engenho Velho, where the houses owned by Maria Julia Figueiredo were built on property owned by Dr. Jose Carneiro de Campos.[109] The *terreiro* allowed for far greater possibilities in the consecration of sacred spaces than those afforded by the private home chapel. It enabled priests to organize using the same principles informing the design of eighteenth- and nineteenth-century Yoruba cities.

Peter Morton-Williams describes a three-dimensional structure of the Yoruba cosmos that included the Houses of the Sky, the Earth, and the inhabited World (Ilê Aiye).[110] A variety of deities and spirits exist in the Sky (orixa) and the Earth (Egungun ancestral spirits). Humans inhabit the World, but exist in all three realms at some point. They interact with the other realms with the assistance of sacred cult leaders, all of whom were represented in the governing bodies of Oyo. The representatives of the Sky in the inhabited world were the Alafin of Oyo (a direct descendant of the orixa), and the high priests of the cults of the principal orixa. The representatives of the Earth were the high priests of Egungun, as well as other Earth cults. Each realm of the cosmos was thus represented in the government of eighteenth-century Oyo, which consisted of the Alafin and the Oyo Mesi, a governing council on which sat priests of both Earth and Sky cults. These governing bodies were compelled to oversee the worship of all deities, so that none would be neglected and create an imbalance of spiritual forces. The government mediated worldly affairs, but its structure implied an additional role in service of a higher unity, one that kept the cosmic realms in harmony. Morton-Williams comments: "[L]ife in the third cosmic realm, Ilê Aiye, the House of the World, is good only when good relationships are maintained with the gods and spirits of the other two."[111] In Brazil, the candomblé hierarchy included a council of senior priests, whose role, much like that of the Oyo Mesi, was to assist the Iyalorixa in matters of governance and representation of the candomblé in public affairs as well as to execute specific sacred obligations. Candomblé focused on orixa worship, although it appears that the Egungun cult of the dead, or some form of ancestor worship, also continued as part of Yoruba cosmology in Bahia. The extreme secrecy surrounding the cult and the lack of documentation have led some historians to conclude that it did not play a significant role in Bahian candomblé.[112]

Another Yoruba principle reflected in Bahian candomblé was the importance of maintaining the cults of all the deities of the pantheon. Because certain towns and special sites such as sacred rivers had patron orixa, their cults were concentrated in diverse areas of the Oyo Empire. An empire of conquest, Oyo permitted tributary states to maintain their patron deities and often adopted them into its own pantheon. A consolidation of sorts was undertaken in Oyo when the relocated capital was divided into districts dedicated to various deities. Although the Alafin, and by extension Oyo itself, had its royal patron deity, the principal orixas of the empire enjoyed specially consecrated areas of the capital. Engenho Velho adopted this principle. Rather than being a group of Oyo descendants gathering to pay homage to their common protector, Xango, they took responsibility for the worship of all the forces necessary to maintain spiritual and temporal harmony. Thus the functions of the essential institutions of the Oyo Empire were brought under the single administration of the Iyalorixa. The *terreiro* was thus a world of spiritual harmony in the context of African cosmology.

"Engenho Velho is the head, and Opô Afonjá is the arm," was a favorite saying of Mãe Aninha. Edison Carneiro wrote that she would have been more correct in saying that Engenho Velho was the trunk and Opô Afonjá was the head.[113] For it was Eugenia Anna dos Santos who went further than any other priest in transforming the *terreiro* into an alternative, African world in the heart of Brazil.

Eugenia Anna dos Santos reflected the ways in which the candomblé community was part of the larger Afro-Bahian community. Not only was she an Iyalorixa and independent businesswoman, she was also active in the prestigious black Catholic brotherhoods. As a woman of means, Aninha was in a position to contribute the hefty annual dues required of the top female officers in the brotherhoods. She served as *prioreza* (chief female officer) of the Rosário brotherhood and of the Bôa Morte sisterhood. This was not necessarily religious hypocrisy. For many Africans, Catholicism represented a supplementary belief system that could be held simultaneously with their own. It was perfectly acceptable to belong both to the candomblé and to the Catholic Church.[114] As the candomblés continued to flourish, it no longer mattered that African deities could not be formally venerated within church walls. Catholic saints, however, continued to be honored in many candomblés as parallel representations of African deities.

Aninha inaugurated the Ilê do Axé Opô Afonjá in 1910. Its design followed the traditions of Engenho Velho and Gantois. Areas were set aside and consecrated to various orixas, and a main hall *(barracão)* was built for public ceremonies. The construction was simple, with thatched roofs and wattle and daub walls. The *barracão* itself began as little more than a large shack built with widely spaced sticks. This was a luxury, for there existed only a few *terreiros* built expressly for candomblé. Those operating in private homes made do with a space in the backyard.[115] Some of the senior priestesses lived in spare accommodations at the *terreiro*. In a rare description of daily life at Engenho Velho, Edison Carneiro depicted the cramped and stuffy quarters of the residents. Interestingly, their lives were very individualized in secular matters.

> Meals are not taken together. Despite the fact that they live under the same roof, each woman has her own meal and they all must cook it on the same stove, with charcoal or wood procured by each herself. The dinner hour, therefore, is uncertain, but in general it varies between 4 and 6 in the afternoon, sometimes the only meal of the day. This gives rise to headaches, fainting, and nutritional ailments, which I was able to verify in several candomblés. . . .
>
> Inside the walls of the house lives a humanity which has solidarity only in religious matters, but independence in civil life. In fact, each woman lives her own life—and has her own candle, her own food, her own water, sometimes her own house. The *casa grande* (big house) serves only as the common meeting ground.[116]

Aninha modeled Opô Afonjá on Engenho Velho, but went further than any other candomblé of her time in her crusade to follow faithfully the traditions of the Yoruba, although it is unclear whether her *terreiro* traced its lineage to either Oyo or Ketu specifically.[117] Although she was not a Nagô by birth, Aninha was nevertheless well grounded in Oyo language and history as a result of her collaboration over many years with Martiniano Eliseu do Bomfim. As an adolescent, Bomfim was sent by his parents to Nigeria, where he was educated in the Yoruba language, philosophy, and religion.[118] When he returned to Brazil, he served as the principal consultant for Nina Rodrigues in the preparation of *L'Animisme Fétichiste*. Over the course of several visits to Nigeria, Bomfim was initiated as a *babalawo,* becoming one of few Brazilians fully trained in the Ifá divination oracle. Together, Aninha and Bomfim set out to make Opô Afonjá an African village to the fullest extent possible. Aninha declared that Yoruba would be the official language of the *terreiro,* and all her initiates received instruction.[119] She also established a council called the Obas of Xango, which became one of her proudest accomplishments.

The Obas of Xango are one of the clearest examples of the reinvention of African tradition in the diaspora. Martiniano do Bomfim himself explained the origin of the tradition at Opô Afonjá in a paper submitted to the Afro-Brazilian Congress of 1937. According to Bomfim, Xango was a praise-name of the third Alafin to succeed Abiodun, who ruled in the late eighteenth century.[120] A power struggle with two military officers prompted Xango to leave the world of humans and transform himself into a deity. Sometime later, a council made up of the twelve ministers who had served him on earth was organized to maintain the cult of Xango there. "Because of this," wrote Bomfim, "in the Centro Cruz Santa do Ache de Opô Afonjá, in São Gonçalo do Retiro, this year was carried out the festival enthroning the twelve ministers of Xango, chosen from among the eldest and most prestigious ogans of the candomblé. This candomblé, erected in honor of Xango, is the only one in Bahia, and perhaps Brazil, to realize this festival, which brings back such good memories for the spiritual children of the African continent."[121] Bomfim's understanding of this institution was probably based on his experiences in early twentieth-century Nigeria. There is no reference to a ministerial council of Xango in Oyo's state structure (although it may refer to an exclusively religious priesthood structure), but it embodies important principles of Oyo's civil organization. The Ministers of Xango were divided into those of the Left and those of the Right. From the earliest days of the Yoruba, lineages grouped themselves into a triadic pattern of Ono (the Center), Otun (the Right), and Ohi (the Left).[122] Administrative councils were important in the cults of each deity, the Egungun cult of the dead, and in state government through such structures as the Oyo Mesi and the Ogboni council in New Oyo. As had been the case with the African Carnival groups, Afro-Brazilians were reaching to African history to establish an identity for themselves in modern Brazil. In the assessment of Deoscóredes M. dos Santos, an initiate of Opô Afonjá, "the re-establishment of the ancient tradition of the Obas de Xango gave still more prestige to Opô Afonjá and demonstrated the competence and knowledge of Iyalorixa Aninha Obá Biyi."[123] On both sides of the Atlantic at this juncture, descendants of the Oyo Empire were claiming legitimacy based on tradition. The Yoruba in Africa were seeking to legitimize claims to leadership positions under British colonial government. It was common at that time to present all traditions as ancient, unchanging practice, a synchronic approach most likely underlying Martiniano's instruction. The same emphasis was evident in Brazil. Dos Santos, for example, described the council as a "reestablishment." Similarly, Martiniano was quoted as saying "[Aninha] really tried to study our ancient religion and reestablish it in its African purity."[124] For Afro-Brazilians, this connection with an ancient past firmly grounded their ethnic identity via the candomblé. The accuracy with which they re-created African institutions is less relevant here than the effort itself, and the degree to which African principles were reinterpreted for a Brazilian context.

It appears that many Africans regarded the Brazilian candomblés with skepticism. Nina Rodrigues noted that the Brazilian *terreiros,* through their incomplete understanding of African language and religion, had lost their "primitive purity." Even though some houses worked assiduously to be faithful to tradition, they failed to receive full acceptance by Africans. Nina Rodrigues recalled, "One day I asked an old African woman watching the sacred dances at Gantois from afar whether she had made *santo* [been initiated] and why she didn't dance. She replied that her *terreiro* was of *gente da Costa* (Africans) and was located in Santo Antonio; that the *terreiro* of Gantois was of *gente da terra* (creoles and mulattoes)."[125] Despite the skepticism of Africans, Brazilian candomblés succeeded in fulfilling the needs of their constituents. As a result, they flourished throughout the city.

Bahia's elites were well aware of the spread of candomblé and other Africanisms, and they did not approve. Regulation of African cultural expression had once been the purview of individual slaveowners. The establishment of new *terreiros* was a phenomenon occurring among the free population of color, and could only be regulated by the state's security forces within constitutional parameters. This was not so easily achieved because the rapid pace of change in political structures and urban expansion caused the frequent reorganization of security forces and districts. The public outcry against the candomblés, and its political ramifications, became so pressing that the police responded with a clandestine campaign of terror that has become infamous in Bahian history.

A letter written in 1897 to the editor of the *Jornal de Noticias:*

> Dear Friend Lellis Piedade—
>   This is the second letter I have the honor to direct to you, hoping
> that with your undeniable patriotism you will call the attention of who-
> ever is responsible for the disappearance of these *religious* scenes prac-
> ticed by African fetichists, which *day by day take deeper root here in
> our land*, weakening and bestializing the popular spirit, which, carried
> away with superstition, only can and will degenerate instead of elevat-
> ing itself to the lofty destiny to which it is called.[126]

News of candomblés also appeared in the regular press columns:

> *"Candomblé"*—All day yesterday, there was an infernal *candomblé* in
> a house of Africans on the Rua do Paço. Because, unfortunately, there
> is no law which guarantees the public calm, it is no surprise that right
> in the heart of the city there are taking place shameful spectacles which
> are demonstrative of our customs. It would not surprise the public if
> tomorrow the press announced that the Police Department was having
> festivals in homage of Xango [the Yoruba deity] or whatever other [de-
> ity]. All speaks to the present state of Bahia.[127]

Police records show that arrests and harassment continued after the turn of the
century: "Admitted into this prison, on order of the Subdelegado da Lapinha,
the individual named Tertuliano da Silva [Quatore], 65 years of age, natural of
this state [Bahian born], captured in this district on this date for practicing
witchcraft."[128]

     The oral traditions of Gantois refer to the irony that several members of
the police force frequented their candomblé.[129] The raids they suffered may
well have been staged to placate the public clamor.

> *"Candomblé"*—We have been advised that for the last six days in the
> place known as Gantois, there has been functioning a great *candomblé.*
> The Linha Circular and Transportes trolleys from midday until five
> o'clock in the afternoon passed full of people flocking there. We have
> just been informed that among the people who went to appreciate the
> *candomblé* were one police official, several patrolmen, and some se-
> cret agents of the very same police force.[130]

> At Gantois, second district of Vitória, for days there has been function-
> ing a savage *candomblé*, which until 11 o'clock at night disturbs the
> public peace. It is said there are express orders from the Chief of Po-
> lice against such African diversions. Nonetheless, the orgy continues
> and is almost always repeated there in Gantois.[131]

The police force, which functioned as a military division, lacked oversight and was also known for excesses in other matters.[132] Although it is tempting to view anti-candomblé aggression exclusively as cultural or racial intolerance, it must be placed in the context of a general expansion of police prerogatives under the First Republic. Although many *terreiros* suffered in the short term, police efforts to check the spread of candomblé were met by a number of adaptations that eventually permitted them to flourish and move into the mainstream of Bahian culture. These adaptations became the hallmark of the third phase of candomblé's development.

Raids were taken extremely seriously by candomblé practitioners because not only were people arrested, but the authorities also confiscated the sacred objects by which the deities were housed, nourished, and worshipped.[133] In one instance a mother sought her daughter who was participating in a ceremony in Mata Escura. She arrived to find her daughter Angela "in a state of extreme excitement, like a crazy woman, and was told by those in the orgy that [Angela] was 'with the saint' and that she would be returned when the saint left her. Fortunately, Sr. Dr. Moura of the 1ª Circunscripção [police unit] saw to it that, despite the 'saint', Angela was returned to her mother."[134] Such a violation of the sanctity of the possession ritual was an extremely serious matter for candomblé practitioners.

Faced with the rising tide of repression, Afro-Bahian candomblés began taking steps to protect their right to religious freedom. Their actions introduced a third phase of candomblé history, marked by modifications in the institutional structure of the candomblé to cope with these exigencies. The first response of the candomblés was to follow the tradition of the *quilombos* and take full advantage of natural defenses. As noted earlier, Gantois, Engenho Velho, and Opô Afonjá were all situated atop steep hills, enabling them to see anyone approaching from far off. But this alone was not enough to prevent police incursions. The *terreiros* then began to seek informal protection through well-placed friends. This practice quickly became institutionalized through the office of ogan. Although the priesthood of the Nagô and Jêje houses was dominated by women, those houses reserved the position of ogan for men. The ogan was a ceremonial position, whose principal responsibilities were secular in nature. Many houses had several ogans named by the leadership. According to Manoel Querino, the scope of this position changed in the nineteenth century: "Some people, in whose number here are included individuals of social stature, have become ogans in the candomblés. While Africans directed these functions, nationals [i.e., Brazilian-born blacks] were not admitted as ogans. Later, these latter began to flow in, and were accepted, for the purpose of facilitating police licenses."[135] The importance of the ogans appears to have grown in direct relation to the need for protection. By the 1930s Edison

Carneiro described them as "protectors of the candomblé, with the special, extra-religious function of lending it prestige and providing it money for the sacred ceremonies."[136] What had begun as a position of financial support, reserved for Africans, had now broadened to include the two new functions of protector and public relations representative. Further, it was now open to non-Africans.

Candomblés began to be frequented by members of Bahia's middle and upper classes, including whites, and some moved into the position of ogan. Candomblé, which had already moved from an exclusively African realm into the broader *prêto* community, now began to enter Brazilian popular culture. Many of those who first ventured to the candomblés during this period were the pioneering researchers of Afro-Brazilian culture, and local artists of all disciplines. The presence of such figures as Nina Rodrigues, Arthur Ramos, Edison Carneiro, and Jorge Amado at Engenho Velho, Gantois, and Opô Afonjá was a major factor in bringing these houses to prominence and protecting them from police aggression. Members of the *terreiros* of Gantois, Bogum, Opô Afonjá, and Casa Branca all cite the importance of personal connections in protection from raids. Gantois was especially adept in cultivating relationships with influential people; in Querino's day it was already known as "one of the most popular" candomblés.[137]

Protection was necessary because attacks from the police continued to increase in the first decades of the twentieth century. These became especially frequent and severe under the administration of Pedro Azevedo Gordilho. As chief of police between 1920 and 1927, "Pedrito," as he was popularly known, led a clandestine campaign of terror against candomblé practitioners. Little has been written about Gordilho's crusade against the candomblés, although he is a prominent figure in oral tradition and popular folklore.[138] Because of their clandestine nature, the candomblé raids were not recorded in the police files stored at the Public Archives. They were, however, grist for the local newspapers, whose pages depicted a police force free to trample on the civic freedoms of the lower classes. Even in the early days of his administration, Pedrito inspired fear. After an argument over an outstanding debt, a woman complained to Pedrito that the wife of Felisberto Sowzer was practicing "witchcraft" *(bruxarias)*. Sowzer was reputed to be an influential candomblé priest who had helped initiate Aninha of Opô Afonjá. At the time of this incident, he was serving on the governing board of the Rosário às Portas do Carmo, and had just helped place Aninha in charge of one of the church's chapels.[139] Sowzer was unable to find representation for a retaliatory lawsuit filed in criminal court. "In this capital there is not one legal representative who will accept this criminal suit against Pedro Gordilho, given the panic and terror that everyone has of him," wrote Sowzer in a letter published in *A*

Tarde.[140] "Pedrito currently has secret and undercover police threatening me. If anything should happen to me or my family, or they should suffer in any fashion, it will be Mr. Pedro de Azevedo Gordilho, the Chief of Police of this city, who is responsible."[141] Pedrito was named to head the police force of the entire state in 1930.[142] Police excesses were not limited to candomblé, but were part of a general atmosphere of repression against the popular classes. *A Tarde* reported in 1921 that police had shot in cold blood a prisoner under arrest.[143] Other instances were less serious. The *Diario da Bahia* reported that when a man was taken off a trolley on suspicion of not having paid, officers hit him and a companion in the back. "It is just one effect of bad governors who, arm in arm with tyranny, for quite some time have been ruling by the fists and weapons of their unreined armed forces."[144] Seraphim Rodrigues, the precinct chief of Lapinha, was so notorious that, reporting an incident in which the Lapinha police had severely whipped a young man, *A Tarde* commented that "every day people come in to our offices to complain about the random cruelties of this precinct chief."[145]

As a further means of defending themselves from repression and as a way of maneuvering through an increasingly complex bureaucracy, the candomblé houses began utilizing a corporate body known as the *sociedade civil*. These corporations served as the legal entities through which candomblés conducted such business transactions as land purchases and banking. In addition, they provided protection against individual liability for the candomblé's legal and financial responsibilities. The advent of the *sociedade civil* signaled another major transformation of the candomblé. Through the new structure, priests enabled the candomblé houses to play a much more active role in defense of their rights and in strengthening their religious tradition without compromising it.

Menininha (Maria Escolástica da Conceição Nazareth), who assumed leadership of Gantois in 1926, reorganized the *terreiro* under the name Association of Saint George, subtitled with a Yoruba translation (Ebe Oxossi) identifying the deity with whom Saint George is syncretized. The association consisted of four entities, the General Superintendency, the Religious Council, the Religious Directorate, and the Administrative Directorate. The General Superintendency was the Iyalorixa (chief priestess) herself, the supreme authority responsible for all final decisions and answerable to no one. The four titled religious officials, all women, formed the Religious Council: the Iyalaxé, Iyakekeré, Iyá Dagan, and Iyá Moro. Each was responsible for the sacred obligations of the *terreiro* and its congregation. The Religious Directorate was a separate entity for two officeholders charged with assisting in the various rituals and accommodating visitors at public ceremonies. One, the Director of Obligations, was the woman overseeing the religious obligations. The second was the Director of the House, a male ogan responsible for the preparations for festivals, and dealing with visitors. Each of these first three divisions within the *terreiro* served essential religious functions, and required formal initiation. The Administrative Directorate, however, was the entity through which the candomblé managed its relations with the public. It was under the direction of the Iyalorixa and Iyalaxé, who served as president and vice president respectively, but was a public corporation whose membership was not restricted to candomblé initiates. Its offices included the various public responsibilities of the candomblé: public relations, financial portfolio management, and legal representation. Membership categories included Beneméritos, an honorary membership for those who had provided important services for the candomblé; Protectores, based upon financial contributions; dues-paying members; and members of the religious household, who were exempt from dues.[146]

The articles of incorporation of the *sociedade civil* provided the candomblés with a governing constitution specifying the roles and responsibilities of the entire candomblé community. In the case of the major Ketu houses, it protected the role of women as the principal authorities on religious matters, with public relations delegated specifically to men. The *sociedade civil* also allowed the clear delineation of the public and private spheres of candomblé. The houses were able to operate in the larger society without compromising sacred traditions or incurring personal liability. Because of this, candomblé leaders were better able to protect and preserve the alternative community they had created within Salvador.

The candomblés also offered practical assistance to the poor people who made up candomblé's membership base. Ruth Landes recalled the comment of Edison Carneiro that "the candomblé organization offered the only social insurance of value to the blacks . . . if a man, or a woman, were poor, his temple group would try to help him out. They would try to get him a job or introduce him to somebody useful or, if he were in trouble with the police, would hide him with no questions."[147] In this respect, the ability of candomblés to deliver vital services and resources ensured their popular support in much the same fashion as the Frente Negra Brasileira.

The candomblés were to develop yet another protective mechanism in the 1930s. This was largely the product of efforts by Edison Carneiro, a young Bahian mulatto and aspiring scholar of candomblé. After attending the first Afro-Brazilian Congress, organized in 1934 by Gilberto Freyre in Recife, he gathered a group of colleagues to stage another conference in Salvador. Carneiro, who worked closely with the largely poor candomblé community, was never welcomed by Brazilian academia. "They thought that, for a congress on Africanology to be realized with concrete contributions to its study, it had to have a Gilberto Freyre at its head," wrote Carneiro. Freyre predicted Carneiro's conference would be a dismal failure and declined to attend, as did several other well-known invited speakers.[148] Carneiro, with the help of local Bahian scholars and key candomblé leaders, nevertheless carried off the second Afro-Brazilian Congress with style in January 1937. The conference focused on Bahian candomblé, with many of its events held at Opô Afonjá and with presentations by Aninha, Martiniano do Bomfim, and other priests. This collaboration fostered the idea of organizing a coalition of candomblé houses to protest religious repression on the grounds of its unconstitutionality. Echoing Nina Rodrigues' argument made nearly fifty years earlier, Dario de Bittencourt submitted a paper to the conference tracing the laws guaranteeing the right of religious freedom in the Brazilian constitutions of 1823 through 1934.[149]

The Afro-Brazilian Congress of 1937 had several direct effects upon the candomblé community. It helped give the struggle for religious and cultural freedom an ideological base by valorizing African culture. Its presentations favored a synchronic conceptualization of African cultural traditions, promoting an emphasis on "authenticity" as a means of legitimization among the houses. This coincided with the desire of cultural researchers to investigate "primitive" cultures in their purest forms, thus providing the rationale for the sanctioning of the candomblé houses. Another side effect of the Congress was the preeminence of Nagô culture. Carneiro's persuasion of Iyalorixa Aninha and Martiniano do Bomfim to host most of the Congress sessions at Opô Afonjá resulted in the unprecedented display of a Bahian *terreiro,* especially one of such prestige, to the international community. The interaction led to important research by such scholars as Carneiro and the American Donald Pierson undertaken at Opô Afonjá, and a subsequent bias toward Nagô traditions in the academic literature.[150]

A third repercussion of the Congress was the creation of the União das Seitas Afro-Brasileiras (Union of Afro-Brazilian Sects) in September 1937. The Union was the brainchild of Edison Carneiro, who enlisted the help of Martiniano do Bomfim to serve as its president. Sixty-seven candomblés of various nations enrolled in the organization, whose stated purpose was to "fight for black people's religious freedom."[151] The candomblé leaders were each asked to identify their *nação,* their responses a testament to the fluidity and diversity of ethnic identity within the context of candomblé (see Table 12). In Carneiro's estimation, the many designations were misleading. Noting the degree of cultural borrowing between supposedly distinct "nations," he described the Amerindian *caboclos* as "degraded forms of Jêje-Nagô candomblés" and noted in the Angolan candomblés only minor differences of dances, rhythms, and language in what was essentially Jêje-Nagô ritual.[152] An interest-

TABLE 12. *Membership by* Nação, *Union of Afro-Brazilian Sects, 1937*

Nação	Number
Angola	15
Caboclo	15
Ketu	10
Jêje	8
Ijêxá	4
Congo	3
Ilú-Ijêxá	2
Alaketo	1
Muçurumim (Malê)	1
Nagô	1
Africano	1
Dahoméa	1
Yoruba	1
Môxe-Congo	1
Angola-Congo	1
Congo-Caboclo	1
Angolinha	1
Total	67

SOURCE: Edison Carneiro, *Candomblés da Bahia*, 3d ed. (Rio de Janeiro: Conquista, 1961), 57.

ing counterpoint exists between, on the one hand, increasing cultural similarities as more candomblés tended to assimilate a Yoruba-derived ritual and, on the other, a resistance to homogenization as reflected in the diversity of self-described *nações*.

A possible reason for the proliferation of "new" candomblé nations was the potential for males to assume leadership roles outside the Jêje-Nagô houses. Male senior priests were the exception in the latter; most were concentrated in the Angola, Congo, and, increasingly, *caboclo* houses. Of the sixty-seven houses participating in the Union, thirty-seven were led by men. Carneiro noted that the priesthood was considered a traditionally female role, and that male priests were derided either as homosexuals or as charlatans seeking to earn money for magical spells.[153] In the ritual itself as practiced in early twentieth-century Salvador, women held special positions as mediums for African deities. In the sacred dances invoking the presence of the deities, only women were expected to become possessed. A man experiencing possession was considered weak and unable to exert self-control. The "traditional" Jêge-Nagô houses placed firm restrictions on male participation, prompting some men to establish their own candomblés and, in the process, create their own "nations." The proliferation of self-annointed priests and a host of new houses paved the way for the popularization of candomblé well beyond the African community. It also strengthened the emphasis on traditionalism in such houses as Engenho Velho, Gantois, and Opô Afonjá. These developments led to further evolutions of candomblé in the middle and late twentieth century, in the fourth phase of its modernization.

As a political entity, the Union was quite short-lived. Shut down as a result of Vargas' prohibition on political activities, it managed only to hold a few organizational meetings.[154] It is, nonetheless, a development in Afro-Bahian history that raises provocative questions. Given that the impetus for its creation came largely from Edison Carneiro, was it in fact an expression of community activism? Carneiro was a friend of the candomblé, an ogan, but this was the equivalent of the guest invited into a home, but welcomed only as far as the living room instead of the more intimate kitchen. The candomblés of the 1930s appeared more heterogeneous, as each sought to establish its uniqueness and validity amid an increasing number of reputed charlatans. Nevertheless, sixty-seven congregations committed themselves to the Union's effort. Carneiro did not assume leadership, serving only as one of eleven members of the Executive Board. Despite any differences that may have existed, the Union is a testament to the candomblé community's recognition of the need to form alliances in order to effect political change.

Here we return to the initial question underlying the comparison between São Paulo and Salvador. The reason activism focused on culture rather than color in Salvador was twofold. First, the historical development of the Afro-Bahian community had contributed to an ethnicity centered in the concept of *nações*. Second, discrimination against Afro-Brazilians there was directed at the cultural expressions of the *nações* and not uniformly against all "black" people. As in São Paulo, activism in Salvador was a direct response to discrimination. Both the formulation of ethnicity within the population of African descent and the modalities of discrimination against the population are therefore intrinsic elements of self-determination struggles in the post-abolition diaspora.

"Full Free"

The Brazilian government intended the centennial anniversary of abolition to be a celebration. Indeed, Afro-Brazilians participated in many of the official events. Around the country, however, Afro-Brazilian activists and their supporters mobilized highly visible protests to denounce what they called a "false freedom." This gulf in perception reveals much about the nature of abolition in the Afro-Atlantic world. The diversity of Afro-Brazilian opinions is equally important to note. Reflecting the heterogeneity that characterizes Afro-Atlantic diasporan communities, there were many who supported the official ideology. At heart is the ambiguous and subjective notion of freedom itself. Although the word abolition implies an end, in historical terms it is best understood as a transition. Societies predicated on clear distinctions between the enslaved and the free had to develop a new social contract for delimiting boundaries, sanctions, and power. Such negotiations are hidden deep beneath the historical surface. It has been the intent of this book to explore the propaganda and politics to better understand the underlying dynamics of abolition in the Afro-Atlantic diaspora, for Afro-Brazilians were not alone in challenging the meaning of freedom when it was limited by imposed constraints. The "false freedom" denounced by Afro-Brazilians in 1988 was, they argued, a new system of oppression in which African descent continued to constitute a barrier to full and equal participation in all aspects of Brazilian life. There is an implicit dismissal of abolition as the dawn of freedom in the Afro-Atlantic world. Ostensibly an event of great import, abolition is not widely commemorated by the descendants of freedpersons. In the United States, a relatively small number of African Americans celebrate the cynically fictitious "Juneteenth"—a nonexistent date. According to oral tradition, slaves were told that freedom would be conferred on "Juneteenth," and thus they toiled on, their lives unchanging, despite the passage of the Emancipation Proclamation. Whether abolition came via legislation or warfare, freedpersons fully expected the end of slavery to signal the start of their complete and equal participation in the larger society. They greeted abolition with hope; their disillusion and protest began only after they had tested old boundaries and found them as intransigent as ever. In this new era, freedom had taken on very different meaning; people of African descent had to clarify that what they wanted was a "full free," not a hypocritical paper freedom that would continue to force them into the position of lackeys to a ruling authority.

For the privileged classes of the Americas, the meaning of abolition was considerably different. It implied freedom in the sense of not a social laissez-faire but, rather, a shift in the civil and economic order. The social order was to be protected to the extent possible, as reflected in post-abolition elite initiatives. Brazil was not unique in this regard, which is why this work has implications for the reinterpretation of the broader Afro-Atlantic diasporan experience. A comprehensive assessment of the actions of the privileged classes of the Americas reveals that those who had once profited from the enslavement of Africans instituted means by which to continue to exercise control over their lives and labor after abolition.

There are many dynamics of abolition that may be illuminated through comparative study. Certainly, the evolution of economic systems has been a major focus of historical research.[1] Here I have concentrated specifically on African descendants, looking at how, within the changing conditions of abolition, they set a political agenda and employed strategies to achieve their goals. Rather than view Afro-Atlantic initiatives exclusively as a response to imposed constraints, I argue that, in the context of those constraints, African descendants determined their own political agenda that was as much a product of internal factors from within the diasporan community as of external conditions.

At abolition, elites and African descendants were engaged in different ideological debates. First, whereas elites were concerned with the consolidation of power, the fundamental political issue facing people of African descent was the choice either to become part of the dominant society (integration) or to withdraw from it (separatism). Abolition removed the constraints barring Africans from their homeland, although for most, slavery had so completely uprooted them that a true return was no longer viable. Second, by reclassifying the emancipated slaves as human beings instead of property, American nations admitted them as citizens, albeit generally with reluctance and with limits firmly placed on the extent of their participation. Thus abolition forced upon freedpersons the choice of accepting their citizenship in the New World and the challenge of making that citizenship yield its greatest potential.

Although abolition introduced new conditions affecting political ideologies and strategies along the integration-separatism continuum, the centrality of the continuum in Afro-Atlantic self-determination was well established.

Older studies frequently presented it as a dichotomy between African reten-tions and rebellion, on the one hand, and accommodationism, on the other. In his classic study of creole society in Jamaica, Edward Brathwaite describes this division:

> Within the slave section of Jamaican society, therefore, there was also (as within the Establishment), a dichotomy—a tension of values, an in-hibiting choice of possibilities. One impulse tended towards an identi-fication with and reinterpretation of their own folk and remembered African culture (such were the obeah-men and some of the more "ex-treme" Black Baptists); the other tended towards coming to terms with their situation within their masters' image of them (such was Quashie-Sambo, and, though they were not technically slaves, many of the free colored). The creolization of the slaves, in other words, had a choice of forms, depending on the attitude, aptitude and opportunities of the par-ticular slave or group of slaves, on the one hand; and on the degree of control and coercion (both physical and psychological) exerted by the master or, more effectively, by the white society as a whole, through its institutions. The development of the slave within creole society de-pended, to put it another way, as much on the efficiency of the white Establishment as on his own socio-cultural equipment and adaptability.[2]

It has been my attempt to explore the nuances of this dynamic in the abolition era and place it in its historical context. What Brathwaite identifies as indicators of political ideology may be grouped into the broad categories of external ("the efficiency of the white Establishment") and internal ("his own socio-cultural equipment and adaptability") factors. I examine the former in terms of an elite defined by its social, political, and economic power, which utilized the politics of ethnicity as an instrument of hegemony. In that regard, elites created conditions that affected Afro-Atlantic political ideology. African descendants, however, were the ultimate arbiters of a political debate that they themselves established. Integration versus separatism as a polemic indeed arose from the external conditions of enslavement and oppression, but its pri-macy and ubiquity were equally the product of factors from within the Afro-Atlantic community. To that end, I have focused here on the internal dynamics of diasporan communities, their effect on political ideology, and how African descendants utilized ethnic identity as a strategic tool of self-determination.

Elites: Consolidating Hegemony

Because this study concentrates explicitly on African descendants, it re-fers only peripherally to elites and is therefore not a complete exploration of this proposed framework. Elites left a rich written record, and their actions have been meticulously examined elsewhere.[3] Several key factors, however, affected their shaping of abolition.

In discussing abolition in a comparative Atlantic context, it is necessary to use broad generalizations to illuminate transnational patterns and trends. Thus references here to "elites" will not take into account the specific composition of the upper social strata in any single country. It must also be noted that this is a sociopolitical, not an ethnic, construct. Members of Latin American elites frequently had indigenous and/or African ancestry, though they typically preferred to emphasize only their European forebears. In Haiti, for example, creole elites shared African ancestry with the rest of the population. Usages of ethnic identity, in this case the division between "mulattoes" and "blacks," should be understood in the context of the consolidation of power. In other words, there is nothing intrinsically ethnic about the creole elite class, but ethnicity did become a tool of hegemony. Finally, I use this term to refer not only to the wealthy but also to those who affected policy decisions and those privileged by the social relationships of slavery.

As with all generalizations, exceptions abound, particularly in the amorphous realm of intent. One important point to clarify is that elites were not necessarily omnipotent or homogeneous. In Brazil, for example, slaving interests in the northeast demanded indemnification but were denied it by a congress dominated by southern states. In the colonial settings of the Caribbean there were power struggles between local elites and influential political factions in the home country. Nonetheless, patterns exist. In the Americas and the Caribbean, the totality of both conscious and consequential factors combined to protect the hegemony of a wealthy, educated, and disproportionately white elite. Prevailing racist theories of African inferiority marginalized African descendants and their culture, and limited their possibilities of upward mobility and social acceptance.

In Brazil, freedpersons had little access to wealth. They found themselves in the least productive sectors of the Brazilian economy with no mechanisms in place to assist them in the transition into the existing free labor market. In areas such as the coffee region, where plantations were still quite lucrative, the labor pool had already been flooded with immigrant workers, thereby forcing down wages and minimizing the bargaining power of the recently emancipated. Negative attitudes about blacks, the equation of blackness with poverty and social marginality, and the idealization of "whitening" severely restricted Afro-Brazilian social space in terms of both quality and quantity. By the time of abolition, Brazilian elites had already created an exclusionary barrier around their ranks composed of social, economic, psychological, and political restrictions on the upward mobility of people of African descent.

The myth of racial democracy, an integral part of this barrier, was the illusion of equality of opportunity for all Afro-Brazilians. In reality, not only were the viable avenues of access limited, but they also exacted a high price in the currency of assimilation. Assimilation is a conditional form of integration. For Afro-Brazilians seeking integration via sanctioned modes of access, wealth and influential connections alone were not sufficient keys to upward mobility. Cultural and/or genetic assimilation was also necessary. "Whitening," as it came to be known, required some degree of rejection of African heritage and culture, yet did not ensure access to the highest echelons of society and power. Those who tried other options, the alternative integrationism of such entities as the Frente Negra and the African Carnival clubs, were challenged.

The specific mechanisms of abolition, and their effect on the prerogatives of freedpersons, varied according to geography, economy, demography, and political conditions around the hemisphere. Yet American societies bore significant similarities that, in turn, led to approaches to abolition comparable to that of the Brazilian elite. Each point of commonality is reflective of the historical forces sweeping the Americas over the course of the nineteenth century.

First, creole elites were primarily concerned with the consolidation of their own power and not with the abolition of slavery.[4] When, in the nineteenth century, both the independence and the abolition movements coincided, elites who gained independence considered abolition in terms of how it might best serve their own interests. Under colonialism there existed a pyramidal system of sociopolitical power, favoring Europeans at top, followed by the local entrepreneurial class, free persons, and finally, the enslaved.[5] As the nineteenth century progressed, creole elites who had grown rich from the slave-based export economy increasingly used this wealth as a basis for political influence, moving to occupy the top echelon of American societies either alongside, or in place of, the European-born. Two aspects of this phenomenon are of interest here. Politically, these shifts were to determine who would shape the legislation of abolition and its subsequent labor policies. Socially, creole elites bolstered their position through hegemonic ideologies, policies, and practices that impeded the ascent of freedpersons after abolition.

In most of the continental Americas, creole elites assumed leadership through wars of independence. These "revolutions," though they were modeled on the French Revolution and often adopted the language of the Enlightenment, were, in fact, socially conservative. Local elites sought to displace Europeans, but did not want to encourage any further social reorganization for fear of mass uprisings that would, in turn, jeopardize their own position.[6]

In some instances, abolition was closely linked to secessionist struggles.

African descendants tried wherever possible to exercise their leverage in this regard, viewing their military service as a key to attaining freedom.[7] When Simón Bolívar sought aid from the recently independent Haiti for his South American independence movement, he was pressured to promise to abolish slavery.[8] Elites also manipulated the promise of abolition. It became a central issue in Cuba's first war of independence (1868–1878), particularly as a bargaining chip to enlist black military assistance and international political support. In Brazil, mulatto soldiers had participated in a secessionist revolt in the province of Pernambuco in 1817. In the first days of the revolution, which was ultimately unsuccessful, the leaders of the uprising went to great pains to squelch rumors that they would immediately emancipate the slaves. The secessionists' statement borrowed the rationales of the authors of the United States Constitution:

> Suspicion has been excited among slave-holders. They believe that the benevolent tendency of the present liberal revolution has for its end the indirect emancipation of the people of color, the slaves. The government excuses them for a suspicion that does it honor. Educated in generous sentiments, it can never allow that men, because their complexions happen to be of a darker shade, should on that account be deprived of their liberty. The government is also well-convinced, that the basis of all regular society is the inviolability of every kind of property. Impelled by these principles, it desires an emancipation which shall no longer permit the cancer of slavery to increase among us, but at the same time to effect this emancipation in a slow, regular, and legal manner.[9]

At no point was abolition a primary objective of American creole elites. In the cynical words of one Cuban planter in 1873, "[T]he word abolition should be only a myth, dust to throw in the eyes of those English and American rogues who want to force themselves into our affairs."[10] Once they had replaced Europeans, the newly empowered elites used any ideological justification at their disposal to safeguard their hegemony. Beyond economic and political tactics, myths of black inferiority along with a continuation of the social relationships of slavery helped shape, in countries such as the United States and Cuba, a race-based, antiblack basis for exclusion.[11] More generally, American republican movements essentially shifted the boundaries between center and periphery to include creole elites in the hub of power while perpetuating the subordinate status of other sectors of society.

African descendants felt especially betrayed when ethnic exclusion continued despite the fact that they had participated in wars in which abolition was achieved. In the words of a black Civil War veteran from Louisiana, "There is no set of Men More willing to serve the United States Than ourselves and we intended to fight for The country expecting to be treated as human beings."[12] In Cuba, where Afro-Cuban military support had been key to the ultimate success of the independence wars, exclusion of blacks in positions of power led to the creation of a national race-based political party, the Partido Independiente de Color. Typically, once military objectives were won, the new ruling class used legislation and discriminatory social ideologies to safeguard its position. The United States exemplifies this phenomenon, and recent scholarship has provided excellent documentation of similar circumstances in Cuba.[13] It is a pattern repeated throughout the Americas, including, in some cases, nonwhite creole elites as well as lesser-known autonomist struggles that ended in defeat. In Haiti, an educated, wealthy, and predominantly mulatto class replaced the largely absentee French planter-landlords after the revolution. The masses of African- and Caribbean-born slaves who had participated in the armed insurrection did not enjoy equal participation in the new nation's power structure, which led eventually to a color-based caste society in which lighter-skinned persons enjoyed greater socioeconomic privilege.[14]

The anticolonial military struggles illustrate the same dynamics of the renegotiation of social roles that characterized abolition. The breaches caused by major sociopolitical transitions in the nineteenth century were seized upon by Americans of all classes to improve their positions. Black soldiers, and the African-descended population in general, had hoped to take advantage of the wars to win their freedom, just as creoles sought to secure new power for themselves. Abolition may be considered in this regard as part of a pattern of social change typical of the Americas. In these comparatively new societies, boundaries were ever shifting and subject to contestation.

A second dimension of the elite approach to abolition in the Afro-Atlantic world is its implicit conferring of the right to appropriate not merely the labor of African descendants, but the people themselves. Elites, in their concern for economic stability once slavery ended, were willing to exercise the implicit right to place constraints on the mobility and bargaining power of freedpersons. This resulted in labor legislation that checked the ability of freedpersons to compete in the new economic order.[15] Individuals and the laws they fashioned did not readily relinquish the prerogative of dictating the role of African descendants.

The third aspect of Afro-Atlantic abolition that characterizes elite understandings is its ideological underpinnings drawn from Positivism. Darwinism and Positivism deeply affected elite beliefs about the nature of the societies in which they lived, and their ability to manipulate society in the interest of development and the protection of class-based prerogatives. Positivistic notions of biological and environmental determinism were uniquely interpreted in the Americas, where large populations of color and warm climates were thought to be detrimental to a progress conceived in linear terms. As in the case of Brazil, elites viewed people of African descent as a developmental liability, further compounding negative stereotyping of blackness.

The nature of elite perspectives on abolition had another pervasive and lasting impact. The dissolution of the civil categories of slave and free upset an intrinsic element of the rationale of social organization in the Americas. The close correlation between European descent and social class, along with the prevailing ideology of racialist biological determinism, served as a convenient new hegemonic justification for the exclusion of nonelites, extending to indigenous Americans as well as to African descendants. Abolition became a watershed for the politicization of ethnic identity in the Americas, and set the tone for the subsequent evolution of race relations. People of African descent did not thereafter operate under the same conditions as did immigrants. They remained under the constraints of a new form of manipulation that limited the opportunities not only of freedpersons specifically but, by predicating itself on ethnicity, now extended to the entire population of African descent.

The fact that abolition occurred at different times in the historical trajectories of individual nations does not negate the similarities in elite intent around the pan-American region. Abolition occurred contemporaneously with the consolidation of power by regional elites over the course of the nineteenth century. This mitigated the breadth of freedoms conferred, thus setting the parameters for subsequent negotiations by freedpersons seeking to realize their own notions of the meaning of abolition.

African Descendants and Self-Determination: Shaping a Role in Post-Abolition Society

The similarity of modes of oppression throughout the Afro-Atlantic diaspora suggests a corresponding similarity of response and, hence, the basis for a comparative framework for analyzing political strategies of African descendants during the transitional period from slavery to freedom. This study began with the hypothesis that abolition was a historical moment of special significance for African descendants. It was a new opportunity for self-determination and self-fulfillment. To that end, every community of the Afro-Atlantic diaspora would be presumed to have manifested some form of response to what each perceived as the new social conditions brought about by abolition. Yet this was apparently not the case, even within a single nation. In contradiction of this hypothesis, the large African-descended population of the northeastern states of Brazil manifested virtually no political organization during the post-abolition years. It seemed extraordinary, particularly in light of the groundbreaking activism of the Frente Negra Brasileira, that an organization directed at harnessing the potential political influence of all people of African descent would find so little support in a region where Afro-Brazilians made up the majority of the population.

It soon became clear that what had initially appeared to North American eyes to be a large "black" population, was, in fact, a heterogeneous group of many smaller communities. Despite the shared heritage of enslavement and connection to the continent of Africa, there existed no unifying ethnic identity to forge a true community from this large and diverse demographic group. The existence of such a community is often taken for granted when viewed through the prism of the U.S. experience. "Blackness" did not arise intrinsically out of the fact of African heritage, but was conditioned and modeled by the historical dynamics of each specific slave society. In response to different historical trajectories and modalities of ethnic exclusion, the African-descended population in São Paulo thus developed an identity based on racial differences, whereas that of Salvador was predicated on cultural differences. The strategic use of identity by each community, however, was remarkably similar. In each case, Afro-Brazilians appropriated the identity of exclusion, a tool of oppression, and used it as a strategy of empowerment.

Part of slavery's legacy to modern Brazil was a tradition of fragmentation, based upon differences of nationality, color, and culture, within the African-descended population. Whereas slave status had once been a basis for exclusion that encompassed the vast majority of African descendants, the growth of a free population of color had given rise to broader-based exclusionary ideologies. Elites were taking advantage of the malleability of ethnicity and using it as a strategy to protect the insularity of their group. Afro-Brazilians also began to manipulate imposed identities as a strategy of their own. Discrimination against Afro-Brazilians as "blacks" or "Africans" provided them with both common cause for protest and a collective identity that would foster ethnic solidarity. Their use of these broader ethnicities emphasized greater levels of inclusion; for the first time, the notion of blackness in São Paulo now included mulattoes, and the concept of Africanity in Salvador came to embrace all adherents regardless of birthplace or even skin color. This understanding of identity not as a fixed variable, but as a social strategy, refines the research question by directing it toward a search for patterns of response that are obscured by external differences of form.

These patterns began to suggest themselves after a survey of a wide range of Afro-Brazilian collective activities, including many that were not explicitly political. To the extent that collectives are predicated on the perception of shared identity, they served as clues to Afro-Brazilian social strategies, the basic elements of self-determination. São Paulo and Salvador each had a dominant mode of self-determination coexisting with a multiplicity of other responses. In São Paulo, collectives oriented toward equality of opportunity and the dismantling of segregation became the most vocal, and black social clubs born of racial exclusion became a highly popular expression of ethnic solidarity and community support. In Salvador, an African-born community forced underground as a result of nineteenth-century repression re-created itself as a vital alternative community with its own cultural constructs that counteracted the detrimental effects of an oppressive mainstream society. Although it became an integral element of contemporary Afro-Bahian society, it was but one form of collective adaptation in the post-abolition era.

Each of the popular responses to post-abolition conditions highlighted here had parallels elsewhere in the Afro-Atlantic world. The civil rights activism of the Frente Negra Brasileira shared important features, such as its political orientation and focus on constitutional law, with Cuba's Independent Party of Color (Partido Independiente de Color), founded in 1907.[16] The religious and cultural enclaves of the candomblé (often established on the sites of former *quilombos*) were mirrored in Pinnacle, the early Jamaican Rastafari community founded in 1940 (in the hills that once sheltered Maroons). Both established alternative social spaces that were sanctuaries from mainstream societies and police harassment.[17] This separatist orientation also bore resemblances to those among the Garífuna on the Atlantic coast of Nicaragua.[18] Were these false friends, or were they parts of a pattern of responses to abolition in the Afro-Atlantic diaspora? I suggest that the decisions of individuals and communities were neither entirely random nor unique to each locale. Just as there are parallels in strategies of hegemony, there exist patterns of black response based on discrete structural, historical, and personal factors that are applicable throughout the former slave societies of the Americas and the Caribbean.

Three essential modes of response at abolition have been identified broadly here as integrationism, alternative integrationism, and separatism. The factors influencing the choice toward either integrationism or separatism fall into two general categories—structural and individual. Both elements are necessary because, whereas external conditions may facilitate certain outcomes, human behavior is ultimately a product of individual choices.

Individual factors hinge on the possession of sanctioned modes of access and the personal choice of whether or not to utilize them. While the fundamental problem is exclusion from the prerogatives enjoyed by a restricted social group, discrimination is not applied evenly to the population of African descent. Therefore responses may be categorized in relation to the terms of individual exclusion. Each society has distinct criteria for admission to its upper echelons. Light skin color, wealth, social connections, and command of Euro-Brazilian culture were keys to upward mobility in Brazil. People of African descent who held these keys could reasonably expect to share in many of the prerogatives of the elite (albeit with the tacit acceptance of the unbreachable color line). The command of sanctioned modes of access appears to indicate a proclivity toward integrationism. The alternative integrationist either cannot, or will not, utilize the sanctioned modes of access. Instead, in this modality, individuals seek to establish new bases for entrée.[19] The Frente Negra Brasileira exemplified this strategy when, without otherwise challenging the tenets of sociopolitical organization, it demanded that criteria for social and political inclusion be expanded to include blacks. The separatist is not oriented toward inclusion, seeking instead that which is unavailable from the mainstream society in a separate environment. It bears noting that the participants in the alternative integrationist and separatist collectives studied here did not possess all the keys to social ascent in Brazilian life.

This formulation allows for personal choice while recognizing the differential application of exclusionary practices. It also deliberately avoids being specific to Brazil, and can be applied to any African diaspora community by considering the mechanisms of access available in each geographical context.[20] Nonetheless, it must be remembered that these are broad patterns, not hard and fast categories, that can vary to a greater or lesser extent with the choices made by individuals throughout their lives.

The structural factors affecting Afro-Atlantic political strategies relate to the composition of the African diaspora community. In this regard I have isolated the existence of a distinct "black" world as its most critical component. This may either take the form of a parallel community, in which the institutions of the dominant society are reproduced for the isolated group, generally a function of segregationist policies, or be expressed as an alternative community. In the latter case, the diasporan community maintains its own cultural constructs and unique worldview, and is far more likely to develop a separatist political orientation than those dependent on mainstream culture and institutions. The degree to which a diasporan community may develop either as parallel or as an alternative to the dominant culture depends largely on historical and demographic considerations.

In this study, the black middle-class society of São Paulo most closely fits the description of a parallel community. It was a world distinct from mainstream society that was born of exclusionary practices. It gave rise to reinvented collective identities; by the 1930s, a new ethnicity as black Paulistanos was superseding original identities based on hometown networks and affiliations. Members of parallel communities create institutions that serve as counterparts of those in the mainstream society, such as banks, social clubs, and athletic teams. In some instances, parallel institutions are inferior substitutes for those of the mainstream. Others have unique qualities that derive from commonalities of culture and experience. Thus the black beauty salon or barber shop takes on additional meaning as a source of ethnic cohesion, culture, and support.

To the extent that imposed segregation limits the prospects of the excluded group, it invites protest oriented toward the dismantling of parallel institutions and integrating those of the mainstream. Once the basis of exclusion is removed, this type of community is subject to dissolution and weakening. Some institutions perceived to have intrinsic value may continue, while others may falter in the face of competition with the greater resources of mainstream counterparts. An example of this was the disappearance of Afro-Brazilian soccer leagues once black players were admitted to professional white clubs, while social clubs and the community press became permanent features of black Paulistano society.[21]

The second type of "black world," the alternative community, generally develops in areas where there has been a strong demographic influence of individuals from a point of origin other than that of the mainstream society. Using different cultural constructs, these individuals create a distinct society that coexists with the mainstream as an alternative. In the Afro-Atlantic diaspora, areas that continued to import large numbers of Africans late in the slave trade frequently developed the alternative model, particularly when the enslaved came from the same cultural area. This was the case in Bahia; an influx of Yoruba peoples in the early nineteenth century heightened the potential for the development of the alternative candomblé community that eventually evolved.

Alternative communities are not necessarily direct retentions of homeland cultures, and are often creoles and blends. Their key feature lies in the perceived differences between the alternative community and the mainstream. Because of the diverse backgrounds of many slave societies, an important factor contributing to successful alternative communities was the creation of pan-ethnic cultures bridging the differences within a heterogeneous slave population. Some incorporated indigenous elements, or patched together aspects of a variety of African cultures. Syncretism and fluidity allowed some New World African cultures to flourish more than those more rigidly construed. Consider the trajectories of Yoruban and Islamic cultures in Salvador. Both were strongly represented in the incoming African population of the late eighteenth and early nineteenth centuries, and followers of both traditions came from approximately the same areas of origin. Throughout the nineteenth century, each religion was forced underground, but the Islamic tradition foundered in contrast to the spread of Yoruban candomblé. What differentiates the two is the fact that, unlike Islam, candomblé was easily adaptable to a broad spectrum of beliefs and, hence, accessible to a larger cross-section of the Afro-Bahian population. The same pattern is seen in Rio de Janeiro's macumba, Haitian vodoun, Cuban santería, and Jamaican myalism, each of which, like candomblé, adopted widely understood elements of Central African, West African, and European belief systems.[22]

What is known in twentieth-century parlance as "counter-culture" is a manifestation of the alternative community in which the culture is largely invented, rather than adopted or transformed. As direct African retentions diminished in the Afro-Brazilian population, alternative communities increasingly took on this form. Private worlds organized around samba, soccer, capoeira, and candomblé created for many Afro-Brazilians in the post-abolition era an environment in which they were not subject to the limitations based on their African heritage that they faced in the mainstream society.

As a form of response, alternative societies are inherently separatist. Their objective is a withdrawal, to varying degrees, from the larger society. The retreat to an alternative society is a modification of marronage serving much the same function as it did during slavery—a revitalizing sanctuary enabling individuals to withstand the dehumanizing effects of oppression or to completely withdraw from those conditions.

There are two important differences between parallel and alternative communities. The first is the element of choice. Whereas the parallel community is the product of forced segregation, the alternative community reflects the conscious choice of individuals to create an insular world. The second difference is that the raison d'être of the alternative community is its unique worldview which provides such intangibles as dignity and self-worth, denied in the mainstream. To protect that sheltering and nurturing function, some alternative communities develop a supportive infrastructure of institutions that mirror those of the larger society. It is necessary to understand the history of each community to determine whether equivalent institutions are the product of segregation or the complements of alternative societies.

This degree of separatism is rare in the African diaspora in the Americas, although it is evident among segments of other American populations such as the Hasidim and the Amish. This is attributable to the fact that, with rare exceptions, American cultures of African descent are blends of the same cultural elements that created American culture as a whole. They are truly more American than African even though African elements may play a more prominent role in their alternative communities than in those of European descent.

It is necessary to offer a caveat about the concept of cultural separatism. Separatists do not typically relinquish their constitutional rights and protections as citizens of the larger society. It will be recalled that the candomblé communities justified their right to religious freedom with a constitutional argument. Separatism is a mode of citizenship created by a discriminated group as a coping mechanism.

Other elements, such as community size and ethnic demography, must be included as intrinsic to the model, but further research is needed regarding their exact role. The small size of the Afro-Paulistano community vis-à-vis other ethnic groups in the city no doubt contributed to a sense of solidarity. Similarly, the larger Afro-Bahian community of Salvador had the "luxury" of greater heterogeneity given the extent of its subcommunities. There arises the question whether or not a critical mass of population is needed to influence formulations of identity and degree of solidarity within communities of African descent. But, without a far more detailed understanding of both São Paulo and Salvador's black population, it is premature to hazard a hypothesis in this regard.[23]

One provocative piece of information related to community size and ethnic demography may be obtained by comparing São Paulo with Porto Alegre in the state of Rio Grande do Sul, another city with an active Frente Negra contingent, but not in the immediate vicinity of the São Paulo networks. In both Porto Alegre and São Paulo, the Afro-Brazilian population was small, there was a high ratio of *prêtos* to *pardos,* and both were active in the alternative integrationist mode. The *prêto* to *pardo* ratio may be of significance, because the former generally had less chance of gaining access to mainstream society through traditional means. A demographic analysis of all Brazilian cities might reveal a connection between these variables and Afro-Brazilian post-abolition strategies.

A full exploration of parallels between Brazil and other Afro-Atlantic communities is a subject for future research. Nonetheless, a consideration of one set of similarities with Cuba merits further discussion. Afro-Cuban history bears striking resemblances to that of both Salvador and São Paulo. In Cuba, the abolition era began in earnest with the Ten Year's War of 1868–1878, and was eventually enacted in an apprenticeship lasting from 1880 to 1886. Prior to this, one of the most important forms of Afro-Cuban collectives was the cabildo, a form of mutual aid society that, in its early manifestations, united Africans of common cultural and linguistic origins. According to Philip Howard, the cabildos became bases of conspiracy in the early nineteenth century, culminating in the slave revolt of La Escalera in 1844.[24] The repression of African cultural institutions in the aftermath of La Escalera appears to parallel that which followed Bahia's Revolt of the Malês in 1835. Of note is the elite concern with the spread of African culture to the creole population, which Cuban authorities sought to impede by restricting cabildo membership to the African-born. In addition, a mythology of evil African witchcraft arose as a mainstay of racial discrimination.

By the latter half of the nineteenth century, the focus of the historiography on Afro-Cubans shifts to features that appear closer to the São Paulo pattern than to that of Salvador. After the enforced cooptation of the cabildos by the Catholic Church, the need for mutual aid societies was increasingly filled by *sociedades de color*. These institutions represented a new form of Afro-Cuban collective that was pan-ethnic in character, organizing on the basis of African descent in general, rather than from any specific African nation. Unlike the cabildos, which emphasized the maintenance of distinct African cultures, the *sociedades de color* behaved much like São Paulo's social clubs. Like the Paulistanos, Afro-Cuban *sociedades de color* organized parallel social functions but eventually became politicized and advocated against racial discrimination. They organized an umbrella organization, the Directorio de las Sociedades de Color, and a newspaper founded in 1904, *El Nuevo Criollo,* voiced their opinions. Ultimately, they formed a national party of people of color in 1907.

The framework outlined in this book suggests new ways to examine the Afro-Cuban case, and new questions to ask. It demands a closer analysis of such differences as region and class among the Afro-Cuban population. For example, historians have noted that, in Oriente Province (the site of the massacre of 1912), the activists of the Partido Independiente de Color were ambitious people who felt entitled to positions within the national government, whereas the majority of Afro-Cuban residents had little practical involvement with the party.[25] This lends support to the argument that alternative integrationist activism is typical of the aspirant segment of Afro-Atlantic communities. If so, it forces a reconsideration of what happened to that portion of the community from which the cabildos sprang. Was there simultaneously an adjustment to post-abolition conditions from the separatist sector? Hints in that direction have been suggested by scholarship on the secret Abakuá societies, but there exists as yet no complete overview of the variety of responses across the spectrum of the Afro-Cuban population. The present framework may provide a mechanism for approaching this material in a way that allows insight into larger dynamics of Atlantic abolition from the perspective of the Afro-Atlantic diaspora.

Understanding the relationship between the factors shaping Afro-Atlantic communities and those affecting personal political choices may explain why the civil rights movement was spearheaded by highly segregated black communities in the southern United States. Or why Rastafarianism was born in Jamaica where the Maroon tradition was strong, and why Rastafarians established their first base in what was essentially a Maroon stronghold. Or why Garvey's message of repatriation was roundly rejected by thousands of diasporan peoples determined to make good in the Americas, which they considered their rightful home, and not Africa. If, indeed, there exists a rationale of African diaspora response, a contextual framework such as that offered here may begin to uncover its structure.

These are the outlines of a model for the analysis of responses to abolition in the Afro-Atlantic diaspora. Based exclusively on case studies in São Paulo and Salvador, the model remains to be tested and refined in other settings both in and outside Brazil. It is specifically designed for the unique historical situation of the Americas and the Caribbean, slave societies born of similar roots in the colonial mercantile era. Its explanatory power comes from its specificity to a historical moment and geographical area. Nonetheless, it may serve to shed light on the experiences of other diasporas as well as those of the African diaspora in other parts of the world. The imposition of geographic boundaries in the aftermath of the conquests and wars of the nineteenth and twentieth centuries created hosts of groups who, like the Afro-Atlantic diaspora, were cultural nations without a physical homeland of their own. Ethnic politics and cultural nationalism have become potent forces of social and political change in the twentieth century, and may become even greater in the future. Closer scrutiny of the dynamics of diasporas may deepen our understanding of ethnonationalism in general.

A diaspora is more than the dispersal of a people. It is a complex historical process whose contemporary dynamics of culture and power are related to four dimensions of the diasporan experience: first, the reasons for and conditions of relocation; second, relationships with the host country; third, relationships with the homeland; and, finally, interrelationships within the diaspora group. This last dimension distinguishes diasporas from emigrant communities, and its corresponding form of identity has only recently come into the consciousness of the Afro-Atlantic diaspora. The Afro-Atlantic diaspora, like the Indian, Chinese, and other diasporas, has been established in scores of nations. It has also undergone subsequent migrations since the initial dislocation. As communications technology and transportation grew increasingly accessible and people of African descent discovered counterparts around the hemisphere with shared histories and struggles, they developed a new psychological and social ethnicity. Marcus Garvey was the first to address this new diasporan consciousness with the Universal Negro Improvement Association, an organization that brought together African descendants in Brooklyn and Bridgetown, Panama City and Port-of-Spain, Caracas and Kingston.

The UNIA reflected an emerging self-awareness as an historically interconnected Afro-Atlantic people. The discourse about this new identity contained in the pages of the *Negro World* passed through the hands of West Indian seamen, through a Bahian English teacher, to the black newspapers of São Paulo at the very time that Afro-Brazilians were reshaping social identities. It was also during the post-abolition era that Robert Abbott of the *Chicago Defender* opened lines of communication between the black communities of Brazil and the United States. The early relationships between Afro-Brazilians and other African and African-descended populations are as yet an understudied aspect of their history that contains important insights into the constructions and uses of identity. In addition, ties to African peoples around the world have informed Afro-Brazilian activism and political philosophy throughout the twentieth century. This was especially true during the liberation struggles of Lusophone Africa and the black power movement in the U.S., which coincided with a political opening and the rise of the contemporary black consciousness movement in Brazil.[26]

The experience of Afro-Brazilians cannot be fully understood in its national context alone. As an Afro-Atlantic people, they share the sense of twoness expressed by W.E.B. du Bois in *The Souls of Black Folk;* they are linked simultaneously to an American nation and to the international African community. This duality has thus far been the defining feature of Afro-Atlantic identity, and lies at the heart of black philosophy, arts, and culture. A diasporan perspective is, therefore, the indispensable complement to understanding the history and thought of Afro-Brazilians or any peoples of the Afro-Atlantic world. It is only through this lens that we will be able to see how, in the words of Lélia Gonzalez with which we began, "the struggle of the Black people of Brazil is an aspect of a much larger struggle: the struggle of the Black people of the world."

There is a fifth dimension to diasporan analysis which synthesizes and analyzes the entire diasporan group in a comparative framework. Resonating through the histories of all diasporan peoples are complex struggles over identity, belonging, acculturation, and separatism. Each diaspora has unique historical circumstances. In the case of the Afro-Atlantic diaspora, the experience of enslavement framed the discourse over those issues; for the Jewish diaspora, it was religious persecution. As we begin to study these and other diasporas comparatively, however, it quickly becomes clear that choices of identity and integration vary within diasporan groups, and are affected by a host of factors.[27] More nuanced study of these issues will shed light on the critical and urgent dynamics of ethnonationalism as it plays an ever more salient role in world history.

For Afro-Brazilian history, and that of the Afro-Atlantic in general, the analytical frameworks of diasporas help frame and address important questions. Is it possible to speak of a "black" community? How do outcomes differ in white-majority versus black-majority societies? Is separatism ultimately more profitable than integrationism? These politically charged questions demand further historical analysis.

People of African descent have spent half a millennium in the Americas and the Caribbean, creating a home out of what began as a world of sorrow. Much progress has been made since the last shackle was removed from the last slave. African descendants have met the challenge of forcing freedom to yield its jealously guarded fruits. North Americans are familiar with stories of black southerners who dared to vote knowing that lynch mobs might hang them, and of the Freedom Riders attacked by dogs, billy clubs, and fire hoses for the simple right to buy a lunch at a counter next to a white person. These were but the most violent expressions of a multifaceted and pan-continental effort to achieve human rights. Alongside these are the thousands of others who somehow wrested dignity from societies in which white progress depended upon the oppression of people of color. The Frente Negra youths in their best clothes boldly setting foot in the chic downtown plazas of São Paulo, the candomblé initiate reconstructing the spiritual world of African ancestors, the Carnival revelers filling the Brazilian summer with drum, dance, and song—all were confronting the same challenges as their North American counterparts. The people of the African diaspora in the Americas and the Caribbean began a history together linked by chains since replaced by links of struggle. Until their "full free" is realized, that struggle will continue to be a fundamental dynamic of American life.

NOTES

INTRODUCTION   *Recontextualizing Abolition*

1. Lélia Gonzalez, "The Unified Black Movement: A New Stage in Black Political Mobilization," in Pierre-Michel Fontaine, ed., *Race, Class, and Power in Brazil* (Los Angeles: University of California/Center for Afro-American Studies, 1985), 132.
2. This estimate includes all persons with some degree of African ancestry. Minority Rights Group, ed., *No Longer Invisible: Afro-Latin Americans Today* (London: Minority Rights Publications, 1995), xiii. Brazil's official estimates from the 1991 census (which did not include race in its questionnaire), are 7,335,130 blacks *(prêtos)* and 62,316,085 browns *(pardos)*. The latter category refers to people of partial African ancestry. African descendants tend to be underestimated in official statistics because blackness continues to bear negative social connotations in the minds of many Brazilians. Brazil, Instituto Brasileiro de Geografia e Estatística, *Censo Demográfico,* 1991 [on-line database]; available from http://www.sidra.ibge.gov.br/cgi-bin/v/m/pcbr; Internet; accessed 8 May 1997.
3. See Minority Rights Group, ed., *No Longer Invisible: Afro-Latin Americans Today*; for Brazil, see also Nelson do Valle Silva, "Updating the Cost of Not Being White in Brazil," in Fontaine, *Race, Class, and Power in Brazil,* 42–55; Carlos A. Hasenbalg, "Race and Socioeconomic Inequalities in Brazil," in Fontaine, *Race, Class, and Power in Brazil,* 25–41; George Reid Andrews, "Racial Inequality in Brazil and the United States: A Statistical Comparison," *Journal of Social History* 26:2 (1992), 229–263.
4. Gonzalez, "The Unified Black Movement," 132.
5. On the exclusionary nature of colonial Brazilian society, see Stuart B. Schwartz, "Plantations and Peripheries," in Leslie Bethell, ed., *Colonial Brazil* (Cambridge: Cambridge University Press, 1987), 135–144.
6. Saraiva-Cotegipe Law, 28 September 1885, "Of the Freedoms, and of the Freed Slaves," article III, sections 3c and 15, reprinted in Robert Conrad, *The Destruction of Brazilian Slavery, 1850–1888* (Berkeley: University of California Press, 1972), 313 (emphasis added). Such restrictions were not uncommon; "apprenticeships" and other transitional programs in the British Caribbean, Puerto Rico, and Cuba freed slaves but obligated them to continue working in assigned jobs for several years.
7. Herbert S. Klein and Stanley L. Engerman, "The Transition from Slave to Free

Labor: Notes on a Comparative Economic Model," in Mario Moreno Fraginals, Frank Moya Pons, and Stanley L. Engerman, eds., *Between Slavery and Free labor: The Spanish-Speaking Caribbean in the Nineteenth Century* (Baltimore: Johns Hopkins University Press, 1985), 255–269; Francisco A. Scarano, "Labor and Society in the Nineteenth Century," in Franklin W. Knight and Colin A. Palmer, eds., *The Modern Caribbean* (Chapel Hill: University of North Carolina Press, 1989), 51–84; Eric Foner, *Nothing but Freedom: Emancipation and Its Legacy* (Baton Rouge: Louisiana State University Press, 1983), 10–28.

8. More common is the pattern in which light-skinned mixed-bloods occupy an intermediate socioeconomic stratum between dark blacks and whites. See H. Hoetink, *Slavery and Race Relations in the Americas: Comparative Notes on Their Nature and Nexus* (New York: Harper and Row, 1973).

9. Emilia Viotti da Costa, "1870–1889," in Leslie Bethell, ed., *Brazil: Empire and Republic, 1822–1930* (Cambridge: Cambridge University Press, 1989), 164; see also Conrad, *Destruction of Brazilian Slavery,* 281–285.

10. Abolition legislation, quoted in Robert Brent Toplin, *The Abolition of Slavery in Brazil* (New York: Atheneum, 1972), 243.

11. There is an emerging body of scholarship on Afro-Brazilians during the post-abolition era (1888 through the 1930s) in Rio de Janeiro. See, for example, Sam Adamo, "The Broken Promise: Race, Health, and Justice in Rio de Janeiro, 1890–1940" (Ph.D. diss., University of New Mexico, 1983); Adamo, "Order and Progress for Some—Death and Disease for Others: Living Conditions of Nonwhites in Rio de Janeiro, 1890–1940," *West Georgia College Studies in the Social Sciences* 25 (1986), 17–30; Alison Raphael, "Samba Schools in Brazil," *International Journal of Oral History* 10:3 (1989), 256–269.

12. The full name of the city of Salvador is "São Salvador da Bahia de Todos os Santos." The preferred adjectival form is Bahian; many people also refer to the city as Bahia, although the precise short name is Salvador.

13. Through the nineteenth century, parish baptismal records routinely indicated race. In Salvador, after 1892–93, scribes rarely noted race. Arquivo da Curia Metropolitana de Salvador (ACMS), Batismos, Casamentos, Óbitos (organized by parish).

14. Boris Fausto observes that police officers routinely noted the race of detainees in the margins of arrest forms, although this information was not required. Fausto, *Crime e Cotidiano: A Criminalidade em São Paulo, 1880–1924* (São Paulo: Editora Brasiliense, 1984), 52. Prison records in Salvador in the 1890s noted name, nationality, color, profession, civil status, age, criminal charge, and authority ordering imprisonment. These forms were subsequently simplified to note only district, name, age, and crime. Arquivo Público do Estado da Bahia (APEB), Secretaria de Segurança Pública, box 03–1 (1892), folder: "Preso"; box 13 (1918–1923), file: "Subdelegacia de Policia, 1921." (Box numbers from the APEB and the Arquivo Municipal de Salvador are temporary numbers assigned during the cataloguing process, 1991–92. I have given all possible identifying information in this and subsequent references available at the time of my research from November 1991 through November 1992.)

15. One such example is the oral history project at the Pontífica Universidade Católica (PUC) in São Paulo, which recorded memories of slavery through several generations of black families. "Projecto Memoria de Escravidão em Familias Negras de

São Paulo," 30 boxes (1987–88), PUC, Central de Documentação e Informação Científica Professor Casemiro dos Reis Filho. The principal primary sources for the São Paulo segment of this book are black newspapers and oral histories. The chapters on Bahia rely more heavily on secondary sources, but greatly benefited from informal oral traditions.

16. The works discussed here published prior to 1965 were not specifically analyses of the post-abolition era. I have highlighted only their implications for that analysis.

17. *O Animismo Fetichista dos Negros Bahianos* first appeared in installments in the *Revista Brasileira* between April and September 1896. To these was added a final chapter which appeared in volume 9 of the *Revista Brasileira* in 1897. These articles were subsequently published in book form in 1900 as *L'Animisme Fétichiste des Nègres de Bahia*. Raymundo Nina Rodrigues, *O Animismo Fetichista dos Negros Bahianos* (Rio de Janeiro: Civilização Brasileira, 1935), 7–8.

18. Gilberto Freyre, *The Masters and the Slaves* (Casa-Grande e Senzala), trans. Samuel Putnam, second English-language edition, revised (New York: Alfred A. Knopf, 1978).

19. Arthur Ramos, *The Negro in Brazil* (Washington, D.C.: Associated Publishers, 1939). Ramos subsequently played a central role in reactivating scholarship in Afro-Brazilian studies as a series editor for a Brazilian publishing company. See also Waldir Freitas Oliveira and Vivaldo da Costa Lima, eds., *Cartas de Edison Carneiro a Arthur Ramos* (São Paulo: Corrupio, 1987).

20. Florestan Fernandes, *A Integração do Negro na Sociedade de Classes,* 2 vols. (São Paulo: Dominus Editora, 1965). This work followed an exhaustive sociological survey of contemporary race relations in São Paulo by Fernandes and Roger Bastide, *Brancos e Negros em São Paulo: Ensaio Sociológico sôbre Aspectos da Formação, Manifestações Atuais e Efeitos do Preconceito de Côr na Sociedade Paulistana,* 3d ed. (São Paulo: Companhia Editora Nacional, 1971), originally published in 1955 as *Relações Raciais entre Negros e Brancos em São Paulo.*

21. Fernandes, *A Integração do Negro na Sociedade de Classes,* 7.

22. Florestan Fernandes, *The Negro in Brazilian Society* (translation of *A Integração do Negro na Sociedade de Classes*) (New York: Atheneum, 1971), 39.

23. Ibid., 12.

24. A Paulistano is a resident of the city of São Paulo; a Paulista is a resident of the state of São Paulo.

25. Fernandes, *The Negro,* 226.

26. Ibid., 227.

27. Carlos A. Hasenbalg, *Discriminação e Desigualdades Raciais no Brasil* (Rio de Janeiro: Graal, 1979). See also Octavio Ianni, *Escravidão e Racismo,* 2d ed. (São Paulo: Hucitec, 1988), and *Raças e Classes Sociais no Brasil,* 3d ed. (São Paulo: Brasiliense, 1987); Abdias do Nascimento, *Brazil: Mixture or Massacre? Essays in the Genocide of a Black People,* 2d rev. ed. (Dover, Mass: Majority Press, 1989); Clovis Moura, *Rebeliões da Senzala* (São Paulo: Edições Zumbi, 1959); idem, *O Negro, de Bom Escravo a Mau Cidadão?* (Rio de Janeiro: Conquista, 1977); and idem, *Brasil: Raizes do Protesto Negro* (São Paulo: Global Editora, 1983).

28. Hasenbalg, "Race and Socioeconomic Inequalities." Nelson do Valle Silva went so far as to calculate the cost of being nonwhite at 566 cruzeiros in 1976, attributing a significant portion of the income differential as a direct result of discriminatory practices. Silva, "Updating the Cost of Not Being White in Brazil."

29. George Reid Andrews, *Blacks and Whites in São Paulo, Brazil, 1888–1988* (Madison: University of Wisconsin Press, 1991).

30. Fernandes, *The Negro,* 232.

31. Roger Bastide, "A Imprensa Negra do Estado de São Paulo." Faculdade de Filosofia, Ciencias e Letras, *Boletim CSSI, Sociologia,* no. 2, *Estudos Afro-Brasileiros,* 2a serie (1951).

32. Fernandes, *The Negro,* 192; Michael Mitchell, "Racial Consciousness and the Political Attitudes and Behavior of Blacks in São Paulo, Brazil" Ph.D. diss., Indiana University, 1977. Both Mitchell and Miriam Nicolau Ferrara's *A Imprensa Negra Paulista, 1915–1963* (São Paulo: FFLCH-USP, 1986), included the post-Vargas era in their studies.

33. Iêda Marques Britto, *Samba na Cidade de São Paulo, 1900–1930: Um Exercício de Resistencia Cultural* (São Paulo: FFLCH-USP, 1986).

34. José Carlos Gomes da Silva, "Os Sub-Urbanos e a Outra Face da Cidade. Negros em São Paulo, 1900–1930: Cotidiano, Lazer e Cidadania," M.A. thesis, Universidade Estadual de Campinas, 1990.

35. Michael Mitchell made an invaluable contribution when he microfilmed the Afro-Paulista newspapers from the personal collections of several of their editors. Michael Mitchell, ed., *The Black Press of Brazil, 1916–1969* (Firestone Library; Princeton: Princeton University, n.d., microfilm). A subsequent film was made by Miriam Nicolau Ferrara that differs slightly in content, and is housed at the Universidade de São Paulo.

36. Renato Jardim Ferreira and José Correia Leite, "Movimentos Sociais no Meio Negro" n.d., unpublished manuscript, cited in Fernandes, *The Negro.* Michael Mitchell conducted interviews in 1970 and 1972 with *Clarim* members Leite and Henrique Cunha, and former Frente Negra leaders. Miriam Nicolau Ferrara studied the press itself, but also cited undated interviews with Leite, Amaral, and Pedro Paulo Barbosa, among others. Ferrara, *A Imprensa Negra de São Paulo.*

37. The São Paulo poet and activist Cuti [Luiz Silva] has compiled a rich collection of interviews, articles, photographs, and artworks of José Correia Leite in Leite and Cuti, . . . *E Disse o Velho Militante José Correia Leite* (São Paulo: Secretaria Municipal de Cultura, 1992). In this book, Leite recounts much of the information provided to researchers over the course of his life. Because the interview tapes and transcripts are not accessible to the public at this time, this volume is presently the richest source of oral history on early twentieth-century Afro-Brazilian activism in São Paulo.

38. See complete list of oral histories in the Bibliography. All interviews adhere strictly to methodological conventions. The 1989 group was approved by the Institutional Review Board of Howard University, Washington D.C.

39. See Chapter 5 for a brief account of the efforts to operate a Frente Negra branch in Salvador.

40. This group of scholars included Nina Rodrigues, Manuel Querino, Gilberto Freyre, Arthur Ramos, Roger Bastide, Donald Pierson, and Edison Carneiro, among others. This literature will be discussed in greater detail in Chapter 1.

41. During my residence in Brazil between 1991 and 1992, I became aware of several Bahian scholars actively involved in research on this topic.

CHAPTER 1   *"Order and Progress": Elites and Abolition*

1. Raymundo Nina Rodrigues, *Os Africanos no Brasil* (São Paulo: Cia. Editora Nacional, 1932), 18.

2. Richard Graham, *Patronage and Politics in Nineteenth-Century Brazil* (Stanford: Stanford University Press, 1990), 23–24. Graham looks at patronage and regionalism as the two basic elements of social organization in Brazil. See also Joseph Love, "Political Participation in Brazil," *Luso-Brazilian Review* 7:2 (1970), 11–12; Eul-Soo Pang, "Coronelismo in Northeast Brazil," in Robert Kern, ed., *The Caciques: Oligarchical Politics and the System of Caciquismo in the Luso-Hispanic World* (Albuquerque: University of New Mexico Press, 1973), 65–88; Marshall R. Nason, "The Literary Evidence, Part III: The Cacique in Latin American Literature," in Kern, *Caciques,* 112–116.

3. Seminal works in this area include Linda Lewin, *Politics and Parentela in Paraíba: A Case Study of Family-Based Oligarchy in Brazil* (Princeton: Princeton University Press, 1987); Eul-Soo Pang, *Bahia in the First Brazilian Republic: Coronelismo and Oligarchies, 1889–1934* (Gainesville: University of Florida Press, 1979); Graham, *Patronage and Politics.*

4. Katia M. de Queirós Mattoso, *Bahia, Século XIX: Uma Província no Império* (Rio de Janeiro: Nova Fronteira, 1992), 175.

5. Pang, *Bahia in the First Brazilian Republic*, 26.

6. Ibid., 3–6.

7. Ibid., 7.

8. On this mode of power, known broadly in Latin America as "caciquismo," see Robert Kern, ed., *The Caciques: Oligarchical Politics and the System of Caciquismo in the Luso-Hispanic World* (Albuquerque: University of New Mexico Press, 1973).

9. It was customary for Brazilian children to receive a daily blessing *(tomar benção)* from their parents. Josepha da Silva Santos to Chief of Police, 22 January 1895, Arquivo Público do Estado da Bahia, Secretaria de Segurança Pública, caixa 5, folder: Occurência Policial 1895.

10. Graham, *Patronage and Politics,* 30.

11. The diary of Carolina Maria de Jesus details the experiences of a young woman who arrived in São Paulo from Minas Gerais in 1929 and eventually landed in a *favela* as a single mother. De Jesus, *Child of the Dark*, trans. David St. Clair (New York: Mentor, 1962). Her story and its implication are revisited in Robert M. Levine and José Carlos Sebe Bom Meihy, *The Life and Death of Carolina Maria de Jesus* (Albuquerque: University of New Mexico Press, 1995).

12. Florestan Fernandes, *The Negro in Brazilian Society* (New York: Atheneum, 1971), 194.

13. Thales de Azevedo, *As Elites de Côr: Um Estudo de Ascensão Social* (São Paulo: Companhia Editora Nacional, 1955*)*, 102.

14. Francisco Lucrecio, interview by author, São Paulo, 10 January 1898.

15. Henrique Cunha, Jr., interview by author, São Paulo, 7 October 1992.

16. Arquivo Público do Estado da Bahia, Registro de Testamento, 63, 29 July 1890, will dated 21 August 1855.

17. Arquivo da Curia Metropolitana de Salvador, "Irmandades: 1858–1903" [portfolio], records from Irmandade de São Benedicto, 1890–91, 1891–92, 1892–93, 1894–95, 1896–97; Arquivo da Venerável Ordem Terceira do Rosário às Portas do Carmo (AVOR), boxes 12–14, Annual Balances, 1890–91, 1891–92, 1892–93, 1895, 1897.

18. AVOR, boxes 18–1g, 19–1a, 18–1q.

19. A *terreiro* is the sacred space where candomblé ceremonies are held. Its modern meaning may also refer to the private compounds that combine residences with ritual spaces, or to the members of a candomblé congregation.

20. The dynamics of patronage within the context of candomblé are slightly different in that priests, invested with ritual knowledge and power, theoretically held both positive and negative incentives over their clients.

21. A.J.R. Russell-Wood, *A World on the Move: The Portuguese in Africa, Asia, and America, 1415–1808* (New York: St. Martin's Press, 1992), 62.

22. Nineteenth-century Latin American elites often portrayed their problem as either a struggle against the forces propelling them toward the negative end of a scale ranging from "barbarity" to "civilization," or an outright war between the two extremes. See, for example, Argentina's classic work by Domingo Faustino Sarmiento, *Facundo, Civilización y Barbarie* (Barcelona: Planeta, 1986 [1845]); or Venezuela's Julio César Sala Uzcátegui, *Civilización y Barbarie: Estudios Sociológicos Americanos* (Barcelona: Lux, 1919). See also E. Bradford Burns, "Cultures in Conflict: The Implication of Modernization in Nineteenth Century Latin America," in Virginia Bernhard, ed., *Elites, Masses, and Modernization in Latin America, 1850–1930* (Austin: University of Texas Press, 1979), 15–20.

23. On the structure and development of the First Republic, see Robert Wesson and David W. Fleischer, *Brazil in Transition* (New York: Praeger, 1983), 7–8; Kenneth Erickson, *The Brazilian Corporative State and Working-Class Politics* (Berkeley: University of California Press, 1977), 11–12; Peter Flynn, *Brazil: A Political Analysis* (London: Ernest Benn, 1978); Thomas W. Merrick and Douglas H. Graham, *Population and Economic Development in Brazil, 1800 to the Present* (Baltimore: Johns Hopkins University Press, 1979); Boris Fausto, ed., *O Brasil Republicano,* 5 vols., tome III of Sergio Buarque de Hollanda, *Historia Geral da Civilização Brasileira* (Rio de Janeiro: DIFEL, 1977).

24. Brazil, Directoria Geral da Estatística, *Resumo de Varias Estatísticas Econômico-Financeiras.* (Rio de Janeiro: Typografia da Estatística, 1924), 45.

25. The integration of a port, capital, and agricultural zone has historically been a prerequisite for regional economic development in Latin America. See James Lockhart and Stuart B. Schwartz, *Early Latin America* (Cambridge: Cambridge University Press, 1983), 86–88.

26. On abolition in Brazil, see Leslie Bethell, *The Abolition of the Brazilian Slave Trade: Britain, Brazil, and the Slave Trade Question, 1807–1869* (Cambridge: Cambridge University Press, 1970); Richard Graham, *Britain and the Onset of Modernization in Brazil, 1850–1914* (Cambridge: Cambridge University Press, 1968), 160–186; Emilia Viotti da Costa, *The Brazilian Empire: Myths and Histories*, 125–132.

27. Philip Curtin, *The Atlantic Slave Trade: A Census* (Madison: University of Wisconsin Press, 1969), 240–241.

28. Celso Furtado, *The Economic Growth of Brazil: A Survey from Colonial to Modern Times*, trans. Ricardo W. de Aguiar and Eric Charles Drysdale (Westport, Conn.: Greenwood Press, 1984), 138–140.

29. Robert Conrad, *The Destruction of Brazilian Slavery, 1850–1888* (Berkeley: University of California Press, 1972), 30–33. See also Bethell, *The Abolition of the Brazilian Slave Trade,* 72.

30. "A lavoura não pode contar com eles, não só pela indolencia herdada dos escravos

e nacionais, como porque em geral os libertos preferem o mercantilismo." Relatorio do Clube da Lavoura, testimony presented to the Assembleia Geral, 17 May 1880, cited in Paula Beiguelman, *A Formação do Povo no Complexo Cafeeiro: Aspectos Políticos* (São Paulo: Livraria Pioneira Editora, 1968), 133.

31. Flynn, *Brazil: A Political Analysis,* 18.

32. Carl Solberg, *Immigration and Nationalism: Argentina and Chile, 1890–1914* (Austin: University of Texas Press, 1970).

33. Furtado, *Economic Growth,* 138. For a detailed look at *colono* life, see Viotti da Costa, *Brazilian Empire,* 94–124.

34. Furtado, *Economic Growth,* 138–140.

35. Beiguelman, *Formação do Povo,* 94–96.

36. Warren Dean, *The Industrialization of São Paulo, 1880–1945* (Austin: University of Texas Press, 1969), 36.

37. This figure is read as 414 *contos* and 882,124 *milréis* (a *conto* equals 1,000 *milréis*), and represents the total paid in the initial distribution of 1876. AMSP, Secção Historica, book 603, "Relação dos municipios da provincia e dos escravos matriculados em cada um delles . . . ," 20 November 1876. For an in-depth analysis of the issues affecting abolition legislation, see Conrad, *Destruction of Brazilian Slavery.*

38. Robert Brent Toplin, *The Abolition of Slavery in Brazil* (New York: Atheneum, 1972), 251–253.

39. AMSP, Secção Historica, book 603, "Relação dos municipios da provincia e dos escravos matriculados em cada um delles . . . ," undated entry entitled "Pecúlio com que contribuiram os escravos." The per capita distribution under the 1871 law was 2$624, as compared with sums slightly over 1:000$000 (1 *conto*) for manumissions partly subsidized by freedpersons. See also Chapter 3.

40. Relatively little research has been done on the subject of *quilombos* in São Paulo. A fairly thorough treatment of the subject is Suely Robles de Queroz, *Escravidão Negra em São Paulo* (Rio de Janeiro: Livraria José Olympio Editora, 1977). See also José Maria dos Santos, *Os Republicanos e a Abolição* (São Paulo: Livraria Martins, 1942), 177–184; Ann M. Pescatello, "Prêto Power, Brazilian Style: Modes of Re-Actions to Slavery in the Nineteenth Century," in Ann M. Pescatello, ed., *Old Roots in New Lands: Historical and Anthropological Perspectives on Black Experiences in the Americas* (Westport, Conn.: Greenwood Press, 1977), 77–106.

41. Arquivo do Estado de São Paulo, MSS, cs. do Ministerio, Rio de Janeiro, 1887; complaints about fugitives: AESP, MSS, Juiz de Paz no. 5846, Juiz de Paz of Piracicaba to Chief of Police, São Paulo, 24 December 1887; João Morato de Carvalho to President of the Province of São Paulo, 19 December 1887. See also Robles de Queroz, *Escravidão Negra,* 141–144, for *quilombo* activity in São Paulo dating from 1778.

42. Marronage refers to the practice of escape from slavery, or the establishment of fugitive communities. The fugitives themselves were known as Maroons in English (derived from the spanish *cimarrón* meaning "wild horse"). The term Maroon is most closely associated with two large fugitive communities in Jamaica who negotiated a treaty with the British allowing for the autonomy of their territories from colonial control.

43. Brazil, Directoria Geral da Estatística, *Resumo de Varias Estatísticas Econômico-Financeiras,* 45.

44. Brazil, *Recenseamento Geral de 1940,* Censo Demográfico, Estado da Bahia, 24.
45. Eul-Soo Pang, "Agrarian Change in the Northeast," in Michael L. Conniff and Frank D. McCann, eds., *Modern Brazil: Elites and Masses in Historical Perspective* (Lincoln: University of Nebraska Press, 1991), 124–125. Pang notes how this gave rise to banditry throughout the region.
46. Brazil, *Recenseamento Geral de 1940,* Censo Demográfico, Estado da Bahia, 24; Censo Comercial, Estado da Bahia, 328–329.
47. Brazil, *Recenseamento Geral de 1940*, Censo Industrial, Estado da Bahia, 292.
48. Eul-Soo Pang provides an excellent study of *coronelismo* in *Bahia in the First Brazilian Republic.*
49. Only 5,052 naturalizations were granted between 1889 and 1912, while imigration between 1890 and 1909 alone was 1,820,734. Brazil, *Anuario Estatístico, 1908–1912*, 190–191; Merrick and Graham, *Population*, 92.
50. Sheldon L. Maram, "Labor and the Left in Brazil, 1890–1921: A Movement Aborted," *Hispanic American Historical Review* 57:2 (1977), 261–263.
51. Frank D. McCann, "The Formative Period of Twentieth-Century Brazilian Army Thought, 1900–1922," *Hispanic American Historical Review* 64:4 (November 1984), 753.
52. Jordan M. Young, *The Brazilian Revolution and the Aftermath* (New Brunswick, N.J.: Rutgers University Press, 1967), 25.
53. Wesson and Fleischer, *Brazil in Transition,* 9–10.
54. Boris Fausto, *O Brasil Republicano,* 3:91.
55. Steven Topik, *The Political Economy of the Brazilian State, 1889–1930* (Austin: University of Texas Press, 1987), 74–77.
56. On coffee protectionism in Brazilian economic policy, see Celso Furtado, *The Economic Growth of Brazil: A Survey from Colonial to Modern Times*, trans. Ricardo W. de Aguiar and Eric Charles Drysdale (Berkeley: University of California Press, 1968), 203–213.
57. Wesson and Fleisher, *Brazil in Transition*, 10–11.
58. Kenneth Erickson, *The Brazilian Corporative State and Working-Class Politics* (Berkeley: University of California Press, 1977), 2–3.
59. Nathaniel Leff, *Economic Policy-Making and Development in Brazil, 1947–1964* (New York: John Wiley and Sons, 1968), 120.
60. These included the Brazilian Academy of the Forgotten (Salvador, 1724–25), the Academy of the Happy (Rio de Janeiro, 1736–1740), the Academy of the Select (Rio de Janeiro, 1751–52), the Brazilian Academy of the Reborn (Salvador, 1759–60), the Academy of Science (Rio de Janeiro, 1772–1779) and the Literary Society (Rio de Janeiro, 1786–1790, and 1794). E. Bradford Burns, "The Intellectuals as Agents of Change," in A.J.R. Russell-Wood, ed., *From Colony to Nation* (Baltimore: Johns Hopkins University Press, 1975), 217; Emilia Viotti da Costa, "The Political Emancipation of Brazil" in Russell-Wood, *From Colony to Nation*, 61–62.
61. E. Bradford Burns, "The Role of Azeredo Coutinho in the Enlightenment of Brazil," *Hispanic American Historical Review* 44:2 (May 1964), 154–157. See also Burns, "The Intellectuals as Agents of Change," and Burns, "Cultures in Conflict," 11–77.
62. Arthur de Gobineau, cited in Georges Raeders, *O Inimigo Cordial do Brasil: O Conde de Gobineau no Brasil,* trans. Rosa Reire d'Aguiar (Rio de Janeiro: Paz e Terra, 1988), 90.

63. The full French introduction is transcribed in the 1935 Brazilian edition. Nina Rodrigues refers to "une contribution à la solution du *Problème de la race noire dans l'Amérique Portugaise*" (emphasis in original) and " . . . l'élucidation des graves questions sociales relatives à notre destinée de peuple en voie de formation." Raymundo Nina Rodrigues, *O Animismo Fetichista dos Negros Bahianos* (Rio de Janeiro: Civilização Brasileira, 1935), 9. Other American scholars published comparable seminal studies of their African-descended population around this time, including Fernando Ortiz Fernandez, *Hampa Afro-Cubana: Los Negros Brujos. Apuntes para um estudio de etnologia criminal* (Madrid, 1906); and Gonzalo Aguirre-Beltran, *La Población Negra de México: Estudio Etnohistorico,* 2d ed. (Mexico: Fondo de Cultura Economica, 1972). It is interesting to note that both Nina Rodrigues and Ortiz contextualized their ethnographies as inquiries into criminal pathology.

64. Da Cunha's work followed the tradition of Domingo Faustino Sarmiento, a nineteenth-century Argentine president who linked human evolutionary typology to the natural environment in a classic study first published in 1845. Domingo Faustino Sarmiento, *Facundo: Civilización y Barbárie* (Barcelona: Planeta, 1986).

65. Da Cunha characterized the concept of the creation of one new race out of the admixture of Europeans, Africans, and indigenous Americans as "too abstract and inflexible." Rather, he stressed the variability of miscegenation and the effects of diverse natural environments, thus setting the context for his biography of the messianic leader Antonio Conselheiro as "a natural representative of the milieu into which he was born." Euclides da Cunha, *Rebellion in the Backlands* (Os Sertões), trans. Samuel Putnam (Chicago: University of Chicago Press, 1944), 50–121.

66. Writers such as da Cunha did, however, introduce an important dimension of the cultural debate—Europe could not simply be re-created in Brazil. Rather, goals of modernization would have to be tempered by, and adapted to, Brazil's own demographic, environmental, and technological conditions.

67. Carvalho Netto, quoted in Fidelis Reis, *Paiz a Organizar* (Rio de Janeiro: Coelho Branco, 1931), 235. He added, "In the United States, they [blacks] constitute a permanent danger."

68. Nancy Leys Stepan, *"The Hour of Eugenics": Race, Gender, and Nation in Latin America* (Ithaca: Cornell University Press, 1991), 155.

69. Euclides da Cunha, *Rebellion in the Backlands* (Os Sertões), trans. Samuel Putnam (Chicago: University of Chicago Press, 1944), 84–85.

70. Nancy Leys Stepan, "Eugenics in Brazil, 1917–1940," in Mark B. Adams, ed., *The Wellborn Science: Eugenics in Germany, France, Brazil, and Russia* (New York: Oxford University Press, 1990).

71. Ibid., 119.

72. Brazil, *Collecção das Leis da Republica dos Estados Unidos Brasileiros de 1892* (Rio de Janeiro: Imprensa Nacional, 1893), Ato do Poder Legislativo, Lei 97, 5 October 1892.

73. Fidelis Reis, "O Problema Immigratorio e Seus Aspectos Ethnicos," in Reis, *Paiz a Organizar*, 231.

74. Parecer to deputado Dr. Oliveira Botelho, appresentado em 8 de julho de 1925 a Commissão de Financas da Camara dos Deputados [national], sobre o projeto n. 391 de 1923 in Brazil, Congresso, Camara dos Deputados, *A Imigração Japonesa* (Rio de Janeiro, 1925), 43. Similar sentiments were offered by Aureliano Candido

Tavares Bastos, *Os Males do Presente e as Esperanças do Futuro* (São Paulo: Nacional, 1939), 20.

75. Reis, *Paiz a Organizar,* 234.

76. Cyril Briggs, cited in Teresa Meade and Gregory Alonso Pirio, "In Search of the Afro-American 'Eldorado': Attempts by North American Blacks to Enter Brazil in the 1920s," *Luso-Brazilian Review* 25:1 (1988), 89.

77. Meade and Pirio, "In Search of the Afro-American 'Eldorado'," 90–91.

78. George Creese, cited in ibid., 95.

79. Reis, *Paiz a Organizar*, 234.

80. Meade and Pirio, "In Search of the Afro-American 'Eldorado,'" 96–98.

81. F. J. Oliveira Vianna, "O Povo Brasileiro e sua Evolução," in Brazil, Directoria Geral de Estatística, *Recenseamento do Brazil, 1 Setembro 1920*, vol. I (Rio de Janeiro: Typ. da Estatistica, 1922), 329.

82. Sam Adamo, "Race and Povo," in Conniff and McCann, *Modern Brazil*, 201–202; see also José Carlos Gomes da Silva, "Os Sub-Urbanos e a Outra Face da Cidade. Negros em São Paulo, 1900–1930: Cotidiano, Lazer e Cidadania," M.A. thesis, Universidade Estadual de Campinas, 1990. As noted by Robert Levine, elite efforts at controlling popular culture extended to the entire urban poor, regardless of race. See Robert M. Levine, "Elite Intervention in Urban Popular Culture in Modern Brazil," *Luso-Brazilian Review* 21:2 (Winter 1984), 9–22.

83. Macumba is used in Brazil to refer to Afro-Brazilian religious traditions of strong Central African influence. Adamo, "Race and Povo," 203.

84. Oliveira Vianna, "O Povo Brasileiro e sua Evolução," 320.

85. Leonido Ribeiro, W. Berardinelli, and Isaac Brown, "Estudo Biotypologico de Negros e Mulatos Brasileiros Normaes e Delinquentes," in Gilberto Freyre, ed., *Novos Estudos Afro-Brasileiros: Trabalhos Apresentados ao 1º Congresso Afro-Brasileiro do Recife,* reprint (Recife: Fundação Joaquim Nabuco, 1988), 151–152.

86. Bastos de Avila, "Contribuição ao Estudo do Indice de Lapicque," in Gilberto Freyre, ed., *Estudos Afro-Brasileiros: Trabalhos Apresentados ao 1º Congresso Afro-Brasileiro Realizado no Recife, em 1934*, reprint (Recife: Fundação Joaquim Nabuco, 1988), 35.

87. Abelardo Duarte, "Grupos Sanguinarios da Raça Negra," in Freyre, *Estudos Afro-Brasileiros*, 179.

88. Robert M. Levine, "The First Afro-Brazilian Congress: Opportunities for the Study of Race in the Brazilian Northeast," *Race* (London) 15:2 (1973), 187.

89. Melville Herskovits, "The Negro in the New World: The Statement of a Problem," *American Anthropologist*, 32 (1930), 145–155.

90. Ibid., 154.

91. Gilberto Freyre, *The Masters and the Slaves* (Casa-Grande e Senzala), trans. Samuel Putnam, second English-language edition, revised. (New York: Alfred A. Knopf, 1978).

91. See, for example, comments by Mario Melo, cited in Levine, "Congress," 186. For a thorough discussion of "whitening" see Thomas E. Skidmore, *Black into White: Race and Nationality in Brazilian Thought* (London: Oxford University Press, 1974).

93. In fact, the notion of such a conference so disturbed local conservatives that it was forcibly closed by the state police. Robert M. Levine, "Turning on the Lights: Brazilian Slavery Reconsidered One Hundred Years after Abolition," *Latin American Research Review* 24:2 (1989), 204.

94. Gilberto Freyre, "O Que Foi o Primeiro Congresso Afro-Brasileiro do Recife," in Gilberto Freyre, ed., *Novos Estudos Afro-Brasileiros,* 351, translation mine.
95. "[O]s nomes vulgares prêto, caboclo, mulato, etc., estavam secularmente consagrados a todo individuo pertencente aos contingentes raciaes, *sem qualquer definida caracterisação anthropologica systematica.*" E. Roquette-Pinto, preface, in Freyre, *Estudos Afro-Brasileiros,* ii. Emphasis in original.
96. Edison Carneiro and Aydano do Couto Ferras, "O Congresso Afro-Brasileiro da Bahia," in Congresso Afro-Brasileiro (second), *O Negro no Brasil,* 7.
97. Ademar Vidal, "Costumes e practicas do Negro," in *O Negro,* 39.
98. Ademar Vidal, "Costumes e Practicas do Negro," in Congresso Afro-Brasileiro (second), *O Negro no Brasil* (Rio de Janeiro: Civilização Brasileira, 1940), 57.
99. Manuel Querino, *Costumes Africanos no Brasil,* 123.
100. José Correia Leite, interview by author, Tape recording, São Paulo, 5 January 1989.
101. Dario de Bittencourt, "A Liberdade Religiosa no Brasil: A Macumba e o Batuque em Face da Lei," in *O Negro,* 169–202. I was unable to locate biographical information on Bittencourt. His dedication, however, suggests he was white: "To the memory of the old negress Senhorinha, who was slave to my maternal ancestors and also to my sweet, good and patient 'mammy' [*Mãe Preta*], in repentance of my pranks in a distant childhood."
102. Carneiro and do Couto Ferras, "O Congresso Afro-Brasileiro da Bahia," *O Negro,* 11.
103. Carlos Alfredo Hasenbalg, *Discriminação e Desigualdades Raciais no Brasil* (Rio de Janeiro: Graal, 1979), 167; Celso Furtado, *Economic Growth of Brazil,* 134–140; Boris Fausto, "Society and Politics," in Leslie Bethell, ed., *Brazil: Empire and Republic, 1822–1930* (Cambridge: Cambridge University Press, 1989), 259–260.
104. Brazil, census 1890, 2–3. Regional designations are based on those used in the 1940 census. The Federal District differed from all other eastern states in its demographic concentration of whites (62.8 percent), approximating more closely the southern regional average white population of 67.3 percent than the eastern average of 38 percent. The terms *prêto, caboclo,* and *mestiço* refer, respectively, to black, indigenous, and mixed-race persons.
105. Andrews, *Blacks and Whites in Sao Paulo, Brazil, 1888–1988* (Madison: University of Wisconsin Press, 1991); Fernandes, *The Negro,* 8–12.

CHAPTER 2   *Self-Determination: The Politics of Identity*

1. Arquivo Público do Estado da Bahia (APEB), Chefes de Policia, Maço 2961, 1 June 1863.
2. Arrests of candomblé practitioners are scattered throughout nineteenth-century police records. See, for example, APEB, Chefes de Policia, Maço 2961, 20 July 1860; Maço 2959, 18 August 1866; Maço 2956, 21 September 1863.
3. Raymundo Nina Rodrigues, *O Animismo Fetichista dos Negros Bahianos* (Rio de Janeiro: Civilização Brasileira, 1935); idem, *Os Africanos no Brasil* (São Paulo: Companhia Editora Nacional, 1932).
4. Carneiro hosted the second Afro-Brazilian Congress in Salvador in 1937, many sessions of which were held within the confines of leading *terreiros.* See Carneiro, *Candomblés da Bahia* [c. 1948], 3d ed. (Rio de Janeiro: Conquista, 1961).
5. Lélia Gonzalez, "The Unified Black Movement: A New Stage in Black Political

Mobilization," in Pierre-Michel Fontaine, ed., *Race, Class, and Power in Brazil.* Los Angeles: University of California/Center for Afro-American Studies, 1985.

6. Ashley Montagu, *Man's Most Dangerous Myth: The Fallacy of Race* [1942], 5th ed. (New York: Oxford University Press, 1974).

7. Marvin Harris, *Patterns of Race in the Americas* (New York: Walker and Company, 1964), 57.

8. A 1994 book by a survivor of a lynch mob captures the full impact of such brutality from the victims' perspective. James Cameron, *A Time of Terror: A Survivor's Story* (Baltimore: Black Classic Press, 1994).

9. Richard Graham, "Introduction," in Graham, ed., *The Idea of Race in Latin America, 1870–1940* (Austin: University of Texas Press, 1990), 1.

10. I regard race as a social construct and not objective biological fact, while I simultaneously recognize it as a social reality of undeniable impact.

11. Brazilians have a special appellation for this group (*branco da Bahia*) to distinguish these fair mulattoes from "true" whites. Thales de Azevedo, *As Elites de Côr: Um Estudo de Ascensão Social* (São Paulo: Companhia Editora Nacional, 1955), 25–27.

12. I recognize the limitations of contemporary U.S. racial terminology in accurately reflecting the diversity of Afro-Atlantic ethnic self-representations. I therefore limit my use of the word "black" to the extent possible.

13. Charles Joyner, *Down by the Riverside: A South Carolina Slave Community* (Urbana and Chicago: University of Illinois Press, 1984), xvi–xvii.

14. For a historical perspective on ethnic and racial distinctions among Afro-Brazilians, see Mary C. Karasch, *Slave Life in Rio de Janeiro 1808–1850* (Princeton: Princeton University Press, 1987), 4–11.

15. Azevedo, *Elites de Côr,* 25–26. There are also colloquial usages of terminologies of blackness (e.g., *"neguinha," "nego"*) to express affection and to refer to "ordinary" people, that may be applied regardless of a person's actual skin color.

16. An often-quoted example of how "whitening" functions is offered by Henry Koster, an Englishman who traveled and resided in Brazil around 1817. He wrote, "In conversing on one occasion with a man of colour who was in my service, I asked him if a certain *Capitam-mor* was not a mulatto man; he answered, 'he was, but is not now.' I begged him to explain when he added, 'Can a *Capitam-mor* be a mulatto man?'" Henry Koster, *Travels in Brazil,* 2 vols. (London: Longman et al., 1817), 2:209–210.

17. Emilia Viotti da Costa, *The Brazilian Empire: Myths and Histories* (Chicago: University of Chicago Press, 1985), 241.

18. Gilberto Freyre, "Human Factors behind Brazilian Development," *Progress* (Winter 1951–52); reprint, Ispwich: W. S. Cowell, n.d., 6 (reprint edition).

19. For a thorough treatment of this topic, see Thomas E. Skidmore, *Black into White: Race and Nationality in Brazilian Thought* (London: Oxford University Press, 1974).

20. H. Hoetink, *Slavery and Race Relations in the Americas: Comparative Notes on Their Nature and Nexus* (New York: Harper and Row, 1973), 3–45, 13.

21. See, in particular, Karasch, *Slave Life in Rio de Janeiro.*

22. Mieko Nishida, "Gender, Ethnicity, and Kinship in the Urban African Diaspora: Salvador, Brazil, 1808–1888" (Ph.D. diss., Johns Hopkins University, 1991), 197–211; Nishida, "Manumission and Ethnicity in Urban Slavery: Salvador, Brazil, 1808–1888," *Hispanic American Historical Review* 73:3 (August 1993), 361–391.

See also João José Reis' nuanced analysis of ethnicity in Salvador at the time of the 1835 revolt. Reis, *Slave Rebellion in Brazil: The Muslim Uprising of 1835 in Bahia,* trans. Arthur Brakel (Baltimore: Johns Hopkins University Press, 1993), 139–159.

23. Brazilian-born children of Africans may have had a different structural relationship to the African-born community.

24. A.J.R. Russell-Wood, "Examination of Selected Statutes of Three African Brotherhoods," in Russell-Wood, *Society and Government in Colonial Brazil, 1500–1822* (Hampshire, U.K., and Brookfield, Vt.: Variorum/Ashgate Publishing, 1992), section VI.

25. Arquivo do Venerável Ordem Terceira do Rosário às Portas do Carmo, Salvador, Compromisso da Irmandade de Nossa Senhora do Rosário dos Homens Prêtos, revised. 1820. Box 1–1. João Reis also notes ethnic rivalry in Afro-Brazilian brotherhoods, which began to decline in the late nineteenth century. João José Reis, *A Morte é Uma Festa: Ritos Fúnebres e Revolta Popular no Brasil do Século XIX* (São Paulo: Companhia das Letras, 1991), 55–56.

26. Mattoso, *To Be a Slave in Brazil,* trans. Arthur Goldhammer (New Brunswick, N.J.: Rutgers University Press, 1991), 92.

27. Deoscóredes M. dos Santos, *Axé Opô Afonjá* (Rio de Janeiro: Instituto Brasileiro de Estudos Afro-Asiáticos, 1962), 17.

28. Monica Schuler, *Alas, Alas Kongo: A Social History of Indentured African Immigrants into Jamaica, 1841–1865* (Baltimore: Johns Hopkins University Press, 1980), 33–34.

29. Ibid., 65–70.

30. AVOR, box 1–2.

31. Florestan Fernandes, *The Negro in Brazilian Society* (New York: Atheneum, 1971), 61; the figure of 108,682 includes *prêto* and *pardo* categories and excludes *amarelo* and *côr não declarada.* Brazil, *Recenseamento Geral de 1940,* part 17, tome 1.

32. Fernandes, *The Negro,* 61. Fernandes bases this estimate on demographic growth rates from 1886 to 1893, and from 1940 to 1950, census data, and a general proportion of Afro-Brazilians in the city's population of 8–12 percent.

33. "Hypocrisia da côr," *Liberdade,* 28 December 1919.

34. Karasch, *Slave Life in Rio de Janeiro,* 5. See also Azevedo, *Elites de Côr,* 27–28.

35. *O Bandeirante,* 1919; *O Menelik,* 1916; *O Alfinete,* 1921; *A Liberdade,* 1919.

36. *Clarim,* 1924–1928; *Progresso,* 1928.

37. *A Voz da Raça,* 26 May 1934.

38. This was the case in the United States, where enforced segregation provided both a collective "black" identity and the common goal of dismantling discriminatory practices.

39. An alternative way to posit the politicization of identity is to view ethnicity as the basis of nationalism. However, I avoid the concept of ethnicity as derived primarily from "inborn attributes" and focus instead on the effects of sociopolitical factors. See James G. Kellas, *The Politics of Nationalism and Identity* (New York: St. Martin's Press, 1991), 4.

40. Statutes of the Frente Negra Brasileira, *Diario Oficial de São Paulo,* 4 November 1931, 12; *Diario de São Paulo,* 17 September 1931.

41. Sidney Mintz and Richard Price, *The Birth of African-American Culture: An Anthropological Perspective* (Boston: Beacon Press, 1992).

42. See, for example, Sterling Stuckey, *Slave Culture: Nationalist Theory and the Foundations of Black America* (New York: Oxford University Press, 1987; Mechal Sobel, *The World They Made Together: Black and White Values in Eighteenth-Century Virginia* (Princeton: Princeton University Press, 1987).

43. Kwame Anthony Appiah, *In My Father's House: Africa in the Philosophy of Culture* (New York: Oxford University Press, 1992), 9.

44. Ibid.

45. On the Central African component of these traditions see, for example, Robert Farris Thompson, "Kongo Influences on African-American Artistic Culture," in Joseph E. Holloway, ed., *Africanisms in American Culture* (Bloomington: Indiana University Press, 1990), 148–184; Luc de Heusch, "Kongo in Haiti: A New Approach to Religious Syncretism," in Darién J. Davis, ed., *Slavery and Beyond: The African Impact on Latin America and the Caribbean* (Wilmington, Del.: Scholarly Resources, 1995), 103–119.

46. This was the experiment of the Rastafarian community in Jamaica in the 1940s and 1950s when they established the commune of Pinnacle. Earlier examples are the large maroon societies such as Palmares in Brazil and the Jamaican maroon settlements under Nanny, Cudjoe, and Accompong. Leonard E. Barrett, Sr., *The Rastafarians: Sounds of Cultural Dissonance* (Boston: Beacon Press, 1988), 86–89; Richard Price, ed., *Maroon Societies: Rebel Slave Communities in the Americas*, 2d ed. (Baltimore: Johns Hopkins University Press, 1979).

47. I am referring here to choices made by people of African descent, which is different from enforced segregation imposed by the dominant society.

48. Leo Spitzer, *Lives in Between: Assimilation and Marginality in Austria, Brazil, and West Africa, 1780–1945* (Cambridge: Cambridge University Press, 1989), 129–130. This is consistent with Gramsci's concept of cultural hegemony as summarized in Walter L. Adamson, *Hegemony and Revolution: A Study of Antonio Gramsci's Political and Cultural Theory* (Berkeley: University of California Press, 1980), 170–171.

49. Spitzer, *Lives in Between,* 122.

50. Capistrano de Abreu, quoted in Spitzer, *Lives in Between,* 106 (translation revised).

51. Aline Helg notes the same tripartite classification in Cuba. Helg, *Our Rightful Share: The Afro-Cuban Struggle for Equality, 1886–1912* (Chapel Hill: University of North Carolina Press, 1995), 33.

52. Because nationalism is so closely associated with the physical possession of territory, "black nationalism" came to describe the shared feelings of a nation conceived on the basis of race rather than land when discussing the experience of African Americans in the United States. I use the term "ethnonationalism" because it is a universal concept not limited by race.

CHAPTER 3   *São Paulo: The New City—The New* Negro

1. Aristides Barbosa, interview by author, tape recording, São Paulo, 21 January 1989.

2. As noted earlier, Paulista is an adjective denoting São Paulo origin; Paulistano refers specifically to the city of São Paulo.

3. Brazil, *Recenseamento Geral da População,* 1890; 1940, 60. Because of changes in demographic categories between census years, "Afro-Brazilian" as used here is the combined total of *prêto* and *mestiço* for 1890 and *prêto, pardo,* and *côr não*

declarada for 1940. The 1940 total without the "undeclared" category is 108,682.

4. Although much data necessary for a detailed social history of Afro-Paulistanos during this period were never recorded, the following sources provide fairly comprehensive overviews: Roger Bastide and Florestan Fernandes, *Brancos e Negros em São Paulo,* 3d ed. (São Paulo: Companhia Editora Nacional, 1971); Florestan Fernandes, *A Integração do Negro na Sociedade de Classes,* 2 vols. (São Paulo: Editora Ática, 1978); George Reid Andrews, *Blacks and Whites in São Paulo Brazil, 1888–1988* (Madison: University of Wisconsin Press, 1991); José Carlos Gomes da Silva, "Os Sub-Urbanos e a Outra Face da Cidade. Negros em São Paulo, 1900–1930: Cotidiano, Lazer e Cidadania" (M.A. thesis, Universidade Estadual de Campinas, 1990); Iêda Marques Britto, *Samba na Cidade de São Paulo, 1900–1930: Um Exercício de Resistencia Cultural* (São Paulo: FFLCH-USP, 1986).

5. Leslie Bethell, ed., *Colonial Brazil* (Cambridge: Cambridge University Press, 1987), 24.

6. Richard M. Morse, *From Community to Metropolis: A Biography of São Paulo, Brazil* (New York: Octagon Books, 1974), 113; Robert H. Mattoon, Jr., "Railroads, Coffee, and the Growth of Big Business in São Paulo, Brazil," *Hispanic American Historical Review* 57:2 (May 1977), 276.

7. São Paulo's 1874 slave population was 174,622 as compared with 165,403 in Bahia and 106,236 in Pernambuco. Robert Conrad, *The Destruction of Brazilian Slavery, 1850–1888* (Berkeley: University of California Press, 1972), 285.

8. Bastide and Fernandes, *Brancos e Negros,* 52, 63.

9. Fernandes, *The Negro in Brazilian Society* (New York: Atheneum, 1971), 17; Bastide and Fernandes, *Brancos e Negros,* 52–54.

10. Brazil, *Anuario Estatístico, 1908–1912.*

11. Arlinda Rocha Nogueira, *Imigração Japonesa na Historia Contemporanea do Brasil* (São Paulo: Centro de Estudos Nipo-Brasileiros, Massao Ohno Editora, 1984).

12. "A lavoura não pode contar com eles, não só pela indolencia herdada dos escravos e nacionais, como porque em geral os libertos preferem o mercantilismo." Relatorio do Clube da Lavoura, testimony presented to Assembleia Geral, 17 May 1880, cited in Paula Beiguelman, *A Formação do Povo no Complexo Cafeeiro: Aspectos Políticos* (São Paulo: Livaria Pioneira Editova, 1968), 133. Some coffee growers used the excuse that Afro-Brazilians preferred trade to agriculture in an attempt to justify increased subsidies for the *colono* program.

13. This movement was specifically toward the capital. Of São Paulo's other large cities, Santos had the second-largest population of *prêtos* and *pardos* in 1940, at 15,068 (13.5 percent of the total in the capital). Brazil, *Recenseamento Geral da População,* 1940, part 17, tome 1, 60.

14. Fernandes, *The Negro,* 11. See also Warren Dean, *The Industrialization of São Paulo, 1880–1945* (Austin: University of Texas Press, 1969), 49–66.

15. Dean, *Industrialization,* 8; Mattoon, "Railroads, Coffee, and the Growth of Big Business, 273–295.

16. Brazil, *Recenseamento Geral de 1940,* part 17, tome 3, 462–463.

17. Rollie E. Poppino, *Brazil: The Land and People* (New York: Oxford University Press, 1968), 228–230.

18. Morse, *From Community to Metropolis,* 132; Frederick Luebke, *Germans in Brazil: A Comparative History of Cultural Conflict during World War I* (Baton Rouge: Louisiana State University Press, 1987), 47–49; Robert Ernst, *Immigrant Life in*

New York City, 1825–1863 (New York: King's Crown Press/Columbia University, 1949).

19. Fernandes, *The Negro,* 61, 70. Fernandes bases this estimate on demographic growth rates from 1886 to 1893 and 1940 to 1950, census data, and a general proportion of Afro-Brazilians in the city's population between 8–12 percent. On immigration figures to São Paulo, see Thomas Holloway, *Immigrants on the Land: Coffee and Society in São Paulo, 1886–1934* (Chapel Hill: University of North Carolina Press, 1980), 179; Dean, *Industrialization,* 153.

20. The figure of 108,682 includes *prêto* and *pardo* categories and excludes *amarelo* and *côr não declarada.* Brazil, *Recenseamento Geral de 1940,* part 17, tome 1.

21. Fidelis Reis, *Paiz a Organizar* (Rio de Janeiro: Coelho Branco, 1931), 236.

22. Henrique Cunha, interview by author, São Paulo, 20 January 1989. *Pinga* is slang for a strong cane liquor.

23. Aristides Barbosa, interview by author, São Paulo, 21 January 1989.

24. Fernandes, *The Negro,* 70.

25. AMSP, book 603, "Pecúlio com que contribuiram os escravos." These slaves were all married. This entry has no date but follows earlier entries dated 1876. The total amounts received by slaveowners in this record are striking, given the fact that other provincial payments were extremely limited. The province compensated planters at the rate of 2$624 *milréis* per slave after the 1871 law freeing children born of slave mothers, and an 1882 distribution paid owners 1$593 *milréis* per slave for 174,622 *libertos.* AMSP, book 603, "Relação dos municipios da provincia e dos escravos matriculados em cada um delles, aos que cabe as quantias abaixo mencionadas, destinadas á sua libertação em virtude da lei de 28 de Setembro de 1871," 20 November 1876; book 603, untitled entry of distributions to 109 *municipios* dated 1 September 1882.

26. A small number of slaves belonging to the state were freed, under compulsory labor and residence provisions for a period of five years under article 6 of the Rio Branco Law. Conrad, *The Destruction of Brazilian,* 305–309. Some letters of manumission under this provision have been preserved in the state archives of São Paulo. AMSP, Registro de Cartas de Liberdade, Secção Historia, no. de ordem 602.

27. One of the best, though brief, discussions of urban black residence patterns is Britto, *Samba na Cidade,* 37–41. On the lack of ethnic statistics, José Carlos Gomes da Silva noted, "The exclusion of blacks from the narrative of the principal historians of the city is a precise reflection of the intellectuals' perspective—that blacks were not part of the cosmopolitan life of São Paulo." Gomes da Silva, "Os Sub-Urbanos," 32.

28. Bernard Gontier, *Bexiga* (São Paulo: Mundo Impresso, 1990), 16–19; Britto, *Samba na Cidade,* 40–41.

29. Mattoon, "Railroads, Coffee, and the Growth of Big Business," 274.

30. Nancy Leys Stepan discusses the impact of health concerns on social policy in "Eugenics in Brazil, 1917–1940," in Mark B. Adams, ed., *The Wellborn Science: Eugenics in Germany, France, Brazil, and Russia.* (New York: Oxford University Press, 1990), 113.

31. Gomes da Silva, "Os Sub-Urbanos," 47–49. Some *cortiços* were constructed expressly for that purpose, although Florestan Fernandes notes that "the most well-known were constructed for commercial, not residential, ends." Fernandes, *The Negro,* 81.

32. Gomes da Silva, "Os Sub-Urbanos," 54–58; Britto, *Samba na Cidade,* 38–39.
33. Alberto Alves da Silva, interview by author, 17 April 1992.
34. Aristides Barbosa, interview by author, 21 January 1989.
35. Francisco Lucrecio, interview by author, 10 January 1989.
36. Censo Escolar, 1934, in *Diario Oficial de São Paulo,* 14 June 1936.
37. Samuel H. Lowrie, "O Elemento Negro na População de Sao Paulo," in *Revista do Archivo Municipal de São Paulo,* ano IV, vol. 48 (June 1938), 54.
38. Carlota de Oliveira Galdino Silva, interview by author, São Paulo, 7 October 1992.
39. Branco, cited in Gomes, "Os Sub-Urbanos," 51; see also Fernandes, *The Negro,* 80–81.
40. Henrique Cunha, Jr., interview by author, 7 October 1992.
41. Censo Escolar, 1934, in *Diario Oficial de São Paulo,* 14 June 1936; Joseph Love, *São Paulo in the Brazilian Federation, 1889–1937* (Stanford: Stanford University Press, 1980), 12–13.
42. George Reid Andrews, *Blacks and Whites in São Paulo, Brazil, 1888–1988* (Madison: University of Wisconsin Press, 1991), 92–101. Andrews relied principally on case studies of the Jafet textile factory and São Paulo Tramway, Light, and Power, the city's electrical and trolley utility. The author himself recognized that, although his is one of the most detailed studies to date on post-abolition labor patterns among blacks in São Paulo, it can only offer preliminary hypotheses owing to the lack of data collected by race during this period.
43. AESP, MSS, no. de ordem 614.
44. Raul Joviano de Amaral, *Os Prêtos do Rosário de São Paulo: Subsidios Historicos* (São Paulo: Alarico, 1954), 35; José Correia Leite and Cuti [Luiz Silva], *. . . E Disse o Velho Militante José Correia Leite* (São Paulo: Secretaria Municipal de Cultura, 1992), 56–57. Approximately 200 brotherhoods were registered in São Paulo between 1864 and 1883, during the city's initial expansion. AESP, mss., 614 and 618.
45. Amaral, *Os Prêtos do Rosário,* 99–109.
46. Lack of documentation does not permit detailed analysis of the role of Catholic brotherhoods in Afro-Paulistano social life between 1888 and 1938, but the topic merits further study. There is ample information on Afro-Brazilian brotherhoods prior to 1888, including A.J.R. Russell-Wood, "Black and Mulatto Brotherhoods in Colonial Brazil: A Study in Collective Behavior," *Hispanic American Historical Review,* 54:4 (1974), 567–602; Russell-Wood, *The Black Man in Slavery and* Freedom (New York: St. Martin's Press, 1982), 128–160, 254–301; Patricia A. Mulvey, "Black Brothers and Sisters: Membership in the Black Lay Brotherhoods of Colonial Brazil," *Luso-Brazilian Review* 17:2 (Winter 1980), 253–279; Mulvey, "Slave Confraternities in Brazil: Their Role in Colonial Society," *The Americas* 39:1 (July 1982), 39–68; and Mary C. Karasch, *Slave Life in Rio de Janeiro, 1808–1850* (Princeton: Princeton University Press, 1987), 82–87. Amaral's *Os Prêtos do Rosário de São Paulo* is the only published source currently available on these institutions in the city of São Paulo between 1888 and 1938. The vibrant history of the political organizations, social clubs, and samba groups has attracted the majority of research attention, obscuring developments within the brotherhoods that may shed further light on black life and history in São Paulo.
47. Gomes da Silva, "Os Sub-Urbanos," 62–63.
48. Britto, *Samba na Cidade,* 62–65.

49. It is unclear whether this is the same Eunice associated with the Campos Eliseos club.
50. Britto, *Samba na Cidade,* 70.
51. The thirteenth of May was the anniversary of abolition, traditionally given over to festivities in the black Paulistano community. Britto, *Samba na Cidade,* 70.
52. Roberto Moura, *Tia Ciatá e a Pequena África do Rio de Janeiro* (Rio de Janeiro: Funarte/MEC-Secretaria de Cultura, n.d.). The title "Aunt" is frequently used as a form of address for older black women to denote respect and affection.
53. A *pandeiro* is a tambourine integral to samba music. When Alberto Alves da Silva founded his own samba school, he renamed himself "Nenê da Vila Matilde," the name of the neighborhood.
54. "Nenê da Vila Matilde" (Alberto Alves da Silva), interview by author, São Paulo, 17 April 1992.
55. Soccer was an important organizational base within the black community that merits further study. Many black players aspired to play professionally with São Paulo's Corinthians. On soccer in Barra Funda, see Gomes da Silva, "Os Sub-Urbanos," 67–68.
56. Ibid., 64; Britto, *Samba na Cidade,* 77.
57. Britto, *Samba na Cidade,* 81.
58. Ibid., 84.
59. Ibid., 62–63; "Zulu" (Antônio Pereira da Silva Neto), interview by author, São Paulo, 18 April 1992.
60. Gomes da Silva, "Os Sub-Urbanos," 69.
61. Ibid., 81–82; Fausto, *Crime e Cotidiano: A Criminalidade em São paulo, 1880–1924* (São Paulo: Editora Brasiliense, 1984), 52.
62. Zezinho-da-Casa-Verde, cited in Gomes da Silva, "Os Sub-Urbanos," 93–94. In the original Portuguese, he uses *negro* colloquially to mean "folks" when referring to a black milieu.
63. *Progresso,* 24 November 1929. The editorial also noticed the prevalence of crime in the slums. The image of the *cortiços* as a haven for squalor, violence, promiscuity, and poverty was popularized by Aluísio Azevedo in his novel *O Cortiço* (Rio de Janeiro: H. Garnier, 1890).
64. Gomes uses the categories *pardos* and *negros*. Gomes da Silva, "Os Sub-Urbanos," 64.
65. On ethnic associations, see Morse, *From Community to Metropolis,* 132; Luebke, *Germans in Brazil,* 47–49.
66. Andrews, *Blacks and Whites,* 141.
67. Michael Mitchell, "Racial Consciousness and the Political Attitudes and Behavior of Blacks in São Paulo, Brazil" (Ph.D. diss., Indiana University, 1997), 125; Michael Mitchell, ed., *The Black Press of Brazil,* Firestone Library (Princeton: Princeton University, n.d., microfilm); Miriam Nicolau Ferrara, ed., *Jornais da Raça Negra,* Instituto de Estudos Brasileiros (São Paulo: Universidade de São Paulo, n.d., microfilm). See also Table 6.
68. *O Kosmos,* 25 January 1925.
69. *Bandeirante,* August 1918; *A Sentinella,* 10 October 1920. Further research into the women's clubs would provide us with rare insight into the lives of black women during this period.
70. *A Liberdade,* 3 August 1919. The practice of using club names as identifiers is still common among samba singers today, including Martinho da Vila, Graça do Salgueiro, Neguinho da Beija-Flor, and Jorginho do Imperio, popular singers of,

respectively, Vila Isabel, Salgueiro, Beija-Flor and Imperio Serrano *escolas de samba* in Rio.

71. *Alfinete,* 3 September 1918.
72. Gastão R. Silva, "Os Agentes da Policia em Acção," *Bandeirante,* April 1919.
73. *A Voz da Raça,* 18 March 1933.
74. J. D'Alencastro, "Em Ferro Frio," *O Bandeirante,* April 1919.
75. José Correia Leite, "O Verbo do Prêto," *O Clarim,* 7 December 1924.
76. Britto, *Samba na Cidade,* 64–65.
77. I include my own master's thesis in this category. This view was first articulated in a chapter entitled "The Negro in Politics" in Arthur Ramos's *The Negro in Brazil* (Washington, D.C.: Associated Publishers, 1939), and remains a topic of debate among researchers.
78. In his study of Afro-Brazilian penetration into the Paulista work force, George Reid Andrews notes the greater ease with which *pardos* were able to find jobs as compared with *prêtos.* Andrews, *Blacks and Whites,* 107.

CHAPTER 4   *The Politics of Race in São Paulo*

1. Michael Mitchell, "Racial Consciousness and the Political Attitudes and Behavior of Blacks in São Paulo, Brazil" (Ph.D. diss., Indiana University, 1977), 159. The most significant and complete studies of São Paulo's black press to date are Roger Bastide, "A Imprensa Negra do Estado de São Paulo," Faculdade de Filosofia, Ciencias e Letras, *Boletim CSSI, Sociologia,* no. 2, *Estudos Afro-Brasileiros,* 2a serie, 1951; Mitchell, "Racial Consciousness," esp. chapter 4; and Miriam Nicolau Ferrara, *A Imprensa Negra Paulista, 1915–1963* (São Paulo: FFLCH, 1986).
2. "Bourgeoisie" is used here in the context of the Afro-Brazilian population alone and is not equivalent to the bourgeoisie of Brazilian society as a whole.
3. George Reid Andrews, *Blacks and Whites in São Paulo, Brazil, 1888–1988* (Madison: University of Wisconsin Press, 1991), 141.
4. Bastide, "Imprensa," 50.
5. I found some inaccuracy in Bastide's dates, such as *A Voz da Raça* listed for 1936 when it was first published in 1933, and 1918 rather than 1919 listed for *A Liberdade*'s first edition. Bastide is the only author to cite *O Getulino* in 1919 when all other sources give its first date as 1923. My sources are microfilmed copies of first editions in Michael Mitchell, ed., *The Black Press of Brazil, 1916–1969,* Firestone Library (Princeton: Princeton University, n.d., microfilm). Bastide, "Imprensa Negra," 52–53. The words "O" and "A" preceding a newspaper title are the Brazilian article ("The"), and are omitted in the text when following the word "the" in English.
6. *O Menelick,* cited in Bastide, "Imprensa Negra," 52. It is possible that another paper, *O Baluarte,* appeared in São Paulo in 1904.
7. Examples of election results: *A Liberdade,* 14 July, 28 December 1919, *A Sentinella,* 10 October 1920; upcoming events: *O Kosmos,* October 1922, *O Xauter,* 16 May 1916; Pirapora festival reminder: *A Liberdade,* 14 July 1919.
8. *O Kosmos,* October 1922.
9. *A Liberdade,* 9 May 1920.
10. *A Liberdade,* 28 December 1919.
11. *Elite,* 20 January 1924; *Liberdade,* 28 December 11.

12. *Elite,* 20 January 1924.
13. *A Liberdade,* 14 July 1919.
14. *A Rua,* 24 February 1916.
15. *A Liberdade,* 28 December 1919.
16. *Elite,* 20 January 1924.
17. *O Xauter,* 16 May 1916. Lest anyone miss the point, they added that the writers from *A Rua* and the members of Kosmos were the "idiot companions of Deocleciano [Nascimento, editor of *A Rua*]."
18. *O Alfinete,* 3 September 1918.
19. Joaquim Cambará, "Deputado de Côr," *O Bandeirante,* August 1918.
20. *A Liberdade,* 9 May 1920.
21. Joaquim Domingues, "Hypocrisia da Côr," *Liberdade,* 28 December 1919. *Moreno* literally means "brunette," but could also be used as a "polite" Brazilian racial euphemism for people of color.
22. José Benedicto Martins, "Os Prêtos e o Progresso," *O Alfinete,* 3 September 1918.
23. *A Liberdade,* 14 July 1919; *O Bandeirante,* April 1919.
24. *O Menelick,* 1 January 1916.
25. Abilio Rodrigues, "Comentando," *O Elite,* 20 January 1924.
26. *O Getulino* of Campinas, first published in 1923, was also a highly influential, ideologically oriented paper. Its editors eventually moved to the capital and founded *Progresso.*
27. José Correia Leite, interview by author, São Paulo, 5 January 1989; José Correia Leite quoted in Ferrara, *Imprensa Negra Paulista,* 56; José Correia Leite and Cuti [Luiz Silva], . . . *E Disse o Velho Militante José Correia Leite* (São Paulo: Secretaria Municipal de Cultura, 1992), 26–33.
28. The most thorough treatment of Leite's life and philosophy is Leite and Cuti, *E Disse o Velho Militante,* an edited collection of most of his writings.
29. José Correia Leite, "Valor da Raça," *O Clarim,* 6 April 1924.
30. *O Clarim,* 25 January 1925.
31. José Correia Leite, "O Verbo do Prêto," *O Clarim,* 7 December 1924.
32. See, for example, "Os Homens Prêtos e a Instrucção," *Progresso,* 23 June 1928; Luís de Souza, "O Momento," *Clarim,* 3 March 1929.
33. Andrews, *Blacks and Whites,* 137.
34. José Correia Leite, interview by author, São Paulo, 5 January 1989.
35. Henrique Cunha, interview by author, São Paulo, 20 January 1989.
36. José Correia Leite, interview by author, São Paulo, 5 January 1989.
37. Florestan Fernandes, *The Negro in Brazilian Society* (New York: Atheneum, 1971), 192.
38. *Progresso,* 24 March 1929.
39. R. K. Kent, "Palmares: An African State in Brazil," *Journal of African History* 6 (1965), 161–175; reprinted in Richard Price, ed., *Maroon Societies: Rebel Slave Communities in the Americas* (Baltimore: Johns Hopkins University Press, 1979).
40. The histories of Afro-Brazilian communities in Campinas and the capital are very closely linked in the post-abolition era. For a social history of Afro-Brazilians in Campinas, see Cleber da Silva Maciel, *Discriminações Raciais: Negros em Campinas, 1888–1921* (Campinas: Editora da UNICAMP, 1987).
41. José Correia Leite, interview by author, São Paulo, 5 January 1989; Mitchell, "Racial Consciousness," 127; Ferrara, *Imprensa Negra Paulista,* 54–55.

42. José Correia Leite, interview by author, São Paulo, 5 January 1989; Renato Jardim Moreira and José Correia Leite, "Movimentos Sociais no Meio Negro," unpublished manuscript, cited in Florestan Fernandes, *A Integração do Negro na Sociedade de Classes,* 2 vols., 1st ed. (São Paulo: Dominus Editora, 1965), 2:14; *Progresso,* 24 March 1929.

43. *Progresso,* 7 September 1928.

44. *Auriverde,* 29 April 1928; *Progresso,* 23 June 1928.

45. *Progresso,* 23 June 1928.

46. *Progresso,* 7 September 1928.

47. Speech reprinted in *A Gazeta,* 25 August 1928, cited in Mitchell, "Racial Consciousness," 149; *Progresso,* 19 August 1928.

48. *Progresso,* 24 March 1929.

49. Mitchell, "Racial Consciousness," 126; Henrique Cunha, interview by author, São Paulo, 20 January 1989; Fernandes, *Integração,* 2:14.

50. Many of Aguiar's contributions were editorials in support of *Clarim's* goals, for example, *Clarim,* 2 December 1928; 6 January 1929; 3 March 1929.

51. *Progresso,* 16 December 1928; 13 January 1929.

52. *Progresso,* 13 January 1929.

53. *Progresso,* 13 January 1929. Emphasis added by *Progresso.*

54. Manoel Antonio dos Santos, "Trajectoria do Ideal," *Tribuna Negra,* September 1935. This paper was affiliated with the Leite group.

55. Horacio da Cunha, "Os Homens Prêtos e a Evolução Social," *Auriverde,* 29 April 1928.

56. In their study *Poor People's Movements,* the political scientists Piven and Cloward maintain that inequities alone are insufficient to motivate protest. "For a protest movement to arise out of [the] traumas of daily life, people have to perceive the deprivation and disorganization they experience as both wrong, and subject to redress." Frances Fox Piven and Richard A. Cloward, *Poor People's Movements: Why They Succeed, How They Fail* (New York: Random House/Vintage Books, 1979), 12.

57. *Progresso,* 24 February 1929.

58. *Progresso,* 13 January 1929. Interestingly, they still used the term *prêto* for general discussion.

59. *Progresso,* 16 December 1928; 24 March 1929.

60. *Progresso,* 24 February 1929.

61. "Desapparecerão os Prêtos de Brasil?" *Progresso,* 13 January 1929.

62. *Progresso,* 12 October 1928.

63. *Progresso,* 24 February 1929; 28 April 1929; 23 June 1929.

64. *Progresso,* 15 November 1930.

65. *Progresso,* 13 January 1929 and 24 February 1929. On the microfilm, these issues were filmed together, so it is not clear which articles appeared in which issues.

66. The first installment of "O Mundo Negro" appeared in *O Clarim,* 7 December 1930.

67. José Correia Leite, interview by author, São Paulo, 7 January 1989.

68. José Correia Leite, "Valor da Raça," *O Clarim,* 6 April 1924.

69. *O Clarim,* 3 February 1929.

70. "Negros de São Paulo e do Brasil, O Congresso da Mocidade Negra é o verdadeiro e único caminho para tratarmos da edificação da nossa obra de resistência, para a formação definitiva da nossa frente única, para a consolidação firme das nossas ideias, e a base fundamental da regeneração da nossa collectividade." *O Clarim,* 3 February 1929.

71. The sixteen groups invited were Campos Eliseos, Auriverde, *União Militar, Club Atletico Brasil,* 13 de Maio, *Rio Branco, Kosmos, Paulistano, União da Mocidade, Flor do Norte,* 28 de Setembro, Auriverde Futebol Clube, Princeza do Norte, *Eden Juvenil, Iris Maranhão,* and the *Congresso dos Soberanos Carnavalescos.* The groups in italics sent representatives. *O Clarim,* 7 April 1929.
72. *O Clarim,* 4 April 1929; 13 May 1929.
73. *O Clarim,* 9 June 1929.
74. *O Clarim,* 9 June 1929.
75. *O Clarim,* 14 July 1929.
76. *O Clarim,* 18 August 1929.
77. *Progresso,* 31 August 1929.
78. *O Clarim,* 28 September 1929; 27 October 1929.
79. *O Clarim,* 25 January 1930.
80. *Progresso,* 24 February 1929; 31 October 1929.
81. *O Clarim,* 18 August 1929; 27 October 1929.
82. *Progresso,* 19 August 1928; see also *Progresso,* 15 November 1928.
83. Frederico Baptista de Souza, "O Negro Deve Ser Político?" *Clarim,* 27 October 1929.
84. Margaret Todaro Williams, "Integralism and the Brazilian Catholic Church," *Hispanic American Historical Review* 54:3 (August 1974), 433.
85. Ilan Rachum, "Feminism, Woman Suffrage, and National Politics in Brazil, 1922–1937," *Luso-Brazilian Review* 14:1 (Summer 1977), 126.
86. *Diario de São Paulo,* 17 September 1931, 5.
87. *Diario Oficial de São Paulo,* 4 November 1931, 12. Governing board members: President, Arlindo Veiga dos Santos; Secretary, Isaltino Benedicto Veiga dos Santos; Official Speaker, Alberto Orlando; Council Members, Francisco Costa Santos, David Soares, Horacio Arruda, Vitor de Sousa, João Francisco de Araujo, Alfredo Eugenio da Silva, Isaltino Benedicto Veiga dos Santos, Alberto Orlando, Arlindo Veiga dos Santos, and Oscar de Barros Leite.
88. Arlindo Veiga dos Santos, quoted in Fernandes, *Integração,* 2:43.
89. Citations from *Diario de São Paulo,* 18 December 1931, 12; see also Mitchell, "Racial Consciousness," 131; Arlindo Veiga dos Santos cited in Fernandes, *Integração,* 2:43–44.
90. Francisco Lucrecio, interview by author, São Paulo, 10 January 1989; Arlindo Veiga dos Santos quoted in Fernandes, *Integração,* 2:43. It should be noted that this information is based exclusively on Frente Negra sources. I have been unable to find corroborating sources to prove that this type of protest was organized FNB action.
91. Photographs of Fernando Lucrecio's Frente Negra identification card appear in Ferrara, *Imprensa Negra,* 70–71.
92. Ferrara, *Imprensa Negra,* 67.
93. Aristides Barbosa, interview by author, São Paulo, 21 January 1989.
94. Ibid.
95. José Correia Leite, interview by author, São Paulo, 7 January 1989.
96. *Clarim,* December 1931.
97. Fernandes, *Integração,* 2:35.
98. José Correia Leite, interview by author, São Paulo, 7 January 1989.
99. Within the first few months of operation, the Frente was estimated to have 6,000 members in the capital and 2,000 in Santos (São Paulo). Mitchell, "Racial Consciousness," 131.

100. Fernandes, *Integração*, 2:43.
101. Moreira and Leite, "Movimentos Sociais," cited in Fernandes, *Integração*, 2:47.
102. *A Voz da Raça*, 29 April 1933.
103. *A Voz da Raça*, 6 May 1933.
104. The Frente Negra subsequently registered as a political party in 1936, but was never able to effectively operate as such because of the ban on political activities under the Estado Novo, declared the following year. Ferrara, *Imprensa Negra*, 74.
105. *A Voz da Raça*, 20 May 1933.
106. All quotations of Veiga in this paragraph are from *A Voz da Raça*, 29 April 1933.
107. *A Voz da Raça*, 10 June 1933.
108. *A Voz da Raça*, 29 April 1933.
109. Ibid. Emphasis in original.
110. *A Voz da Raça*, 6 May 1933.
111. *A Voz da Raça*, 1 July 1933.
112. Fernandes, *Integração*, 2:25; Arlindo Veiga dos Santos, quoted in Fernandes, ibid., 44.
113. Jeffrey Lesser, *Welcoming the Undesirables: Brazil and the Jewish Question* (Berkeley: University of California Press, 1995), 46–82.
114. Raul Joviano de Amaral, "A Frente Negra Brasileira: Suas Finalidades e Obras Realizadas," cited in Fernandes, *Integração*, 2:46. Veiga did not "direct" the monarchist movement, but was one of its most vocal advocates in the black community.
115. The percentage of Roman Catholics in the state was 99.7 percent in 1872, 98.8 percent in 1890, 92.0 percent in 1900, and 92.1 percent in 1940. Brasil, *Recenseamento Geral de 1940*, part 17, tome 1, 1.
116. I thank Dr. Michael Mitchell for this biographical information.
117. Williams, "Integralism," 42.
118. *A Voz da Raça*, 1 July 1933.
119. José Correia Leite, interview by author, São Paulo, 7 January 1989.
120. *Clarim*, November 1931.
121. The Grand Council at that time consisted of eighteen members: Arlindo Veiga dos Santos, his brother Isaltino Veiga dos Santos, Alfredo Eugenio da Silva, Victor de Souza, Sebastião Costa, Justiniano Costa, Irineu B. Silva, David Soares, João Francisco P. de Araujo, Horacio Arruda, Dinas de Campos, José Correia Leite, Antônio Alves, Cristovam Brasil, Alberto de Barros, José Celestino Franco, Horacio da Silva Paranhos, and Alberto Orlando. *Clarim*, December 1931.
122. Mitchell, "Racial Consciousness," 124.
123. *A Chibata*, February 1932.
124. *A Chibata*, February 1932. See also Cunha's comment on the oppressive aspects of church teachings in Chapter 2.
125. José Correia Leite, interview by author, São Paulo, 7 January 1989.
126. *A Chibata* published a satirical samba about da Costa entitled "Agora Vae" (Now Go): "O Senhor Xico da Costa / Agora é Xico da Frente/ Por causa do secretario / Está ficando valente / Homenzinho do elite / Que tem moral de primeira / Só anda dando palpite / Defendendo a bandalheira / Oi, sae da frente." *A Chibata*, February 1932; José Correia Leite, interview by author, São Paulo, 7 January 1989.
127. Francisco Lucrecio, interview by author, São Paulo, 10 January 1989.
128. Francisco Lucrecio, interview by author, São Paulo, 10 January 1989; José Correia

Leite, interview by author, São Paulo, 5 January 1989; Mitchell, "Racial Consciousness," 136; *Clarim,* March 1932.

129. Mitchell, "Racial Consciousness," 136–137.

130. *Brasil Novo,* 3 April 1933; Henrique Cunha, interview by author, São Paulo, 20 January 1989. This is not to be confused with the Black Guard, a short-lived Rio-based black organization loyal to Isabel "the Redeemer" that reflected anti-Republican sentiments in the first years of the regime. Michael R. Trochim, "The Brazilian Black Guard: Racial Conflict in Post-Abolition Brazil," *The Americas* 44 (January 1988), 285–300.

131. *Brasil Novo,* 3 April 1933.

132. Fernandes, *Integração,* 2:47; *Voz da Raça,* 15 July 1933.

133. Henrique Cunha, interview by author, São Paulo, 20 January 1989.

134. Iêda Marques Britto, *Samba na Cidade de São Paulo, 1900–1930: Um Exercîcio de Resistencia Cultural* (São Paulo: FFLCH–USP, 1986); Robert M. Levine, "Elite Intervention in Urban Popular Culture in Modern Brazil," *Luso-Brazilian Review* 21:1 (Winter 1984), 9–22.

135. *Cultura,* January 1934.

136. *Clarim,* March 1935.

137. *Clarim,* May 1935.

138. Fernandes, *Integração,* 2:71–73.

139. Aristides Barbosa, interview by author, São Paulo, 21 January 1989.

140. Robert M. Levine, *The Vargas Regime: The Critical Years, 1934–1938* (New York: Columbia University Press, 1970), 138–158.

141. Ibid., 161.

142. Aristides Barbosa, interview by author, São Paulo, 21 January 1989.

143. Ferrara, *Imprensa Negra,* 76.

CHAPTER 5   *Salvador: Afro-Bahia in an Era of Change*

1. Marcos Rodrigues dos Santos to Sociedade Protectora dos Desvalidos, 20 November 1932, 15 December 1932, Anuario 1929–1932; Livro de Visitantes, 16 September 1932, ASPD.

2. Marcos Rodrigues dos Santos interview, *Diario da Bahia,* 16 November 1932, cited in Jeferson Bacelar, "A Frente Negra Brasileira na Bahia," *Afro-Ásia* 17 (1996), 75. Arthur Ramos's chapter on black social movements identifies dos Santos as the founder of the Associação dos Brasileiros de Côr, along the lines of the Frente Negra, in the city of Santos, São Paulo. In his interview, dos Santos describes himself as the founder of the Santos branch of the Frente Negra, with a membership of 4,000. Arthur Ramos, *The Negro in Brazil,* 2d ed. (Washington, D.C.: Associated Publishers, 1951), 178–179.

3. Thales de Azevedo, *As Elites de Côr: Um Estudo de Ascensão Social* (São Paulo: Companhia Editora Nacional, 1955), 102–103.

4. Bacelar, "Frente Negra Brasileira na Bahia," 17 (1996), 73–85.

5. Ibid., 79–80; Azevedo, *Elites de Côr,* 186.

6. See Chapter 2.

7. Jeferson Bacelar notes the existence of the Henrique Dias League (named for a black military hero of the struggle to recapture northeastern Brazil from a Dutch invasion in the mid-seventeenth century). A 1917 notice in a daily newspaper an-

nounced a meeting to address a school's refusal to admit a black student, the only documentation discovered about this organization to date. Bacelar, "Frente Negra Brasileira da Bahia," 74. According to Thales de Azevedo, a Sociedade Henrique Dias was formed in early 1937 by Afro-Bahian professionals to promote interracial understanding. Its members, however, were reluctant to identify themselves as *negros* because such a position implied an affiliation with communism. Azevedo, *Elites de Côr,* 187–188.

8. *Prêtos* and *mestiços* made up 61.4 percent of Salvador's population in 1890.

9. Eul-Soo Pang, "Coronelismo in Northeast Brazil," in Robert Kern, ed., *The Caciques: Oligarchical Politics and the System of Caciquismo in the Luso-Hispanic World* (Albuquerque: University of New Mexico Press, 1973), 65–88. Pang emphasizes the prevalence of *coronelismo* in a variety of political contexts, whereas Victor Nunes Leal emphasizes it as a phenomenon of the backlands. Nunes Leal also highlights its unique transitional role during the First Republic in negotiating a compromise between "private power in its decline and a much strengthened public authority." Victor Nunes Leal, *Coronelismo: The Municipality and Representative Government in Brazil,* trans. June Henfrey (Cambridge: Cambridge University Press, 1977), 136.

10. Chapter 6 discusses these struggles against cultural repression in post-abolition Salvador.

11. The 1940 census classified the population into black, white, and yellow. Any other response (for example, *caboclo, mulato, moreno*) was subsumed into the *pardo* category. The introduction to the census explained that "omission of response signified, in many cases, reluctance to expressly declare mixed heritage." Brazil, *Recenseamento Geral de 1940,* xv.

12. Capoeira is a martial art, probably of Central African origin, developed by Brazilian slaves as a form of self-defense. The seminal work on the subject is Waldeloir Rego, *Capoeira Angola* (Salvador: Editora Itapuã, 1968).

13. In this section, the Portuguese feminine forms *prêta* and *mestiça* refer to women; the masculine forms are *prêto* and *mestiço.*

14. These figures are inexact because the census does not note multiple marriages. For this time period, however, the rates of widowhood and divorce were relatively low.

15. Brazil, *Recenseamento Geral 1940,* part 12, tome 1, 59.

16. Arquivo Público do Estado da Bahia (hereafter APEB), Registro de Testamento, 63, 13 May 1889, will dated 11 September 1882.

17. Manuel Querino, *Costumes Africanos no Brasil,* 2d ed. (Recife: Fundação Joaquim Nabuco, 1988), 58–59.

18. APEB, SSP, caixa 2, folder "Ex-Escravo," correspondence of Chief of Police, 8 October 1890.

19. Arquivo Municipal de Salvador, loose documents grouped in 1992 by *secretaria* and year pending permanent classification. File: "Comando da Guarda Cívica, 1890," números de ordem 63, 72, 75, 91, 92, 97, 99, 100, 107, 127.

20. Roberto Moura, *Tia Ciatá e a Pequena Africa no Rio de Janeiro* (Rio de Janeiro: Funarte/MEC-Secretaria de Cultura, n.d.), 46.

21. Arquivo Municipal de Salvador, file: "Sociedades," correspondence dated 2 September 1895. Correspondence from Cabelleireiros, 11 October 1899, was in a loose pile of documents pending cataloguing.

22. Ricardo Martins Ferreira was librarian and Caetano Porfirio da Silva Campos was

254 Notes to Pages 139–146

deputy visitor (responsible for home visits to pension recipients). ASPD, yearbook, 15 July 1898.

23. ASPD, Yearbook, 12 June 1894; 28 June 1897.

24. ASPD, Yearbook, 11 April 1894, 4 June 1902, 6 May 1926, 16 September 1927; AVOR, box 5–1.

25. Because archival records from this era were being catalogued at the time of my visit in 1991–92, and because references to race were often omitted, these samples merely represent data on race and occupation available during the course of field research.

26. APEB, Obitos, livro 5, Distrito do Paço, 1919–20.

27. Correspondence, Centro Operario to Sociedade Protectora dos Desvalidos, ASPD, Yearbook, 1 July 1893.

28. Correspondence, Sociedade Beneficente das Classes Proletarias to Sociedade Protectora dos Desvalidos, ASPD, Yearbook, 27 January 1925.

29. Pierre Verger, *Fluxo e Refluxo do Tráfico de Escravos entre o Golfo do Benin e a Bahia de Todos os Santos dos Séculos XVII a XIX*, 3d ed., trans. Tasso Gadzanis (São Paulo: Corrupio, 1987), 525.

30. On the return to Africa, see J. Michael Turner, "Les Brésiliens: The Impact of Former Brazilian Slaves upon Dahomey" (Ph.D. diss., Boston University, 1975); Manuela Carneiro da Cunha, *Negros, Estrangeiros: Os Escravos Libertos e Sua Volta a África* (São Paulo: Brasiliense, 1985).

31. Verger, *Fluxo e Refluxo*, 599, 633. I have estimated 135 African passports for 1857, the only incomplete year in the sample, on the basis of a monthly average of 11.25 for the eight months for which data are available.

32. Hygerio was sixty-five in 1892 when he was arrested for robbery, and had most likely been in Brazil for decades. His nationality was recorded as African; the concept of naturalized citizenship was rarely, if ever, applied to Africans. APEB, Mappa de Movimento da Cadeia de Correcção, 20 September 1892.

33. APEB, Commissariado da Policia do Porto, *Registro de Sahida de Passageiros*, books 54–58 (1882–1903). See Figure 2.

34. It is not clear to what extent notions of *nação* differed among West and Central Africans in this respect. The most common references to *nação* groups around the turn of the century (Jêje, Nagô, and so on) are of West African origin, suggesting that Central Africans had formed a more homogeneous identity.

35. A *cria* was the free child of a slave for whom the slave's master was responsible.

36. APEB, Registro de Testamento, 63, 29 July 1890, will dated 21 Aug 1855.

37. Mieko Nishida, "Gender, Ethnicity and Kinship in the Urban African Diaspora: Salvador, Brazil, 1808–1888" (Ph.D. diss., Johns Hopkins University, 1991), 193–194.

38. APEB, Testamentos, Secção Judiciaria 07/2966/34, Manoel do Bomfim Galliza, 24 August 1908, will dated 5 July 1903.

38. APEB, Registro de Testamento, 63, 22 June 1889.

40. APEB, Registro de Testamento, 63, 27 August 1889, will dated 2 October 1888.

41. When an individual becomes the godparent of a child, he or she also becomes the *compadre* (masculine) or *comadre* (feminine) of the child's parents. In Latin America, the *compadre* relationship is regarded as one of lifelong assistance and friendship.

42. APEB, Registro de Testamento, 63, 9 January 1890, will dated 2 September 1889.

43. APEB, Registro de Testamento, 63, 29 October 1889, will dated 15 June 1887. A

conto (written 1:000$000) was the largest unit of currency and represented 1,000 *milréis*.

44. APEB, Registro de Testamento, 63, 29 July 1890, will dated 21 April 1885.
45. Joana Maria da Conceição to Chief of Public Security, 14 August 1893, APEB, SSP box 4 (1893–1894; "Preso" folder).
46. APEB, Registro de Testamento, book 63, will dated 18 December 1871; died 18 October 1890.
47. Raymundo Nina Rodrigues, *O Animismo Fetichista dos Negros Bahianos* (Rio de Janeiro: Civilização Brasileira, 1935), 167–199.
48. This section deals with the branch of the Rosário brotherhood elevated to a Third Order in 1899 and whose full name is Venerável Ordem Terceira de Nossa Senhora do Rosário às Portas do Carmo. For brevity, I sometimes refer to it simply as the Rosário. A.J.R. Russell-Wood, *The Black Man in Slavery and Freedom* (New York: St. Martin's Press, 1982), 160.
49. Arquivo do Curia Metropolitana de Salvador (ACMS), "Irmandades, 1858–1903".
50. On the social importance of Third Orders, see A.J.R. Russell-Wood, "Prestige, Power, and Piety in Colonial Brazil: The Third Orders of Salvador," reprinted in Russell-Wood, *Society and Government in Colonial Brazil, 1500–1822* (Hampshire, U.K. and Brookfield, Vt,: Variorum/Ashgate Publishing, 1992), section 5, 61–89.
51. ACMS, "Diversos sobre irmandades" (portfolio), 10 December 1862. Vigario Jozé Pereira de Araújo, "Relação das Irmandades existentes na Freguezia da Nossa Senhora da Victoria da Cidade da Bahia e dos bens que constitue seos patrimonios."
52. AVOR, Rosário to Archbishop, 25 June 1889; Archbishop to Rosário, 28 June 1889, transcribed in Livro de Actas (box 4, doc. 5), 19 March 1891.
53. AVOR, Livro de Actas, caixa 4, doc. 5, 5 October 1899.
54. AVOR, box 1–3, "Compromisso da Venerável Ordem Terceira do Rosário de Nossa Senhora às Portas do Carmo," 31 May 1900.
55. AVOR, box 5–3, minutes, 20 May 1917.
56. AVOR, box 18, doc. 3–L, 1 May 1864.
57. AVOR, box 18, doc. 3–H, 2 March 1856.
58. I am translating *apolice* as "bonds" on the basis of the Rosário's financial reports, although the Michaelis dictionary also offers "stocks" as an alternative translation.
59. AVOR, box 12–14, "Contas—receita e despesa, 1890–99."
60. AVOR, box 12–14, "Contas—receita e despesa, 1890–1895."
61. AVOR, box 19–1a. The Sociedade Protectora dos Desvalidos owned a building on this plot. Because many members belonged to both organizations simultaneously, an amicable settlement was arranged.
62. AVOR, box 9–1, "Entradas, 1879–1889," Martins registered 19 July 1887.
63. AVOR, box 3–5, 15 March 1905.
64. AVOR, box 3–5; boxes 5–1 through 5–3, Atas 1907–1936.
65. AVOR, box 5–3, 16 September 1917.
66. AVOR, box 5–3, Atas, 1 August 1920–14 October 1921.
67. AVOR, box 5–3, Atas, 4 September 1921, 14 May 1922.
68. AVOR, box 12–14, 13–1.
69. J. da Silva Campos, "Procissões Tradicionais da Bahia," *Anais do Arquivo Publico da Bahia* 27 (1941), 456.
70. Excludes dividend income. ACMS, "Irmandades, 1858–1903."
71. This supports A.J.R. Russell-Wood's conclusions in "Black and Mulatto Brotherhoods

in Colonial Brazil: A Study in Collective Behavior," *Hispanic American Historical Review* 54:4 (1974), 567–602.

72. APEB, Testamentos, Secção Judiciaria 07/2966/34. A *sobrado* is a large townhouse suitable for conversion into a multifamily dwelling and/or commercial shops. The men of the Fernandes Galliza family seem to have been artisans and tradesmen. Although they inherited property that increased in value over time, these were most likely working class people. Their history is difficult to reconstruct from Sociedade records alone because the descendants of Benedicto and his slave João used the same last name. Xavier Fernandes Galliza entered the SPD as a barber in the 1890s, as did stonemason João Fernandes Galliza. ASPD, Livro de Matrículas, nos. 29, 165.

73. Silva Campos, "Procissões Tradicionais da Bahia," 459–460.

74. The Juiza was the highest female office in a brotherhood. The title Prioreza (Prioress) was only used for a Third Order. The full name of this sisterhood was Nossa Senhora da Bôa Morte (Our Lady of Good Death).

75. APEB, Testamentos TE08/3296/01, 24 December 1918, died 6 January 1919 (this testament transcribed from Livro 230, Fls. 17a).

76. Iyalorixa is the title accorded the senior priestess of a candomblé congregation.

77. *Babalawo* is a candomblé title for a priest initiated into the Ifa divination system.

78. The identity of Felizberto Sowzer is not completely clear. My informants told me he was also known as Rodolfo "Tio" Bamboucher (Bambuxé), but this may not be accurate. Edison Carneiro identifies Sowzer as Benzinho and maintains that these were two different individuals. Pierre Verger refers to an African named Bangboxé who moved to Bahia in the nineteenth century with two important candomblé priestesses and took the name Rodolfo Martins de Andrade. Another informant at the Ilê Opô Afonjá who knew Sowzer says that his name was an Anglicized spelling of Souza. I suspect Rodolfo and Felizberto were close relatives, and the Anglicization may have been the result of travel to English-speaking Nigeria. Edison Carneiro, *Candomblés da Bahia*, 3d ed. (Rio de Janeiro: Conquista, 1961), appendix; AVOR, box 10–6; Pierre Verger, "Primeiros Terreiros de Candomblé," in Carybé, ed., *Iconografia dos Deuses Africanos nos Candomblés da Bahia* (São Paulo: Editora Raizes Artes Gráficas, 1980).

79. The Sociedade Protectora dos Desvalidos is commonly referred to as the Sociedade, the Protectora, or the SPD.

80. APEB, Judiciaria, Testamento 07/2892/13.

81. ASPD, "Escrituras de Propriedades com todos os comodos," 1933.

82. ASPD, Livro de Matrículas, 1888–1938.

83. ASPD, Yearbook, 1893, nos. 8080, 8088, 8096, 8099, 9082; 1894, nos. 10040, 10052, 11008, 12034; 9 February 1896.

84. ASPD, Yearbook, 12 July 1926, 19 July 1926, 23 July 1927.

85. ASPD, Yearbooks, 1893, 1894, 1897, 1898, 1900.

86. ASPD, Yearbook, 23 June 1923.

87. ASPD, Actas do Conselho Administrativo, 1869–1898, 17 January 1883; 13 July 1883.

88. AMS, "Sociedades" (uncatalogued file of correspondence of the Conselho Municipal). Exemptions were noted for the following organizations: Sociedade Beneficente Bolsa dos Patriotas (20 November 1900), Sociedade Beneficente de Sant'Anna (9 January 1899), Sociedade Beneficente União Philantropica dos Artistas (28 July 1898), Sociedade Beneficencia Caixeiral (14 October 1898).

89. ASPD, Atas da Assembleia Geral, 28 August 1889.
90. AMS, "Juntas Distritais," correspondence of the Intendencia and Conselho Municipal; 12 August 1893, 23 August 1893, 25 August 1893.
91. ASPD, Atas do Conselho Administrativo, 1869–1898, 10 December 1891; Yearbook, 23 October 1889.
92. ASPD, Yearbooks, 24 December 1893, 29 April 1894, 3 May 1894, 17 June 1894, 28 October 1894.
93. One of the qualifications of membership was that the applicant be a *prêto*. A favorite SPD saying repeated to me in 1992 was that dark skin alone was not enough to qualify as a member; one had to have black gums to prove one wasn't a light-skinned person with a tan.
94. ASPD, Yearbook, 26 July 1911 (Ata de Conselho).
95. ASPD, Yearbook, 13 April 1921, 8 June 1921.
96. ASPD, Yearbook, 14 May 1925.
97. ASPD, Livro de Atas, 1929–1938, 20 March 1929.
98. ASPD, Yearbook, 10 May 1892, 24 May 1892, 25 May 1892.
99. ASPD, Yearbook, 1 August 1894, 22 August 1894.
100. ASPD, Yearbook, 3 February 1896.
101. ASPD, Yearbook, 5 August 1896, 31 December 1896.
102. ASPD, Atas do Conselho Administrativo, 1869–1898; Yearbook, 30 September 1910.
103. ASPD, Livro de Balanço Geral, 1918–1923.
104. ASPD, Yearbook, 9 June 1913, 6 August 1913.

CHAPTER 6   *The Politics of Culture in Salvador*

1. One of the earliest observations of this phenomenon is found in Raymundo Nina Rodrigues, *O Animismo Fetichista dos Negros Bahianos* (Rio de Janeiro: Civilização Brasileira, 1935), 173.
2. Manuel Querino, *Costumes Africanos no Brasil*, 2d ed. (Recife: Fundação Joaquim Nabuco, 1988), 58–59.
3. Interestingly, in 1952, Bahian scholar Thales de Azevedo introduced his study on Afro-Bahian elites by noting that "Bahia today is considered the most European city in Brazil." Thales de Azevedo, *As Elites de Côr: Um Estudo de Ascensão Social* (São Paulo: Companhia Editora Nacional, 1955), 25.
4. In using the term "creole African" I am referring to the culture created in Jamaica by Africans and descendants. This is different from creole culture based upon European precepts.
5. Monica Schuler, *Alas, Alas Kongo: A Social History of Indentured African Immigrants into Jamaica, 1841–1865* (Baltimore: Johns Hopkins University Press, 1980), 32–37.
6. Nina Rodrigues, *O Animismo Fetichista dos Negros Bahianos*, 171.
7. Deoscóredes M. dos Santos ("Mestre Didi") recounts his own experiences as co-founder of a Carnival group. In 1935 he and a group of young people found a tree stump in the shape of a man which they christened "Pai Burukô." In 1942 they formed the Pai Burukô Revelers (Troça do Pai Burukô) and paraded in that year's Carnival. Deoscóredes M. dos Santos, *Axé Opô Afonjá* (Rio de Janeiro: Instituto Brasileiro de Estudos Afro-Asiáticos, 1962), 90–95.

8. João José Reis, *Slave Rebellion in Brazil: The Muslim Uprising of 1835 in Bahia*, trans. Arthur Brakel (Baltimore: Johns Hopkins University Press, 1993), 40–69.

9. Donald Ramos, "Social Revolution Frustrated: The Conspiracy of the Tailors in Bahia, 1798," *Luso-Brazilian Review* 13:1 (1976), 74–90.

10. Bahian Chief of Police Francisco Gonçalves Martins, cited in Reis, *Slave Rebellion*, 192.

11. Reis, *Slave Rebellion,* 203.

12. Ibid., 142.

13. A *roda de capoeira* is the circle in which the martial art of *capoeira* is practiced to the accompaniment of a stringed bow *(berimbau),* tambourines and drums. *Batuques* (literally, "drumming") is a term for the sacred drumming of the candomblé, but was applied generically to all types of Afro-Bahian merrymaking at which drums were played.

14. In the northeast, this may have been due to the fact that Carnival generally took place during the time of the sugar harvest. The traditional time for festivities was in honor of São João in June, after the harvest was over.

15. Peter Fry, Sérgio Carrara, and Ana Luiza Martins-Costa, "Negros e Brancos no Carnaval da Velha Republica," in João José Reis, *Escravidão e a Invenção da Liberdade: Estudos sobre o negro no Brasil* (São Paulo: Editora Brasiliense, 1988), 241.

16. Fernando Denis, *O Brasil*, cited in Olga Rodrigues de Moraes von Simpson, "Family and Carnival in Brazil during the Nineteenth Century," *Loisir et Société [Society and Leisure]* (Quebec: Les Presses de l'Université du Québec) 1:2 (November 1978), 329.

17. John Luccock, *Notas sobre o Rio de Janeiro e Partes Meridionais do Brasil,* cited in von Simpson, "Family and Carnival," 329.

18. Mello Moraes Filho, *Festas e Tradições Populares do Brasil,* cited in von Simpson, "Family and Carnival," 330 (translation altered).

19. Moraes Filho, cited in von Simpson, "Family and Carnival," 329–330 (translation slightly altered).

20. Denis, cited in Fry, Carrara, and Martins-Costa, "Negros e Brancos no Carnaval," 243–44.

21. Fry, Carrara, and Martins-Costa, "Negros e Brancos no Carnaval," 243.

22. Quotes from Jean Baptiste Debret, *Viagem Pitoresca e Histórica ao Brasil*, 4th ed., vol. 1, (São Paulo: Livraria Martins, 1949), 220.

23. Debret, *Viagem Pitoresca,* 220.

24. Fry, Carrara, and Martins-Costa, "Negros e Brancos no Carnaval," 244.

25. Ibid.

26. *Jornal de Noticias,* 23 February 1884, cited in ibid., 246.

27. Some issues raised by these *carros de crítica* were abolitionism, republicanism, and gambling. Fry, Carrara, and Martins-Costa, "Negros e Brancos no Carnaval," 249; *Jornal de Noticias,* review of the Baralho Carnavelsco ("Carnival Playing-Cards") club, 23 February 1898.

28. The Secretaria de Segurança Pública, in conjunction with police precinct officials, appointed the neighborhood decorating commissions. See for example, *Jornal de Noticias,* 10 February 1899.

29. Fry, Carrara, and Martins-Costa, "Negros e Brancos no Carnaval," 249.

30. The only reference I located for the ethnicity of the Embaixada's organizers was

Raymundo Nina Rodrigues, who referred to them as "some Africans, Brazilian-born blacks, and mulattoes [*alguns africanos, negros crioulos e mestiços*]." Nina Rodrigues, *Os Africanos no Brasil* (São Paulo: Companhia Editora Nacional, 1932), 270.

31. *Vatapá* is an Afro-Brazilian culinary delicacy and one of the ritual foods of candomblé. *Jornal de Noticias,* 27 February 1895.

32. Fry, Carrara, and Martins-Costa, date the appearance of both groups to between 1892 and 1895, "No Carnaval da Velha Republica," 250. The earliest reference I found for the Embaixada was in 1895. The date for the Pandego's emergence is based on an 1899 review which referred to an Embaixada-Pandegos rivalry of three years. *Jornal de Noticias,* 27 February 1895; 15 February 1899.

33. *Jornal de Noticias,* 19 February 1896, emphasis in original.

34. *Jornal de Noticias,* 23 February 1898; 16 February 1901; 21 February 1903; 25 February 1903; *Diario de Noticias,* 26 February 1900.

35. *Jornal de Noticias,* 3 March 1897.

36. *Jornal de Noticias,* 23 February 1898.

37. *Jornal de Noticias,* 3 March 1897.

38. Person of mixed Portuguese-African origin from the Luanda region of Central Africa, specifically, from the Portuguese slave trading town of Ambaca. Joseph C. Miller, "The Slave Trade in Congo and Angola," in Martin L. Kilson and Robert I. Rotberg, eds., *The African Diaspora* (Cambridge: Harvard University Press, 1976), 110.

39. That is, to play African music.

40. *Jornal de Noticias,* 19 February 1898. It is unclear to what type of "model" they were referring.

41. *Jornal de Noticias,* 15 February 1899.

42. *Jornal de Noticias,* 13 February 1899.

43. *Jornal de Noticias,* 11 February 1899. A Fluminense is someone from one of the districts of Rio de Janeiro.

44. *Jornal de Noticias,* 28 February 1898.

45. *Jornal de Noticias,* 22 January 1902. Emphasis added.

46. *Jornal de Noticias,* 25 January 1902. Emphasis in original.

47. *Jornal de Noticias,* 23 February 1901.

48. Fry, Carrara, and Martins-Costa, "Negros e Brancos no Carnaval," 259.

49. *Jornal de Noticias,* 7 February 1902.

50. *Jornal de Noticias,* 5 February 1902. Emphasis in original.

51. *Jornal de Noticias,* 23 February 1903. Portions of this letter appeared in Jorge Amado's fictionalized account of this debate in his novel *Tent of Miracles* (New York: Avon, 1988), 86.

52. According to Emilia Viotti da Costa, the expression was used by whites to describe their black friends, or, in U.S. parlance, "good Negroes." *Da Monarquia à República: Momentos Decisivos* (São Paulo: Grijalbo, 1977), 235.

53. Fry, Carrara, and Martins-Costa, "Negros e Brancos no Carnaval," 258.

54. Nina Rodrigues, *Os Africanos no Brasil,* 271.

55. *Jornal de Noticias,* 16 February 1901.

56. " . . . a idéia dominante dos negros mais intelligentes ou melhor adaptados, é a celebração de uma sobrevivencia, de uma tradição. Os personagens e o motivo são tomados aos povos cultos da Africa, Egypcios, Abyssinios, etc." It is significant

that cultures from which most of Bahia's Africans had come were not included in this list of "refined peoples." Nina Rodrigues, *Os Africanos no Brasil,* 270.

57. Nina Rodrigues, *Os Africanos no Brasil,* 236.

58. The Filhos de Gandhi Carnival club, founded in 1949 and drawing predominantly from the Afro-Brazilian stevedores, is credited with restoring the sacred *afoxé* rhythms of Nagô-Gegê candomblé to Bahia's carnival, and generally revitalizing black participation. "Earlier in the century, *afoxé* members were usually candomblé devotees, and their music and dances came straight out of that religion." Chris McGowan and Ricardo Pessanha, *The Brazilian Sound* (New York: Billboard Books, 1991), 126.

59. Querino, *Costumes Africanos no Brasil,* 220.

60. *Jornal de Noticias,* 19 January 1897.

61. J. da Silva Campos, "Procissões Tradicionais da Bahia," *Anais do Arquivo Publico da Bahia* 27 (1941), 492–493; Estelita "da Bôa Morte" [last name not available], president of the Sisterhood of Bôa Morte, interview by author, Cachoeira, Bahia, 21 August 1992. Another source, though incorrect in some assertions, is Luiz Cláudio Nascimento, *A Bôa Morte em Cachoeira: Contribuição para o Estudo Etnológico* (Cachoeira, Bahia: Centro de Estudos, Pesquisa e Ação Sócio-Cultural de Cachoeira, 1988), 16–24.

62. Querino, *Costumes Africanos no Brasil,* 199.

63. Waldeloir Rego, *Capoeira Angola* (Salvador: Editora Itapuã, 1968), 98. He has written all the songs out phonetically.

64. Rego uses both *capoeira* and *capoeirista* to describe practitioners. Bahian capoeira master Moraes (Pedro Moraes Trindade) told me in 1992 that purists today prefer the former.

65. Rego, *Capoeira Angola,* 282.

66. Ibid., 283.

67. Ibid., 287.

68. Ibid., 282–290; see also Querino, *Costumes Africanos no Brasil,* 195–199.

69. J. da Silva Campos, "Procissões Tradicionais da Bahia," 381.

70. *A Tarde,* 24 August 1929, 1–3.

71. *A Tarde,* 24 August 1929, 1–3.

72. Waldeloir Rego uses this image in his essay, "Mitos e Ritos Africanos da Bahia," in Carybé, *Iconografia dos Deuses Africanos no Candomblé da Bahia* (São Paulo: Editora Raizes Artes Gráficas, 1980), pages unnumbered.

73. Nina Rodrigues, *Os Africanos no Brasil,* 156–157; Mieko Nishida, "Gender, Ethnicity, and Kinship in the Urban African Diaspora: Salvador, Brazil, 1808–1888" (Ph.D. diss., Johns Hopkins University, 1991), 43–73.

74. Nina Rodrigues, *O Animismo Fetichista dos Negros Bahianos,* 146–147.

75. Subsequent references to candomblé practices and rituals are based on the Nagô (Oyo) tradition. Bahian candomblé is extremely "Oyocentric" in that the Nagô houses (such as Gantois and Opô Afonjá) have been preeminent throughout the twentieth century. Most of the literature is focused on these traditions, and it appears that other cultures borrowed liberally from the Oyo liturgy. It is hoped that future research into other traditions will enable their fuller study.

76. Writing in the 1890s, Raymundo Nina Rodrigues estimated a total of no more than 15 or 20 *terreiros* in the entire city of Salvador. *O Animismo Fetichista,* 62.

77. The most significant of their publications in this regard are Nina Rodrigues,

L'Animisme Fétichiste des Nègres de Bahia and *Os Africanos no Brasil;* Manuel Querino, *A Raça Africana e Seus Costumes na Bahia*, republished in Querino, *Costumes Africanos no Brasil*.

78. See, for example, Edison Carneiro, *Candomblés da Bahia*, 3d ed. (Rio de Janeiro: Conquista, 1961); Roger Bastide, *O Candomblé da Bahia*, 2d ed. (São Paulo: Nacional, 1978) and *As Religiões Africanas no Brasil: Contribuição a uma Sociologia das Interpentrações de Civilizações*, trans. Maria Eloisa Capellato and Olívia Krähenbühl (São Paulo: Livraria Pioneira Editôra, 1971); Donald Pierson, *Negroes in Brazil: A Study of Race Contact at Bahia* (Chicago: University of Chicago Press, 1944).

79. Monica Schuler notes the same process in Jamaica, where religious institutions "constituted the basis of a functional African counterculture in a system dominated by Europeans." Schuler, *Alas, Alas Kongo*, 32.

80. See, for example, John S. Mbiti, *Introduction to African Religion*, 2d ed. (London: Heineman, 1991).

81. On the process of cultural regenesis in the African diaspora, see Sidney Mintz and Richard Price, *An Anthropological Approach to the Afro-American Past: A Caribbean Perspective* (Philadelphia: Institute for the Study of Human Issues, 1976).

82. The origin of this term has long been a matter of debate, summarized briefly by Reis in *Slave Rebellion in Brazil*, 96–97.

83. Sociedade Fiéis de São Bartolomeu, "Zoogodo Bogum Malê Rundo, Terreiro do Bogum, Terreio Gege do Bogum," unpublished paper (May 1992); Jehova de Carvalho, "Nação-Jeje," in Centro de Estudos Afro-Orientais, *Encontro de Nações de Candomblé* (Salvador: Universidade Federal da Bahia, 1984), 55–56.

84. The early history of Bahian candomblé is difficult to retrace because of the paucity of written documentation. The research of 1890–1940 is based almost entirely on oral history and personal observation, which resulted in much conflicting or incorrect data. Edison Carneiro estimated Ilê Iya Nassô's foundation as 1830, although he cited some who dated it as early as the mid-eighteenth century. Carneiro, *Candomblés da Bahia,* 61. His estimate is likely; Iyalorixas generally assumed their position at an advanced age. There were two Iyalorixas prior to 1849, making it probable that the candomblé was founded anywhere between 1800 and 1830. See also succession chart, Vivaldo da Costa Lima, "A Familia de Santo nos Candomblés Jeje-Nagos da Bahia: Um Estudo de Relações Intra-Grupais," M.A. thesis, Universidade Federal da Bahia, Salvador, 1977. Costa Lima's genealogy may be somewhat incorrect; he omits the eight-year reign of Maria da Gloria Nazareth at Gantois between 1918 and1926.

85. This was understood as a complement to, not a replacement for, Catholicism. As previously noted, numerous members of the candomblé community, including its senior clergy, were active members of Catholic lay brotherhoods as well.

86. Melville Herskovits, *The Myth of the Negro Past* (Boston: Beacon Press, 1958), 86–87.

87. Sidney Mintz and Richard Price emphasized that the creation of institutions was the immediate first stage in creating creole cultures, prior to which Africans in the New World were little more than "very heterogeneous crowds." Mintz and Price, *An Anthropological Approach to the Afro-American Past* (Philadelphia: ISHI, 1976), 9.

88. The traditions set forth by the three principal Nagô houses (Casa Branca, Gantois,

and Opô Afonjá) are popularly called "Ketu." However, Gantois traces its lineage directly to Abeokuta, and the name of Opô Afonjá suggests a link with Afonja, an Oyo dissident who led the unsuccessful mutiny that touched off the Islamic *jihad* and the eventual destruction of Oyo Ilê. J.F.A. Ajayi, "The Aftermath of the Fall of Old Oyo," in J.F.A. Ajayi and Michael Crowder, eds., *The History of West Africa*, vol. 2, 3rd ed. (London: Longman, 1985), 141–144.

89. APEB, Chefes de Policia, Maço 2959, 18 August 1866.

90. APEB, Chefes de Policia, Maço 2956, 21 September 1863.

91. Agostinho Luís to Chief of Police, APEB, Chefes de Policia, Maço 2961, 20 July 1860.

92. Nina Rodrigues, *O Animismo Fetichista dos Negros Bahianos*, 61.

93. There are several older women living in *terreiros* such as Opô Afonjá who rarely leave the grounds.

94. These divisions were not absolute; Reis notes that both Jejes and Nagôs could be found in brotherhoods founded by other Africans. Pierre Verger, "Primeiros Terreiros de Candomblé," in Carybé, *Iconografia dos Deuses Africanos nos Candomblés da Bahia*, unnumbered pages; João José Reis, *A Morte é uma Festa: Ritos Fúnebres e Revolta Popular no Brasil do Seculo XIX* (São Paulo: Companhía das Letras, 1991), 55; Reis, *Slave Rebellion in Brazil*, 150–151.

95. Verger uses the masculine form to refer to this person, and "Baba" is the Yoruba word for father ("Iya" means mother).

96. Verger, "Primeiros Terreiros." A third version of this oral history, offered by Edison Carneiro, was that Engenho Velho was founded by three women, Adetá, Iya Kalá, and Iya Nassô. Carneiro, *Candomblés da Bahia*, 61. Vivaldo da Costa Lima disputes this widely cited account. He maintains that the three names given for the founder refer to a single woman whose administrative title, Iya Nassô, was a title for the priestess of the royal cult of Xango. Costa Lima credits Mãe Senhora, then Iyalorixa of Opô Afonjá, with this interpretation. Senhora herself was a recipient of the honorific title of Iya Nassô conferred by Oba Adeniran Adeyemi, Alafin of Oyo (sent via Pierre Verger) in 1952. Ironically, this differs significantly from Verger's version, which he also attributes to Mãe Senhora. Vivaldo da Costa Lima, "Nações de Candomblé," *Encontro de Nações de Candomblé* (Salvador: Ianama/UFBA, 1984), 23–24; Deoscóredes M. dos Santos, *Axé Opô Afonjá* (Rio de Janeiro: Instituto Brasileiro de Estudos Afro-Asiáticos, 1962), 30.

97. Verger, "Primeiros Terreiros," unnumbered pages.

98. One of the difficulties in researching Oyo traditions in the diaspora is that the Western system of education is antithetical to African pedagogy. Further, the inextricable nexus of sacred and secular poses difficulties for those who have not been fully trained in religious precepts. The uninitiated are not privy to spiritual knowledge which is necessary to understand the finer points of secular matters. Because of the insistence of Western-trained researchers on obtaining restricted information, a good deal of misinformation has made its way into the scholarship.

99. Edison Carneiro, *Candomblés da Bahia*, 62–63. The 1849 date is taken from the *Estatutos da Associação de São Jorge (Ebe Oxossi)*, microfilm document 2560, Cartorio Santos Silva, 113° vara civil das Pessôas Juridicas, 2° Oficio, Salvador, Bahia; APEB, Testamento de Marcelina da Silva, 03–1276–1745–08. Will dated 5 April 1881, died 27 June 1885.

100. Nina Rodrigues personally observed Pulcheria's apprenticeship. Nina Rodrigues,

O Animismo Fetichista dos Negros Bahianos, 157; Statutes of Gantois, *Estatutos da Associação de São Jorge (Ebe Oxossi)*, 2.

101. There are many conflicting accounts of her spiritual kinship at Engenho Velho. Deoscóredes M. dos Santos claims she was the goddaughter of Maria Julia Figueiredo and the godsister of Marcelina da Silva. However, this is unlikely because it implies that da Silva was named Iyalorixa prior to her own godmother. More recent oral tradition at Opô Afonjá says Aninha was the goddaughter of Marcelina. Dos Santos, *Axé Opô Afonjá,* 17; Stella Azevedo and Cleo Martins, *E Daí Aconteceu o Encanto* (Salvador: Axé Opô Afonjá, 1988), 16–17; Vivaldo da Costa Lima, "A Familia de Santo," 198.

102. Maria Julia Figueiredo died 6 March 1890. APEB, Arrecadação 03–1011–1480–20.

103. Dos Santos, *Axé Opô Afonjá,* 18; on the details of Aninha's reasons for leaving, see also Carneiro, *Candomblés da Bahia,* 63; and Azevedo and Martins, *E Daí Aconteceu o Encanto,* 17–19.

104. Deoscóredes M. dos Santos dates the beginning of Tia Massi's administration as 1925. This date indicates a long gap between administrations, although there is a period during which a candomblé is closed after the death of an Iyalorixa. Dos Santos, *Axé Opô Afonjá,* 86.

105. Dos Santos, *Axé Opô Afonjá,* 18.

106. APEB, Arrecadação 03–1011–1480–20 (Maria Julia Figueiredo); Testamento 03–1276–1745–08 (Marcelina da Silva).

107. APEB, Affidavit of Miguel Vieira, 10 September 1887, Testamento de Marcelina da Silva, 03–1276–1745–08.

108. Ruth Landes, *The City of Women* (New York: Macmillan, 1947), 147–148.

109. APEB, Arrecadação da propriedade de Maria Julia Figueiredo, 03–1011–1480–20.

110. Peter Morton-Williams, "An Outline of the Cosmology and Cult Organization of the Oyo Yoruba," *Africa* (London), 34 (1964), 243–260.

111. Ibid., 246.

112. Katia Mattoso questioned the importance of the ancestral cult in Brazil. However, ancestral worship was and is part of Bahian candomblé, and Deoscóredes M. dos Santos participated in at least one formal Egungun cult on the island of Itaparica. Mattoso, *To Be a Slave in Brazil* (New Brunswick, N.J.: Rutgers University Press, 1991), 127.

113. Carneiro, *Candomblés da Bahia,* 63.

114. I was told by the senior priestess of the Bôa Morte sisterhood in 1992, that candomblé and Catholicism could coexist as long as clear distinctions were made between the two realms. "The majority of members participate in candomblé, but not within Catholicism. Each one participates in their house or terreiro, but not here in the church." Estelita "da Bôa Morte" [last name not available], interview by author, Cachoeira, Bahia, 21 August 1992.

115. Carneiro, *Candomblés da Bahia,* 42.

116. Ibid., 48–49.

117. See note 88.

118. The exact course of Martiniano's travels would yield vital insight into the basis for Opô Afonjá's traditions.

119. Personal communication from one of Aninha's initiates (who wished to remain anonymous), aged ninety-two in 1992 and resident at Opô Afonjá.

120. Bomfim writes that Awole succeeded Abiodun (whom he calls "one of the first kings of the Nagô people"), but abdicated in favor of Arogangan. The latter was followed by Beri, who became known as Xango. Martiniano do Bomfim, "Os Ministros de Xango," Congresso Afro-Brasileiro (second), in *O Negro no Brasil* (Rio de Janeiro: Civilização Brasileira, 1940), 233–236. Johnson, however, notes that Abiodun was the *last* Oyo king to retain effective control of the empire. Samuel Johnson, *The History of the Yorubas from the Earliest Times to the Beginning of the British Protectorate* (London: Routledge, 1921; reprint, 1969), 187.

121. Martiniano do Bomfim, "Os Ministros de Xango," 236.

122. Ade M. Obayemi, "The Yoruba and Edo-speaking Peoples and Their Neighbours before 1600 A.D.," in Ajayi and Crowder, *History of West Africa*, 1:264.

123. Dos Santos, *Axé Opô Afonjá*, 21.

124. Landes, *City of Women*, 28.

125. Nina Rodrigues, *O Animismo Fetichista dos Negros Bahianos*, 171.

126. *Jornal de Noticias*, 22 May 1897, cited in Nina Rodrigues, *Os Africanos no Brasil*, 356. (emphasis in original). The citations by Nina Rodrigues are at present the single best source for contemporary newspaper accounts. The original newspapers have deteriorated seriously, perhaps beyond repair, at Bahian libraries and archives.

127. *O Republicano*, 7 June 1897, cited in Nina Rodrigues, *Os Africanos no Brasil*, 358.

128. APEB, SSP, file: Preso, "Captura—feitiçarias," 1 November 1915.

129. Gantois is also well known today for its connections to high-ranking politicians as well as to artists, scholars, and writers.

130. *Diario de Noticias*, 5 October 1896, cited in Nina Rodrigues, *Os Africanos no Brasil*, 355.

131. *A Bahia*, 4 January 1900, cited in Nina Rodrigues, *Os Africanos no Brasil*, 359.

132. There were occasional reports of police brutality in the files of the Secretaria de Segurança Publica. See, for example, complaint by residents of the district of Sto. Amaro do Ipitanga, APEB, SSP, box 7, 10 December 1899; report of abuse of prisoner, APEB, SSP, box 10, file: Ocurrencia, 22 October 1912.

133. *Diario de Noticias*, 4 July 1905, cited in Nina Rodrigues, *Os Africanos no Brasil*, 368–369.

134. *A Bahia*, 13 January 1900, cited in Nina Rodrigues, *Os Africanos no Brasil*, 360.

135. Querino, *Costumes Africanos no Brasil*, 56.

136. Nina Rodrigues, *Os Africanos no Brasil*, 348–352; Edison Carneiro, *Candomblés da Bahia*, 138.

137. Querino, *Costumes Africanos no Brasil*, 38.

138. Pedrito appears as a character in Jorge Amado's novel set in post-abolition Bahia, *Tenda dos Milagres*, published in English as *Tent of Miracles* (New York: Knopf/Avon, 1971).

139. AVOR, box 5–3, 15 May 1921.

140. *A Tarde*, 9 July 1921, 3.

141. *A Tarde*, 9 July 1921, 3.

142. Portaria do Governo do Estado da Bahia, 10 October 1930, APEB, SSP, box 16, folder: Gabinete do Secretario, 1930.

143. *A Tarde*, 5 July 1921.

144. *Diario da Bahia*, 19 January 1921.

145. *A Tarde*, 12 July 1921.

146. Statues of Gantois, *Estatutos da Associação de São Jorge (Ebe Oxossi)*, microfilm

document 2560, Cartório Santos Silva, 113º Vara Civil das Pessôas Jurídicas, 2º Oficio, Salvador, Bahia.

147. Landes, *City of Women,* 147. Carneiro himself was to be the beneficiary of candomblé's protection when he was forced into hiding at Opô Afonjá during the Vargas regime.

148. Edison Carneiro and Aydano do Couto Ferras, "O Congresso Afro-Brasileiro da Bahia," in Congresso Afro-Brasileiro (second), *O Negro no Brasil,* 7. See also Chapter 1.

149. Dario de Bittencourt, "A Liberdade Religiosa no Brasil: A Macumba e o Batuque em Face da Lei," *O Negro,* 169–199.

150. See Carneiro, *Candomblés da Bahia,* Donald Pierson, *Negroes in Brazil: A Study of Race Contact at Bahia* (Chicago: University of Chicago Press, 1941).

151. Carneiro, *Candomblés da Bahia,* 56–57; Carneiro and Ferras, "O Congresso Afro-Brasileiro da Bahia," 11.

152. Carneiro, *Candomblés da Bahia,* 57–58.

153. Ibid., 126–130.

154. Meeting announcements in *Estado da Bahia,* 4 September 1937 (2d ed.), 2; 30 September 1937, 8.

CONCLUSION   *"Full Free"*

1. Nancy Naro, "Revision and Persistence: Recent Historiography on the Transition from Slave to Free Labor in Rural Brazil." *Slavery and Abolition* (UK) 13:2 (1992), 68–85; Rebecca Scott, "Comparing Emancipations: A Review Essay," *Journal of Social History* 20:3 (Spring 1987), 565–83.

2. Edward Brathwaite, *The Development of Creole Society in Jamaica, 1770–1820* (Oxford: Oxford University Press, 1971), 244.

3. For an excellent overview, see E. Bradford Burns, "Cultures in Conflict: The Implication of Modernization in Nineteenth-Century Latin America," in Virginia Bernhard, ed., *Elites, Masses, and Modernization in Latin America, 1850–1930* (Austin: University of Texas Press, 1979), 11–77.

4. Consolidation of creole power is more clearly evident in the nations of the continental Americas as they established political autonomy from Europe. This shift was problematic in those areas highly dependent on European investment capital, as noted by Kathleen Mary Butler in Barbados and Jamaica. Despite their many encumbrances, the Caribbean "planter class" is the operative local elite for purposes of the present discussion. Kathleen Mary Butler, *The Economics of Emancipation: Jamaica and Barbados* (Chapel Hill: University of North Carolina Press, 1995).

5. Depending on local demographics, socioeconomic stratification correlated closely with racial/ethnic distinctions. The literature for those regions tends to emphasize ethno-social categorizations. On the structure of colonial societies in the Afro-Atlantic world see, for example, David Nicholls, *Haiti in Caribbean Context: Ethnicity, Economy, and Revolt* (New York: St. Martin's Press, 1985), 22–23; Franklin W. Knight, *Slave Society in Cuba* (Madison: University of Wisconsin Press, 1970), 85–120; Stuart B. Schwartz, *Sugar Plantations in the Formation of Brazilian Society: Bahia, 1550–1835* (Cambridge: Cambridge University Press, 1985), 245–412.

6. For example, Jamaican planters relinquished much of their political autonomy

vis-à-vis the colonial government after the Morant Bay rebellion of 1865. Gad Heuman, *"The Killing Time": The Morant Bay Rebellion in Jamaica* (Knoxville: University of Tennessee Press, 1994).

7. Peter M. Voelz, *Slave and Soldier: The Military Impact of Blacks in the Colonial Americas* (New York: Garland, 1993).

8. Rout, *African Experience in Spanish America,* 176.

9. Statement of the Provisional Government dated 15 March 1817, reprinted in the *Patriot* (Boston), 24 May 1817.

10. Letter signed Tricanga, 13 February 1873, quoted in Rebecca Scott, *Slave Emancipation in Cuba* (Princeton: Princeton University Press, 1985), 112.

11. Aline Helg meticulously details this process in Cuba in *Our Rightful Share,* especially 227–248. Helg, *Our Rightful Share: The Afro-Cuban Struggle for Equality, 1886–1912* (Chapel Hill: University of North Carolina Press, 1995).

12. Berlin et al., *Freedom: A Documentary History of Emancipation,* cited in Rebecca J. Scott, "Comparing Emancipations," 569.

13. Scott, *Slave Emancipation in Cuba*; Helg, *Our Rightful Share*; Philip A. Howard, "The Spanish Colonial Government's Responses to the Pan-Nationalist Agenda of the Afro-Cuban Mutual Aid Societies, 1868–1895," *Revista/Review Interamericana,* 22:1–2 (1992), 155–157.

14. David Nicholls addresses the nuances of ethnicity and class in Haiti in *Haiti in Caribbean Context,* 21–35.

15. Eric Foner, *Nothing But Freedom: Emancipation and Its Legacy* (Baton Rouge: Louisiana State University Press, 1983); O. Nigel Bolland, "Systems of Domination after Slavery: The Control of Land and Labor in the British West Indies after 1838," *Comparative Studies in Society and History* 23:4 (October 1981), 591–619; Walter Rodney, *A History of the Guyanese Working People, 1881–1905* (Baltimore: Johns Hopkins University Press, 1981), 31–59; Monica Schuler, *Alas, Alas Kongo: A Social History of Indentured African Immigrants into Jamaica, 1841–1865* (Baltimore: Johns Hopkins University Press, 1980); Herbert S. Klein and Stanley L. Engerman, "The Transition from Slave to Free Labor," in Mario Moreno Fraginals, Frank Moya Pons, and Stanley L. Engerman, eds., *Between Slavery and Free Labor: The Spanish-Speaking Caribbean in the Nineteenth Century* (Baltimore: Johns Hopkins University Press, 1985), 255–269; Francisco A. Scarano, "Labor and Society in the Nineteenth Century," in Franklin W. Knight and Colin A. Palmer, eds., *The Modern Caribbean* (Chapel Hill: University of North Carolina Press, 1989), 51–84.

16. Louis A. Pérez, Jr., "Politics, Peasants and People of Color: The 1912 'Race War' in Cuba Reconsidered," *Hispanic American Historical Review* 66:3 (1986), 509–539; Helg, *Our Rightful Share,* 141–191.

17. Leonard Barrett, Sr., *The Rastafarians: Sounds of Cultural Dissonance* (Boston: Beacon Press, 1988), 84.

18. Jane Freeland, "Nicaragua," in Minority Rights Group, ed., *Afro-Latin Americans Today: No Longer Invisible* (London: Minority Rights Publications, 1995), 192–195.

19. Although I focus here on the issue of access at the time of abolition, this concept may be broadened to include reformists in general.

20. In Haiti, for example, the military provided access. David Nicholls, *Haiti in Caribbean Context,* 27.

21. Similarly, Negro League baseball and the black motion picture industry in the United States disappeared after the passage of integration legislation, whereas other black institutions continued.

22. Roger Bastide, *African Civilisations in the New World,* trans. Peter Green (New York: Harper and Row, 1971), 168–169; Luc de Heusch, "Kongo in Haiti: A New Approach to Religious Syncretism" in Darién J. Davis, ed., *Slavery and Beyond: The African Impact on Latin America and the Caribbean* (Wilmington, Del.: Scholarly Resources), 103–119; Schuler, *Alas, Alas Kongo.*

23. Interestingly, the organizers of Cuba's Partido Independiente de Color encountered substantial support among the Afro-Cuban minority in Santa Clara province, but had difficulty forming committees in many areas where Afro-Cubans were in the majority. Helg, *Our Rightful Share,* 156.

24. Howard, "Spanish Colonial Government's Responses to the Pan-Nationalist Agenda"; Robert L. Pacquette, *Sugar Is Made with Blood: The Conspiracy of La Escalera and the Conflict Between Empires over Slavery in Cuba* (Middletown, Conn.: Wesleyan University Press, 1988).

25. Pérez, "Politics, Peasants, and People of Color," 526–530. Aline Helg describes more broad-based ideological support for the Partido Independiente de Color, notably among immigrant workers of African descent. She nonetheless concurs with Pérez that, at the start of the protests, most of the participants were directly linked to the Partido. Helg, *Our Rightful Share,* 207–209.

26. Michael Mitchell, "Blacks and the Abertura Democrática," and Anani Dzidzienyo, "The African Connection and the Afro-Brazilian Condition," in Pierre Michel Fontaine, ed. *Race, Class, and Power in Brazil* (Los Angeles: CAAS/UCLA, 1985), 95–119, 135–153; Michael George Hanchard, *Orpheus and Power: The Movimento Negro of Rio de Janeiro and São Paulo, Brazil, 1945–1988* (Princeton: Princeton University Press, 1994), 111–119.

27. Evelyn Hu-Dehart has made important contributions in this line of research and analysis. See, for example, Hu-Dehart, "Coolies, Shopkeepers, Pioneers: The Chinese of Mexico and Peru, 1849–1930," *Amerasia* 15:2 (1989), 91–116.

GLOSSARY

acarajé (ah-car-a-JAY): fritter of seasoned and skinned black-eyed peas, fried in palm oil

agôgô (ah-go-GO): type of bell

atabaque (ah-ta-BAH-kee): type of drum used in candomblé

Babalawo (ba-ba-LAU-oh): male priest specializing in the Ifá divination system of the Yoruba

Babalorixa (ba-ba-low-REE-sha): candomblé priest

batuque (bah-TOO-kee): generic Brazilian term for drumming, especially at candomblé ceremonies

berimbau (bee-reem-BAU): musical instrument of African origin, consisting of a bow strung with a wire and an open gourd that is played with a stick while simultaneously shaking a small seed-filled rattle (caxixi)

caboclo (ca-BO-cloo): term referring to indigenous people in Brazil; candomblé incorporating indigenous elements

cachaça (ca-SHA-sa): liquor distilled from sugar cane

candomblé (cahn-dome-BLAY): Afro-Brazilian religion derived in large measure from the Yoruba culture of Nigeria

cantos (CAHN-toos): gathering points for Afro-Brazilians to offer their services for hire

capoeira (ca-poo-A-rah): Afro-Brazilian martial art form

cavaquinho (cah-vah-KEEN-yoo): stringed musical instrument, similar to a small high-pitched guitar, typically used in samba

conto (CONE-toe): Brazilian currency unit of 1,000 milréis

crioulo, creoulo (cree-OH-loo): antiquated term for a black person born in Brazil

feijoada (fay-jo-AH-da): traditional bean stew flavored with meats and spices

festa (FEST-ah): festival, usually in honor of a Catholic saint

ingenuo (in-JEN-yoo-oh): free child of enslaved mother

Iyalorixa (EE-ya-lore-ee-SHA): candomblé priestess; leader of candomblé congregation

lavagem (la-VA-gen): literally cleansing; the *lavagem* of Bomfim in Bahia was a festival in which Afro-Brazilian cleansed the church of a Catholic saint equated with the Yoruba diety Oxala

Malês (mah-LAYS): Brazilian term for African Muslims, especially from Dahomey

milréis (meal-HACE): Brazilian currency unit, written as 1$000, of one thousand réis

nação (nahs-AUN): nation; term for the African nationalities of slaves

nações (nah-SO-ees): plural of nação

Nagô (nah-GO): Brazilian term for Yoruba Africans

ogan (oh-GAHN): officer of candomblé communities

orixa (oh-REE-sha): deities of the Yoruba tradition; each represents an archetype of divine energy

pandeiro (pan-DAY-roo): instrument similar to a tambourine used especially in samba

pano da costa (pa-noo-da-COAST-ah): African cloth, similar to Kente cloth, worn by Afro-Brazilian women

pardo (PAHR-doo): "brown" person, i.e., mulatto

prêto (PRAY-too): "black," i.e., dark-skinned person

réis (HACE): Brazilian currency

samba (SAM-ba): a traditional Afro-Brazilian rhythmic music and dance form

terreiro (tay-HAY-roo): consecrated land used for candomblé ceremonies; generic term for candomblé congregations

vatapá (vah-tah-PAH): puree of dried shrimp, bread, palm oil, and spices; ritual food of candomblé

yayá (ya-YA): Africanized version of the Portutguese *Senhora* (madam, mistress); possibly jointly derived from the Yoruba word *Iya* (mother). *Senhora* was also Africanized as *Sinhá*

yoyô (yo-YAW): Africanized version of the Portuguese *Senhor* (sir, master)

BIBLIOGRAPHY

Archives

SÃO PAULO

Arquivo do Estado de São Paulo (AESP)
Arquivo Municipal de São Paulo (AMSP)

SALVADOR

Arquivo da Curia Metropolitana de Salvador (ACMS)
Arquivo Municipal de Salvador (AMS)
Arquivo Público do Estado da Bahia (APEB)
Arquivo da Sociedade Protectora dos Desvalidos (Salvador) (ASPD)
Arquivo da Venerável Ordem Terceira da Nossa Senhora do Rosário às Portas do Carmo
(Salvador) (AVOR)

Manuscripts and Unpublished Materials

Adamo, Sam. "The Broken Promise: Race, Health, and Justice in Rio de Janeiro, 1890–
1940." Ph.D. diss., University of New Mexico, 1983.
Costa Lima, Vivaldo da. "A Familia de Santo nos Candomblés Jeje-Nagos da Bahia: Um
Estudo de Relações Intra-Grupais." M.A. thesis, Universidade Federal da Bahia,
Salvador, 1977.
Estatutos da Associação de São Jorge (Ebe Oxossi), microfilm document 2560, Cartorio
Santos Silva, 113º Vara Civil das Pessoas Juridicas, 2º Oficio, Salvador, Bahia.
Ferrara, Miriam Nicolau, ed. *Jornais da Raça Negra.* Instituto de Estudos Brasileiros;
São Paulo: Universidade de São Paulo, n.d., microfilm.
Gomes da Silva, José Carlos. "Os Sub-Urbanos e a Outra Face da Cidade. Negros em
São Paulo, 1900–1930: Cotidiano, Lazer e Cidadania." M.A. thesis, Universidade
Estadual de Campinas, 1990.
Mitchell, Michael. "Racial Consciousness and the Political Attitudes and Behavior of
Blacks in São Paulo, Brazil." Ph.D. diss., Indiana University, 1977.
Mitchell, Michael, ed. *The Black Press of Brazil, 1916–1969.* Firestone Library. Princeton:
Princeton University, n.d., microfilm.
Nishida, Mieko. "Gender, Ethnicity, and Kinship in the Urban African Diaspora: Salva-
dor, Brazil, 1808–1888." Ph.D. diss., Johns Hopkins University, 1991.

Pontífica Universidade Católica. "Projecto Memoria de Escravidão em Familias Negras de São Paulo." 30 boxes. Central de Documentação e Informação Científica Professor Casemiro dos Reis Filho, 1987–88.

Raphael, Alison. "Samba and Social Control: Popular Culture and Racial Democracy in Rio de Janeiro." Ph.D. diss., Columbia University, 1980.

Sociedade Fiéis de São Bartolomeu. "Zoogodo Bogum Malê Rundo, Terreiro do Bogum, Terreio Gege do Bogum." [May 1992].

Turner, J. Michael. "Les Brésiliens: The Impact of Former Brazilian Slaves upon Dahomey." Ph.D. diss., Boston University, 1975.

Newspapers

São Paulo

Diario Oficial de São Paulo, 4 November 1931, 14 June 1936.
Diario de São Paulo, 17 September 1931, 18 December 1931.

Salvador

Diario da Bahia, 19 January 1921.
Diario de Noticias, 26 February 1900.
Estado da Bahia, 4 September 1937.
Jornal de Noticias, 27 February 1895; 19 February 1896; 19 January 1897; 3 March 1897; 18, 19, 23, 28 February 1898; 10, 11, 13, 15 February 1899; 16, 23 February 1901; 22, 25 January 1902; 5, 7 February 1902; 21, 23 February 1903.
A Tarde, 5, 9, 12 July 1921.

Afro-Brazilian Newspapers (São Paulo)

O Alfinete, 3 September 1918; 28 August 1921.
Auriverde, 29 April 1928.
O Bandeirante, August 1918; April 1919.
Brasil Novo (weekly), 3, 10, 17 April 1933; 17 July 1933.
A Chibata (monthly), February, March 1932.
O Clarim (monthly), February, March, April 1924.
O Clarim (monthly). February–May 1935.
O Clarim da Alvorada (spelled alternatively as "d'Alvorada" in some editions) (monthly), May, June, October, December 1924; January, August, November, December 1925; April, May, July, August, September, October 1926; January, February, April, May, June, July, October 1927.
O Clarim da Alvorada (Second Phase) (monthly). February, April, May, June, September, October, November, December 1928; January–November 1929; January, April, May, July, August, September, December 1930; May, June, July, August, September, November, December 1931; January, March, May 1932.
Elite, 20 January 1924.
O Kosmos, October 1922; January 1925.
A Liberdade, 14 July 1919; 3 August 1919; 23 November 1919; 14 December 1919; 28 December 1919; 7 March 1920; 9 May 1920.
O Menelick, 1 January 1916.

Progresso (monthly), June 1928–August 1932 (except July, August 1928; May 1929; March, May, October 1930; December 1931; February, March, May, June 1932)
A Rua, 24 February 1916.
A Sentinella, 10 October 1920.
A Voz da Raça (weekly), 18 March 1933–15 July 1933 (nos. 1–17).
A Voz da Raça (biweekly), 5 August 1933–29 December 1934 (nos. 18–44; except 23, 37, 42).
A Voz da Raça (monthly), May 1935–November 1937 (nos. 45–70; except 48, 63, 68.)
O Xauter, 16 May 1916.

Interviews

Barbosa, Aristides. 1989. Interviewed by author, 21 January, São Paulo. Tape recording.
Cunha, Eunice. 1989. Interviewed by author, 20 January, São Paulo. Tape recording.
Cunha, Henrique. 1989. Interviewed by author, 20 January, São Paulo. Tape recording.
Cunha, Jr., Henrique. 1992. Interviewed by author, 7, 10 October, São Paulo. Tape recording.
Estelita "da Bôa Morte" [last name not available]. 1992. Interviewed by author, 21 August, Cachoeira, Bahia. Tape recording.
Ferreira, Leocadio Pires. 1991. Interviewed by author, 12 December, Salvador. Tape recording.
Leite, José Correia. 1989. Interviewed by author, 5, 7 January, São Paulo. Tape recording.
Leite, Ricarda. 1992. Interviewed by author, 10 October, São Paulo. Tape recording.
Lucrecio, Francisco. 1989. Interviewed by author, 10 January, São Paulo. Tape recording.
Ribeiro, Marcello Orlando. 1989. Interviewed by author, 10 January, São Paulo. Tape recording.
Santana, Antônio Albérico. 1992. Interviewed by author, 4 September, Salvador. Tape recording.
Silva, Alberto Alves da ("Nenê da Vila Matilde"). 1992. Interviewed by author, 17 April, São Paulo. Tape recording.
Silva, Carlota de Oliveira Galdino. 1992. Interviewed by author, 7 October, São Paulo. Tape recording.
Silva, Júlio. 1991. Interviewed by author, 13 December, Salvador. Tape recording.
Silva Neto, Antônio Pereira da ("Zulu"). 1992. Interviewed by author, 18 April, São Paulo. Tape recording.
Sodré Pereira, Henrique Jarbas. 1992. Interviewed by author, 24, 30 July, Salvador. Tape recording.

Books and Articles

Adamo, Sam. "Order and Progress for Some—Death and Disease for Others: Living Conditions of Nonwhites in Rio de Janeiro, 1890–1940." *West Georgia College Studies in the Social Sciences,* 25 (1986), 17–30.
———. "Race and Povo." In Michael L. Conniff and Frank D. McCann, eds., *Modern Brazil: Elites and Masses in Historical Perspective.* Lincoln: University of Nebraska Press, 1989.

Adams, Mark B., ed. *The Wellborn Science: Eugenics in Germany, France, Brazil, and Russia.* New York: Oxford University Press, 1990.

Adamson, Walter L. *Hegemony and Revolution: A Study of Antonio Gramsci's Political and Cultural* Theory. Berkeley: University of California Press, 1980.

Ajayi, J. F. A., and Michael Crowder, eds. *History of West Africa,* 2 vols., 3d ed. London: Longman, 1985.

Amado, Jorge. *Tent of Miracles.* New York: Avon, 1988.

Amaral, Raul Joviano de. *Os Prêtos do Rosário de São Paulo: Subsidios Historicos.* São Paulo: Alarico, 1954.

Andrews, George Reid. *Blacks and Whites in São Paulo, Brazil, 1888–1988.* Madison: University of Wisconsin Press, 1991.

Appiah, Kwame Anthony. *In My Father's House: Africa in the Philosophy of Culture.* New York: Oxford University Press, 1992.

Avila, Bastos de. "Contribuição ao Estudo do Indice de Lapicque." In Gilberto Freyre, ed., *Estudos Afro-Brasileiros.* Reprint. Recife: Fundação Joaquim Nabuco, 1988.

Azevedo, Aluísio. *O Cortiço.* Rio de Janeiro: H. Garnier, 1890.

Azevedo, Stella, and Cleo Martins. *E Daí Aconteceu o Encanto.* Salvador: Axé Opô Afonjá, 1988.

Azevedo, Thales de. *As Elites de Côr: Um Estudo de Ascensão Social.* São Paulo: Companhia Editora Nacional, 1955.

Bacelar, Jeferson. "A Frente Negra Brasileira da Bahia." *Afro-Ásia* 17 (1996), 73–85.

Barrett, Sr., Leonard. *The Rastafarians: Sounds of Cultural Dissonance.* Boston: Beacon Press, 1988.

Bastide, Roger. *African Civilisations in the New World,* trans. Peter Green. New York: Harper and Row, 1971.

———. *O Candomblé da Bahia,* 2d ed. São Paulo: Nacional, 1978.

———. "A Imprensa Negra do Estado de São Paulo." Faculdade de Filosofia, Ciencias e Letras, *Boletim CSSI, Sociologia,* no. 2, *Estudos Afro-Brasileiros,* 2a serie (1951).

———. *As Religiões Africanas no Brasil: Contribuição a uma Sociologia das Interpentrações de Civilizações,* trans. Maria Eloisa Capellato and Olívia Krähenbühl. São Paulo: Livraria Pioneira Editôra, 1971.

Bastide, Roger, and Florestan Fernandes. *Brancos e Negros em São Paulo,* 3d ed. São Paulo: Companhia Editora Nacional, 1971.

Beiguelman, Paula. *A Formação do Povo no Complexo Cafeeiro: Aspectos Políticos.* São Paulo: Livaria Pioneira Editora, 1968.

Bethell, Leslie. *The Abolition of the Brazilian Slave Trade: Britain, Brazil, and the Slave Trade Question, 1807–1869.* Cambridge: Cambridge University Press, 1970.

Bethell, Leslie, ed. *Colonial Brazil.* Cambridge: Cambridge University Press, 1987.

Bolland, O. Nigel. "Systems of Domination after Slavery: The Control of Land and Labor in the British West Indies after 1838." *Comparative Studies in Society and History* 23:4 (October 1981), 591–619.

Brathwaite, Edward. *The Development of Creole Society in Jamaica, 1770–1820.* Oxford: Oxford University Press, 1971.

Brazil. *Collecção das Leis da Republica dos Estados Unidos Brasileiros de 1892.* Rio de Janeiro: Imprensa Nacional, 1893.

Brazil. Congresso, Camara dos Deputados. *A Imigração Japonesa.* Rio de Janeiro, 1925.

Brazil. Directoria Geral de Estatística. *Recenseamento do Brazil, 1 Setembro 1920,* vol. 1. Rio de Janeiro: Typ. da Estatística, 1922.

Brazil. Directoria Geral da Estatística. *Resumo de Varias Estatísticas Econômico-Financeiras*. Rio de Janeiro: Typografia da Estatística, 1924.

———. *Sexo, Raça, e Estado Civil . . . da População Recenseada em 31 de Dezembro de 1890*. Rio de Janeiro: Oficina da Estatística, 1898.

Brazil. Instituto Brasileiro de Geografia e Estatística. *Recenseamento Geral do Brazil, 1º de Setembro de 1940*. Rio de Janeiro: Serviço Gráfico do Instituto Brasileiro de Geografia e Estatística, 1950.

Britto, Iêda Marques. *Samba na Cidade de São Paulo, 1900–1930: Um Exercício de Resistencia Cultural*. São Paulo: FFLCH-USP, 1986.

Buarque de Hollanda, Sergio. *Historia Geral da Civilização Brasileira*, vol. 3, *O Brasil Republicano*, ed. Boris Fausto, 5 vols. Rio de Janeiro: DIFEL, 1977.

Burns, E. Bradford. "Cultures in Conflict: The Implication of Modernization in Nineteenth Century Latin America." In Virginia Bernhard, ed., *Elites, Masses, and Modernization in Latin America, 1850–1930*. Austin: University of Texas Press, 1979.

———. "The Intellectuals as Agents of Change." In A.J.R. Russell-Wood, ed., *From Colony to Nation*. Baltimore: Johns Hopkins University Press, 1975.

———. "The Role of Azeredo Coutinho in the Enlightenment of Brazil." *Hispanic American Historical Review* 44:2 (May 1964).

Butler, Kathleen Mary. *The Economics of Emancipation: Jamaica and Barbados*. Chapel Hill: University of North Carolina Press, 1995.

Carneiro, Edison. *Candomblés da Bahia* [c. 1948], 3d ed. Rio de Janeiro: Conquista, 1961.

Carneiro, Edison, and Aydano do Couto Ferras, "O Congresso Afro-Brasileiro da Bahia." In Congresso Afro-Brasileiro (second), *O Negro no Brasil*. Rio de Janeiro: Civilização Brasileira, 1940.

Carneiro da Cunha, Manuela. *Negros, Estrangeiros: Os Escravos Libertos e Sua Volta a Africa*. São Paulo: Brasiliense, 1985.

Carvalho, Jehova de. "Nação-Jeje." In Centro de Estudos Afro-Orientais, *Encontro de Nações de Candomblé*. Salvador: Universidade Federal da Bahia, 1984.

Carybé. *Iconografia dos Deuses Africanos no Candomblé da Bahia*. São Paulo: Editora Raizes Artes Gráficas, 1980.

Centro de Estudos Afro-Orientais. *Encontro de Nações de Candomblé*. Salvador: Universidade Federal da Bahia, 1984.

Congresso Afro-Brasileiro (second). *O Negro no Brasil*. Rio de Janeiro: Civilização Brasileira, 1940.

Conniff, Michael, and Frank McCann, eds. *Modern Brazil: Elites and Masses in Historical Perspective*. Lincoln: University of Nebraska Press, 1989.

Conrad, Robert. *The Destruction of Brazilian Slavery, 1850–1888*. Berkeley: University of California Press, 1972.

Costa Lima, Vivaldo, "Nações de Candomblé." In *Encontro de Nações de Candomblé*, 11–26. Salvador: Ianama/UFBA, 1984.

Curtin, Philip D. *The Atlantic Slave Trade: A Census*. Madison: University of Wisconsin Press, 1969.

Da Cunha, Euclides. *Rebellion in the Backlands* (Os Sertões), trans. Samuel Putnam. Chicago: University of Chicago Press, 1944.

De Avila, Bastos. "Contribuição ao Estudo do Indice de Lapicque." In Gilberto Freyre, ed., *Estudos Afro-Brasileiros: Trabalhos Apresentados ao 1º Congresso Afro-Brasileiro Realizado no Recife, em 1934*, 29–38. Reprint. Recife: Fundação Joaquim Nabuco, 1988

De Jesus, Carolina. *Child of the Dark,* trans. David St. Clair. New York: Mentor, 1962.

Dean, Warren. *The Industrialization of São Paulo, 1880–1945.* Austin: University of Texas Press, 1969.

Debret, Jean Baptiste. *Viagem Pitoresca e Histórica ao Brasil,* 4th ed., 2 vols. São Paulo: Livraria Martins, 1949.

Dos Santos, Deoscóredes M. *Axé Opô Afonjá.* Rio de Janeiro: Instituto Brasileiro de Estudos Afro-Asiáticos, 1962.

Dos Santos, José Maria. *Os Republicanos e a Abolição.* São Paulo: Livraria Martins, 1942.

Duarte, Abelardo. "Grupos Sanguinarios da Raça Negra." In Gilberto Freyre, ed., *Estudos Afro-Brasileiros: Trabalhos Apresentados ao 1º Congresso Afro-Brasileiro Realizado no Recife, em 1934,* 171–180. Reprint. Recife: Fundação Joaquim Nabuco, 1988.

Ellis, Jr., Alfredo B. *Populações Paulistas.* São Paulo: Companhia Editora Nacional, 1934.

Engerman, Stanley L. "Slavery and Emancipation in Comparative Perspective: A Look at Some Recent Debates." *Journal of Economic History* 46 (June 1986), 317–339.

Erickson, Kenneth. *The Brazilian Corporative State and Working-Class Politics.* Berkeley: University of California Press, 1977.

Ernst, Robert. *Immigrant Life in New York City, 1825–1863.* New York: King's Crown Press/Columbia University, 1949.

Fausto, Boris. *Crime e Cotidiano: A Criminalidade em São Paulo, 1880–1924.* São Paulo: Editora Brasiliense, 1984.

Fausto, Boris, ed. *O Brasil Republicano,* 5 vols., São Paulo: DIFEL, 1986: tome III of Sergio Buarque de Hollanda, ed., *Historia Geral da Civilização Brasileira.* Rio de Janeiro: DIFEL, 1977.

Fernandes, Florestan. *A Integração do Negro na Sociedade de Classes,* 2 vols. 2d ed. São Paulo: Editora Ática, 1978 (1st ed., São Paulo: Dominus, 1965).

———. *The Negro in Brazilian Society* (translation of *A Integração do Negro na Sociedade de Classes*). New York: Atheneum, 1971.

Ferrara, Miriam Nicolau. *A Imprensa Negra Paulista, 1915–1963.* São Paulo: FFLCH-USP, 1986.

Flynn, Peter. *Brazil: A Political Analysis.* London: Ernest Benn, 1978.

Foner, Eric. *Nothing but Freedom: Emancipation and Its Legacy.* Baton Rouge: Louisiana State University Press, 1983.

Fontaine, Pierre-Michel. *Race, Class, and Power in Brazil.* Los Angeles: CAAS/UCLA, 1985.

Fraginals, Mario Moreno, Frank Moya Pons, and Stanley L. Engerman, eds. *Between Slavery and Free Labor: The Spanish-Speaking Caribbean in the Nineteenth Century.* Baltimore: Johns Hopkins University Press, 1985.

Freitas Oliveira, Waldir, and Vivaldo da Costa Lima, eds. *Cartas de Edison Carneiro a Arthur Ramos: De 4 de Janeiro de 1936 a 6 de Dezembro de 1938.* São Paulo: Corrupio, 1987.

Freyre, Gilberto. *The Masters and the Slaves* (Casa-Grande e Senzala), trans. Samuel Putnam, second English-language edition, revised. New York: Alfred A. Knopf, 1978.

———. "Human Factors behind Brazilian Development." *Progress* (Winter 1951–52); reprint, Ispwich: W. S. Cowell, n.d.

Freyre, Gilberto, ed. *Estudos Afro-Brasileiros: Trabalhos Apresentados ao 1º Congresso Afro-Brasileiro Realizado no Recife, em 1934.* Reprint. Recife: Fundação Joaquim Nabuco, 1988.

———. *Novos Estudos Afro-Brasileiros: Trabalhos Apresentados ao 1º Congresso Afro-Brasileiro do Recife.* Reprint. Recife: Fundação Joaquim Nabuco, 1988.

Fry, Peter, Sérgio Carrara, and Ana Luiza Martins-Costa. "Negros e Brancos no Carnaval da Velha Republica." In João José Reis, ed., *Escravidão e a Invenção da Liberdade: Estudos sobre o Negro no Brasil*. São Paulo: Editora Brasiliense, 1988.

Furtado, Celso. *The Economic Growth of Brazil: A Survey from Colonial to Modern Times*, trans. Ricardo W. de Aguiar and Eric Charles Drysdale. Berkeley: University of California Press, 1968.

Geggus, David. "The Haitian Revolution." In Franklin W. Knight and Colin A. Palmer, eds., *The Modern Caribbean*, 21–50. Chapel Hill: University of North Carolina Press.

Gontier, Bernard. *Bexiga*. São Paulo: Mundo Impresso, 1990.

Gonzalez, Lélia. "The Unified Black Movement: A New Stage in Black Political Mobilization." In Pierre-Michel Fontaine, ed., *Race, Class, and Power in Brazil*. Los Angeles: University of California/Center for Afro-American Studies, 1985.

Graham, Richard, ed. *Britain and the Onset of Modernization in Brazil, 1850–1914*. Cambridge: Cambridge University Press, 1968.

———. *The Idea of Race in Latin America, 1870–1940*. Austin: University of Texas Press, 1990.

———. *Patronage and Politics in Nineteenth-Century Brazil*. Stanford: Stanford University Press, 1990.

Hamilton, Ruth Sims, ed. *Creating a Paradigm and Research Agenda for Comparative Studies of the Worldwide Dispersion of African Peoples*. East Lansing: African Diaspora Research Project, Michigan State University, 1990.

Harris, Joseph, ed. *Global Dimensions of the African Diaspora*. Washington, D.C.: Howard University Press, 1982.

Harris, Marvin. *Patterns of Race in the Americas*. New York: Walker and Company, 1964.

Hasenbalg, Carlos Alfredo. *Discriminação e Desigualdades Raciais no Brasil*. Rio de Janeiro: Graal, 1979.

Helg, Aline. *Our Rightful Share: The Afro-Cuban Struggle for Equality, 1886–1912*. Chapel Hill: University of North Carolina Press, 1995.

Herskovits, Melville. *The Myth of the Negro Past*. Boston: Beacon Press, 1958.

———. "The Negro in the New World: The Statement of a Problem." *American Anthropologist* 32 (1930), 145–155.

Heusch, Luc de. "Kongo in Haiti: A New Approach to Religious Syncretism." In Darién J. Davis, ed., *Slavery and Beyond: The African Impact on Latin America and the Caribbean*, 103–119. Wilmington, Del,.: Scholarly Resources, 1995.

Hoetink, H. *Slavery and Race Relations in the Americas: Comparative Notes on Their Nature and Nexus*. New York: Harper and Row, 1973.

Holloway, Thomas. *Immigrants on the Land: Coffee and Society in São Paulo, 1886–1934*. Chapel Hill: University of North Carolina Press, 1980.

Howard, Philip A. "The Spanish Colonial Government's Responses to the Pan-Nationalist Agenda of the Afro-Cuban Mutual Aid Societies, 1868–1895." *Revista/Review Interamericana* 22:1–2 (1992), 151–167.

Hu-Dehart, Evelyn. "Coolies, Shopkeepers, Pioneers: The Chinese of Mexico and Peru, 1849–1930." *Amerasia* 15:2 (1989), 91–116.

Ianni, Octavio. *Escravidão e Racismo,* 2d ed. São Paulo: Hucitec, 1988.

———. *Raças e Classes Sociais no Brasil,* 3d ed. São Paulo: Brasiliense, 1987.

Johnson, Samuel. *The History of the Yorubas from the Earliest Times to the Beginning of the British Protectorate*. London: Routledge, 1921; reprint, 1969.

Joyner, Charles. *Down by the Riverside: A South Carolina Slave Community*. Urbana and Chicago: University of Illinois Press, 1984.

Karasch, Mary C. *Slave Life in Rio de Janeiro, 1808–1850*. Princeton: Princeton University Press, 1987.

Kellas, James G. *The Politics of Nationalism and Identity*. New York: St. Martin's Press, 1991.

Kent, R. K. "Palmares: An African State in Brazil." *Journal of African History* 6 (1965), 161–175.

Kern, Robert, ed. *The Caciques: Oligarchical Politics and the System of Caciquismo in the Luso-Hispanic World*. Albuquerque: University of New Mexico Press, 1973.

Klein, Herbert S., and Stanley L. Engerman, "The Transition from Slave to Free Labor: Notes on a Comparative Economic Model." In Mario Moreno Fraginals, Frank Moya Pons, and Stanley L. Engerman, eds., *Between Slavery and Free Labor: The Spanish-Speaking Caribbean in the Nineteenth Century*. Baltimore: Johns Hopkins University Press, 1985.

Knight, Franklin W., and Colin A. Palmer, eds. *The Modern Caribbean*. Chapel Hill: University of North Carolina Press, 1989.

Koster, Henry. *Travels in Brazil*, vol. 2. London: Longman et al., 1817.

Kuhn, Thomas S. *The Structure of Scientific Revolutions,* 2d ed. Chicago: University of Chicago Press, 1970.

Landes, Ruth. *The City of Women*. New York: Macmillan, 1947.

Leff, Nathaniel. *Economic Policy-Making and Development in Brazil, 1947–1964*. New York: John Wiley and Sons, 1968.

Leite, José Correia, and Cuti [Luiz Silva]. *...E Disse o Velho Militante José Correia Leite*. São Paulo: Secretaria Municipal de Cultura, 1992.

Lesser, Jeffrey. *Welcoming the Undesirables: Brazil and the Jewish Question*. Berkeley: University of California Press, 1995.

Levine, Robert M. "Elite Intervention in Urban Popular Culture in Modern Brazil." *Luso-Brazilian Review* 21:2 (Winter 1984), 9–22.

———. "The First Afro-Brazilian Congress: Opportunities for the Study of Race in the Brazilian Northeast." *Race* (London) 15:2 (1973).

———. "Turning on the Lights: Brazilian Slavery Reconsidered One Hundred Years after Abolition." *Latin American Research Review* 24:2 (1989), 201–217.

———. *The Vargas Regime: The Critical Years, 1934–1938*. New York: Columbia University Press, 1970.

Levine, Robert M., and José Carlos Sebe Bom Meihy. *The Life and Death of Carolina Maria de Jesus*. Albuquerque: University of New Mexico Press, 1995.

Lewin, Linda. *Politics and Parentela in Paraíba: A Case Study of Family-Based Oligarchy in Brazil*. Princeton: Princeton University Press, 1987.

Lockhart, James, and Stuart B. Schwartz. *Early Latin America*. Cambridge: Cambridge University Press, 1983.

Love, Joseph. "Political Participation in Brazil." *Luso-Brazilian Review* 7:2 (1970) .

———. *São Paulo in the Brazilian Federation, 1889–1937*. Stanford: Stanford University Press, 1980.

Lowrie, Samuel H. "O Elemento Negro na População de Sao Paulo." In *Revista do Archivo Municipal de São Paulo*, ano IV, vol. 48 (June 1938).

Luebke, Frederick. *Germans in Brazil: A Comparative History of Cultural Conflict during World War I*. Baton Rouge: Louisiana State University Press, 1987.

Maciel, Cleber da Silva. *Discriminações Raciais: Negros em Campinas, 1888–1921.* Campinas: Editora da UNICAMP, 1987.

Maram, Sheldon L. "Labor and the Left in Brazil, 1890–1921: A Movement Aborted," *Hispanic American Historical Review* 57:2 (1977), 254–272.

Mattoon, Jr., Robert H. "Railroads, Coffee, and the Growth of Big Business in São Paulo, Brazil." *Hispanic American Historical Review* 57:2 (May 1977), 273–295.

Mattoso, Katia M. de Queirós. *Bahia, Século XIX: Uma Província no Império.* Rio de Janeiro: Nova Fronteira, 1992.

———. *To Be a Slave in Brazil,* trans. Arthur Goldhammer. New Brunswick, N.J.: Rutgers University Press, 1991.

Mbiti, John S. *Introduction to African Religion,* 2d ed. London: Heineman, 1991.

McCann, Frank D. "The Formative Period of Twentieth-Century Brazilian Army Thought, 1900–1922." *Hispanic American Historical Review* 64:4 (November 1984).

McGowan, Chris, and Ricardo Pessanha. *The Brazilian Sound.* New York: Billboard Books, 1991.

Meade, Teresa, and Gregory Alonso Pirio. "In Search of the Afro-American 'Eldorado': Attempts by North American Blacks to Enter Brazil in the 1920s." *Luso-Brazilian Review* 25:1 (1988), 85–110.

Merrick, Thomas W., and Douglas H. Graham. *Population and Economic Development in Brazil, 1800 to the Present.* Baltimore: Johns Hopkins University Press, 1979.

Miller, Joseph C. "The Slave Trade in Congo and Angola." In Martin L. Kilson and Robert I. Rotberg, eds., *The African Diaspora.* Cambridge: Harvard University Press, 1976.

Minority Rights Group, ed. *No Longer Invisible: Afro-Latin Americans Today.* London: Minority Rights Publications, 1995.

Mintz, Sidney, and Richard Price. *An Anthropological Approach to the Afro-American Past: A Caribbean Perspective.* Philadelphia: Institute for the Study of Human Issues, 1976.

———. *The Birth of African-American Culture: An Anthropological Perspective.* Boston: Beacon Press, 1992.

Montagu, Ashley. *Man's Most Dangerous Myth: The Fallacy of Race* [1942], 5th ed. New York: Oxford University Press, 1974.

Morse, Richard M. *From Community to Metropolis: A Biography of São Paulo, Brazil.* New York: Octagon Books, 1974.

Morton-Williams, Peter. "An Outline of the Cosmology and Cult Organization of the Oyo Yoruba." *Africa* (London) 34 (1964), 243–260.

Moura, Clovis. *Rebeliões da Senzala.* São Paulo: Edições Zumbi, 1959.

———. *O Negro, de Bom Escravo a Mau Cidadão?* Rio de Janeiro: Conquista, 1977.

———. *Brasil: Raizes do Protesto Negro.* São Paulo: Global Editora, 1983.

Moura, Roberto. *Tia Ciatá e a Pequena África do Rio de Janeiro.* Rio de Janeiro: Funarte/ MEC-Secretaria de Cultura, n.d.

Mulvey, Patricia A. "Black Brothers and Sisters: Membership in the Black Lay Brotherhoods of Colonial Brazil." *Luso-Brazilian Review* 17:2 (Winter 1980), 253–279.

———. "Slave Confraternities in Brazil: Their Role in Colonial Society." *The Americas* 39:1 (July 1982), 39–68.

Naro, Nancy. "Revision and Persistence: Recent Historiography on the Transition from Slave to Free Labor in Rural Brazil." *Slavery and Abolition* (UK) 13:2 (1992), 68–85.

Nascímento, Abdias do. *Brazil: Mixture or Massacre? Essays in the Genocide of a Black People*. 2nd rev. ed. Dover, Mass.: Majority Press, 1989.

Nascimento, Luiz Cláudio. *A Bôa Morte em Cachoeira: Contribuição para o Estudo Etnológico*. Cachoeira, Bahia: Centro de Estudos, Pesquisa e Ação Sócio-Cultural de Cachoeira, 1988.

Nash, Roy. "Is Race Prejudice on the Increase in Brazil?" *The Crisis* (April 1951), 247–254.

Nicholls, David. *Haiti in Caribbean Context: Ethnicity, Economy, and Revolt*. New York: St. Martin's Press, 1985.

Nina Rodrigues, Raymundo. *Os Africanos no Brasil*. São Paulo: Companhia Editora Nacional, 1932.

————. *O Animismo Fetichista dos Negros Bahianos*. Rio de Janeiro: Civilização Brasileira, 1935.

Nishida, Mieko. "Manumission and Ethnicity in Urban Slavery: Salvador, Brazil, 1808–1888." *Hispanic American Historical Review* 73:3 (August 1993), 361–391.

Nunes Leal, Victor. *Coronelismo: The Municipality and Representative Government in Brazil*, trans. June Henfrey. Cambridge: Cambridge University Press, 1977.

Oliveira Vianna, F. J. "O Povo Brasileiro e sua Evolução." In Brasil, Directoria Geral de Estatística, *Recenseamento do Brasil, 1 Setembro 1920*, vol. 1. Rio de Janeiro: Typ. da Estatística, 1922.

Pang, Eul-Soo. "Agrarian Change in the Northeast." In Michael L. Conniff and Frank D. McCann, eds., *Modern Brazil: Elites and Masses in Historical Perspective*, 123–139. Lincoln: University of Nebraska Press, 1991.

————. *Bahia in the First Brazilian Republic: Coronelismo and Oligarchies, 1889–1934*. Gainesville: University of Florida Press, 1979.

————. "Coronelismo in Northeast Brazil." In Robert Kern, ed., *The Caciques: Oligarchical Politics and the System of Caciquismo in the Luso-Hispanic World*, 65–88. Albuquerque: University of New Mexico Press, 1973.

Pérez, Jr., Louis A. "Politics, Peasants, and People of Color: The 1912 'Race War' in Cuba Reconsidered." *Hispanic American Historical Review* 66:3 (1986), 509–539.

Pescatello, Ann M. "Prêto Power, Brazilian Style: Modes of Re-Actions to Slavery in the Nineteenth Century." In Ann M. Pescatello, ed., *Old Roots in New Lands: Historical and Anthropological Perspectives on Black Experiences in the Americas*. Westport, Conn.: Greenwood Press, 1977.

Pierson, Donald. *Negroes in Brazil: A Study of Race Contact at Bahia*. Chicago: University of Chicago Press, 1944.

Piven, Frances Fox, and Richard A. Cloward. *Poor People's Movements: Why They Succeed, How They Fail*. New York: Random House/Vintage Books, 1979.

Poppino, Rollie E. *Brazil: The Land and People*. New York: Oxford University Press, 1968.

Price, Richard, ed. *Maroon Societies: Rebel Slave Communities in the Americas*. 2d ed. Baltimore: Johns Hopkins University Press, 1979.

Querino, Manuel. *Costumes Africanos no Brasil*, 2d ed. Recife: Fundação Joaquim Nabuco, 1988.

Rachum, Ilan. "Feminism, Woman Suffrage, and National Politics in Brazil: 1922–1937." *Luso-Brazilian Review* 14:1 (Summer 1977), 118–134.

Raeders, Georges. *O Inimigo Cordial do Brasil: O Conde de Gobineau no Brasil*. Trans. Rosa Reire d' Aguiar. Rio de Janeiro: Paz e Terra, 1988.

Ramos, Arthur. *The Negro in Brazil*. Washington, D.C.: Associated Publishers, 1939.

Ramos, Donald. "Social Revolution Frustrated: The Conspiracy of the Tailors in Bahia, 1798." *Luso-Brazilian Review* 13:1 (1976), 74–90.

Raphael, Alison. "Samba Schools in Brazil." *International Journal of Oral History* 10:3 (1989), 256–269.

Rego, Waldeloir. *Capoeira Angola*. Salvador: Editora Itapuã, 1968.

―――. "Mitos e Ritos Africanos da Bahia." In Carybé, *Iconografia dos Deuses Africanos no Candomblé da Bahia*. São Paulo: Editora Raizes Artes Gráficas, 1980.

Reis, Fidelis. *Paiz a Organizar*. Rio de Janeiro: Coelho Branco, 1931.

Reis, João José. *A Morte é Uma Festa: Ritos Fúnebres e Revolta Popular no Brasil do Século XIX*. São Paulo: Companhia das Letras, 1991.

―――. *Escravidão e a Invenção da Liberdade: Estudos sobre o Negro no Brasil*. São Paulo: Editora Brasiliense, 1988.

―――. *Slave Rebellion in Brazil: The Muslim Uprising of 1835 in Bahia,* trans. Arthur Brakel. Baltimore: Johns Hopkins University Press, 1993.

Ribeiro, Leonido, W. Berardinelli, and Isaac Brown. "Estudo Biotypologico de Negros e Mulatos Brasileiros Normaes e Delinquentes." In Gilberto Freyre, ed., *Novos Estudos Afro-Brasileiros: Trabalhos Apresentados ao 1º Congresso Afro-Brasileiro do Recife*, 151–170. Reprint. Recife: Fundação Joaquim Nabuco, 1988.

Robles de Queroz, Suely. *Escravidão Negra em São Paulo*. Rio de Janeiro: Livraria José Olympio Editora, 1977.

Rocha Nogueira, Arlinda. *Imigração Japonesa na Historia Contemporanea do Brasil*. São Paulo: Centro de Estudos Nipo-Brasileiros, Massao Ohno Editora, 1984.

Rodney, Waller. *A History of the Guyanese Working People, 1881–1905*. Baltimore: Johns Hopkins University Press, 1981.

Russell-Wood, A.J.R. *A World on the Move: The Portuguese in Africa, Asia, and America, 1415–1808*. New York: St. Martin's Press, 1992.

―――. *The Black Man in Slavery and Freedom*. New York: St. Martin's Press, 1982.

―――. "Black and Mulatto Brotherhoods in Colonial Brazil: A Study in Collective Behavior." *Hispanic American Historical Review* 54:4 (1974), 567–602.

―――. *From Colony to Nation: Essays on the Independence of Brazil*. Baltimore: Johns Hopkins University Press, 1975.

―――. "Prestige, Power, and Piety in Colonial Brazil: The Third Orders of Salvador," in Russell-Wood, *Society and Government in Colonial Brazil, 1500–1822*, section 5, pp. 61–89. Hampshire, U.K., and Brookfield, Vt.: Variorum/Ashgate Publishing, 1992, section V, 61–89.

Schuler, Monica. *Alas, Alas Kongo: A Social History of Indentured African Immigrants into Jamaica, 1841–1865*. Baltimore: Johns Hopkins University Press, 1980.

Schwartz, Stuart B. "Plantations and Peripheries." In Leslie Bethell, ed., *Colonial Brazil*. Cambridge: Cambridge University Press, 1987.

Scott, Rebecca. *Slave Emancipation in Cuba*. Princeton: Princeton University Press, 1985.

―――. "Comparing Emancipations: A Review Essay." *Journal of Social History* 20:3 (Spring 1987), 565–583.

―――. "Exploring the Meaning of Freedom: Brazilian Abolition in Comparative Perspective." *Hispanic American Historical Review* 68:3 (August 1988), 407–428.

Silva, Nelson do Vale. "Updating the Cost of Not Being White in Brazil." In Michel Fontaine, ed., *Race, Class, and Power in Brazil*. Los Angeles: CAAS/UCLA, 1985.

Silva Campos, J. da. "Procissões Tradicionais da Bahia." *Anais do Arquivo Público da Bahia*, 27 (1941).

Skidmore, Thomas E. *Black into White: Race and Nationality in Brazilian Thought*. London: Oxford University Press, 1974.

———. "Racial Ideas and Social Policy in Brazil, 1870–1940." In Richard Graham, ed., *The Idea of Race in Latin America, 1870–1940*. Austin: University of Texas Press, 1990.

Sobel, Mechal. *The World They Made Together: Black and White Values in Eighteenth-Century Virginia*. Princeton: Princeton Univeristy Press, 1987.

Solberg, Carl E. *Immigration and Nationalism: Argentina and Chile, 1890–1914*. Austin: University of Texas Press, 1970.

Spitzer, Leo. *Lives in Between: Assimilation and Marginality in Austria, Brazil, and West Africa, 1780–1945*. Cambridge: Cambridge University Press, 1989.

Stepan, Nancy Leys. "Eugenics in Brazil, 1917–1940." In Mark B. Adams, ed., *The Wellborn Science: Eugenics in Germany, France, Brazil, and Russia*. New York: Oxford University Press, 1990.

———. *"The Hour of Eugenics": Race, Gender, and Nation in Latin America*. Ithaca: Cornell University Press, 1991.

Stuckey, Sterling. *Slave Culture: Nationalist Theory and the Foundations of Black America*. New York: Oxford University Press, 1987.

Tavares Bastos, Aureliano Candido. *Os Males do Presente e as Esperanças do Futuro*. São Paulo: Nacional, 1939.

Thompson, Robert Farris. "Kongo Influences on African-American Artistic Culture." In Joseph E. Holloway, ed., *Africanisms in American Culture*, 148–184. Bloomington: Indiana University Press, 1990.

Topik, Steven. *The Political Economy of the Brazilian State, 1889–1930*. Austin: University of Texas Press, 1987.

Toplin, Robert Brent. *The Abolition of Slavery in Brazil*. New York: Atheneum, 1972.

Trochim, Michael R. "The Brazilian Black Guard: Racial Conflict in Post-Abolition Brazil." *The Americas* 44 (January 1988), 285–300.

Verger, Pierre. *Fluxo e Refluxo do Tráfico de Escravos entre o Golfo do Benin e a Bahia de Todos os Santos dos Séculos XVII a XIX*, 3d ed., trans. Tasso Gadzanis. São Paulo: Corrupio, 1987.

———. "Primeiros Terreiros de Candomblé." In Carybé, ed., *Iconografia dos Deuses Africanos nos Candomblés da Bahia*. São Paulo: Editora Raizes Artes Gráficas, 1980.

Viotti da Costa, Emilia. *The Brazilian Empire: Myths and Histories*. Chicago: University of Chicago Press, 1985.

———. *Da Monarquia à República: Momentos Decisivos*. São Paulo: Grijalbo, 1977.

Von Simpson, Olga Rodrigues de Moraes. "Family and Carnival in Brazil during the Nineteenth Century." *Loisir et Société [Society and Leisure]*, (Les Presses de l'Université du Québec) 1:2 (November 1978), 325–343.

Wesson, Robert, and David W. Fleischer. *Brazil in Transition*. New York: Praeger, 1983.

Williams, Margaret Todaro. "Integralism and the Brazilian Catholic Church." *Hispanic American Historical Review* 54:3 (August 1974), 431–452.

Young, Jordan M. *The Brazilian Revolution and the Aftermath*. New Brunswick, N.J.: Rutgers University Press, 1967.

INDEX

Abbott, Robert, 101, 108, 225
abolition, 2–7, 26, 59, 210–227; and
  indemnification, 6, 27–28, 73; and
  transitional labor legislation, 6, 26,
  216
Africans, 133, 136–138, 141, 142–147,
  168–169, 189–193, 196; attitudes
  toward, 33–36, 40, 169, 170–171, 181–
  189, 213, 223; back-to-Africa
  migration of, 5, 142–144; and mutual
  aid, 141, 144–147
Afro-Brazilian: newspapers, 10, 13, 83–
  86, 89–112 (*see also* O Bandeirante; A
  Chibata; O Clarim d'Alvorada; A Voz
  da Raça*); organizations, 80, 82–83,
  92, 102–128 (*see also* Centro Cívico
  Palmares; Clube Negra de Cultura
  Social; Frente Negra Brasileira;
  Legião Negra; Sociedade Protectora
  dos Desvalidos)
Afro-Brazilian Congress of 1934 (Recife),
  42–43, 206
Afro-Brazilian Congress of 1937
  (Salvador), 43–45, 206–207
Afro-Brazilians: attitudes toward, 39–40,
  44, 171, 181–189, 213; economic
  conditions of, 45–46, 136–140, 156;
  and interaction with international
  black community, 226; migration and
  residential patterns of, 71–77, 133–
  135 (*see also* Barra Funda; Bela Vista)
Aguiar, Jayme de, 13, 97–98, 101–102,
  103, 111, 117

alternative communities, 62, 219, 220,
  221–222. *See also* parallel communi-
  ties
Amaral, Raul Joviano de, 13
Andrews, George Reid, 12, 101
Anninha, *see* Santos, Eugenia Anna dos
Associação dos Negros Brasileiros
  (Association of Brazilian Blacks), 126
Azevedo, Thales de, 21–22

Bahia, economic change in, 29–30
O Bandeirante (São Paulo), 83–86, 94
Barbosa, Aristides, 67
Barra Funda, São Paulo, 74
Bastide, Roger, 13
Bela Vista (Bexiga), São Paulo, 73–74
Bento, Antônio, 28
Bexiga, *see* Bela Vista
Black Legion (Legião Negra), 124
Bôa Morte sisterhood (Bahia), 157, 186,
  193, 199
Bomfim, Martino Eliseo do, 158, 200,
  207
botequins, 81–83
Britto, Iêda Marques, 13
brotherhoods, 14, 22, 147; in São Paulo,
  78; in Salvador, 147–158. *See also*
  Bôa Morte sisterhood; Rosário,
  Venerável Ordem Terceira do

candomblé, 8, 23, 40, 47, 141, 157–158,
  169–170, 171, 183, 184, 185, 186,
  189–209, 222; historical phases of,

ABOUT THE AUTHOR

Kim D. Butler is an associate professor of history in the Department of Africana Studies at Rutgers University.